COMMON PROBLEMS/
PROPER SOLUTIONS

SOME OTHER VOLUMES IN THE
SAGE FOCUS EDITIONS

COMMON PROBLEMS/ PROPER SOLUTIONS
Avoiding Error in Quantitative Research

Edited by
J. Scott Long

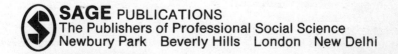
SAGE PUBLICATIONS
The Publishers of Professional Social Science
Newbury Park   Beverly Hills   London   New Delhi

To

Robert McGinnis

For information address:

SAGE Publications, Inc.
2111 West Hillcrest Drive
Newbury Park, California 91320

SAGE Publications Inc.
275 South Beverly Drive
Beverly Hills
California 90212

SAGE Publications Ltd.
28 Banner Street
London EC1Y 8QE
England

SAGE PUBLICATIONS India Pvt. Ltd.
M-32 Market
Greater Kailash I
New Delhi 110 048 India

Printed in the United States of America

Library of Congress Cataloging-in-Publication Data

Main entry under title:

Common problems/proper solutions.

(Sage focus editions ; v. 94)
Bibliography: p.
1. Social sciences—Statistical methods.
I. Long, J. Scott.
HA29.C7325 1987   300'.72   87-20625
ISBN 0-8039-2806-8
ISBN 0-8039-2807-6 (pbk.)

Contents

Acknowledgments

Many people contributed to the completion of this volume. The initial ideas emerged out of discussions with George W. Bohrnstedt. Carol A. Bailey, George W. Bohrnstedt, Clifford C. Clogg, Lowell L. Hargens, Robert M. Hauser, Robert McGinnis, and Michael E. Sobel provided suggestions for topics and/or discussed various aspects of the project. Paul D. Allison, Carol A. Bailey, Peter M. Bentler, Clifford C. Clogg, Gene Fisher, Lowell L. Hargens, Kinley Larntz, Monica Seff, Michael E. Sobel, and Blair Wheaton served as reviewers. Michael P. Allen, Carol A. Bailey, Lowell L. Hargens, and Robert McGinnis provided valuable comments on the introduction. The encouragement of Mitch Allen at Sage was always appreciated. The contributions of each of these people is gratefully acknowledged. Finally, I would like to thank the authors for accepting my invitation to write a paper, and for doing so with such care and insight.

My wife Valerie and daughter Megan made their own unique contributions. Thanks.

This book is dedicated to Robert McGinnis who is my teacher, colleague, and friend. It is but meager payment for his generous support and encouragement over many years and in many ways.

—*J. Scott Long*

Introduction

J. SCOTT LONG

During the past 20 years, there has been rapid growth in the variety and complexity of methods available for quantitative social research. Statistical analyses that taxed the largest computers of 20 years past are now routinely accomplished on microcomputers. The availability of computing has, in turn, stimulated the development of techniques that require intensive computing. Many of today's most important statistical techniques were introduced to social sciences during this period. Regression and path analysis emerged from econometrics and biometrics with H. M. Blalock's 1964 *Causal Inferences in Nonexperimental Research* and O. D. Duncan's 1966 article "Path Analysis." After many years of development in statistical journals, log-linear models for the analysis of cross-tabulated data were introduced to social scientists with L. A. Goodman's 1972 article "A Modified Multiple Regression Approach to the Analysis of Dichotomous Variables," R. E. Fay and L. A. Goodman's 1975 program ECTA, and Y.M.M. Bishop et al.'s 1975 *Discrete Multivariate Analysis*. A general and systematic method for dealing with errors in variables and errors in equations was presented by K. G. Jöreskog's 1973 paper "A General Method for Estimating a Linear Structural Equation System" and by K. G. Jöreskog and M. van Thillo's 1972 program LISREL. Methods for dealing with duration data were adapted from work in engineering and biometrics to the social sciences with N. B. Tuma's 1976 paper "Rewards, Resources and the Rate of Mobility" accompanied the

7

same year by N. B. Tuma and D. Crockford's program RATE. To appreciate the impact these methods have had on substantive applications in the social sciences, one needs only to compare the articles in leading substantive journals in the social sciences from the 1960s to the 1980s.

While progress has been made, the availability of new techniques has not been fully translated into improvements in quantitative social research. The success with which quantitative methodologists have mastered these techniques has not been matched by an equal success in having these methods widely adopted and fruitfully applied to substantive problems. Indeed, the idea for this volume grew out of my experiences with refereeing substantive papers and seeing a number of recurring errors that could have been avoided with appropriate statistical methods. While these errors occur frequently and usually have solutions in the statistical literature, often there are no articles or books that provide clear, practical, and accurate discussions of the issues.

Common mistakes in quantitative social research are of both omission and commission. Errors of omission occur when researchers fail to apply methods that are ideally suited to the topic at hand. For example, in research focusing on differences among groups (e.g., male versus females, ethnic groups), it commonly occurs that statistical analyses are made of the relationships among variables within a group, but statistical comparisons across groups are not made. Errors of commission occur when a technique is inappropriately applied. One of the most damaging instances of such errors occurs when a faddish technique is used but not well understood, or is applied to data for which it is not suited. Many instances of this occurred (and probably still occur) after path models, log-linear models, and LISREL were introduced.

Errors of omission and commission can be traced to two sources. First with the increasing sophistication of quantitative methods, there has not been a corresponding enhancement in the methodological training of new Ph.D.s or of those who received their degrees prior to the introduction of the new methods (although exceptions certainly exist). While new techniques are increasingly dependent upon sophisticated mathematics, the average mathematical level of social scientists has not increased accordingly. The second and related source of the problem lies with the methodologists who have mastered or developed these techniques, but have placed relatively little emphasis on conveying these methods to nonspecialists. It is informative that while there are scores of textbooks on quantitative methods written by economists to train economists, there are only a handful written by social scientists in other disciplines. Pedagogical efforts in statistical methods have not been given a high priority in social sciences. Indeed, several of the authors of the papers in this volume were pleased to have the chance to write pedagogical papers that they had neglected to write in the past because they felt that there wasn't an appropriate outlet.[1]

As quantitative techniques have become more sophisticated, they have overcome many of the criticisms of those who argued that the models are too unrealistic to be informative. These developments have been made at the cost of increasing demands on the mathematical preparation of the users. If social scientists are to realize the potential of these methods fully, *undergraduate* training in the social sciences must strongly encourage, if not require, students to take courses in statistics and mathematics, especially for those going on to graduate school. At the same time, graduate programs must enhance the statistical and methodological training of those students who plan to do quantitative work.

As the idea for this project developed, a second sense of the term *common problem* emerged—problems in the sense of difficulties commonly encountered in applying quantitative methods to real data. Anyone who has used the covariance structure model (e.g., LISREL) soon realizes that few models converge so nicely or fit so well as the often used example from Duncan et al. (1968). Or, anyone fitting a log-linear model is likely to find that most tables do not produce as elegant results as those obtained from analyzing the Stouffer data for military camp preference (see Goodman, 1972). Difficulties emerge when the analyses do not conform to the standard model, when convergence does not occur, when the sampling scheme is complex, or when data are missing, among other reasons. Often there are no clear answers to be found in the statistical literature. Or, the answers are found only in the latest technical writings that have not been disseminated to typical users. It takes time to determine how new methods can be appropriately applied, and indeed to know what is appropriate. The tacit knowledge gained from the use of a technique in applied research lags behind the technical knowledge.

Each of the 11 chapters in this volume addresses specific aspects of the general issues described above. They are written by experts who routinely use the methods or who have contributed to the development of the method discussed. The authors have attempted to approach the issues rigorously and to anticipate difficulties that are frequently encountered and errors that are commonly made in applying the methods, but at the same time to avoid unnecessary complications. This is not to say that the presentations are nonmathematical or based solely on intuitive explanations of the issues. Efforts can be made to minimize difficulties, but the development of quantitative methods has and will continue to place increasing demands on the mathematical abilities of applied researchers.

ABOUT THE CHAPTERS

The first section deals with issues related to the general linear model, which remains the most commonly applied statistical technique in the social sciences. These chapters assume familiarity with the regression model at the level of an introductory course or text in regression analysis. The first chapter, by Duane F. Alwin, considers the interpretation of regression coefficients and the choice between standardized and unstandardized coefficients. Rather than simply providing rules of thumb, Alwin carefully develops the issues that determine what scaling should be used to compare coefficients within and across equations. The chapter shows that interpretations often involve consideration of direct and indirect effects. This issue is considered in detail in the following chapter by Michael E. Sobel. After reviewing the computation and interpretation of total, direct, and indirect effects in recursive regression models, Sobel provides a nonmathematical treatment of his research on statistical inferences on indirect effects. By focusing on the application of these techniques to the simplest, and also the most common, cases, Sobel's chapter is designed to encourage the use of statistical testing of indirect effects. Another complication that is encountered when systems of equations are considered is addressed in Lowell L. Hargens's chapter on correlated errors. Correlated errors are most commonly considered in systems of equations with reciprocal causality. Hargens's chapter is particularly useful in demonstrating the need to consider correlated errors in systems of equations without reciprocal relationships. Given the increasing availability of software for estimating such systems, their use is likely to increase.

Gene A. Fisher's chapter considers regression models that contain product terms. He begins by considering substantive reasons that require the use of product terms. On this framework, he addresses issues of interpretation, estimation, and hypothesis testing. The following chapter, by J. Scott Long and Terance D. Miethe, considers a particular type of model that includes product variables, namely, regression models for the comparison of groups. A substantive example is developed to illustrate how group differences can be incorporated into the regression model, how such models can be estimated and tested, and the implications of inadequately testing for group differences. The idea of models incorporating group differences is extended in the chapter by Robert D. Mare and Christopher Winship on switching regressions. In the models considered by Long and Miethe it is assumed that group membership (e.g., sex or race) is not determined by the independent variables in the model. In cases where group membership is determined by the same factors determining the dependent variable, switching regressions are necessary to avoid biased estimates of the effects of independent variables. Mare and Winship present an example that applies switching regressions to the allocation of students to college and noncollege tracks within secondary schools, and the effects of tracks on mathematics achievement. The example clearly illustrates how more complex models, which incorporate substantively more realistic assumptions, can provide important substantive insights.

The next two chapters deal with the covariance structure model, often referred to as the LISREL model. The chapter by P. M. Bentler and Chih-Ping Chou reviews the latest literature on the covariance structure model. It provides a comprehensive review of the problems that are commonly encountered and suggests solutions to these difficulties. Much of the practical advice that is given is scattered widely throughout the literature or is unavailable in published sources. Anyone who has suffered frustrations in setting up and estimating a covariance structure model will find this chapter extremely helpful. The chapter by Blair Wheaton expands upon the issue of assessing goodness of fit, which is discussed briefly in the chapter by Bentler and Chou. It makes a valuable contribution by summarizing our knowledge in this area and by systematically considering the strengths and weaknesses of alternative measures.

The final section of the book includes three chapters dealing with the analysis of cross-tabular data. The chapter by Clifford C. Clogg and Scott R. Eliason considers five problems that are commonly encountered in applying log-linear models: determining degrees of freedom, analyzing sparse data, analyzing weighted data, modeling rates, and interpreting results. Not only are these difficulties that often must be dealt with in substantive applications, but they also represent sources of common errors made in applying log-linear models. By providing a state-of-the-art review of advances in log-linear methods, the authors provide a chapter that should benefit students, teachers, and practitioners. The following chapter by Richard D. Alba focuses on what may be the greatest practical problem in applying log-linear models—the interpretation of parameters. The chapter is a model of clear exposition of a complex issue. The final chapter by James W. Shockey, deals with an important class of log-linear models that is receiving increasing attention—models for latent class analysis. These models introduce the use of latent variables into models for cross-classified data. Shockey's chapter introduces the reader to these models by means of series of examples that illustrate not only the statistical issues involved, but also how these models can further our understanding of substantive issues.

EXCLUDED TOPICS

While the chapters cover a wide variety of the most important topics, some areas have been excluded due to oversight, a lack of success in finding someone to write the chapter, known and unknown biases of the editor, and limited space. In other cases, the availability of other published materials made the writing of a new paper unnecessary. It is useful to mention these other sources (although I have undoubtedly missed other sources that should be included). Full references are in the bibliography.

While many of the chapters deal with nonlinear models and many errors are made using or failing to use nonlinear models, no chapter in the volume explicitly considers this topic. R. M. Stolzenberg's "The Measurement and Decomposition of Causal Effects in Nonlinear and Nonadditive Models" (1980) and M. A. Stoto and J. D. Emerson's "Power Transformations for Data Analysis" (1983) provide excellent introductions to this topic. Biases introduced by sampling are receiving increasing and necessary attention; R. A. Berk's "An Introduction to Sample Selection Bias in Sociological Data" (1983) provides an excellent review of this issue. The limitations of cross-sectional research are receiving increasing attention and a variety of methods are being developed to handle data involving time. P. D. Allison's *Event History Analysis* (1984), R. McCleary and R. A. Hay, Jr.'s *Applied Time Series Analysis* (1980), and R. C. Kessler and D. F. Greenberg's *Linear Panel Analysis* (1981) provide useful introductions to alternative models for dealing with time. Finally, the last decade has witnessed the development of numerous methods for dealing with ordinal and nominal variables, often referred to as quantal response models or models for limited dependent variables. Errors such as running regressions on nominal variables can be avoided by using these methods. A mathematically demanding treatment of these models is provided by G. S. Maddala's *Limited-Dependent and Qualitative Variables in Econometrics* (1983). More accessible introductions are provided by J. H. Aldrich and F. D. Nelson's *Linear Probability, Logit, and Probit Models* (1984) and C. Winship and R. D. Mare's papers "Structural Equations and Path Analysis for Discrete Data" (1983) and "Regression Models with Ordinal Variables" (1984).

CONCLUSIONS

It is hoped that these chapters will accomplish three objectives. First, that they will provide clear and accurate statements concerning methodological issues commonly facing quantitative researchers. Second, that they will encourage further efforts at communication between methodological specialists and quantitative researchers. Third, that they will highlight the important relationship between substantive research and statistical methods. Each chapter places a high priority on the substantive problem motivating the research. The argument is made uniformly that the subject matter must point the way to the model, a method must not be applied for the sake of using a method, and vacuous specification searches must be avoided. To the extent that these goals are achieved, training in quantitative methods can be improved, which in turn will improve the quality of social research.

NOTE

1. Other authors had to be coerced.

1

Measurement and the Interpretation of Effects in Structural Equation Models

DUANE F. ALWIN

Issues of measurement are intimately linked to the analysis and interpretation of empirical data. A central element of measurement tied to such issues involves the *units of magnitude* used to express variation in the qualities measured. Measurement implies units of magnitude, and researchers assume that their variables have some meaningful units designating relevant theoretical quantities. As Kaplan (1964) has pointed out, the essence of measurement lies in the principle of "standardization," that is, the principle that units of magnitude have a constancy across time and space. Although some such units of measure seem *natural*, many are arbitrary, and standardization in Kaplan's sense is often more of an objective than a reality.[1] But it seems impossible to make comparisons across units of observation if one were not reasonably sure of the standardization of units of measurement in this sense.

These matters come to the fore when researchers utilize statistical models that express the effects of variables on other variables, as in structural equation models. The language used in the interpretation of coefficients expressing such effects assumes units of magnitude having the above-mentioned properties, making it reasonable (or possible) to regard effects as expressions involving relationships between variables in terms of units of both variables. Thus the coefficients in linear models of the type $y = \gamma x + \zeta$ are interpreted as the number of units (γ) in the dependent variable (y) associated with a one-unit change in an independent variable (x), holding constant the influences of prior and contemporaneous influences (reflected in ζ).[2]

Units for measuring such effects are a matter of choice in most instances, and the choice of units for the measurement of variables used in structural equation models determines the particular interpretation of effects of variables. One of the most common practices in the social and behavioral sciences is the "standardization" of metric (as distinct from the type of standardization referred to by Kaplan), wherein variables are scaled or normalized to have means of zero and standard deviations of one. This type of standardization is obtained by centering the variable(s) and scaling this deviation score by the reciprocal of the standard deviation(s), that is, $(y - \mu_y)/\sigma_y$.

Additionally, one occasionally encounters the argument that the measures social scientists frequently use have no "real" units of measurement; and there is often little choice but to "standardize" variables on their "population-specific" distribution (see, e.g., Hargens, 1976; Bielby, 1986). Despite these arguments, many uses of structural equation models in sociology and economics report "metric" coefficients because of the theoretical importance placed on units of measurement.[3]

The question for the user of structural equation models, then, is how to determine the choice of metric for analysis and interpretation? In addressing this question, I assume there exist some acceptable units designating magnitudes of theoretical quantities, and that in principle such units differ from variable to variable. Moreover, I assume that there is some choice, however arbitrary, in the units of measurement. Given these assumptions, I argue that the choice of units of measurement devolves to the scaling of coefficients in structural equation models (or vice versa), and is governed by two categories of purpose: (1) assessing the relative importance of variables, and (2) making interpopulation assessments of the relative magnitudes of effects across distinct populations or subpopulations.

STRUCTURAL COEFFICIENTS

The focus of the present discussion is on the parameters of structural equation models, which are assumed to reflect fundamental causal mechanisms linking variables of theoretical interest in the populations studied. Such structural parameters reflect "the invariant features of the mechanisms that generate observable variables" (Goldberger, 1973: 6). In referring to these invariant properties of structural parameters I assume that the interest is in the primary causal interconnections among variables representing aspects of social relations and social structure in a given spatiotemporal context, rather than simply in their levels of association. And while knowledge of the correlations among variables is valuable information, just as are means and variances, the exclusive focus on correlational data perhaps reflects a misplaced emphasis (see Duncan, 1975a).

It is common practice in econometrics, as among sociologists writing about econometric techniques (e.g., Duncan, 1975a), to reserve the term *structural relations* to specified causal relations expressed in the original metric of the variables of interest. That is, "structural" coefficients are inherently "*un*standardized." This is in part mere convention, in that economists have traditionally dealt with variables whose meters were reasonably interpretable. This has been less the case in the social and behavioral sciences, where expositions of structural equation models often rely on the conventions of path analysis, which is routinely formulated for variables that are "standardized" (see Wright, 1934, 1954; Duncan, 1966, 1975; Heise, 1968, 1975; Land, 1968; Kenny, 1979).

Thus in the present discussion I refer to both scalings—the metric and the standard forms—as structural coefficients. I see no reason to limit the definition of a structural coefficient to the metric form, because if the metric form expresses an invariant relationship between two variables, then this information can be recovered from the standard-form coefficient, given knowledge of the distributional properties of the variables for a particular population. It is in fact an empirical question whether the metric coefficients are invariant, an issue to which I return briefly below (see also Long and Miethe, this volume).

SOME INTERPRETATIONS AND ALGEBRAIC EQUIVALENCES

While the simple bivariate form of a structural equation model, involving a single dependent variable (y) and a single independent variable (x), is rarely one of interest, it is nonetheless of use in demonstrating certain algebraic equivalences among coefficients of interest, which can be generalized to the multivariate case. This simple bivariate form is expressed as follows: $y = \gamma_{yx} x + \zeta$, where x and y are empirical variables presumed to represent the theoretical variables in the causal model, γ_{yx} is the structural parameter expressing the causal connection between them, and ζ represents the other causes of y.[4] The coefficient γ_{yx} is interpreted as the number of units change in y that are associated with a unit of change in x. This type of change interpretation is often simply an analogue to the idea of a change in one variable forcing a change, or leading to a change, in another (see Blalock, 1961), because often the "change" in the causal variable has not been measured in the research design, for instance, in cross-sectional data. In this case, the coefficient of the type referred to above (i.e., γ_{yx}) represents the expected difference in the outcome variable associated with one unit of difference in a given causal variable.

In its metric form, the coefficient γ_{yx} is defined as $\gamma_{yx} = \sigma_{yx}/\sigma_x^2$. In its standardized form, the coefficient is defined as $\gamma_{yx}^* = \sigma_{yx}/\sigma_x\sigma_y$. From this it is seen that each of these coefficients reflects *different scalings of the same relationship between x and y, namely the covariance* σ_{yx}. The metric coefficient scales this covariance by $1/\sigma_x^2$, and the standardized coefficient scales this covariance by $1/\sigma_x\sigma_y$. Thus these two types of coefficients— standardized and unstandardized—are different scalings of the same information.

Because of their dependence on the same covariance information (σ_{yx}), it is thus a simple matter to translate one type of coefficient into the other. The relation between the metric structural coefficient and the standardized structural coefficient is as follows: $\gamma_{yx}^* = \gamma_{yx}\sigma_x/\sigma_y$. The standardized structural coefficient in this bivariate case is, of course, equal to the zero-order product-moment correlation coefficient, that is, $\gamma_{yx}^* = \rho_{yx}$.

These relationships demonstrate how both the metric and the standardized forms of the structural coefficient are intimately tied to the covariance between x and y, as well as to their variances. It is often argued that the metric structural coefficient is unaffected by population variances (Blalock, 1964, 1967b; Tukey, 1969), yet it is clear from the definition of γ_{yx} given here that this coefficient is intimately linked to the variance of the independent variable. Note also that because $\sigma_{yx} = \rho_{yx}\sigma_x\sigma_y$, it is difficult to say that either coefficient is any more or less so affected by the distributional properties of the variables involved.

The observations made above, of course, generalize to the multivariate case. Note that the relation between metric and standardized coefficients given above permits one to move between standardized and metric coefficients using an appropriate ratio of standard deviations. In an equation of the type: $y = \gamma_1^* x_1 + \gamma_2^* x_2 + \ldots + \gamma_p^* x_p$, the γ^*-coefficients equal $\gamma_i \sigma_{x_i} / \sigma_y$. In such a model an independent change in x_1, x_2, or x_p produces change in y, independently of one another, with these changes scaled in standard units. Thus in the context of this more complex, multivariate model it is possible to conceive of the standardized and unstandardized coefficients as rescalings of the same information, as above.

These algebraic equivalences suggest that these two major scalings of coefficients in structural equation models both convey useful information. Each is intimately linked by the properties of the population or populations of interest. Both forms are valuable and, in many cases, both should be reported. Each conveys something important about the processes that generate the distributions and joint distributions of the observed variables (Goldberger, 1973). This conclusion reiterates one given by Sewall Wright (1960: 202), who suggested that standardized and unstandardized regression coefficients should be thought of as complementary rather than alternative concepts. They should be looked upon, he concluded, "as aspects of a single theory rather than as alternatives . . . [they] correspond to different modes of interpretation which taken together give a deeper understanding of a situation than either can give by itself."

CHOICE OF SCALE—
THE CONVENTIONAL WISDOM

The conventional logic governing the choice of metric for variables or the scaling of coefficients in structural equation models is usually given as follows. *In order to compare the effects of variables in a given equation or set of equations in terms of their relative importance, one refers to coefficients for variables scaled in a common metric*, typically variables scaled to have a standard deviation of unity, that is, standardized coefficients.

Owing to the difficulty of interpreting the magnitudes of coefficients of variables in differing units of measurement, this form of standardization is believed to allow comparison of the sizes of coefficients (see, e.g., Schoenberg, 1972; Specht and Warren, 1976; Kim and Mueller, 1976).[5]

By contrast, when the objective is *to compare the magnitudes of coefficients for a given variable in equations specified in different populations, the general practice is to compare the regression coefficients in their original metric*, rather than to rely on standardized units. Differing magnitudes of coefficients reflect both the units of measurement and the sizes of effects, and because the magnitudes of such standardized coefficients are clearly dependent upon within-population variances, and to the extent these vary significantly across populations/subpopulations, it is generally thought that the unstandardized values are the more stable and therefore the more appropriate (see Schoenberg, 1972; Specht and Warren, 1976; Kim and Mueller, 1976). As the discussion above suggests, it is not simply because these metric coefficients are unaffected by interpopulation differences in variation that they are of value for this purpose, as is often supposed. The rationale in fact is different: structural coefficients are often assumed to be invariant reflections of the causal processes generating the distributions and joint distributions of variables.[6]

In what follows I review the arguments often advanced for these conventional practices, and while I cannot fault the general logic set forth for these guidelines, there are several difficulties that must be faced in the application of the above principles. I turn now to the two major purposes to which structural coefficients are put, *evaluating the relative importance of variables and making comparisons of effects of variables across populations*, and I discuss some of the major problems in applying the above guidelines in pursuit of these objectives.

ASSESSING THE RELATIVE IMPORTANCE OF VARIABLES

Research in the social sciences often raises questions about the relative importance of variables or sets of variables in terms of their causal impact. For example, one of the conclusions of the landmark study by Coleman et al. (1966) of school effects on student achievement was that variation in family background (variation occurring within schools) was more important than variation in factors differentiating schools from one another (between-school variation) in producing individual differences among students in achievement (see also Jencks et al., 1972). Other examples abound. Kohn and his colleagues (Kohn and Schooler, 1973; Kohn et al., 1983), for example, have been arguing for several years that the "socialization" effects of jobs are stronger in their influence on "personality" than is the magnitude of the effect of personal factors in job "selection." And, the debate about the "heritability" of test scores (e.g., Jensen, 1969) is essentially a debate about the relative importance of genetic inheritance versus the environment in shaping individual differences in IQ scores. All of these efforts using structural equations, by necessity, rely on some use of *standardized coefficients* of one form or another.

There are several points of view on whether it is possible or appropriate to evaluate the importance or relative importance of variables or sets of variables using the types of statistical techniques of concern here. There are two fundamental problems. First, causal importance need not be related to variance and the covariation among causal and caused variables (see Lieberson, 1985). Conditions reflecting causal impact for a particular phenomenon of interest may not vary in the populations we study, and although they may be *necessary causal agents* they would be assigned little causal importance if measurements of their variation were entered into the types of equations referred to here. And yet, it would be difficult to establish their causal importance from the use of such statistical modeling strategies. For example, few persons would argue that the existence of schools (as we know them, or in some imagined world) are unnecessary for school learning, although when differences among schools are assessed and entered into analytic models aimed at assigning relative importance to causal factors, school-to-school differences do not appear to be very important. It would be a grave error in such a situatiuon to conclude that schools do not influence achievement. Thus, from this example, and others that are possible, it should be readily clear that we can assess the relative importance of variables in only a limited way.

A second fundamental problem facing the analyst interested in assessing the relative importance of variables is that in non-experimental research designs, measured causal factors are often correlated, and it is therefore difficult to distinguish relative importance (see Gordon, 1968). While the general practice among social scientists using these models is to infer the relative importance of variables from the relative size of coefficients, the relative redundancy of variables poses a serious problem in the interpretation of relative importance of variables. Some statistical writers have even argued that it is *never possible* to assess relative importance in the presence of correlation among causal variables. It has been the contention of research methodologists of the social sciences, however, that given a causal model relating variables in a multivariate system (e.g., Blalock, 1961; Duncan, 1966), it is possible to interpret the coefficients in these models in terms of causal importance. Before examining the problem of redundancy in somewhat greater detail, I first review the common practices in social and behavioral science in assessing the relative importance of variables.

CRUDE INDICATIONS OF RELATIVE IMPORTANCE

Many of the interests of social scientists in the coefficients in structural equation models simply involve the question of whether a coefficient (or coefficients) is (are) zero or not. Indeed, both the theory of hypothesis-testing in regression-type models and the actual practices of social scientists often phrase the question of relative importance of variables in terms of whether the effects of particular variables can be ruled out as being zero or "nonsignificant." Although this may be considered a crude approach to the assessment of relative importance, and there are clearly difficulties with the uncritical application of statistical inference techniques, this approach is routinely practiced.[7] Regardless of the size of the sample, it is quite common for social scientists to consider statistically significant coefficients as worthy of interpretation and those that are not, unworthy of interpretation.

In using significance tests it matters little whether one uses the standardized or unstandardized coefficients, because the judgment of their significance is identical. Obviously, from the above algebraic equivalences it is clear that if one type of coefficient is zero, so will be the other, so a failure to reject the null hypothesis of a zero metric coefficient will coincide with a failure to reject the null hypothesis of a zero standardized coefficient. It can be shown that the t-statistics (or F-ratios) for the two types of coefficients are the same, so the result of a test of the null hypothesis will be the same. It may also be of value to note that the *t-statistics* associated with comparable *partial correlation coefficients* and *part correlation coefficients* would also have identical values (see Linn and Werts, 1969; Cohen, 1968; Darlington, 1968).

COMPARISONS OF RELATIVE IMPORTANCE

Many efforts to assess the relative importance of variables go beyond the simple assessment of the "statistical significance" of variables. Comparisons are typically made between the relative magnitudes of the coefficients. As I illustrate in the example given below, analysts often desire to answer questions of the type: Is x_1 more important than x_2 in its influence on y? If particular structural coefficients are judged to be nonzero on the basis of statistical criteria, and if the variables are considered to be conceptually distinct, then it is possible to interpret the relative sizes of the coefficients in terms of relative importance.

Consider the simple model where y is a function of three variables, $y = \gamma_1^* x_1 + \gamma_2^* x_2 + \gamma_3^* x_3 + u$, as shown in the diagram in Figure 1, part A. In this simple model the variables are standardized on their population distributions and, as above, the γ^*'s are *in standard form*. Suppose $\gamma_1^* = .2$, $\gamma_2^* = .2$, and $\gamma_3^* = .4$ and that all are judged to be nonzero in the population, that is, having a small probability of Type I error. Here it is possible to assert that y_3 is two times more influential in producing variation in y than are x_1 and x_2, because a standard deviation unit change in x_3 produces a standard deviation change in y that is two times what would be produced by a standard deviation change in x_1 or x_2.

Although such an approach is routinely practiced by social scientists, it is more often than not plagued with difficulties. I have already mentioned the problem of redundancy. In the above example, the relative magnitudes of the coefficients for γ_1^* and γ_2^* would be less clearly interpretable if x_1 were known to be

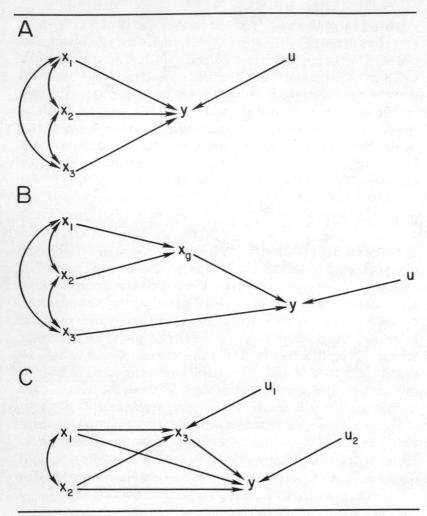

Figure 1: Causal Models Involving Comparisons of Relative Importance

highly redundant with respect to x_2, say correlated in the range .5 or above, and if both were relatively independent of x_3. In this situation one should be cautious in making the type of interpretation suggested above.

In such a situation it might be more appropriate to consider the combined effects of x_1 and x_2 relative to that of x_3 rather than their independent effects. Figure 1, part B, presents a diagram of a causal model that presents an alternative to the interpretation of their independent effects. In this model the effects of x_1 and x_2 on y are represented by the effect of x_g on y, and the model to be estimated is $y = \gamma_{yg}x_g + \gamma_{y3}x_3 + u$, and $x_g = \gamma_{gx_1}x_1 + \gamma_{gx_2}x_2 + \gamma_{gx_3}x_3$ (see Hauser and Goldberger, 1971; Hauser, 1972; Heise, 1972; Hauser et al., 1983). Of course, such a model that combines the effects of x_1 and x_2 may not be desirable, sepecially if they are considered conceptually distinct.

In many cases the assessment of relative importance of variables or sets of variables in multivariate models needs to consider the causal ordering of the variables involved (see Sobel, this volume). Consider the model depicted in Figure 1, part C, wherein x_3 mediates the effects of x_1 and x_2 on y. In such a model it would make little sense to compare the γ_1^*, γ_2^*, and γ_3^* coefficients in the regression of y on x_1, x_2, and x_3, associated with the model depicted in Figure 1, part A. Because these are direct effects and do not represent the total effects of x_1 and x_2 on y in this model, the comparison will potentially underrepresent their effects. If, for example, the path-coefficients in the model $x_3 = \gamma_1^*x_1 + \gamma_2^*x_2 + u$, equal .5, and, as above, $\gamma_{y1}^* = \gamma_{y2}^* = .2$ and $\gamma_{y3}^* = .4$, then there would be no basis for claiming x_3 to be more important than x_1 and x_2. In this case the total effects of x_1 and x_2 would equal $(\gamma_{y1}^* + [\gamma_{31}^*\gamma_{y3}^*]) = (\gamma_{y2}^* + [\gamma_{32}^*\gamma_{y3}^*]) = (.2 + [.4 \times .5]) = .4$, which is the same magnitude of the effect of x_3 on y.

In other words, when the variables in an equation are themselves causally ordered, it may be more appropriate to compare the total effects of variables both within and between populations. I return to these issues in the empirical example presented later in the chapter.

INTERPOPULATION COMPARISONS

One of the reactions to Duncan's (1966) introduction of path analysis to sociologists was Blalock's (1967a, see also 1967b) contention that for some purposes it is desirable to interpret the unstandardized or metric structural coefficients—the so-called path-regression coefficients—rather than the standardized path coefficients. Specifically, Blalock argued that in situations where one wishes to compare structural coefficients across populations or subpopulations of the same population, it is desirable to make use of a metric that is common across populations or subpopulations (hereafter populations).

Because standardized variables are presumably affected by population variances, they are less immune to the uniqueness of the population. And because metric structural coefficients are believed to be less dependent upon distributional properties of the population, it is often assumed that they are more likely to be invariant (see Blalock, 1964, 1967b; Schoenberg, 1972; Specht and Warren, 1976). This argument has certain appeal, given that it squares with the econometric practice of defining structural coefficients as inherently in metric form. In other ways it seems spurious, because it is simply not the case that metric structural coefficients are unaffected by population or subpopulation variances. Metric coefficients are a function of both variances and covariances, and it is possibly misleading to state that they are invariant due to their independence from the distributional properties of the variables involved (see Wright, 1960).

The standard methods for comparing the effects of variables across populations involve tests for the statistical significance of differences between structural coefficients *in metric form* across two or more populations. The standard methods for accomplishing such interpopulation comparisons are reviewed by Long and Miethe (this volume; see also Allison, 1977), and I will not review these here. Suffice it to say that the comparison of *un*standardized coefficients of structural equation models across populations carries with it the same general considerations discussed above with regard to the comparison of standardized coefficients within populations. That is, one must be reasonably certain that the variables are conceptually distinct and that redundancy of variables is not taken as problematic.

Perhaps the most creative solution to the problem of which coefficient to evaluate in the interpretation of research results is what Hotchkiss (1976) refers to as *standardized path regression coefficients*. These coefficients rescale the unstandardized regression coefficients in interpopulation comparisons by the pooled standard deviations, rather than by the within-population standard deviations. The point here is that as long as metric coefficients are rescaled by the same standard deviation estimates, the standardized coefficients in such regression results can be used to perform judgments about relative importance (within populations) *and* the relative sizes of coefficients across populations (see Jöreskog and Sörbom, 1986).

AN EXAMPLE—SOCIOECONOMIC
BACKGROUND AND ACHIEVEMENT

As a didactic example of the application of recursive structural equation models in the interpretation of the relative importance of variables and in the comparison of coefficients across populations, I rely on an example of the development of socioeconomic achievement over the life cycle. I draw on the work of Duncan et al. (1972), who present estimates of their central model of occupational status attainment separately by age cohorts. I here reproduce their analyses in order to illustrate the concepts involved in the interpretation of the coefficients of these models. This application is of interest because it points to some of the difficulties of making judgments about the relative importance of theoretical domains of influence and to the vagaries of the interpretation of cross-population differences in structural coefficients.

Duncan et al. (1972) consider the interrelationships among six variables assessing socioeconomic background and achievements among nonblack men of nonfarm origins in the experienced civilian labor force, ages 20 to 64, who were respondents to the March 1962 Current Population Survey. Correlational data are provided for four age-groups—25-34, 35-44, 45-54, and 55-64—from the over 27,000 men in this sample. The variables considered are as follows: x_1 = father's (or family head's) educational attainment, measured in years of schooling completed; x_2 = father's (or family head's) occupational status, measured as the score on Duncan's Socio-Economic Index (SEI); x_3 = the respondent's number of siblings; y_1 = respondent's educational attainment, also measured in years of schooling; y_2 = respondent's occupational status, also measured by Duncan's SEI; and y_3 = respondent's income in 1961. Table 1 presents the correlations, means, and standard deviations for these six variables.[8]

The basic model used by Duncan et al. (1972) for the process of achievement, considered separately for each of the aforementioned age cohorts, is given in Figure 2. In this causal model respondent's education (y_1) is shown to depend directly upon all three socioeconomic background variables (x_1, x_2, and x_3); respondent's occupational status attainment (y_2) depends directly upon father's occupational status (x_2), respondent's number of siblings (x_3), and respondent's education (y_1); and respondent's

TABLE 1

Simple Correlations Between Variables Entering into the Basic Model, for Non-Black Men with Nonfarm Background, in Experienced Civilian Labor Force, by Age: March 1962

Age Group and Variable*	Correlation with					Mean	Standard Deviation
	x_2	x_3	y_1	y_2	y_3		
25-34 (n = 3141)							
x_1	.4885	-.2691	.4017	.3420	.1534	9.17	3.53
x_2	—	-.2290	.4133	.3534	.2019	34.59	22.35
x_3	—	—	-.3262	-.2475	-.1523	3.49	2.86
y_1	—	—	—	.6510	.2726	12.38	3.04
y_2	—	—	—	—	.3369	43.34	25.01
y_3	—	—	—	—	—	6.14	4.29
35-44 (n = 3214)							
x_1	.5300	-.2871	.4048	.3194	.2332	8.55	3.72
x_2	—	-.2476	.4341	.3899	.2587	34.41	23.14
x_3	—	—	-.3311	-.2751	-.1752	3.77	2.88
y_1	—	—	—	.6426	.3759	11.95	3.20
y_2	—	—	—	—	.4418	44.78	24.71
y_3	—	—	—	—	—	7.50	5.36
45-54 (n = 2596)							
x_1	.4863	-.2395	.3685	.2517	.1902	8.15	3.69
x_2	—	-.2301	.4454	.3777	.3032	32.99	22.35
x_3	—	—	-.2997	-.2341	-.1329	4.09	2.96
y_1	—	—	—	.5949	.3635	11.25	3.28
y_2	—	—	—	—	.4376	42.41	23.76
y_3	—	—	—	—	—	7.74	6.81
55-64 (n = 1482)							
x_1	.5313	-.2749	.3534	.3022	.1595	8.38	3.66
x_2	—	-.2398	.3879	.3543	.1871	34.06	23.16
x_3	—	—	-.2817	-.2565	-.1122	4.46	3.09
y_1	—	—	—	.5576	.3071	10.47	3.61
y_2	—	—	—	—	.3799	42.73	24.62
y_3	—	—	—	—	—	6.99	6.37

SOURCE: Duncan et al. (1972: 38).

*x_1, Father's (or family head's) educational attainment; x_2, father's (or family head's) occupational status; x_3, respondent's number of siblings; y_1, respondent's educational attainment; y_2, respondent's occupational status, March 1962; y_3, respondent's income in 1961 (in thousands); from OCG data set.

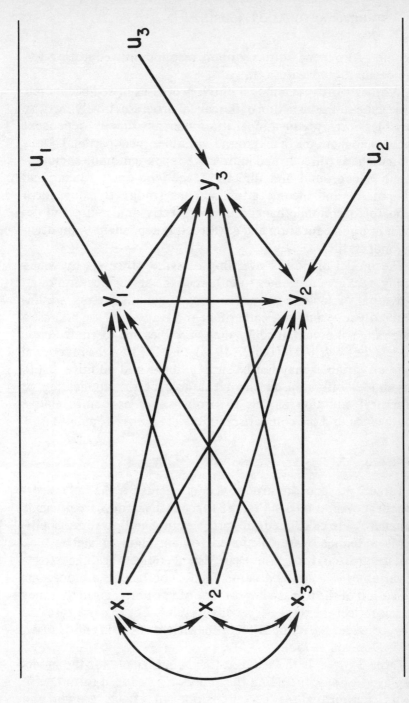

Figure 2: A Causal Model of Socioeconomic Background and Achievement

income (y_3) depends directly upon respondent's education (y_1) and occupational status (y_2).

In other words, as a model of the processes of socioeconomic achievement, the depiction of the causal processes involving these variables portrays educational attainment as (directly) dependent upon socioeconomic background variables, occupational status attainment as (directly and indirectly) dependent upon socioeconomic background and directly dependent upon educational attainment, and income attainment as (indirectly) dependent upon socioeconomic background, (directly and indirectly) dependent upon education and as (directly) dependent upon occupational status.

The model obviously oversimplifies the processes by which family background comes to influence the status position of an individual in society, because other exogenous factors are undoubtedly relevant (see Featherman and Hauser, 1978), because a wide range of potential intervening variables are absent from the model (see Sewell and Hauser, 1975), and because the functional form of variables may not be simply linear and additive.[9] Still, this model offers an excellent example of the application of structural equation models to problems of assessing relative importance and the comparison of effects across populations.

RESULTS

Table 2 presents the structural coefficients for the fully recursive form of the model in Figure 3 for each age group. Coefficients in panel A are calculated for variables in standard form; coefficients in panel B are calculated for variables in metric (i.e., unstandardized) form. These coefficients reflect the direct effects of variables in a given equation. These coefficients are only one indication of the relative importance of variables, given that they do not reflect the total effects of variables. For this purpose one must consider the reduced-form coefficients (Alwin and Hauser, 1975; Duncan, 1975a).

Table 3 presents the reduced-form coefficients for the model displayed above, including the successive reduced-form coefficients, permitting the decomposition of effects (Alwin and Hauser, 1975). In this regard, note that in Table 3 there are two sets of reduced-form coefficients for y_3, one including x_1, x_2,

TABLE 2

Partial Regression Coefficients for Recursive Model
Relating Achieved Statuses to Family Background Factors,
by Age, for Non-Black Men with Nonfarm Background,
in Experienced Civilian Labor Force: March 1962

Age Group and Variable	Independent Variables					Coefficient of Determination
	x_1	x_2	x_3	y_1	y_2	
A. Standard Form Coefficients						Unadjusted
25-34						
y_1	.2194**	.2585**	−.2080**			.263
y_2	.0638**	.0744**	−.0216	.5876**		.436
y_3	−.0124	.0795**	−.0541*	.0555	.2635**	.126
35-44						
y_1	.1985**	.2781**	−.2053**			.269
y_2	.0074	.1266**	−.0540**	.5668**		.431
y_3	.0494*	.0492	−.0200	.1193**	.3247**	.216
45-54						
y_1	.1680**	.3210**	−.1856**			.261
y_2	−.0235	.1441**	−.0494*	.5246**		.372
y_3	.0058	.1298**	.0079	.1153**	.3203**	.222
55-64						
y_1	.1696**	.2562**	−.1737**			.208
y_2	.0460	.1287**	−.0810*	.4686**		.342
y_3	.0122	.0277	.0104	.1294**	.2969**	.159
B. Metric Coefficients						Adjusted
25-34						
y_1	.1890**	.0352**	−.2210**			.262
y_2	.4520**	.0833**	−.1891	4.8348**		.435
y_3	−.0151	.0153**	−.0812*	.0784	.0452**	.125
35-44						
y_1	.1707**	.0385**	−.2281**			.268
y_2	.0490	.1352**	−.4531**	4.3767**		.430
y_3	.0712*	.0114	−.0373	.1998**	.0704**	.215
45-54						
y_1	.1493**	.0471**	−.2057**			.260
y_2	−.1514	.1532**	−.3961*	3.8000**		.371
y_3	.0108	.0396**	.0182	.2395**	.0918**	.220
55-64						
y_1	.1672**	.0399**	−.2029**			.207
y_2	.3091	.1368**	−.6454*	3.1960**		.340
y_3	.0212	.0076	.0215	.2284**	.0768**	.156

SOURCE: Table 1.
*p < .01; **p < .001.

and x_3, and one including these plus y_1. Again, panel A presents the standardized coefficients and panel B the unstandardized coefficients.

The reduced-form coefficients in Table 3 are important for determining the relative importance of variables on the outcomes of interest. As Duncan et al. (1972) note, these coefficients allow one to conclude that aspects of family background have appreciable effects on several elements of achievement in all cohorts. Family background strongly affects length of schooling, occupational status attainment somewhat less so, and income attainment still less. Increases in paternal education and occupational status increase the likelihood of longer schooling, whereas an increase in the number of siblings lowers the expected number of years of schooling completed. Although noting the difficulties in interpreting the relative importance of even modestly correlated variables, Duncan et al. (1972: 41) suggest that "father's occupation is a slightly more weighty factor in educational attainment than either father's education or number of siblings when all three variables are considered simultaneously."

Family background factors similarly affect occupational status and income across all cohorts, although effects on income are of a lesser magnitude. As with son's education, paternal occupational status stands out as the most important predictor of the three, especially in the older cohorts. Such conclusions regarding total effects are drawn from the coefficients in the reduced-form equations in standard form (see Table 3, panel A).

Using the relative magnitudes of "total effect" coefficients as an indication of the relative importance of variables (Alwin and Hauser, 1975), length of schooling is by far the most important in producing differences in status attainment in all cohorts, but family background factors clearly show important "total effects," if not "direct effects." (Compare the standard-form coefficients for y_2 in Tables 2 and 3.) The assessment of the relative magnitudes of effects of the socioeconomic origin variables in this case is problematic, however, because of the redundancy of variables. The correlations in Table 1 indicate that there is a moderate degree of correlation among the three family origin variables. This is especially true of x_1 and x_2. Thus the interpretation of the relative size of the coefficients for these variables in Tables 2 and 3 is not straightforward. We return to this issue in a subsequent section.

TABLE 3
Partial Regression Coefficients for Reduced Form of Recursive Model Relating Achieved Statuses to Family Background Factors, by Age, for Non-Black Men with Nonfarm Background, in Experienced Civilian Labor Force: March 1962

Age Group and Variable	Independent Variables				Coefficient of Determination
	x_1	x_2	x_3	y_1	
A. Standard Form Coefficients					Unadjusted
25-34					
y_1	.2194**	.2585**	−.2080**		.263
y_2	.1928**	.2263**	−.1438**		.182
y_3	.0506	.1535**	−.1036**		.055
y_3	.0044	.0991**	−.0598*	.2104**	.295
35-44					
y_1	.1985**	.2781**	−.2053**		.269
y_2	.1199**	.2842**	−.1703**		.196
y_3	.1120**	.1745**	−.0998**		.089
y_3	.0578*	.0903**	−.0376	.3033**	.156
45-54					
y_1	.1680**	.3210**	−.1856**		.261
y_2	.0646*	.3126**	−.1467**		.169
y_3	.0459	.2670**	−.0605*		.098
y_3	−.0017	.1760**	−.0079	.2834**	.157
55-64					
y_1	.1696**	.2562**	−.1737**		.208
y_2	.1254**	.2487**	−.1624**		.168
y_3	.0713	.1347**	−.0603		.043
y_3	.0258	.0660	−.0136	.2686**	.101
B. Metric Coefficients					Adjusted
25-34					
y_1	.1890**	.0352**	−.2210**		.262
y_2	1.3656**	.2532**	−1.2576**		.181
y_3	.0614	.0295**	−.1553**		.054
y_3	.0053	.0190**	−.0897*	.2969**	.293
35-44					
y_1	.1707**	.0385**	−.2281**		.268
y_2	.7963**	.3035**	−1.4613**		.195
y_3	.1614**	.0405**	−.1858**		.088
y_3	.0746*	.0209**	−.0699	.5080**	.155
45-54					
y_1	.1493**	.0471**	−.2057**		.260
y_2	.4158*	.3323**	−1.1777**		.168
y_3	.0847	.0813**	−.1392*		.097
y_3	−.0031	.0536**	−.0181	.5884**	.156
55-64					
y_1	.1672**	.0399**	−.2029**		.207
y_2	.8436**	.2644**	−1.2938**		.166
y_3	.1242	.0371**	−.1243		.041
y_3	.0449	.0181	−.0281	.4739**	.098

SOURCE: Table 1.
*p < .01; **p < .001.

The role of years of schooling in the determination of occupational status provides an important focal point for the interpretation of stratification processes, demonstrating the importance of considering both the *direct and the indirect effects* of variables in causal models of such processes. Especially interesting in this regard is the part educational attainment plays in the several influences on occupational status.

Educational attainment plays two contrasting roles. First, as a transmitter of the effects of family background on occupational status attainment, education plays a key part in status inheritance, perpetuating status differences between generations. As the decomposition of effects in Table 4 illustrates (see Alwin and Hauser, 1975), length of schooling *interprets* a substantial part of the effects of socioeconomic background. In other words, a substantial part of the effects of family origins operates *indirectly* via educational attainment. Second, to the extent length of schooling is independent of socioeconomic origins, then educational attainment provides a direct influence on occupational status attainment, an influence that is often interpreted as attesting to the "openness" of the status attainment process in American society (see Blau et al., 1967; Duncan et al., 1972; Sewell and Hauser, 1975; Hauser and Featherman, 1977; Featherman and Hauser, 1978).

DEALING WITH REDUNDANCY

Most discussions recommending that standardized coefficients be used to evaluate the relative importance of variables, as above, make the implicit assumption that each variable in the equation is conceptually distinct and not *redundantly related* to other variables in the equation. As Gordon (1968) has shown, it is not always a straightforward exercise therefore to evaluate the relative importance of variables by reading the relative magnitudes of their standardized coefficients. I noted above that the high degree of correlation, or redundancy, among the measures of socioeconomic background in the above example makes it difficult to interpret the relative effects of these variables. It also makes it difficult to assess the relative influence of their combined effects on a given variable, for example, educational attainment, compared to other factors.

TABLE 4
The Decomposition of Effects on Occupational Status
Attainment, by Age Group: Coefficients in Standard Form

Age Group and Variable	Summary of Effect Decomposition			
	Reduced Form Coefficients	Structural Coefficients	Percentage Indirect	Percentage Direct
25-34				
x_1	.193	.064	67%	33%
x_2	.226	.074	67%	33%
x_3	−.144	−.022	85%	15%
y_1		.588		100%
35-44				
x_1	.120	.007	94%	6%
x_2	.284	.127	56%	44%
x_3	−.170	−.054	68%	32%
y_1		.567		100%
45-54				
x_1	.065	−.024	80%	20%
x_2	.313	.144	54%	46%
x_3	−.147	−.049	66%	34%
y_1		.525		100%
55-64				
x_1	.125	.046	63%	37%
x_2	.249	.129	48%	52%
x_3	−.162	−.081	50%	50%
y_1		.469		100%

SOURCE: Tables 2 and 3.

One way to gauge the relative importance of a set of variables, such as the socioeconomic background factors in our example, is to estimate their combined effects by using a composite variable, wherein one simply sums several measures or forms an index in some other way (Alwin, 1973). A composite variable, g, might combine the effects of x_1, x_2, and x_3 as in the following model:

$$g = w_1 x_1 + w_2 x_2 + w_3 x_3$$

where the ws are coefficients that express the weight of the component variable in forming the composite. Then, one might consider the effect of the composite variable, g, on the set of endogenous variables, rather than the independent effects of the components.

The use of such composite variables, while potentially useful in obtaining a summary of the effects of variables in a given domain, leaves certain ambiguity in assessing which of the several variables is generating whatever are the observed effects of the composite. Thus while such coefficients provide some useful information, they obscure certain facts about the individual importance of variables. Recently, however, a number of investigators have made use of composite variables or "induced" variables that are linear combinations of variables, where both the composite and its components are represented in the model (see Heise, 1972; Hauser and Goldberger, 1971; Hauser, 1972; Hauser et al., 1983; Alwin and Thornton, 1984). *This approach represents an important solution to the problem of redundant sets of correlated exogenous variables.*

The principles involved in resolving interpretive difficulties confronted in assessing the relative importance of sets of variables through the use of *induced variables* can be illustrated using our present example. If the effects of the three socioeconomic background factors—father's education, father's occupation, and number of siblings—are "collected" or "combined" in a single composite variable, then the relative effects of socioeconomic background on the endogenous variables in the system will be clarified. The diagram in Figure 3 depicts the nature of the model of interest.

In this model three socioeconomic background factors operate *via* the "composite" or "induced" variable, $g = x_{SES}$. Their weights in forming this composite can be chosen to maximize the relationship of x_{SES} to the endogenous variables, the y's. The effect of socioeconomic origins (SES) on the endogenous variables are thus represented by x_{SES} in the model. The SES composite affects educational attainment directly, SES affects occupational status attainment directly and indirectly *via* education, and SES affects income attainment directly and indirectly *via* education and occupation. Thus this model is identical in several respects to the model used by Duncan et al. (1972), as shown in Figure 2, but it differs in important respects.

The important differences between these two models consists of the ways in which the effects of socioeconomic origins are represented. The model here (see Figure 3) permits one to assess *both* the individual effects of the socioeconomic background factors (operating through the composite SES variable) and their combined effects, represented in the model by x_{SES}. This permits one to make comparisons of the effects of "socioeconomic origins" as a more general concept, and the relative redundancy of the SES factors does not present an obstacle for doing so.

Table 5 presents the estimates of the standardized structural coefficients for this model for each age group. These estimates are computed using Jöreskog and Sörbom's LISREL program (1986), which provides maximum-likelihood estimates of the structural coefficients.[10] These results permit a less ambiguous assessment of the relative effects of family socioeconomic origins than was possible using the results presented by Duncan et al. (1972) (see Table 2).

For example, using this set of results, it is possible to gauge the relative dependence of education (y_1) on socioeconomic origins versus those factors independent of such origins. We may do so by partitioning the total variance in educational attainment into that part that is "explained" by the three socioeconomic origin variables and that part that is "unexplained." The effect of socioeconomic origins on educational attainment in this simple case would be estimated by the multiple correlation, $R_{y_1.x_1,x_2,x_3}$ (see Heise, 1972). The effect of those factors independent of socio-economic origins on educational attainment would be estimated by the square root of $1 - R^2$.[11]

Carrying out the estimation of these components in this case (see Tables 2 and 3), yields proportions of variance in years of schooling completed attributable to family origins ranging from .21 to .27 across age groups. This leaves 74% to 79% of the variance in educational attainment due to factors independent of family origins. From these decompositions of variance, it is possible to calculate the theoretical path coefficient from the composite SES variable, x_{SES}, to educational attainment (y_1). And, from this, one can also calculate the theoretical path coefficient for those residual factors independent of these family origin variables. This latter variable is depicted as u_1 in the model in Figure 3.

Calculating the relevant path coefficients for the two sets of factors in this case yields (across age cohorts from youngest to oldest) $\gamma^*_{yx_{SES}} = .513, .518, .510,$ and $.456$ (see Table 5) and the standardized effect of the disturbance equal to .858, .855, .860, and .890. Then, it would be possible to multiply these direct effects by the effect that education (y_1) has on the later variables.

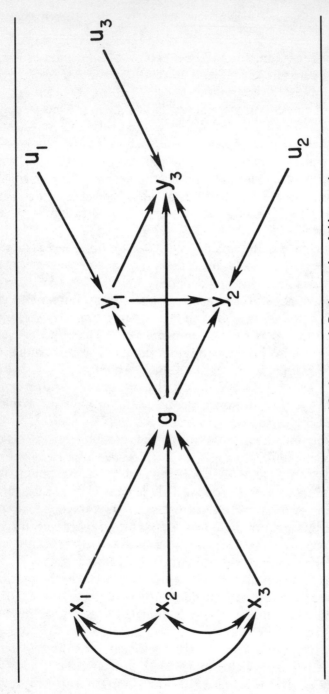

Figure 3: An Induced Variable Model for the Effects of Socioeconomic Background on Achievement

TABLE 5

Standardized Partial Regression Coefficients for
Recursive Model Relating Achieved Statuses to Family
Background Composite Variable for Non-Black Men with
Nonfarm Background, in Experienced Civilian Labor Force,
by Age: March 1962

Age Group and Variable	Independent Variable						R^2
	x_1	x_2	x_3	x_{SES}	y_1	y_2	
25-34							
x_{SES}	.421	.520	−.394	—	—	—	1.000
y_1	—	—	—	.513	—	—	.263
y_2	—	—	—	.124	.587	—	.435
y_3	—	—	—	.089	.056	.263	.124
35-44							
x_{SES}	.356	.566	−.388	—	—	—	1.000
y_1	—	—	—	.518	—	—	.269
y_2	—	—	—	.148	.566	—	.429
y_3	—	—	—	.092	.120	.324	.216
45-54							
x_{SES}	.278	.682	−.344	—	—	—	1.000
y_1	—	—	—	.510	—	—	.260
y_2	—	—	—	.142	.523	—	.369
y_3	—	—	—	.117	.112	.324	.218
55-64							
x_{SES}	.347	.580	−.385	—	—	—	1.000
y_1	—	—	—	.456	—	—	.208
y_2	—	—	—	.196	.468	—	.341
y_3	—	—	—	.027	.129	.297	.158

For example, if one multiplies these effects by the direct effect of education on occupational status, the two sets of factors have influences, via the amount of schooling of $\gamma_{y_1}x_{SES}\gamma_{y_2y_1} = .301$, .294, .268, and .214, and from the disturbance reflecting factors independent of SES origins of .504, .485, .451, and .417.

The important point to emphasize about these results is that the effects of SES origins, as a composite variable, are substantially greater when considered in such a combination than when entered as separate variables (as in Table 2). A comparison of the effects of the composite SES-origins variable in Table 5 with the corresponding effects of the separate variables in Table 2 (see standard-form coefficients), reveals several interesting features of these different results. First, as noted, the composite variable reveals a picture of substantially stronger effects of SES-origins than is the case when the variables are included separately. Second, the results in Table 5 provide estimates of the relative weight of the three SES background factors in the composite variable, which are roughly the same across age groups. Third, it is possible to recover the effects of the separate variables from the coefficients in Table 5, because their products with the coefficients linking x_{SES} to the later endogenous variables are equal (within rounding error) to the structural coefficients given in Table 2. Finally, note that the effects of y_1 on y_2, and y_3, and the effect of y_2 on y_3 registered in Table 5 are equal (within rounding error) to the corresponding coefficients in Table 2 (see the standard-form coefficients). So, these aspects of the earlier estimates are not altered by combining the effects of the exogenous SES-origin variables.

The observation regarding the relative sizes of the composite variable effects in Table 5 (the effect of x_{SES}) compared to the separate effects of the components in Table 2 (the effects of x_1, x_2, and x_3) bears further consideration. To illustrate the value of using such composite representation of sets of variables such as those socioeconomic origin factors, let us return to the question of the relative importance of socioeconomic background factors and schooling in their effects on occupational status attainment, which we considered earlier with respect to the results in Tables 2 and 3. The standardized effects of education (y_1) on occupational status (y_2) in the four age groups (from youngest to oldest) are .587, .566, .523, and .468. The standardized effects of SES-origins (x_{SES}) on occupational status, including both direct and indirect effects, are ($.124 + .301 = .425$), ($.148 + .293 = .441$), ($.142 + .267 = .409$), ($.196 + .213 = .409$).

It is clear from these results that the combined effects of the SES background variables rival those of schooling, and in no instance does it appear that SES-origins is substantially less important than schooling in the attainment of occupational status. The effects of family origins are somewhat smaller in most age groups, but ascribed and achieved influences seem to be nearly equal. And, given the strong possibility that some family origin variables have been omitted, it is difficult to conclude that schooling is any more important for achievement in modern society than are the ascriptive influences of family origins. This is a somewhat different conclusion than that reached by Duncan et al. (1972), owing to the differences in the ways in which socioeconomic origin variables are incorporated into the structural equation model.

A similar exercise could be worked through for the relative effects of SES-origins, education, and occupational status in the determination of income. A full substantive interpretation of these results, while quite compelling, is beyond the scope of this discussion. My purpose, rather, has been to demonstrate one possible solution to the redundancy problem in the specification and intepretation of coefficients in structural equation models. These results clearly show the benefits of incorporating "composite" or "induced" variables into structural equation models to cope with problems of redundancy. And, perhaps more important, they provide graphic evidence of the partialing fallacy referred to by Gordon (1968).

Unless variables in a particular structural equation or system of structural equations (causal models) are conceptually distinct from one another, the interpretation of relative importance of variables is problematic. In the above example I argued that for some purposes it was valuable to aggregate or combine the effects of the redundant set of exogenous factors in Duncan et al.'s (1972) status attainment model. It is clear from this example and from the coefficient estimates given here that *substantive conclusions can be affected by a failure to consider the redundancy of variables in structural equation models.*

INTERPOPULATION COMPARISONS

One final topic for consideration in the context of the present example is the problem of assessing differences across populations in the relative magnitudes of effects. I briefly address this issue within the context of the results presented in Tables 2 and 3. I do not consider these issues in the context of the "induced-variable model" considered directly above, although it would be possible to do so. The relevant question for the present discussion is whether the general pattern of results seems to vary by age group. As noted, I rely on the results in Tables 2 and 3 for these considerations.

These results clearly suggest a declining level of influence of both types of factors—socioeconomic background and educational attainment—with age. The former reflects both a lesser influence of socioeconomic factors on education in older age groups, and as Duncan et al. (1972: 41) observe, a declining role of education in the older age groups. The latter effects reflect the combination of the apparent increasing role of nonorigin factors in educational attainment over age groups and the lesser effects of education on occupational attainments in the older groups. As Duncan et al. (1972: 41) note, however, this finding has at least two competing interpretations, not separable using these data alone. One possible interpretation is that length of time in the labor force provides opportunities and resources for individuals to reduce the dependence of their occupation on their length of school attendance. A second interpretation involves historical time rather than biographical time—the possibility that these data are witness to a time trend in the degree of dependence of occupational status on levels of education.

The role of schooling is also apparent in producing variation in reported income levels, and, as with occupational status, schooling functions both as a transmitter of socioeconomic origins and as a conduit for the operation of factors unrelated to family origins. The effect is weakest in the youngest cohorts and appears to be the strongest in midlife. The largest direct effect on income in the model, however, is occupational status, and due to its important role in generating earnings differentials, the major component of income differences, it is not surprising that it serves to transmit a large portion of the effects of educational attainment (and the effects it conveys) on income attainment. In these data occupational status attainment transmits about three-fourths of the effects of educational attainment on income in the 25-34 age group $(1 - [.0555/.2104])$, roughly 60% of its effect in the middle two cohorts $(1 - [.1193/.3033]$ and $1 - [.1153/.2834])$, and approximately one-half of its effects in the 55-64 age group $(1 - [.1294/.2686])$.

This exercise gives interpretive weight to two types of conclusions in the analysis of status attainment processes over the life cycle. One is that experiences that occur quite early in the life cycle (family origins and length of schooling completed) continue to have an effect on a person's socioeconomic attainments throughout the life course, even into older age. Second, these results suggest that the effects of both types of factors (socioeconomic origins and length of schooling) decline with age. Both such conclusions are consistent with previous research work suggesting that both family origins and educational attainment have a declining effect on occupational status later in the life cycle (Blau et al., 1967; Featherman, 1971; Kelley, 1973). Unfortunately, it is difficult to provide a straightforward interpretation for differences among age cohorts in socioeconomic stratification processes, because as mentioned above, such differences as observed here are potentially due to differences in aging/development over the life cycle and differences in the historical experiences of different cohorts. Featherman and Hauser (1978: 262-287) provide the most complete analyses of these issues to date, analyzing age-specific intercohort differences in occupational stratification.

CLOSING

This chapter began by reviewing the conventional logic of choosing an appropriate scaling of coefficients in structural equation models. This logic encourages the use of standardized coefficients in comparing the relative effects of variables and the use of *un*standardized coefficients in the comparison of effects across populations or subpopulations. While I do not question this basic strategy, I suggested that following these conventions was not a straightforward exercise. I argued that, to the extent that structural coefficients can inform questions of causation and change in indicators of social variables, problems of redundancy of variables are especially problematic when the purpose is to assess the relative influences among included variables. I also suggested that causal modeling strategies may be useful in assessing the relative importance of variables that are themselves causally ordered.

The general conclusion of this work is that, while redundancy and causal specification problems exist, there are approaches for dealing with them. The example worked through above reflects this fact. In the present example, we have applied existing computer programs to these problems. The results show the value of the "induced variable" approach to the solution of redundancy problems, although it is not completely clear that this represents a viable solution in all situations. There are obviously other solutions to the problem of redundancy. One common approach is the use of the common factor model, although this represents a somewhat different structural model. Both approaches are useful, and when combined to counter measurement problems in the use of structural equation models, they may be even more useful (e.g., Alwin and Thornton, 1984).

Whatever the solution to the redundancy problem, the present discussion leads to the conclusion that substantive interpretations of relative importance of sets of factors in structural equation models should be approached with considerable caution. Unless factors are orthogonal by design, the interpretation of the relative effects of variables from coefficients in structural equation models will always be made difficult by the redundancy of variables. And while the use of modern structural equation techniques can be helpful in the interpretation of relative effects, they are no substitute for careful thinking and theoretical knowledge.

Finally, throughout this discussion I have assumed that variables are perfectly measured. Such an assumption is problematic for many variables in social and behavioral science. The effects that certain types of measurement errors have on the coefficients of simple models are well known (e.g., Blalock, 1965: Bohrnstedt and Carter, 1971; Duncan, 1975a). Recent structural equation approaches permit the specification of latent, unobserved variables underlying the observed indicators (see Bentler, 1980, 1982; Bentler and Weeks, 1980; Bielby and Hauser, 1977; Jöreskog and Sörbom, 1986). One of the issues that arises in this literature is the problem of assigning a unit of measure to the latent (or unobserved) variables (see Alwin, 1976; Alwin and Jackson, 1981; Bielby, 1986). The issues discussed here apply equally to the interpretation of coefficients in models where the variables are latent (or unobserved) variables, that is, if one is willing to assume it is possible to assign a metric to latent variables (see Alwin, forthcoming).

NOTES

1. Duncan (1984: 12-36) presents an informative review of the history of measurement, especially the development of standard meters in the natural and social sciences.

2. This discussion is not intended to apply to logistic regression models, log-linear models, or other models in which the dependent variable is limited to binary values.

3. Another form of expressing the metric of variables in structural equation models is simply to center the variables without scaling these deviation scores by $1/\sigma$. This is a convenient way of removing the intercepts from consideration in such equations, but it does not change the metric in which the structural coefficients are expressed.

4. For purposes of this discussion I assume that all variables are continuous interval-level variables and are measaured from their means. This latter condition makes it unnecessary to be concerned with the origins of the variables and the specification of intercepts in equations of the above type.

5. Other types of standardization of metric are possible. For example, Duncan (1975) utilizes a percentile distribution when comparing the distributions of income across two samples of the same metropolitan area obtained at different times.

6. For policy purposes, neither of these types of coefficients is necessarily adequate, and it may ultimately be more desirable to express coefficients in terms of units of benefit for a given unit of cost. Although a given variable (x_1) may appear to be more important in a given population/subpopulation than another (x_2) in affecting an outcome of interest, the costs of policies aimed at changing x_1 may be quite large relative to those costs associated with changing x_2. And thus the coefficients need to take into account effects or benefits relative to the cost needed to generate them (see Cain and Watts, 1970).

7. There is no need to review here the conventional logic of testing the null hypothesis that a particular structural coefficient is zero. Any standard text on regression models will contain such a discussion. In addition, it should be pointed out that the problems of colinearity should not be uncritically ignored in the use of these procedures.

8. The reader is advised to consult Duncan et al. (1972) and Blau et al. (1967) for the technical details relevant to the measurement of variables and selection of the sample.

9. This is not intended as a criticism of Duncan and his colleagues, because many of these potential inadequacies of the model are considered in their monograph. In fact, the potential role of a number of intervening variables that may interpret aspects of the model are explicitly considered by Duncan et al. (1972). Sewell and Hauser (1975) also consider a similar model for educational, occupational status, and income attainments incorporating additional exogenous and a more extensive set of intervening variables.

10. Details on how one sets up a LISREL model involving induced variables may be obtained by consulting Jöreskog and Sörbom (1981, 1986).

11. Although we do not do so here, it is possible to carry out the logic of these procedures for the other endogenous variables as well (y_2 and y_3). Here the relevant equations are the reduced-form equations expressing the total effects of x_1, x_2, and x_3 on y_2 and y_3 in Table 3.

2

Direct and Indirect Effects in Linear Structural Equation Models

MICHAEL E. SOBEL

Linear structural equation models have been widely utilized throughout the social and behavioral sciences (see the review articles by Bentler, 1986, and Bielby and Hauser, 1977a), and the usage of these models comports well with the emphasis in scientific activity on mapping out the mechanisms that link cause and effect (see Harre, 1972, on the subject of cause and effect).

Roughly speaking, a linear structural equation model consists of (1) a set of stochastic linear equations specifying the causal connections between the variables in the model, and (2) various auxiliary assumptions. Because the equations are linear, the direct connection between any cause and any effect is typically specified by the value of the coefficient linking the two variables in question. This coefficient is typically the change in effect produced by a one unit change in the level of the cause, holding constant the other causes. Ordinarily, the value of this coefficient is unknown. The connections in a system may be represented in

AUTHOR'S NOTE: *Thanks are due to Clifford C. Clogg, Roberto Fernandez, Edward H. Freeman, Jr., and J. Scott Long for helpful advice and comments. In addition, J. Scott Long wrote the SAS program in Appendix B.*

various ways. Typically, either the set of equations governing the behavior of the system is specified or a path diagram of the connections among the variables is employed.

Figure 1 depicts the path diagram for a linear structural equation model that describes the achievement process. This model was first considered by Duncan et al. (1972). In this model there are three variables that are causes only. These are father's occupational status (ξ_1), father's education, in years of completed schooling (ξ_2), and the number of siblings in the family of orientation (ξ_3). As indicated by the path diagram, all pairs of variables from this set are linked by curved arrows that indicate that these variables may be correlated, but are not presumed to be causally related. Because the values of these variables are determined outside the operation of the system, these variables are said to be exogenous. In the present case, these variables are also random, but in other instances, the values of the exogenous variables may be fixed by the investigator, as in an experiment. The variables η_1 (respondent's education), η_2 (respondent's occupational status in March 1962), η_3 (respondent's income, in units of thousands, in 1961), are said to be endogenous since their behavior depends stochastically on the operation of the system. The straight arrows leading to each of these variables indicate that the variable at the beginning of an arrow is a cause of the variable at the end of that arrow. The number accompanying each arrow is the sample estimate of the unstandardized effect of the causal variable on the effect variable in question. Finally, the variables ζ_1, ζ_2, and ζ_3 are called disturbances. These random variables are typically assumed to follow a particular probability distribution, often the multivariate normal distribution.

The set of equations for a model may be read directly from the path diagram. Thus, for the model depicted in Figure 1, the equations for any observation are as follows (the subscript indexing sample observations are hereafter suppressed and observations are centered about the means):

$$\eta_1 = \gamma_{11}\xi_1 + \gamma_{12}\xi_2 + \gamma_{13}\xi_3 + \zeta_1 \tag{1a}$$

$$\eta_2 = \gamma_{21}\xi_1 + \gamma_{22}\xi_2 + \gamma_{23}\xi_3 + \beta_{21}\eta_1 + \zeta_2 \tag{1b}$$

$$\eta_3 = \gamma_{31}\xi_1 + \gamma_{32}\xi_2 + \gamma_{33}\xi_3 + \beta_{31}\eta_1 + \beta_{32}\eta_2 + \zeta_3, \tag{1c}$$

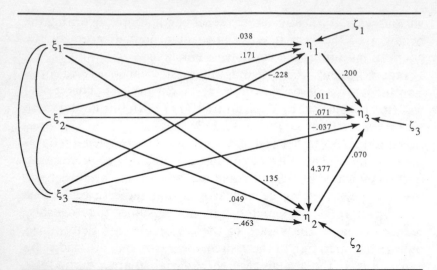

Figure 1: Path Diagram for the Recursive Model of Socioeconomic Achievement

or, in matrix form:

$$\eta = \mathbf{B}\eta + \Gamma\xi + \zeta \qquad [2]$$

where

$$\eta = \begin{pmatrix} \eta_1 \\ \eta_2 \\ \eta_3 \end{pmatrix}, \quad \mathbf{B} = \begin{bmatrix} 0 & 0 & 0 \\ \beta_{21} & 0 & 0 \\ \beta_{31} & \beta_{32} & 0 \end{bmatrix}, \quad \xi = \begin{pmatrix} \xi_1 \\ \xi_2 \\ \xi_3 \end{pmatrix}, \quad \Gamma = \begin{bmatrix} \gamma_{11} & \gamma_{12} & \gamma_{13} \\ \gamma_{21} & \gamma_{22} & \gamma_{23} \\ \gamma_{31} & \gamma_{32} & \gamma_{33} \end{bmatrix}.$$

ζ is a vector of disturbances and the expectation of this vector is assumed to be $\mathbf{0}$. Under this model, it is also assumed, as indicated by the absence of curved arrows among the variables in ζ, that $\operatorname{cov}(\zeta_1, \zeta_2) = \operatorname{cov}(\zeta_1, \zeta_3) = \operatorname{cov}(\zeta_2, \zeta_3) = 0$, where cov is used to denote the covariance operator. Thus, the variance covariance matrix of ζ (hereafter Ψ) is diagonal. The matrix $\mathbf{B}$ represents the direct causal effects of the endogenous variables on the endogenous variables, whereas the matrix Γ represents the direct causal effects of the exogenous variables on the endogenous variables. Finally, the model is recursive, that is, the matrix $\mathbf{B}$ is strictly triangular and the matrix Ψ is diagonal. (A square matrix is said to be strictly triangular if (a) all diagonal elements are 0 and (b) all elements above (or below) the diagonal are 0.)

Although the diagrammatical representation of a model appears to be an awkward substitute for the more compact matrix representation given here, the path diagram calls attention to certain features of the system that are not readily apparent from the alternate form of representation. In particular, inspection of the path diagram reveals that a variable may causally affect another variable not only directly, but also indirectly by affecting one or more intervening variables. Thus, from Figure 1, it is clear that father's occupational status (ξ_1) affects son's occupational status (η_2) directly ($\hat{\gamma}_{21} = .135$), and indirectly ($\hat{\gamma}_{11}\hat{\beta}_{21} = .168$) through the intervening variable son's education (η_1). Similarly, father's occupational status (ξ_1) affects son's income (η_3) both directly ($\hat{\gamma}_{31} = .011$) and indirectly, in three ways: (a) through the chain of arrows leading from father's status (ξ_1) to son's education (η_1) to son's occupational status (η_2) to son's income (η_3), this being a chain of length three; (b) through the chain of arrows leading from father's occupational status (ξ_1) to son's occupational status (η_2) to son's income (η_3), this being a chain of length two; and (c) through the chain leading from father's status (ξ_1) to son's educational status (η_1), to son's income (η_3), this being a chain of length two. The sample total indirect effect is then defined to be the sum of each of the indirect effects above. These are, respectively, $\hat{\beta}_{32}\hat{\beta}_{21}\hat{\gamma}_{11} = (.070)(4.377)(.038) = .012$, $\hat{\beta}_{32}\hat{\gamma}_{21} = (.070)(.135) = .009$, and $\hat{\beta}_{31}\hat{\gamma}_{11} = (.200)(.038) = .008$; thus, the total indirect effect of father's occupational status is .029.

From the analysis above, it appears that father's occupational status affects son's occupational status both directly and indirectly, with the indirect effect being stronger than the direct effect. Thus while fathers appear to transmit occupational advantages directly to their sons, the bulk of the transmission process is indirect, arising because father's occupational status affects son's education, which in turn affects son's status. Similarly, although fathers appear to be transmitting occupational advantages to son's income, the bulk of this effect appears to be indirect, and arises because father's status positively affects earlier achievements of the son.

The preceding example should illustrate that a fuller understanding of the causal process under investigation is obtained by looking at both the direct and indirect effects. Ignoring the indirect effects can yield a misleading impression of the causal process under investigation. Direct effects and indirect effects tap different (though related) aspects of the process, and the failure to distinguish between these two types of effects can create needless confusion and controversy.

The purpose of this article is to address the issues in the paragraph above. First, the various types of causal indirect effects that arise in linear structural equation models are discussed. Second, the subject of statistical inference on the indirect effects is considered, and results obtained by Sobel (1982, 1986) are reviewed. This discussion emphasizes conceptual understanding, and computational procedures for implementing Sobel's methods are largely ignored, in part because several programs for implementing these procedures already exist. To keep matters simple, only the case where the exogenous and endogenous variables are perfectly measured is considered (for the more general case, in which independent and/or endogenous variables are measured with error, see Freeman, 1982; Graff and Schmidt, 1982; Sobel, 1986). In addition, only the case where B is strictly triangular (as in recursive models) is discussed. For a discussion of total indirect effects and statistical inference on total indirect effects in the case where B is not strictly triangular and Ψ is not diagonal, see Sobel (1986).

DEFINITIONS OF TOTAL, DIRECT, AND INDIRECT EFFECTS

Returning to Figure 1, recall that father's occupational status affects son's income both directly and indirectly. The direct effect is a chain of length one, while two of the indirect effects defined in the previous section involve chains of length two, and the third involves a chain of length three. The total effect of father's occupational status on son's income is the sum of all the direct and indirect effects linking these two variables. In this section, the total, direct, and indirect effects are defined, and I show how to work with these definitions, appealing to the reader's intuition that it is reasonable to define the effects by adding up the effects of various lengths, where the effects of a given length are a sum of effects, each effect defined as a product of direct effects.

To begin, let $\boldsymbol{\xi}' = (\xi_1, \ldots, \xi_n)$ be a vector of n exogenous variables and let $\boldsymbol{\eta}' = (\eta_1, \ldots, \eta_m)$ be a vector of m endogenous variables. Suppose the model equations are:

$$\boldsymbol{\eta} = \mathbf{B}\boldsymbol{\eta} + \boldsymbol{\Gamma}\boldsymbol{\xi} + \boldsymbol{\zeta}. \tag{3}$$

By definition, the total effect of any variable (exogenous or endogenous) on an endogenous variable is the sum of the effects of length r, r = 1, ..., provided this sum is finite. When B is strictly triangular, this being the case considered in this article, the sum is always finite, and the question of existence is of no further concern. Therefore, in the following material, the effects of interest always exist. The total indirect effect is now defined as the sum of the effects of length r, r = 2, ..., and this effect may be obtained by subtracting the direct effect from the total effect.

For compactness, it is desirable to collect the various total, total indirect, and direct effects together in matrices. To do so, let $t_{\eta_i\eta_j}$ denote the total effect of η_j on η_i and let $p_{\eta_i\eta_j}$ denote the total indirect effect of η_j on η_i. Now let

$$\mathbf{T}_{\eta\eta} = \begin{bmatrix} t_{\eta_1\eta_1} & \cdots & t_{\eta_1\eta_m} \\ \vdots & & \vdots \\ t_{\eta_m\eta_1} & \cdots & t_{\eta_m\eta_m} \end{bmatrix} \text{ and } \mathbf{P}_{\eta\eta} = \begin{bmatrix} P_{\eta_1\eta_1} & \cdots & P_{\eta_1\eta_m} \\ \vdots & & \vdots \\ P_{\eta_m\eta_1} & \cdots & P_{\eta_m\eta_m} \end{bmatrix}.$$

Similarly, let $t_{\eta_i\xi_j}$ be the total effect of the exogenous variable ξ_j on the endogenous variable η_i, and let

$$\mathbf{T}_{\eta\xi} = \begin{bmatrix} t_{\eta_1\xi_1} & \cdots & t_{\eta_1\xi_n} \\ \vdots & & \vdots \\ t_{\eta_m\xi_1} & \cdots & t_{\eta_m\xi_n} \end{bmatrix} \text{ and } \mathbf{P}_{\eta\xi} = \begin{bmatrix} P_{\eta_1\xi_1} & \cdots & P_{\eta_1\xi_n} \\ \vdots & & \vdots \\ P_{\eta_m\xi_1} & \cdots & P_{\eta_m\xi_n} \end{bmatrix}.$$

Then, since the relevant matrices exist:

$$\mathbf{T}_{\eta\eta} = \mathbf{P}_{\eta\eta} + \mathbf{B} \tag{4}$$

$$\mathbf{T}_{\eta\xi} = \mathbf{P}_{\eta\xi} + \boldsymbol{\Gamma} \tag{5}$$

and thus

$$P_{\eta\eta} = T_{\eta\eta} - B \qquad [6]$$

$$P_{\eta\xi} = T_{\eta\xi} - \Gamma \qquad [7]$$

It is easy to show that $T_{\eta\eta}$ and $T_{\eta\xi}$ exist when B is strictly triangular. Recall that the total effect of a variable on an endogenous variable is defined as the sum of the effects of length r, $r = 1, \ldots$. In the case where B is strictly triangular, it may be seen from the path diagram corresponding to equation 3 that an exogenous variable can indirectly affect an endogenous variable through a chain of length m at most. Similarly, an endogenous variable can affect another endogenous variable through a chain of length m – 1 at most. Because the chains are finite, and the sum of finitely many real numbers is a real number, it is clear that in models where B is strictly triangular, the total and total indirect effects exist.

The total effects are also simple to compute. In Appendix A, it is shown that the effects of the exogenous variables on the endogenous variables of length r are given in the matrix $B^{r-1}\Gamma$, $r = 1, \ldots, m$, and the effects of the endogenous variables of length r, $r = 1, \ldots, m - 1$ appear in the matrix B^r. Thus

$$T_{\eta\eta} = B + B^2 + \ldots + B^{m-1} = (I - B)^{-1} - I, \qquad [8]$$

$$T_{\eta\xi} = \Gamma + B\Gamma + B^2\Gamma + \ldots + B^{m-1}\Gamma = (I - B)^{-1}\Gamma, \qquad [9]$$

where I is the identity matrix of order m. Note that $T_{\eta\xi}$ is the matrix of reduced form coefficients of the model. To understand how the second equality in equations 8 and 9 is obtained, it suffices to note that B^m is the 0 matrix (see Appendix A). With this fact in hand, it may be seen that $(I + T_{\eta\eta})(I - B) = I$, whence $I + T_{\eta\eta} = (I - B)^{-1}$, and the result follows. Note that the result shows also that $(I - B)$ is nonsingular—this is an important point because I have not assumed that $(I - B)$ is invertible. Using essentially the same argument, it is readily determined that $T_{\eta\xi} = (I - B)^{-1}\Gamma$. (Readers who are used to computing the indirect effects directly from the path diagram should note that they are applying equations 8 and 9. See also Alwin and Hauser, 1975, for alternative computational methods in the case where the model is both recursive and just identified.)

As an application, consider the model depicted in Figure 1. Table 1 presents maximum likelihood estimates of the direct and total indirect effects in the model of socioeconomic achievement. The estimates of the direct effects were obtained by applying ordinary least squares to each equation of the system, a procedure that is justifiable if the model is recursive. The maximum likelihood estimates of the total indirect effects were obtained by substituting sample estimates for population values in equations 4 through 9. Readers who want to make sure they understand the material above may wish to calculate these effects by hand and check them against the results reported in Table 1. The computations suggest that father's occupational status positively affects son's status and son's income both directly and indirectly. Similarly, father's education appears to affect son's status and son's income indirectly, but the direct effect of father's status on son's status is not statistically different from 0, at the .05 level. Finally, increases in the number of siblings in the family of orientation affects son's status negatively, both directly and indirectly, but the negative effect on income appears to be indirect, as the direct effect does not differ statistically from 0. For a fuller accounting of the total indirect effects, see Sobel, 1982.

STATISTICAL INFERENCE
ON INDIRECT EFFECTS

In our discussion of the indirect effects in the example above, it would be useful to know which of the indirect effects are statistically different from 0. In this section, I discuss how to obtain confidence intervals for, and test hypotheses about, the magnitude of the indirect effects. The discussion is limited to the information necessary to apply the techniques suggested herein. The reader who desires more detail may consult Bishop et al. (1975), Cox and Hinkley (1974), Rao (1973), and Sobel (1982, 1986). The basic idea is to use information about the distribution of the direct effects to obtain the large sample distribution of the indirect effects under fairly general regularity conditions. With this large

TABLE 1
Maximum Likelihood Estimates of B, Γ, $P_{\eta\eta}$, and $P_{\eta\xi}$ and
Standard Errors (in parentheses) for the
Recursive Model of Achievement

$$
\hat{B} = \begin{bmatrix}
0 & & 0 & & 0 & \\
4.377 & (.120) & 0 & & 0 & \\
.200 & (.036) & .070 & (.004) & 0 &
\end{bmatrix}
$$

$$
\hat{\Gamma} = \begin{bmatrix}
.038 & (.002) & .171 & (.016) & -.228 & (.018) \\
.135 & (.018) & .049 & (.108) & -.463 & (.123) \\
.011 & (.004) & .071 & (.028) & -.037 & (.031)
\end{bmatrix}
$$

$$
\hat{P}_{\eta\eta} = \begin{bmatrix}
0 & & 0 & 0 \\
0 & & 0 & 0 \\
.308 & (.021) & 0 & 0
\end{bmatrix}
$$

$$
\hat{P}_{\eta\xi} = \begin{bmatrix}
0 & & 0 & & 0 & \\
.168 & (.012) & .747 & (.071) & -.998 & (.082) \\
.029 & (.002) & .090 & (.012) & -.148 & (.014)
\end{bmatrix}
$$

NOTE: The sample size is 3214 and the population is nonblack, nonfarm, U.S. men in the experienced civilian labor force, aged 35-44 in March 1962. The analysis is based on the correlation matrix and standard deviations reported by Duncan et al. (1972: 38).

sample distribution in hand, standard errors of the indirect effects can then be estimated, and standard methods of statistical inference can then be employed to assess the significance of an indirect effect or obtain a confidence interval for such an effect.

To obtain the large sample distribution of the indirect effects, the δ method may be used. Heuristically speaking, this method says that if you take an estimator $\hat{\theta}_N$ based on a sample of size N with the property that $\sqrt{N}(\hat{\theta}_N - \theta)$ is normally distributed in "large samples" with mean θ and asymptotic variance $\sigma^2(\theta)$, and then use $f(\hat{\theta}_N)$ to estimate $f(\theta)$, $\sqrt{N}(f(\hat{\theta}_N) - f(\theta))$ is also normally distributed in "large samples," with mean 0 and asymptotic variance $f^1(\theta)^2\sigma^2(\theta)$, where $f^1(\theta)$ is the first derivative of f with respect to θ. It is assumed that f is a differentiable function at the population mean. If, in addition, the first derivative is continuous and if $\sigma^2(\theta)$ is a continuous function of θ, then the δ method can be implemented by estimating the asymptotic variance by $f^1(\hat{\theta}_N)^2 s^2(\hat{\theta}_N)$, where $s^2(\hat{\theta}_N)$ is the sample estimate of $\sigma^2(\theta)$.

To illustrate how to use the δ method, suppose $f(\theta) = \exp(\theta)$. Then, if $\hat{\theta}_N$ is an estimator satisfying the conditions above, $\sqrt{N}(\exp(\hat{\theta}_N) - \exp(\theta))$ is normally distributed in "large samples" with mean 0 and asymptotic variance $\exp(2\theta)\sigma^2(\theta)$ (note: $f^1(\theta)^2 = \exp(2\theta)$). Assuming that $\sigma^2(\theta)$ is a continuous function of θ, then, in a sample of size N (N is a fixed number here) $\exp(\hat{\theta}_N)$ has an approximate normal distribution with mean $\exp(\theta)$ and variance $N^{-1}\exp(2\theta)\sigma^2(\theta)$. This statistic, in conjunction with the estimate $s^2(\hat{\theta}_N)$ and the tabulated standard normal distribution, can be used to construct confidence intervals for the function $\exp(\theta)$. For a concrete example utilizing the exponential function, see Sobel et al.(1986).

The results above are not sufficiently general to permit statistical inferences on the indirect effects, since the indirect effects are a function of many parameters. In this case, $\theta = (\theta_1, \theta_2, \ldots, \theta_u)'$ is a vector of direct effects, and an indirect effect is a function $f(\theta)$. Let $\Sigma(\theta)$ be the asymptotic covariance matrix of $\sqrt{N}\hat{\theta}_N$, and let $f^1(\theta) = (\partial f/\partial\theta_1, \partial f/\partial\theta_2, \ldots, \partial f/\partial\theta_u)'$. Under these conditions, if $\hat{\theta}_N$ is a consistent estimator of θ, and $\sqrt{N}\hat{\theta}_N$ is approximately normally distributed in "large samples" with asymptotic covariance matrix $\Sigma(\theta)$, $\sqrt{N}(f(\hat{\theta}_N) - f(\theta))$ is approximately normally distributed in "large samples" with mean 0 and variance $(f^1(\theta))'\Sigma(\theta)f^1(\theta)$. Then, provided f is continuously differentiable, and $\Sigma(\theta)$ is a continuous function of θ, the statistic $\sqrt{N}(f(\hat{\theta}_N) - f(\theta))/((f^1(\hat{\theta}_N))'S(\hat{\theta}_N)f^1(\hat{\theta}_N))^{1/2}$ is approximately normally distributed in large samples with mean 0 and variance 1, where $S(\theta_N)$ is the sample estimate of $\Sigma(\theta)$. This statistic, in conjunction with the tables for the standard normal distribution, may be used to construct confidence intervals for or test hypotheses about the magnitudes of the indirect effects.

As an application of the material above, consider the indirect effect of father's occupational status on son's occupational status $(\gamma_{11}\beta_{21})$ in the model of the achievement process previously considered. The maximum likelihood estimates of γ_{11} and β_{21} are, respectively, .038 and 4.377, and the maximum likelihood estimate of this indirect effect is .168. Our vector of parameters is $\theta = (\beta_{21}, \gamma_{11})'$, and $f(\theta) = \beta_{21}\gamma_{11}$. To compute the standard error of $f(\hat{\theta})$, estimates of $f^1(\theta)$ and $\Sigma(\theta)$ are needed. Here $f^1(\theta) = (\partial f(\theta)/\partial\beta_{21}, \partial f(\theta)/\partial\gamma_{11})' = (\gamma_{11}, \beta_{21})'$. Estimates of the asymptotic standard errors are, respectively, .002 and .120. (Readers who are not familiar with statistical terminology will want to note that the asymptotic error is defined as N^{-1} (asymptotic variance)). Note that because the model is recursive, the asymptotic covariance between $\hat{\gamma}_{11}$ and $\hat{\beta}_{21}$ is 0 (Sobel, 1982). This allows us to estimate $\Sigma(\theta)$ as:

$$S(\hat{\theta}) = \begin{bmatrix} s^2(\hat{\beta}_{21}) & 0 \\ 0 & s^2(\hat{\gamma}_{11}) \end{bmatrix}.$$

The variance of $f(\hat{\theta})$ can then be estimated as $(\mathbf{f}^1(\hat{\theta}))'S(\hat{\theta})\mathbf{f}^1(\hat{\theta})$. Plugging in our estimates yields:

$$(0.038 \quad 4.377) \begin{pmatrix} (0.120)^2 & 0 \\ 0 & (0.002)^2 \end{pmatrix} \begin{pmatrix} 0.038 \\ 4.377 \end{pmatrix} = 0.0001,$$

That is, the standard error of $(\hat{\gamma}_{11}\hat{\beta}_{21})$ is, by the δ method, $(\beta_{21}^2 \text{var}(\hat{\gamma}_{11}) + \gamma_{11}^2 \text{var}(\hat{\beta}_{21}))^{1/2}$, and the estimated standard error is thus $((.4.377)^2(.002)^2 + (.038)^2(.120)^2)^{1/2} = .010$. Applying standard normal theory, a 95% confidence interval for the indirect effect is thus $(.168 - 1.96(.010), .168 + 1.96(.010)) = (.148, .188)$, which indicates that the indirect effect differs statistically from 0, on the basis of a two tailed test at the .05 level of significance. Inspection of Table 1 reveals that all other possible indirect effects (excluding those that are constrained to be 0) are statistically different from 0, at the .05 level. Thus, son's education affects son's income both directly and indirectly, through son's occupation status. Each of the three background variables affects son's occupational status indirectly, and the direct effect of father's education on son's status is not statistically different from 0. Similarly, the indirect effects of the background variables on son's income are statistically different from 0. In particular, the negative indirect effect of the siblings variable on son's income is statistically different from 0, although the direct effect of this variable is not statistically different from 0.

To obtain the sample indirect effects and their asymptotic variances by the approach above the user must (a) calculate the sample indirect effect $f(\hat{\theta}_N)$, and (b) obtain the vector of partial derivatives $\mathbf{f}^1(\theta)$, evaluate this vector at the value $\hat{\theta}_N$ that maximizes the likelihood function, and calculate the quadratic form $\mathbf{f}^1(\hat{\theta}_N)'\mathbf{S}(\hat{\theta}_N)\mathbf{f}^1(\hat{\theta}_N)$. These calculations can become unwieldy when an indirect effect involves many parameters and/or when one wants to examine many indirect effects. It is therefore desirable to have general expressions for the partial derivatives of the total indirect effects with respect to the parameters of the model.

The first step is to "stack" all of the direct effects in the model to create θ. This can be done by taking all of the direct effects from the first equation in the model and stacking them; then the direct effects from the second equation are stacked below these; and so on for all equations. The resulting vector contains all of the structural coefficients from the model.

Now suppose that each column of $\mathbf{P}_{\eta\eta}$ (see equation 6) is stacked on top of the following column to produce one long vector called $\mathbf{F}(\theta)$. We can differentiate each element of this vector with respect to the direct effects to obtain a matrix $(\partial\mathbf{F}/\partial\theta)$. This has the form

$$
\begin{bmatrix}
\partial f_1/\partial\theta_1 & \cdots & \partial f_k/\partial\theta_1 \\
\vdots & & \vdots \\
\partial f_1/\partial\theta_u & \cdots & \partial f_k/\partial\theta_u
\end{bmatrix}
= \mathbf{V}_B' [(\mathbf{I}-\mathbf{B})^{-1} \otimes ((\mathbf{I}-\mathbf{B})^{-1})' - \mathbf{I}_m \otimes \mathbf{I}_m]
$$

where $\otimes$ denotes the Kronecker product, $K = m^2$, and

$$
\mathbf{V}_B =
\begin{bmatrix}
\partial\beta_{11}/\partial\theta_1 & \cdots & \partial\beta_{11}/\partial\theta_u \\
\partial\beta_{21}/\partial\theta_1 & & \partial\beta_{21}/\partial\theta_u \\
\vdots & & \vdots \\
\partial\beta_{mm}/\partial\theta_1 & \cdots & \partial\beta_{mm}/\partial\theta_u
\end{bmatrix}
$$

The reader who has trouble understanding these expressions is encouraged to take a simple model and work through these operations for himself or herself.

The asymptotic variance covariance matrix of $\sqrt{N}\mathbf{F}(\hat{\theta}_N)$ is then given by $(\partial\mathbf{F}/\partial\theta)'\Sigma(\theta)(\partial\mathbf{F}/\partial\theta)$, where $\Sigma(\theta)$ is the asymptotic variance covariance matrix of the direct effects. Similarly, let $G(\theta)$ be the vector obtained by stacking the columns of $P_{\eta\xi}$ (see equation 7) in the manner just described. Then $(\partial G/\partial\theta)$ is given by

$$
\begin{bmatrix}
\partial g_1/\partial\theta_1 & \cdots & \partial g_L/\partial\theta_1 \\
\vdots & & \vdots \\
\partial g_1/\partial\theta_u & \cdots & \partial g_L/\partial\theta_u
\end{bmatrix}
=
\begin{aligned}
& V_B'[(I-B)^{-1}\Gamma \otimes ((I-B)^{-1})'] + \\
& V_\Gamma'[I_n \otimes ((I-B)^{-1} - I)'],
\end{aligned}
$$

where $L = mn$, and

$$
V_\Gamma =
\begin{bmatrix}
\partial\gamma_{11}/\partial\theta_1 & \cdots & \partial\gamma_{11}/\partial\theta_u \\
\partial\gamma_{21}/\partial\theta_1 & \cdots & \partial\gamma_{21}/\partial\theta_u \\
\vdots & & \vdots \\
\partial\gamma_{mn}/\partial\theta_1 & \cdots & \partial\gamma_{mn}/\partial\theta_u
\end{bmatrix}.
$$

The asymptotic variance-covariance matrix for the total indirect effects of the exogenous variables is thus: $(\partial G/\partial\theta)'\Sigma(\theta)(\partial G/\partial\theta)$. Plugging in sample estimates for the quantities above and dividing by N one obtains estimates of variances and covariances for the approximately normally distributed indirect effects.

Obtaining V_B and V_Γ is a simple task in the case under consideration, for each of these matrices consists entirely of 0's and 1's. The typical element in V_B is of the form $(\partial\beta_{ij}/\partial\theta_K)$. This element is 1 if $\beta_{ij} = \theta_K$, 0 otherwise. Similarly, the typical element of V_Γ, $[\partial\gamma_{ij}/\partial\theta_K]$ is 1 if $\gamma_{ij} = \theta_K$, 0 otherwise. Readers who want to make sure they understand how to construct V_Γ and V_B should consult Table 2, which presents these matrices for the recursive model of achievement depicted in Figure 1.

Readers who wish to obtain standard errors for the total effects (see equations (4) and (5)) should note that this can be done by making trivial modifications to the expressions for $(\partial F/\partial\theta)$ and $(\partial G/\partial\theta)$ and proceeding in the manner described herein.

Several computer programs are available to compute standard errors of indirect effects. The programs by Wolfle and Ethington (1985a, 1985b) are for recursive models without functional rela-

TABLE 2
Partial Derivative Matrices V_B and V_Γ for the Recursive Model of Achievement

$$V_B = \begin{bmatrix} 0 & 0 & 0 & 0 & 0 & 0 & 0 & 0 & 0 & 0 & 0 & 0 \\ 0 & 0 & 0 & 1 & 0 & 0 & 0 & 0 & 0 & 0 & 0 & 0 \\ 0 & 0 & 0 & 0 & 0 & 0 & 0 & 1 & 0 & 0 & 0 & 0 \\ 0 & 0 & 0 & 0 & 0 & 0 & 0 & 0 & 0 & 0 & 0 & 0 \\ 0 & 0 & 0 & 0 & 0 & 0 & 0 & 0 & 0 & 0 & 0 & 0 \\ 0 & 0 & 0 & 0 & 0 & 0 & 0 & 0 & 0 & 0 & 0 & 0 \\ 0 & 0 & 0 & 0 & 0 & 0 & 0 & 0 & 1 & 0 & 0 & 0 \\ 0 & 0 & 0 & 0 & 0 & 0 & 0 & 0 & 0 & 0 & 0 & 0 \\ 0 & 0 & 0 & 0 & 0 & 0 & 0 & 0 & 0 & 0 & 0 & 0 \end{bmatrix}$$

$$V_\Gamma = \begin{bmatrix} 1 & 0 & 0 & 0 & 0 & 0 & 0 & 0 & 0 & 0 & 0 & 0 \\ 0 & 0 & 0 & 0 & 1 & 0 & 0 & 0 & 0 & 0 & 0 & 0 \\ 0 & 0 & 0 & 0 & 0 & 0 & 0 & 0 & 0 & 1 & 0 & 0 \\ 0 & 1 & 0 & 0 & 0 & 0 & 0 & 0 & 0 & 0 & 0 & 0 \\ 0 & 0 & 0 & 0 & 0 & 1 & 0 & 0 & 0 & 0 & 0 & 0 \\ 0 & 0 & 0 & 0 & 0 & 0 & 0 & 0 & 0 & 0 & 1 & 0 \\ 0 & 0 & 1 & 0 & 0 & 0 & 0 & 0 & 0 & 0 & 0 & 0 \\ 0 & 0 & 0 & 0 & 0 & 0 & 1 & 0 & 0 & 0 & 0 & 0 \\ 0 & 0 & 0 & 0 & 0 & 0 & 0 & 0 & 0 & 0 & 0 & 1 \end{bmatrix}$$

NOTE: The mapping from which V_B and V_Γ are constructed is $\gamma_{11} = \theta_1$, $\gamma_{12} = \theta_2$, $\gamma_{13} = \theta_3$, $\beta_{21} = \theta_4$, $\gamma_{21} = \theta_5$, $\gamma_{22} = \theta_6$, $\gamma_{23} = \theta_7$, $\beta_{31} = \theta_8$, $\beta_{32} = \theta_9$, $\gamma_{31} = \theta_{10}$, $\gamma_{32} = \theta_{11}$, $\gamma_{33} = \theta_{12}$.

tionships among the parameters of the model. More general programs are also available. A program by Stone (1985) uses the results obtained by Sobel (1986) to compute standard errors for all the indirect effects in the Jöreskog-Keesling-Wiley covariance structure model (Jöreskog, 1977). Similarly the covariance structure analysis program LINCS (Schoenberg, 1987), written in Gauss programming language, gives standard errors for the indirect effects in the Jöreskog-Keesling-Wiley covariance structure model. A simple program that can be run directly from SAS, and can be easily modified for any matrix language such as MINITAB, APL or GAUSS, is presented in Appendix B. This program is for recursive models.

Researchers who want to use these procedures to assess the statistical significance of an indirect effect should note that the results in this paper are valid in large samples. It is not clear what sample size to associate with the word "large." However, Stone and Sobel are currently conducting a Monte Carlo study to address this issue, and the preliminary results suggest that a sample size of one hundred is sufficient for the types of models considered explicitly in this article.

SUMMARY AND CONCLUSIONS

This article discusses direct and indirect effects in linear structural equation models. Throughout, to keep matters simple, I focus almost exclusively on the case where **B** is strictly triangular. In the first section, I define total indirect effects and show how such effects may be computed and interpreted. Next, I briefly consider how to obtain standard errors for the indirect effects and show how estimates of the standard errors, in conjunction with the estimates of the indirect effects, can be used to test hypotheses about the magnitude of the indirect effects. I also describe several computer programs that can implement the calculations that are required to estimate standard errors for indirect effects and I discuss the type of input that is necessary to use the program in Appendix B.

There are many other topics that also merit attention, but which have been omitted from the current discussion. For example, I have not considered specific indirect effects, i.e., various components of total indirect effects. Readers who are interested in this topic may consult Sobel (1982, 1986) for further discussion. In addition, a manuscript on this subject is being prepared. In this manuscript, I show that current definitions of specific indirect effects are flawed, and I redefine these quantities. Nor have I discussed alternate methods of statistical inference on the indirect effects. A manuscript on this subject is also under preparation.

APPENDIX A

In this appendix, I show that the total effects of (1) η on η and (2) ξ on η exist if B is strictly triangular, and that these effects are given by equations 8 and 9, respectively. These results are already well known. A proof is given for two reasons. First, I could not find an adequate proof in the sociological literature to refer the reader to. Second, the structure of the proof should help the reader to understand the definition of total and indirect effects better and to see how the results are generalized to the case when B is not strictly triangular.

To obtain the results, I first show (a) B^r, $r = 1, \ldots, m - 1$, is the total effect of η on η of length r, and (b) $B^{r-1}\Gamma$ is the total effect of ξ on η of length r, $r = 1, \ldots, m$. With this result in hand, and the definition of the total indirect effect, the first set of equalities in equations 8 and 9 are obtained. It is then shown that the second set of equalities follow.

The first set of results are easily obtained by mathematical induction. Clearly, B is the total effect of η on η of length one. Now suppose the result is true for some integer r, where $r < m - 2$, i.e., B^r is the total effect of η on η of length r. Then, the (ij)th element of B^{r+1} is

$$\sum_{k=1}^{m} c_{ik} \beta_{kj},$$

where c_{ik} is the total effect of η_k on η_i of length r. Thus, $c_{ik}\beta_{kj}$ is the total effect of η_j on η_i of length r + 1 through the variable η_k, $k = 1, \ldots, m$. Adding these total effects together, the (ij)th element of B^{r+1} is the total effect of η_j on η_i. Thus B^{r+1} is the total effect of η on η of length r + 1. A similar argument establishes claim (b).

By the previous result and the definition of $t_{\eta_i\eta_j}$,

$$T_{\eta\eta} = B + B^2 + \ldots + B^{m-1}.$$

Let $G = I + T_{\eta\eta}$, and note that $G - GB = G(I - B) = I - B^m$.

But B^m is a 0 matrix if B is strictly triangular. To see this, use induction. Note that (in the case where the elements on and above the diagonal of B are 0) the first row of $B = B^1$ is a row vector of zeroes. Then note that if the (r)th row of B^r is a row vector of zeroes, the (r+1)th row of B^{r+1} is a row vector of zeroes.

Thus, $G(I - B) = I$, so $G = (I - B)^{-1}$, whence $T_{\eta\eta} = (I - B)^{-1} - I$. Similarly, $T_{\eta\xi} = (I - B)^{-1}\Gamma$.

APPENDIX B
A Matrix Program to Compute Standard Errors of Indirect Effects
(J. Scott Long, Washington State University)

The following program uses PROC MATRIX in SAS to estimate the indirect effects and standard errors for models of the type discussed in the paper. There are two parts to the program.

Part I inputs the information necessary to do the computations. Users can modify this part to make it easier to enter data from the specific regression program being used. All that is necessary is that Part II of the program be passed the following variables:

(continued)

APPENDIX B Continued

(1) A matrix N_ALL contain the names of the endogenous variables followed by the names of the exogenous variables. Names can be up to eight characters.

(2) A matrix BG that contains estimates of the matrix (B|Γ). 999's are entered for fixed coefficients. Be careful that the order of the coefficients corresponds to the order of the variables in N_ALL.

(3) Matrices VB and VG corresponding to V_B and V_Γ in the text. Be very careful that the rows of VB correspond to the coefficients β_{11}, β_{21}, ..., β_{12}, β_{22}, ..., β_{13}, β_{23}, ..., etc; the rows of VG must correspond to the coefficients γ_{11}, γ_{21}, ..., γ_{12}, γ_{22}, ..., γ_{13}, γ_{23}, ..., etc. The columns must correspond to the non-999 coefficients in BG, in the same order as the coefficients in BG.

The data currently in Part I will estimate the results from Table 1 in the text.

Part II computes the indirect effects and the standard errors. You should not need to change this part of the program.

This program can be readily adapted to other matrix languages, such as found in GAUSS, LIMDEP, MINITAB or APL. To run under SAS, enter the following program; comments contained with *...;'s do not need to be typed.

```
PROC MATRIX;
*-------------------------------------------------------------------;
* PART I:  ENTER INFORMATION NECESSARY FOR COMPUTING STANDARD       ;
*          ERRORS.                                                  ;
*                                                                   ;
*          THE USER WILL HAVE TO ENTER INFORMATION AND MAKE         ;
*          CHANGES TO THIS PART OF THE PROGRAM.                     ;
*-------------------------------------------------------------------;
*                                                                   ;
*--- ENTER NAMES OF ENDOGENOUS AND EXOGENOUS VARIABLES -------------;
*          NAMES MUST BE IN THE SAME ORDER AS THE COLUMNS OF THE     ;
*          BETA AND GAMMA MATRICES.  UP TO EIGHT LETTERS PER NAME.   ;
*                                                                   ;
*                                                                   ;
   N_ENDOG = 'ETA1' 'ETA2' 'ETA3';   N_EXOG = 'XI1'  'XI2'  'XI3' ;
   N_ALL   = N_ENDOG || N_EXOG;
*                                                                   ;
*--- ENTER BG MATRIX - BETA NEXT TO GAMMA --------------------------;
*          USE 999S TO INDICATE FIXED COEFFICIENTS                  ;
*          THE METHOD USED HERE MAKES IT EASY TO COPY OUTPUT FROM    ;
*          PROC REG.  BE CERTAIN THAT THE ORDER OF COEFFICIENTS      ;
*          CORRESPONDS TO THE ORDER OF NAMES ENTERED ABOVE.          ;
*                                                                   ;
*          IF MORE THAN THREE EQUATIONS ARE USED, ADD ADDITIONAL     ;
*          LINES FOR BG4, BG5, ETC.                                 ;
*                                                                   ;
BG1 = 999        999        999 0.03845514 0.17074200 -0.22806880;
BG2 = 4.37671018 999        999 0.13516840 0.04900921 -0.46309866;
BG3 = 0.19979074 0.07043015 999 0.01139405 0.07116513 -0.03727020;
*                                                                   ;
*          IF ONLY BG1 AND BG2 ARE NEEDED, DELETE "//BG3".  IF       ;
*          MORE EQUATIONS ARE USED, ADD ADDITIONAL "//BGX"S.         ;
*          FOR EXAMPLE:  BG=BG1//BG2//BG3//BG4//BG5                  ;
*                                                                   ;
   BG=BG1//BG2//BG3;
*                                                                   ;
*--- ENTER VARIANCE/COVARIANCE MATRIX OF ESTIMATES ----------------;
*          SINCE COVARIANCES ACROSS EQUATIONS ARE ZERO, COVARIANCES  ;
```

(continued)

APPENDIX B Continued

```
*       FOR EACH EQUATION ARE ENTERED AND THEN STACKED                    ;
*                                                                         ;
*       THE COLUMNS IN S1 CORRESPOND TO THE NON-999 COEFFICIENTS          ;
*       IN BG1       ; SIMILARLY, S2 TO BG2 AND S3 TO BG3.                ;
*                                                                         ;
*       IF MORE EQUATIONS ARE USED, ADD ADDITIONAL LINES FOR              ;
*       S3, S4, ETC.                                                      ;
*                                                                         ;
S1 = .00000614071 -.0000191042  .00000513175 /
    -.0000191042  0.0002430764  .00005213595 /
     .00000513175  .00005213595 .0003106769   ;

S2 = 0.01446947    -.000556425  -.00247055  0.003300034   /
    -0.000556425  0.0003066151 -.000792329 0.0001114511 /
    -0.00247055   -0.000792329  0.011712    0.001858103  /
     0.003300034   0.0001114511 0.001858103 0.01518264    ;

S3 = 0.001324925   -.0000884125  -.0000241191 -0.000155818   .0001729777  /
    -.0000884125   .00002020069 -.0000027305 -9.90020E-07   .00000935491 /
    -.0000241191  -.0000027305   .00002024509 -.0000512281   .00000596022 /
    -.000155818  -9.90020E-07   -.0000512281  0.0007592669  .0001199912  /
     0.0001729777  .00000935491  .00000596022 0.0001199912  .0009885317   ;
*                                                                         ;
*       IF ADDITIONAL S'S WERE ADDED, ADD THEM TO THE NEXT LINE.          ;
*       FOR EXAMPLE:  S=BLOCK(S1,S2,S3,S4,S5). IF S3 IS NOT               ;
*       USED CHANGE THE NEXT LINE TO:  S=BLOCK(S1,S2)                     ;
*                                                                         ;
   S=BLOCK(S1,S2,S3);
*                                                                         ;
*--- ENTER VB MATRIX ----------------------------------------------------;
*       THE ROWS ARE ASSUMED TO BE IN THE ORDER:                         ;
*       B11, B21, ... , B21, B22, ... , B31, B32, ...                    ;
*                                                                         ;
*       THE COLUMNS ARE IN THE ORDER OF THE NON-999 COEFFICIENTS         ;
*       IN THE BG1, BG2, ... EQUATIONS.                                  ;
*                                                                         ;
VB = 0 0 0 0 0 0 0 0 0 0 0 0 /
     0 0 0 1 0 0 0 0 0 0 0 0 /
     0 0 0 0 0 0 0 1 0 0 0 0 /
     0 0 0 0 0 0 0 0 0 0 0 0 /
     0 0 0 0 0 0 0 0 0 0 0 0 /
     0 0 0 0 0 0 0 0 1 0 0 0 /
     0 0 0 0 0 0 0 0 0 0 0 0 /
     0 0 0 0 0 0 0 0 0 0 0 0 /
     0 0 0 0 0 0 0 0 0 0 0 0 ;
*                                                                         ;
*--- ENTER VG MATRIX ----------------------------------------------------;
*       THE ROWS ARE ASSUMED TO BE IN THE ORDER:                         ;
*       G11, G21, ... , G21, G22, ... , G31, G32, ...                    ;
*                                                                         ;
*       THE COLUMNS ARE IN THE ORDER OF THE NON-999 COEFFICIENTS         ;
*       IN THE BG1, BG2, ... EQUATIONS.                                  ;
*                                                                         ;
*       INCORRECT RESULTS OCCUR IF THE THESE ORDERINGS ARE NOT           ;
*       USED.                                                            ;
*                                                                         ;
VG = 1 0 0 0 0 0 0 0 0 0 0 0 /
     0 0 0 0 1 0 0 0 0 0 0 0 /
     0 0 0 0 0 0 0 0 0 1 0 0 /
     0 1 0 0 0 0 0 0 0 0 0 0 /
     0 0 0 0 0 1 0 0 0 0 0 0 /
     0 0 0 0 0 0 0 0 0 0 1 0 /
     0 0 1 0 0 0 0 0 0 0 0 0 /
     0 0 0 0 0 0 1 0 0 0 0 0 /
     0 0 0 0 0 0 0 0 0 0 0 1 ;
```

(continued)

APPENDIX B Continued

```
*---------------------------------------------------------------;
*                                                               ;
* PART II:   COMPUTE INDIRECT EFFECTS AND STANDARD ERRORS        ;
*                                                               ;
*           NO CHANGES NEED TO BE MADE TO THIS PART OF THE       ;
*           PROGRAM.                                             ;
*                                                               ;
*---------------------------------------------------------------;
*                                                               ;
*--- COMPUTE MATRICES NEEDED IN THE COMPUTATIONS --------------- ;
*                                                               ;
  M = NROW(BG);           N = NCOL(BG)-M;      * COUNT ENDOG & EXOG  ;
  B = BG(,1:M);           G = BG(,M+1:M+N);    * PULL OFF B & G      ;
  B = B#(B\ = 999);       G = G#(G\ = 999);    * ZERO FIXED COEFS    ;
  TEMP = SHAPE(BG,1)-999;                       * SELECT ONLY NON-    ;
  L = LOC(TEMP);          T = TEMP(L,)+999;     *  FIXED COEFS        ;
*                                                               ;
*--- COMPUTE T-VALUE FOR DIRECT EFFECTS ------------------------ ;
*                                                               ;
  SDBG = SQRT(VECDIAG(S));                      * GET SD OF DIRECT EFFECTS;
  TT = T#/SDBG;                                 * COMPUTE T-VALUES    ;
  T_BG = J(M*(M+N),1,-999);                     * STACK T-VALUES      ;
  T_BG(L,) = TT;                                *  TO MATCH BG FORM   ;
  T_BG = SHAPE(T_BG,M+N);
NOTE SKIP = 2 'DIRECT EFFECTS AND THEIR T-VALUES.';
PRINT BG COLNAME=N_ALL ROWNAME=N_ENDOG;
PRINT T_BG COLNAME=N_ALL ROWNAME=N_ENDOG;
*                                                               ;
*--- COMPUTE INDIRECT EFFECTS --------------------------------- ;
*                                                               ;
  IBI = INV(I(M)-B);                            * COMPUTE I-B INVERSE  ;
  TNN = IBI-I(M);                               * COMPUTE TOTAL EFFECTS ;
  TNE = IBI*G;
  PNN = TNN-B;                                  * COMPUTE INDIRECT EFFECTS;
  PNE = TNE-G;
*                                                               ;
*--- COMPUTE T-VALUES FOR INDIRECT EFFECTS -------------------- ;
*                                                               ;
  DFDT = VB'*(IBI@IBI' - I(M)@I(M));            * DF/DTHETA MATRIX     ;
  DGDT = (VB'*((IBI*G) @ IBI')) +
         (VG'*(I(N)@(IBI-I(M))'));              * DG/DTHETA MATRIX     ;
  SF = DFDT'*S*DFDT;                            * COVARIANCE OF INDIRECT ;
  SG = DGDT'*S*DGDT;                            *   EFFECTS            ;
  SDPNN = SQRT(VECDIAG(SF));                    * PULL OF STD DEVS OF  ;
  SDPNE = SQRT(VECDIAG(SG));                    *   INDIRECT EFFECTS   ;
  SDPNN = SHAPE(SDPNN,M)';                      * RESHAPE STD DEVS     ;
  SDPNE = SHAPE(SDPNE,M)';
  T_PNN = PNN#/SDPNN;                           * T'S OF INDIRECT      ;
  T_PNE = PNE#/SDPNE;                           *   EFFECTS            ;
NOTE SKIP = 2 'INDIRECT EFFECTS AND THEIR T-VALUES.';
PRINT PNN COLNAME = N_ENDOG ROWNAME = N_ENDOG;
PRINT T_PNN COLNAME = N_ENDOG ROWNAME = N_ENDOG;
PRINT PNE COLNAME = N_EXOG ROWNAME = N_ENDOG;
PRINT T_PNE COLNAME = N_EXOG ROWNAME = N_ENDOG;
```

3

Estimating Multiequation
Models with
Correlated Disturbances

LOWELL L. HARGENS

The general linear model (GLM) is the foundation of most
of the statistical research carried out by social scientists.
Its dominance is due to several factors, the most important being
its correspondence to common notions of causality and its great
flexibility. The GLM posits that a dependent variable is a linear
function of some independent variables and a disturbance term,
as represented by the equation

$$Y = \beta_0 + \beta_1 X_1 + \beta_2 X_2 + \ldots + \beta_k X_k + e \qquad [1]$$

where Y is the dependent variable, and $X_1 \ldots X_k$ are k independent variables.[1] The coefficients $\beta_1 \ldots \beta_k$ in equation 1 describe
the effects of changes in each of the independent variables on the
dependent variable, and β_0 is the intercept term, which gives the
predicted value of Y when all independent variables equal zero.
The final element in equation 1 is the "error" or "disturbance"
term, e, and it represents the effects on Y of various unobserved
factors, including errors in measuring Y. The presence of the
disturbance term in equation 1 allows for the possibility that the
independent variables do not completely determine the dependent
variable; this stipulation is usually seen as enhancing the model's
realism.[2] Unfortunately, its presence also complicates the estima-

AUTHOR'S NOTE: *This chapter has benefited from advice and assistance given
by J. Scott Long, Barbara F. Reskin, and Robert J. Sampson.*

tion of the β coefficients, and some assumptions about the behavior of e must be made before the β coefficients can be estimated (Hanushek and Jackson, 1977: 27-28).

Too often we view the e term in equation 1 as merely a "residual" that has no substantive meaning or importance. Also, because e is unobservable we may become too cavalier about the assumptions we make about it, because those assumptions usually cannot be checked. Failure to consider e seriously, however, can lead to the use of statistical procedures that yield misleading results. In this chapter I discuss assumptions about correlations between disturbances in different equations of multiequation models. In general, I argue that assuming that disturbances from different equations are uncorrelated is usually unjustifiable, and that estimation procedures that allow them to be correlated are almost always preferable to procedures that do not. I also discuss the effects of using the latter procedures instead of the former when disturbances are in fact correlated. These effects vary for different types of multiequation systems; sometimes only the efficiency of the estimates of the β coefficients is affected, while in other cases those estimates become biased and inconsistent (for a brief presentation of these concepts, see Wonnacott and Wonnacott, 1979: 55-66).

Thus the purpose of this chapter is to demonstrate the importance of explicitly considering assumptions about correlations between disturbances when estimating multiequation models.

ESTIMATION OF
SINGLE-EQUATION GLMs

Although our focus is on multiequation models, we need to consider briefly assumptions about the disturbance term that are made in order to estimate the β coefficients in single-equation models such as equation 1. This is because the questions about disturbances that must be answered to estimate coefficients in single-equation models must also be answered before one can estimate multiequation models. The most widely used technique for obtaining estimates of the β coefficients in equation 1 is ordinary least squares (OLS), and it is based on several assumptions about e, the most important of which are[3]

$$E(e_i X_{ki}) = 0 \quad \text{for} \quad i = 1, 2, \ldots N, \quad k = 1, 2, \ldots K \qquad [2]$$

$$E(e_i e_j) = 0 \quad \text{for} \quad i, j = 1, 2, \ldots N, \quad i \neq j \qquad [3]$$

$$E(e_i)^2 = \sigma^2 \quad \text{for} \quad i = 1, 2, \ldots N \qquad [4]$$

Equation 2 specifies that the expected value of the covariance between e and each of the independent variables is equal to zero. This is a crucial assumption for OLS analysis; if it is not met, OLS estimates of the β coefficients in equation 1 are biased and inconsistent (Hanushek and Jackson, 1977: 49-51). This results from the procedure by which OLS estimates the β coefficients. It produces an estimated equation $Y = b_0 + b_1 X_1 + \ldots + b_k X_k + u$ where u is an estimate of e under the constraint that u is uncorrelated with each of the independent variables. If e *is* correlated with any of the dependent variables, OLS estimates of the β coefficients are biased and inconsistent because e and u do not have the same properties.

In practice, e and the independent variables will be correlated when causes of Y that are not included among the independent variables are correlated with one or more of those independent variables (Hanushek and Jackson, 1977: 79-86). In such cases, the model being used to estimate the effects of the included independent variables is said to be "misspecified." In general, this kind of model misspecification is a theoretical rather than a statistical problem, and inadequate attention to it is probably the chief source of errors in quantitative research in the social sciences (Lieberson, 1985).

The assumptions in equations 3 and 4, respectively, require that the disturbances for different cases be uncorrelated (nonautocorrelation) and that the disturbances for all cases have the same variance (homoscedasticity). When either of these assumptions is violated, OLS estimates of the standard errors of the OLS b coefficients are incorrect. As a result, hypothesis tests involving the OLS estimates are erroneous. Fortunately, *if equation 2 holds*, it is often possible to estimate the variances and covariances of the disturbance terms. When this can be done it is possible to avoid the problem of violating OLS assumptions (3) and (4) by using generalized least squares (GLS) estimation procedures (Hanushek and Jackson, 1977: 146-169).

Thus the most important assumption for estimating single-equation models is that given by equation 2, because if it holds, researchers can deal with violations of the homoscedasticity and nonautocorrelation assumptions. It also bears repeating that before researchers can estimate multiequation models, they must be convinced that equations 2 through 4 hold or that they have dealt with any violations.

A TYPOLOGY OF
MULTIEQUATION MODELS

Because the effects of correlations between disturbances in different equations of multiequation models depend on the type of model, it is necessary to begin by specifying the different forms that such models can assume. To do this it is helpful to specify a general multiequation model as follows:

$$Y_1 = \beta_{12} Y_2 + \ldots + \beta_{1m} Y_m + \gamma_{10} X_0 + \gamma_{11} X_1 + \ldots + \gamma_{1k} X_k + e_1$$

$$Y_2 = \beta_{21} Y_1 + \ldots + \beta_{2m} Y_m + \gamma_{20} X_0 + \gamma_{21} X_1 + \ldots + \gamma_{1k} X_k + e_2$$

$$\vdots$$

$$Y_m = \beta_{m1} Y_1 + \ldots + \beta_{m\,m-1} Y_{m-1} + \gamma_{m0} X_0 + \gamma_{m1} X_1 + \ldots + \gamma_{mk} X_k + e_m$$

Thus the system of equations contains two sets of observed variables. The first consists of m Y variables, each of which appears on the left side of one of the equations and is called an endogenous variable. The remaining k observed variables, the Xs, are never on the left side of an equation, and are called exogenous variables.[4] As before, the m e variables are unobserved disturbances. Finally, there are two types of unobserved coefficients in these equations. Each β_{ij} coefficient represents the effect of the j*th* endogenous variable on the i*th*, and each γ_{ik} coefficient represents the effect of the k*th* exogenous variable on the i*th* endogenous variable. This system of equations can be written more compactly as the matrix equation[5]

$$Y = BY + \Gamma X + e$$

where

$$Y' = (Y_1\, Y_2\, \dots\, Y_m), \quad X' = (X_1\, X_2\, \dots\, X_k), \quad e' = (e_1\, e_2\, \dots\, e_m),$$

and

$$
B = \begin{bmatrix}
0 & \beta_{12} & \beta_{13} & \cdots & \beta_{1m} \\
\beta_{21} & 0 & \beta_{23} & \cdots & \beta_{2m} \\
\vdots & \vdots & \vdots & & \vdots \\
\beta_{m1} & \beta_{m2} & \beta_{m3} & \cdots & 0
\end{bmatrix}
\qquad
\Gamma = \begin{bmatrix}
\gamma_{10} & \gamma_{11} & \cdots & \gamma_{1k} \\
\gamma_{20} & \gamma_{21} & \cdots & \gamma_{2k} \\
\vdots & \vdots & & \vdots \\
\gamma_{m0} & \gamma_{m1} & \cdots & \gamma_{mk}
\end{bmatrix}
$$

We will distinguish between three types of multiequation models in terms of the contents of the B matrix. The first type consists of cases where all elements in B are zero, in other words, where there are no causal links among the endogenous variables. This type is called "seemingly unrelated regression" (SUR) systems of equations. The second type consists of cases where all of the nonzero elements in **B** are below the main diagonal.[6] We will call this type "recursive systems."[7] Finally, "nonrecursive systems" place no restrictions on the elements in B other than that the main diagonal elements all equal zero. Such systems contain direct and/or indirect feedback loops among the endogenous variables.

In the following pages I discuss each of these three types of multiequation models, noting how correlations between the disturbance terms of different equations affect both the estimation of the β and γ coefficients and hypothesis tests about them.

SEEMINGLY UNRELATED REGRESSION SYSTEMS OF EQUATIONS

As defined above, a SUR system exists when the endogenous variables in a model are not causally linked, but the disturbances of the equations are correlated. The former condition often leads researchers to overlook the possibility that the various equations are interrelated. Figure 1 presents one example of a SUR system.

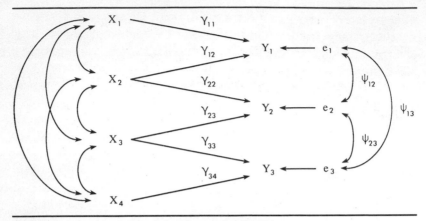

Figure 1: A Seemingly Unrelated Regression System

Note that the independent variables that appear in each of the equations need not be the same. In fact, it is in cases where they differ that there are superior alternatives to OLS estimates of the γ coefficients.

Recently published studies that involve SUR systems include a study of the effects of various metropolitan structural characteristics on rates of four types of violent crime in U.S. SMSAs (Blau and Blau, 1982), research on how social causation and social construction variables affect eight age- and sex-specific suicide rates (Pescosolido and Mendelsohn, 1986), and a study of the effects of several cultural variables on four structural characteristics of business organizations (Lincoln et al., 1978).

In each of these instances, it seems reasonable to expect correlated disturbance terms across equations because omitted variables, presumably uncorrelated with the independent variables in each equation, may still affect the dependent variables in more than one equation. SUR systems typically contain endogenous variables—rates for types of violent crime, age- and sex-specific suicide rates, and so on—that are closely related, although not causally linked with each other. Such endogenous variables are likely to be influenced similarly by variables the disturbance term encompasses. For example, in a study like the Blaus' one might expect that an unusually cool summer in Detroit could depress both murder and assault rates for that city. Weather conditions were not included in the analysis, and even though they might well be uncorrelated with the independent variables that are included, it seems likely that they could contribute to correlations between the disturbances. The alternative, that the disturbances are uncorrelated, seems unlikely. Because the Blaus published the correlations upon which their analysis is based, it is possible to estimate the six correlations between the disturbances for their four types of crime using Jöreskog and Sörbom's LISREL program.[8] The estimates range from .16 to .29, not particularly large but all highly significant statistically (t values range from 3.8 to 5.5).

There are two consequences of cross-equation correlations between the disturbances in SUR systems. First, OLS estimates of the γ coefficients, although still unbiased and consistent, often are not most efficient—that is, they are not minimum variance estimates. This is because OLS estimation ignores information about the cross-equation correlations between disturbances, and procedures that take this additional information into account can be superior to OLS. Second and more important is the fact that tests of hypotheses about γ coefficients in different equations (for example, that $\gamma_{12} = \gamma_{22}$) will give erroneous results if they ignore the correlations between disturbances. OLS-based procedures for testing such hypotheses (Specht and Warren, 1976) give incorrect results because they assume that the disturbances for different equations are uncorrelated. When that assumption is not met, it is necessary to use a test statistic that takes account of the correlated disturbances (Theil, 1971: 312-317).

Let us examine the effects of correlated disturbances on the efficiency of estimates of the γ coefficients in more detail. Kmenta (1970: 520-524) shows that the loss of efficiency resulting from the use of OLS is positively related to (1) the absolute magnitudes of the correlations between the disturbances, and (2) the lack of redundancy between the independent variables in different equations. The first factor is easily understood. When disturbances are uncorrelated, OLS estimates are best linear unbiased estimates; but as the correlations between disturbances increase in magnitude, OLS becomes increasingly inefficient compared to procedures that take the correlations into account. The effect of redundancy is not obvious, but when exactly the same independent variables appear in all equations,[9] OLS procedures are most efficient, even in the presence of correlated disturbances. To the extent that the independent variables in different equations are uncorrelated, OLS estimates are relatively inefficient compared to procedures that take the correlations between disturbances into account. Thus use of the latter procedures will give no advantage over OLS in exploratory studies where several dependent variables are regressed on a common set of independent variables. In instances where an investigator wishes to estimate models for two or more dependent variables and in which proper specification of the models involves sets of independent variables that do not overlap completely, however, estimation procedures that take account of the correlations between disturbances can be expected to yield more accurate estimates of the γ coefficients than OLS.

A study by Sampson (1986) of the determinants of race-specific robbery-offender rates for large U.S. cities exemplifies an analysis that is well suited to SUR estimation techniques. Sampson specified that each race-specific robbery offender rate was a function of five race-specific characteristics of the cities' populations— per-capita income, mean public assistance payments, percentage of female-headed households, male employment ratios, and median age—and various characteristics of the cities as wholes: region, size, density, and so on. Thus each set of race-specific independent variables appears only in the equation for the corresponding race-specific robbery-offender rate, while the city characteristics appear in both equations. The correlation between the disturbances for Sampson's model for the two robbery-offender rates equaled .33 (t = 6.1).

The relative efficiency of two unbiased statistical techniques for estimating a given parameter is usually assessed by computing the ratio of the squared estimated standard errors for the two techniques (Hanushek and Jackson, 1977: 339). For Sampson's analysis, the ratio of the squared maximum likelihood estimated standard errors obtained from the LISREL program to those produced by OLS for the ten race-specific independent variables equal on average .70, whereas these ratios for the independent variables included in both equations average .96. Thus the gains in efficiency that can be realized through the use of SUR estimation techniques were limited to those variables that appeared in only one of the equations in Sampson's model.

Except for economists, social scientists rarely take correlated disturbances into account when analyzing SUR systems; instead, they apply OLS separately to each equation in such systems.[10]

Alternative techniques that take correlated disturbances into account include single-equation methods or system methods.[11] I discuss each of these types in turn. Zellner (1962) developed a single-equation method for estimating SUR systems. Zellner's method begins by estimating the correlations between disturbances from OLS residuals, which are unbiased estimates of the disturbances because OLS estimates of the γ coefficients are unbiased. The estimated correlations are then included in a GLS estimation of all the equations in the SUR system (see Theil, 1971: 297-311). System methods for estimating SUR models include procedures for carrying out full-information maximum likelihood estimation (MLE). MLE estimates can be obtained through general structural equation MLE programs, such as LISREL and EQS, or through iterative GLS programs.[12] The former tend to be more flexible, in that they allow one to estimate SUR models that specify that some, but not all, of the disturbances are correlated, whereas the latter automatically allow correlations between all pairs of disturbances. The latter programs are typically easier to learn and use than the former, however.

Computer program availability is not likely to limit a researcher's choice among these estimation procedures. The two-stage and iterative GLS techniques are available in nearly all econometric estimation packages (Time Series Processor, Shazam, LIMDEP, GAUSS) as well as in SAS; LISREL is available at many locations as part of SPSSX; and EQS as a part of BMDP.

It is worth repeating that if one wishes to test hypotheses about coefficients in different equations of a SUR model, then it is *necessary* to use a program that performs one of the procedures that estimate the correlations among the disturbances and take them into account in carrying out the tests—OLS tests give incorrect results regardless of whether the same independent variables appear in all of the model's equations.

RECURSIVE SYSTEMS OF EQUATIONS

The last two decades have seen a sharp increase in social scientists' use of structural equation models, most involving recursive systems with uncorrelated disturbance terms. This subset has several desirable technical features. First, the β and γ coefficients in these models are best estimated by OLS, a very attractive feature when only OLS computer programs are available. Second, their coefficients are always identifiable, thereby eliminating the identification problems that can result when models are non-recursive or have correlated disturbances.[13] Third, these systems have a simplicity that makes them well suited for pedagogical purposes, and several cohorts of social scientists learned about structural equation models from sources that relied on recursive models with uncorrelated disturbances almost to the exclusion of other types.

Often the stipulation that disturbances in a recursive system are uncorrelated seems to be made for convenience's sake rather than on the basis of any evidence or logical reasoning about the disturbances. Indeed, published reports of research based on recursive models almost never give reasons for this stipulation. Hanushek and Jackson (1977: 229-231; see also Land, 1973: 48), in one of the few discussions of this issue, argue strongly that it is likely that disturbances will be correlated across equations. This is because the variables encompassed in the disturbance term, even though they may be uncorrelated with the exogenous variables in the system, are likely to affect more than one of the endogenous variables. This argument is similar to that given above for why disturbances in SUR systems are likely to be correlated.

If disturbances are correlated across equations, OLS estimates are biased and inconsistent for those equations that contain endogenous variables among the regressors (Hanushek and Jackson, 1977: 229). This occurs because correlated disturbances logically imply that the OLS assumption that the disturbance term is uncorrelated with all of the regressors will be violated. It is worth noting that correlations between disturbances are more damaging to OLS estimates of recursive system parameters than to OLS estimates of parameters in SUR systems, which are unbiased though not efficient. In addition, because OLS estimates are biased and inconsistent for recursive systems with correlated disturbances, using OLS residuals to estimate the correlations between disturbances, appropriate for SUR systems, is inappropriate. Finally, OLS-based procedures for testing hypotheses about coefficients in different equations—for example, $\gamma_{12} = \gamma_{22}$—are inappropriate for both SUR systems and recursive systems when disturbances are correlated across equations.

Thus disturbances are likely to be correlated in recursive systems of equations, and unless researchers can present convincing reasons for believing that disturbances are uncorrelated, they should not use OLS estimation for such systems.

There are both single-equation and system alternatives to OLS for estimating recursive structural-equation models. The most prominent technique in the former category is the instrumental-variable procedure, usually called two-stage least squares (TSLS). To illustrate this procedure briefly, let us consider the structural-equation model:

$$Y_1 = \gamma_{10} + \gamma_{11} X_1 + \gamma_{12} X_2 + e_1 \tag{6}$$

$$Y_2 = \beta_{21} Y_1 + \gamma_{20} + \gamma_{22} X_2 + e_2 \tag{7}$$

with $E(e_1 X_1) = E(e_1 X_2) = E(e_2 X_1) = E(e_2 X_2) = 0$, but $E(e_1 e_2) \neq 0$. This model can be represented by Figure 2.

OLS will yield biased and inconsistent estimates of the coefficients in equation 7 of this model because the equation fails to meet the OLS assumption that the disturbance term is uncorrelated with the regressors. One can see this by multiplying each of the terms in equation 6 by e_2. Taking expectations (see Duncan, 1975: 6-7), one obtains $\text{Cov}(Y1, e_2) = \gamma_{11} \text{Cov}(x_1, e_2) + \gamma_{12} \text{Cov}(x_2, e_2) + \text{Cov}(e_1, e_2)$. Now by assumption $\text{Cov}(X_1, e_2) = \text{Cov}(X_2, e_2) = 0$, and representing $\text{Cov}(e_1, e_2)$ as ψ_{12} we have $\text{Cov}(Y_1, e_2) = \psi_{12}$. If $\psi_{12} \neq 0$, then one of the regressors in equation 7, Y_1, is correlated with the disturbance for that equation.

The instrumental-variable procedure for estimating the coefficients in equation 7 is based on the idea that one can find a proxy variable for Y_1 that is substantially correlated with it, yet uncorrelated with e_1, and thus with e_2. One obtains such a variable, $\hat{Y}_1$, where $\hat{Y}_1 = b_0 + b_1 X_1 + b_2 X_2$, by estimating equation 6 with OLS. Because $\text{Cov}(\hat{Y}_1, e_1) = 0$, and therefore $\text{Cov}(\hat{Y}_1, e_2) = \psi_{12}(0) = 0$, the OLS assumption in equation 2 is met (see Wonnacott and Wonnacott, 1979: 255-262).[14] Therefore, the estimates obtained when one replaces $\hat{Y}_1$ for Y_1 and uses OLS to estimate the "second-stage" equation $Y_2 = \gamma_{20} + \beta_{21} \hat{Y}_1 + \gamma_{22} X_2 + e_2$ are unbiased.

Substituting $\hat{Y}_1$, the "instrumental variable," for Y_1 in estimating equation 7 is not an arbitrary and substantively unjustified step. It is justified by equation 6, which formalizes the researcher's substantive knowledge about Y_1. In general, the adequacy of the instrumental-variable procedure depends upon the

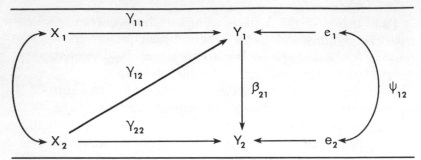

Figure 2: A Recursive System with Correlated Disturbances

adequacy of the researcher's substantive knowledge of the causal processes operating on the endogenous variables. Specifically, when the exogenous variables that are used to create an instrumental variable, $\hat{Y}$, account for only a small fraction of the variance in the corresponding observed variable Y, the efficiency of the parameter estimates TSLS yields will be low compared to situations in which $\hat{Y}$ and Y are highly correlated. Thus when a researcher is unable to explain a substantial proportion of the variance in Y_1, low efficiency will handicap attempts to estimate the model's coefficients. Worse consequences occur when a researcher misspecifies the determinants of Y_1 such that some determinants that are correlated with the exogenous variables in the model are not included among the exogenous variables in the model. In this case the TSLS procedure will produce biased and inconsistent estimates.

When researchers allow disturbances to be correlated across equations they must meet more stringent requirements in order to identify the coefficients in their models. A necessary condition for identifiability in models with correlations among all disturbance terms is the "order condition." One way to state this condition is that the number of exogenous variables in the model that are excluded from a given equation must equal or exceed the number of endogenous variables that are included as independent variables in that equation (Hanushek and Jackson, 1977: 261-262). Both equations in the above model meet this condition; equation 6 excludes neither of the two exogenous variables but it includes no endogenous variables as independent variables, and equation 7 includes one endogenous variable, Y_1, as an independent variable, but also excludes one exogenous variable, X_1.

To illustrate why it is impossible to use TSLS to estimate the coefficients in an equation that does not meet the order condition, let us add a third equation to the two-equation model above.

$$Y_3 = \beta_{32} Y_2 + \gamma_{30} + \gamma_{31} X_1 + \gamma_{32} X_2 + e_3 \qquad [8]$$

As before, we allow e_3 to be correlated with the other disturbance terms in the model. The first step in using TSLS to estimate the coefficients in equation 8 would be to regress Y_2 on X_2 and X_3 using OLS to obtain $\hat{Y}_2$. It is impossible to perform the second stage of the TSLS procedure, however, because $\hat{Y}_2$ is defined as a linear combination of the two exogenous variables, so the three independent variables used in the second stage of the TSLS procedure are perfectly collinear. This makes it impossible to estimate their independent effects on the dependent variable. In sum, only one endogenous variable, Y_2, is included in equation 8, but neither exogenous variable in the system is excluded. As a result, the coefficients in the equation are not identifiable.

The TSLS procedure is not unique in being unable to estimate the coefficients in equation 8; no technique can do so. I use TSLS in the above example because it clearly shows how insufficient information renders TSLS unable to estimate the coefficients in that equation.

In order to estimate the coefficients of the various equations in a recursive system with correlated disturbances, one must usually be able to exclude one or more exogenous variables from each of the equations.[15] This is often difficult because properly specifying a model tends to be incompatible with meeting identification conditions. It is important to remember, however, that when these two goals conflict, proper model specification always takes precedence. For example, suppose that existing theoretical and substantive knowledge leads a researcher to believe that the recursive model in Figure 3 is properly specified. The equations for Y_2 and Y_3 in this model are not identifiable because each includes an endogenous variable as an independent variable but excludes no exogenous variables. Note that dropping the causal impacts of X_1 on Y_2 and Y_3 from the analysis in order to identify the coefficients in the equations for Y_2 and Y_3 will misspecify equations 7 and 8 in the new model, yielding biased and inconsistent estimates for

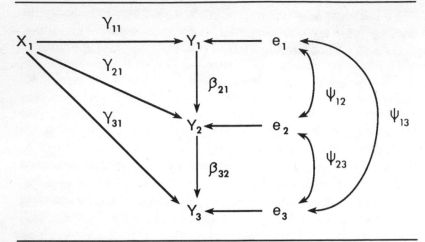

Figure 3: An Unidentified Recursive System

those equations. Similarly, assuming the disturbances are uncorrelated solely to make the coefficients in those equations identifiable will, once again, yield biased and inconsistent estimates. Thus the fact that all coefficients in a recursive system with uncorrelated disturbances are identifiable cannot justify assuming that the disturbances of a particular model are uncorrelated. This assumption must be based on logical or substantive knowledge about the variables the disturbance term subsumes. Without such knowledge, one should not make the assumption.[16]

How can one modify the above model to make all of its equations identifiable? The general strategy is to use one's knowledge about the variables encompassed by the disturbance terms to specify those that affect some endogenous variables but not others. Adding these variables to the appropriate equations will help to identify the coefficients in the equations from which they are excluded, especially if they substantially affect the dependent variables for the equations in which they are included.[17] Identifying additional variables that have the needed causal links to the endogenous variables and obtaining measures of these variables are not easy tasks, and in some cases they may be impossible even in principle. Thus a class of recursive models exists for which the requirements of proper specification and identification are incompatible and, as a result, contain parameters that cannot be estimated.

A final point should be made about the relation between allowing for correlated disturbances and proper model specification. Some argue that using techniques that allow for correlated disturbances helps statistical estimation by guarding against the possibility that variables omitted from a model may lead to biased and inconsistent estimates. This is true only for omitted variables that meet the assumption in equation 2—variables that are uncorrelated with the exogenous variables and are therefore appropriately encompassed by the disturbance term. In contrast, if one has omitted variables that affect the endogenous variables and are correlated with the exogenous variables, allowing for correlated disturbances will not magically undo the violation of equation 2. Only adding the omitted variables to the analysis will remedy this type of misspecification.

The above comments should demonstrate that the major difficulties involved in estimating recursive models with correlated disturbances are theoretical and substantive difficulties rather than technical ones. In fact, computer programs for TSLS estimation are widely available in econometric program packages and in more general packages such as SAS. The TSLS programs are typically quite easy to use. Programs that carry out system estimation of recursive systems with correlated disturbances include three-stage least squares programs and MLE programs. Most of the packages that contain a TSLS program provide the former, and the latter are found in the sources listed in the above discussion of SUR estimation. Researchers should be aware that the system methods tend to be more sensitive to specification errors than single-equation methods such as TSLS. The system methods estimate coefficients for all equations simultaneously, and thus specification errors in one equation can affect estimates in all of the other equations of the model (see Burt, 1976, for an instructive discussion of this problem for models with latent variables). In contrast, because TSLS estimates each equation in a recursive system separately, errors in the specification of one equation are not as likely to affect the estimates of coefficients in other equations.

NONRECURSIVE SYSTEMS OF EQUATIONS

A number of texts discuss the basic principles underlying the estimation of nonrecursive models (see, for example, Berry, 1984; Duncan, 1975), so I will give only a brief treatment here. When the endogenous variables in a multiequation system have direct or indirect causal feedback relationships with each other, their disturbance terms are especially likely to be correlated. Econometric techniques for estimating these systems nearly always assume that all of the disturbances in such systems are correlated. For example, the order and rank conditions for establishing identifiability are based on this assumption, as is the most popular technique for estimating such systems, TSLS. Thus when researchers estimate nonrecursive models, they typically follow the econometricians' lead in assuming that all disturbances are correlated.

As is the case for recursive systems, the chief difficulties in estimating the coefficients in nonrecursive systems involve proper model specification and meeting identification conditions. It is noteworthy that although assumptions that disturbances are uncorrelated will often help the researcher meet identification conditions, this strategy is usually dismissed as a likely source of model misspecification. Hanushek and Jackson (1977: 274) offer an example in which logical grounds suggest the assumption that a subset of the disturbances in a model are uncorrelated, but argue that it is usually difficult to justify this kind of assumption. The reader should be aware that although pedagogical exercises sometimes assume that disturbances are uncorrelated (Jöreskog and Sörbom, 1981: III. 87-90), these exercises should not be construed as advocating the assumption.

Once the researcher is satisfied that a multiequation model is properly specified and meets identifiability conditions, a wide range of computer programs are accessible to carry out the estimation. Previous sections already enumerated some of these programs.

CONCLUSION

In this chapter I have argued that researchers need to consider carefully the assumptions they make about correlations between disturbances when they choose a method for estimating coefficients in multiequation systems. In particular, it is generally unreasonable to assume that disturbances in such models are uncorrelated, and thus OLS is often inappropriate to estimate their parameters. In the past, the lack of computer programs for other estimation procedures contributed to the improper use of OLS, but appropriate programs are now widely available. Although it is a misspecification to posit that disturbances are correlated when they are not, I have emphasized the opposite type of misspecification because researchers tend to assume that disturbances are uncorrelated more frequently than that they are correlated, and because the latter assumption is generally more appropriate than the former.

It should be emphasized, however, that the methods reviewed above for taking correlated disturbances into account are of little value if one's model contains other specification errors. In particular, omitting important independent variables that are correlated with included exogenous variables *always* leads to biased and inconsistent estimates that cannot be remedied by allowing for correlated disturbances. Discussions of model misspecification in textbooks tend to focus on demonstrating the consequences of misspecification rather than providing guidance on how to avoid it. This is because model misspecification usually stems from inadequate theoretical and substantive knowledge rather than inadequate technical procedures. Social scientists increasingly appreciate the dependence of their research procedures on proper model specification (Lieberson, 1985). Greater sensitivity to these issues should enhance awareness of techniques that take account of correlated disturbances, and foster the development of the property specified models on which these techniques depend.

NOTES

1. These variables may be either observed or unobserved. To incorporate unobserved or "latent" variables in the GLM framework, however, one must have observed indicators of them or measures of their causes (Long, 1983). Latent-variable models are subject to the same considerations as those discussed below for models with observed independent and dependent variables.

2. It is usually impossible to include all the causes of a given dependent variable in a model, and some social phenomena may be inherently stochastic.

3. For a more complete discussion of the OLS assumptions, see Hanushek and Jackson (1977: 46-54).

4. The first of these, X_0, equals unity for all cases and is necessary for the determination of the intercept term, γ_{i0}, for each equation.

5. This formalization is just a modification of the general formula for structural equation models. Different authors use different symbols for any or all of these matrices. For example, the LISREL computer program (Jöreskog and Sörbom, 1981), which is referred to at various points below, denotes Y as η, X as ξ, and e as ζ, but uses the same symbols as those below for the two coefficient matrices. In addition, LISREL denotes the variance-covariance matrix of the disturbances as ψ. Long (1983: 25-33) discusses the LISREL structural equation in detail and gives helpful examples of its application to specific problems.

6. The order of the endogenous variables may be rearranged to bring this about. Thus the important feature of these models is that endogenous variables higher in the causal order never affect ones that are lower in the causal order (see Duncan, 1975: 25-28).

7. Different authors define recursive systems differently. Sociologists tend to define them as above, with reference only to the **B** matrix. Econometricians, on the other hand, tend to define recursive systems as having uncorrelated disturbances across equations as well as a triangular **B**. Because the focus of this chapter is on the effects of correlations between disturbances in different equations, it is convenient to follow the former convention.

8. One does this by specifying that the **B** matrix is a zero matrix and that ψ is a nondiagonal symmetric matrix containing free parameters (Jöreskog and Sörbom, 1981).

9. By this I mean that cases have the same values for corresponding variables in the different equations. This is not the same as the situation where independent variables in different equations have the same substantive meaning but different values—a typical occurrence in SUR models for time-series data (see Zellner, 1962). For a more detailed discussion of the conditions under which OLS estimates are most efficient even in the presence of correlated disturbances, see Kmenta (1971: 521-524).

10. This is of no consequence in analyses, such as the Blaus' study of types of violent crime, that include the same exogenous variables in all equations and test no hypotheses about coefficients in different equations.

11. For a more complete discussion of this distinction and the statistical properties of some of the methods that are included in each category, see Long (1983: 42-47).

12. In the latter, the GLS estimates of the coefficients yielded by the two-stage GLS procedure are used to reestimate the correlations between disturbances, which are, in turn, incorporated in a second GLS estimation of the coefficients in the SUR system. This cycle is repeated until estimates of coefficients and correlations between disturbances become stable over successive cycles (Kmenta and Gilbert, 1968). The iterative GLS procedure is asymptotically equivalent to MLE.

13. Discussion of the identification problem is beyond the scope of this chapter. For a good introduction, see Berry (1984: 18-56).

14. Equation 7 is just identified, and "indirect least squares" would yield the same estimates as TSLS (Hanushek and Jackson, 1977: 231-235).

15. This is not true for the first equation in recursive systems because by definition no endogenous variables act as independent variables in those equations.

16. When researchers neglect the possibility that disturbances are correlated across equations, they are likely to conclude mistakenly that the endogenous variables in a system

are causally linked when in reality they form a SUR system.

17 For good introductory discussions of ways to identify unidentified models, see Duncan (1975: 81-90) and Berry (1984: 56-60).

4

Problems in the Use and Interpretation of Product Variables

GENE A. FISHER

Product variables often occur in the context of a theoretically hypothesized interaction. Examples include the effect of "socialization into culture goals" and "access to institutionalized means" on deviant behavior (Merton, 1957); the effect of "prior strain" and "structural conduciveness" on collective outbursts (Smelser, 1962); the effect of education and work experience on income (Stoltzenberg, 1974); and the effects of coping responses, social support, and stress on psychological distress (Pearlin et al., 1981).

A variable X is said to interact with another variable Z or with itself when its relationship to a third variable Y depends in some way on the values of the other variable or on its own value. Product variables[1] are most likely to appear when the interacting variable is thought to "moderate," "buffer," or "facilitate" the *effect* of the other variable. For example, social support *buffers* the effects of stress; structural conduciveness *facilitates* the effect of prior strain.

To see how product terms arise in the specification of statistical models of interaction, consider the relationship between social support and psychological distress. The theory advocated by Brown and Harris (1978) can be represented in this way:

$$Y = \alpha + \beta X + \epsilon \tag{1}$$

$$\beta = \gamma + \delta Z \tag{2}$$

where Y is a random variable measuring distress, and X and Z are measures of stress and social support, respectively. In this model

Z does not have a direct effect on Y. Rather Z affects Y through its effect on the regression coefficient of Y on X.

The theory espoused by Brown and Harris (1978) predicts that the coefficient γ is positive, while δ is negative. This means that when social support (Z) is utterly lacking (i.e., Z = 0), β, the effect of stress (X) on distress (Y) reaches its maximum value, γ; but as social support increases, β decreases. In this way, social support *buffers* the effect of stress.

By substituting equation 2 into equation 1 we obtain the following estimation equation:

$$Y = \alpha + (\gamma + \delta Z)X + \epsilon = \alpha + \gamma X + \delta(XZ) + \epsilon \qquad [3]$$

If the assumptions of the general linear model are met (see Johnston, 1972: 121-123), ordinary least squares applied to equation 3 provide the best linear unbiased estimates of the parameters in equations 1 and 2. Note that the estimating equation 3 contains the product variable XZ, even though the original model was not couched in terms of product variables.

Equations 1 and 2 represent but one of many possible ways of describing the effect of X on Y. One alternative is to specify a different *form* for the effect of Z on the regression coefficient β in equation 1:

$$\beta = \gamma(1 + Z)^{\delta} \qquad [4]$$

In this model the effect of Z on β is nonlinear, because theory suggests not only that the effect of social support (Z) is to reduce the effect of stress (X), but also that this "buffering" effect diminishes as ones's level of social support increases. In other words, the more support one has, the less additional support one needs to relieve distress.

To illustrate, let $\gamma = 2$, and $\delta = -2$. If Z = 0 (no support), then $\beta = 2$, and a unit change in X increases the expected value of Y by 2; if Z = 1 (low support), then $\beta = .5$ and a unit change in X will increase the expected value of Y by .5; if Z = 3 (moderate support), then $\beta = .13$; and if Z = 4 (high support), then $\beta = .08$. The decrease in β is far greater when one moves from Z = 0 to Z = 1 than from Z = 3 to Z = 4, showing that the buffering effect of social support is stronger at low levels of support than at high levels.

The parameters α, γ, and δ of the model represented by equations 1 and 4 are more difficult to estimate than the model represented by equations 1 and 2, because it is not possible to derive a linear estimating equation from equations 1 and 4. Still, it shows that as we find more subtle specifications of the interaction of two variables, we are also likely to develop more complex formulations of their product.

These examples illustrate how product variables arise in the context of studying interactions. They suggest that the parameters of many models involving interaction can be estimated quite easily with conventional regression techniques. But while we may use regression to *estimate* interaction effects, we should not use it to *interpret* such effects. Many errors have been made because regression equations resembling equation 3 were interpreted as modeling the process under investigation. In fact, the problems of interpretation appeared so formidable that at one point it was suggested that models involving product variables were not appropriate (Althauser, 1971: 466; Sockloff, 1976). Subsequent work by Allison (1977), Cohen (1978), and Southwood (1978) provide the guidelines one needs to make appropriate use of product variables. See also Cleary and Kessler (1982), Marsden (1981), and Finney et al. (1984) for excellent recent discussions of the interpretation of interaction effects involving product variables.

This chapter attempts to bring together the advances made in our understanding of the use of product variables during the past decade. The proper specification of interactive models that contain product terms is considered first, with an emphasis on the key role played by substantive theory in deriving the estimating equation. Problems of estimation are considered next. Special consideration is given to estimating nonlinear models of interaction. The goal of this section is to show how estimates of interaction effects are obtained. The next section shows how estimates of parameters and their standard errors are used to test hypotheses about the effects specified in the model. A major concern of this section is to show that different models of interaction require different testing procedures. The crucial distinctions introduced in the development of models involving product variables are reviewed in the final section of the chapter.

SPECIFICATION OF MODELS
CONTAINING PRODUCT VARIABLES

Ideally, product variables are added to a regression equation because the researcher has theoretical reasons for expecting an interaction. If an exploratory analysis uncovers the presence of a statistically significant interaction, the researcher must find a substantive reason to account for it. In either case, the interpretation of the regression coefficient associated with a product variable depends primarily on substantive theory to specify how the variables in the model are related and measured.

THE ROLE OF THEORY IN
SPECIFYING INTERACTION MODELS

Smith and Sasaki (1979) examine the effects of energy consumption (C) and democratic performance (D) on income equality (E). They predicted that energy consumption, taken as an indicator of industrialization and economic development, would have a direct effect on income equality, and that it would also have an *indirect effect* via democratic performance, because, *according to their theory*, with economic development comes a strong pressure toward democratic forms of government. Their model is expressed in the following equations:

$$D = \beta_1 C + u \qquad\qquad [5]$$

$$E = \beta_2 C + \beta_3 D + v \qquad\qquad [6]$$

where β_2 and β_3 are the direct effects of C and D on E, and β_1 is the direct effect of C on D. The indirect effect of C via D is equal to $\beta_1 \beta_2$. The hypotheses then are that all the β's are greater than zero.

An analysis of data from 60 countries yielded the following standardized regression coefficients: $\beta_1 = .56$; $\beta_2 = .05$; and $\beta_3 = .55$. Contrary to theoretical prediction, the direct effect of D on E was very small ($\beta_2 = .05$) and not statistically significant. The effect of C on D was large, as predicted, ($\beta_1 = .56$), but the indirect effect, $\beta_1 \beta_2 = (.56)(.05) = .03$, was negligible and statistically insignificant.

A bit more theoretical reasoning suggested an interactive model. The effect of economic development (measured by energy consumption) should be facilitated by development of democratic institutions, and at the same time the effect of democratic performance would be contingent on the prevailing level of economic development.

The mathematics needed to represent this line of reasoning is more complex than what is required in equations 1-3. Rather than start with an equation for E, we must start with equations for the *effect* of each variable on E. These are *differential* equations, because they show how E changes, given a change in C or D. Then, using the calculus, these equations are *integrated* to get the equation that expresses E as a function solely of C and D.

The application of this method yields the following model: The effect of C on E is

$$\partial E/\partial C = \beta_2 = \alpha_1 + \tau D \qquad [7]$$

The effect of D on E is

$$\partial E/\partial D = \beta_3 = \alpha_2 + \tau E \qquad [8]$$

where $\partial E/\partial C$ represents the change in E for a change in C holding all other variables constant, and similarly, $\partial E/\partial D$ represents the change in E for a change in D, holding all other variables constant. β_2 and β_3 are included in equations 7 and 8 to show how this model builds on the previous model represented by equation 6.

Equations 7 and 8 are integrated to obtain the following estimating equation:

$$E = \alpha_0 + \alpha_1 C + \alpha_2 D + \gamma CD + \epsilon \qquad [9]$$

Smith and Sasaki (1979) found that γ was statistically significant, supporting their theory. But as the model is presently specified, C and D contribute equally to the mutual interaction. That is, the effect of D on the effect of C on E is the same as the effect of C on the effect of D on E. In both cases the effect is γ. Yet one may have a theoretical reason to believe that the facilitating effect of democratic institutions on economic development is greater than the dependency of democratic institutions on the level of economic development. The present specification of the model does not allow one to consider this hypothesis.

Further theoretical reflection suggests another model. The effect of energy consumption, C, may depend both on itself and on income equality, E. If equality is high, the effect of C must diminish, because there is little more equality to achieve. But as C becomes larger, the effect of C should grow stronger, or accelerate. The same sort of argument can be applied to democratic performance, D.

In this model the effect of C on E is specified as

$$\partial E / \partial C = \gamma_1 C / E \qquad [10]$$

and the effect of D on E

$$\partial E / \partial D = \gamma_2 D / E \qquad [11]$$

These equations are integrated to form

$$E = (\alpha + \gamma_1 C^2 + \gamma_2 D^2 + v)^{\frac{1}{2}} \qquad [12]$$

where v has been added as a stochastic error term. If we square E, we have the estimating equation,

$$E^2 = \alpha + \gamma_1 C^2 + \gamma_2 D^2 + v \qquad [13]$$

which can be estimated using OLS. This specification of the effects of C and D allows one to assess the *separate* contributions of C and D to the interaction.

AN ALTERNATIVE SPECIFICATION OF INTERACTION MODELS

So far, we have considered models where the effect of X on Y, defined as the partial derivative of X with respect to Y, was specified first. By integrating the equation for the effect of X on Y, an estimating equation was obtained. But it also happens in some situations that the *entire equation* relating X to Y depends on, or is conditioned by, Z. The model would have this form:

$$Y = \alpha + \beta X + u \qquad [14]$$

$$\alpha = \gamma_1 + \gamma_2 Z \qquad [15]$$

$$\beta = \delta_1 + \delta_2 Z \qquad [16]$$

When equations 15 and 16 are substituted into equation 14, the following estimating equation is obtained:

$$Y = \gamma_1 + \gamma_2 Z + \delta_1 X + \delta_2(XZ) + u \qquad [17]$$

When this model is compared to that represented by equations 1-3, it is evident that a separate term for Z has been added to the estimating equation. Note that a *separate equation* is created for each value of Z. Equation 17 is sometimes written in the following form to emphasize this interpretation:[2]

$$Y = (\gamma_1 + \gamma_2 Z) + (\delta_1 + \delta_2 Z)X + u \qquad [18]$$

For example, if $Z = 0$, equation 18 becomes $Y = \gamma_1 + \delta_1 X + u$; if $Z = 1$, equation 18 becomes: $Y = (\gamma_1 + \gamma_2) + (\delta_1 + \delta_2)X + u$; and similarly for other values of Z. Thus for each value of Z there is in effect a different equation relating X to Y.

There are occasions when separate regression equations for different values of Z express the theoretically expected relationship of X and Y. These are most likely to occur when Z is a categorical variable (see Long and Miethe, this volume). When X is also a categorical variable, the model becomes statistically a two-way analysis of variance with interaction. When Z is a continuous variable, a substantive reason for predicting that the entire relationship between X and Y should change for different values of Z is more difficult to find. Mason et al. (1983), however, provide an important example wherein Z is a continuous, but contextual, variable (a country's Gross National Product) that affects both the intercept of the equation for Y (children ever born) and the slope of an individual level predictor X (mother's education).

A COMPARISON OF THE DIFFERENT MODELS OF INTERACTION

In the examples above, three different types of interaction models were specified. For type I, the effect of X is facilitated or buffered by an interacting variable Z. For type II, X facilities or moderates the effect of Z, while Z simultaneously facilitates or moderates the effect of X. For type III, either Z affects the entire relationship of X to Y, or X affects the entire relationship of Z to Y. The model types are differentiated by the structural equations that specify them: equations 1 and 2 for type I, equations 7 and 8 for type II, and equations 14-16 for type III. The estimating equations for model types II and III, equations 9 and 17, do not differ. Both contain a product term and separate terms for each of the variables in the product. The estimating equation for model type I, shown in equation 3, differs from the other estimating equations only by the omission of a separate term for Z. These comparisons underscore the point made earlier that interpretation of models involving product variables depends on prior theoretical specification.

MEASUREMENT CONSIDERATIONS IN THE SPECIFICATION OF INTERACTIVE MODELS

In specifying interaction models, the scale on which X and Z are measured must be considered. In the example of the buffering effect of social support on the effect of stress (see equations 1-4), both stress (X) and social support (Z) were conceptualized as positive quantities, ranging from no stress or support to high levels of stress or support. The measures of these variables should include zero as the measure of no stress or social support and positive values thereafter. Panel A of Figure 1 illustrates the relationship between stress and distress under the conditions of no support and maximal support, using nonnegative measures of stress and support. This model is also shown in equations 1-3. If stress is zero, distress is at some baseline level, α. When there is no social support, distress increases sharply with increased levels of stress. When support is at its maximal level, the line relating stress to distress is nearly flat.

Suppose that the researcher decided to measure stress as a deviation from the mean value of stress, on the grounds that the amount of stress is difficult to gauge without some standard of comparison. The measure of stress would be $X^* = X - \mu$. Replacing X with $X^* + \mu$ in equation 1 to form equation 1a, and then subsituting equation 2, $\beta = \delta + \gamma Z$, into equation 1a gives us a different estimating equation 3a:

$$Y = \alpha + \beta(X^* + \mu) + \epsilon \qquad [1a]$$

$$Y = \alpha + (\gamma + \delta Z)(X^* + \mu) + \epsilon \qquad [3a]$$

$$= (\alpha + \gamma\mu) + \gamma X^* + \delta\mu Z + \delta(X^*Z) + \epsilon$$

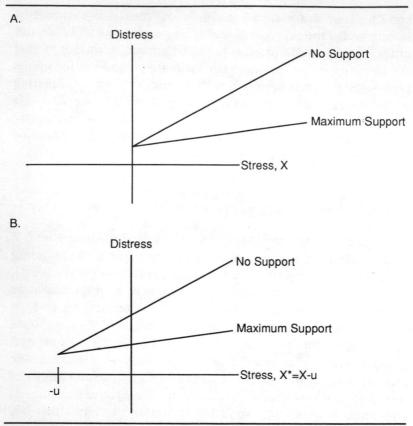

**Figure 1: Two Models of the Relationship of Stress to Distress Under Different
Conditions of Social Support, Based on Different Measures of Stress**

Equation 3a, which will be estimated by OLS, is different from
equation 3, because it has a different product term, X*Z, a
different intercept, $(\alpha + \gamma\mu)$, and, most important, an additional
term, $\delta\mu Z$.

Panel B of Figure 1 graphs the relationship of X to Y for Z = 0
(no support) to Z = max. (full support) where X* is used instead
of X. Comparing Panels A and B in Figure 1, we see that the
regression lines are quite the same, except that in Panel B they
have been shifted laterally to the left. The point where the lines
intersect is now at $X* = -\mu$, whereas in Panel A they intersect at
X = 0. The regression equation relating X* to Y now has a
different intercept for each value of Z. In other words, the specification represented by equations 1a, 2, and 3a is a type III

specification. This example shows how measurement considerations can affect the specification of interaction models.

Changes in measurement are most likely to occur when X or Z are measured on interval scales, because these scales have no fixed zero point. For example, X may consist of an attitude scale that sums 5 Likert-scaled items. The individual items constituting the scale may have been four category Likert scales (1 = strongly disagree, 2 = disagree, 3 = agree, and 4 = strongly agree), where the numbers assigned to the categories have an arbitrary starting point (i.e., one could have used –1 = strongly disagree, –2 = disagree, and so on). The attitude scale constructed by combining the attitudes has no meaningful zero point, unless the scale is transformed (say by adding a constant) so that zero represents a meaningful value, such as the lowest possible score on the scale, or the average score on the scale. When Z is measured on an interval scale, a type III specification is recommended, because deviation scores or some other transformation of Z will be required to obtain a meaningful zero point on the scale.

SPECIFICATION OF MULTIPLE INTERACTIONS

It often happens that a researcher will want to model several interactions within a single system of equations. For example, the effect of stress (X) on distress (Y) may depend on both social support (Z_1) and coping skills (Z_2). In this model the effect of X is specified as

$$\partial Y / \partial X = \alpha_1 + \gamma_1 Z_1 + \gamma_2 Z_2 \qquad [19]$$

which is integrated to yield

$$Y = \alpha_0 + \alpha_1 X + \gamma_1 X Z_1 + \gamma_2 X Z_2 + \epsilon \qquad [20]$$

an OLS estimating equation.

It can also happen that several of the X variables in the model interact with a number of Z (facilitating or moderating) variables. Suppose we theorize that distress (Y) depends on the presence of recent stressful events (X_1) and stressful events from childhood and adolescence (X_2). While informal social support (Z_1) and coping skills (Z_2) may buffer the effects of X_1, professionally given therapy (Z_3) and coping skills (Z_2) may be needed to buffer the effect of X_2. This leads to a more complex model:

$$\partial Y / \partial X_1 = \alpha_1 + \gamma_1 Z_1 + \gamma_2 Z_2 \qquad [21]$$

$$\partial Y / \partial X_2 = \alpha_2 + \gamma_3 Z_3 + \gamma_4 Z_2 \qquad [22]$$

These are integrated to form the estimating equation:

$$Y = \alpha_0 + \alpha_1 X_1 + \alpha_2 X_2 + \gamma_1 X_1 Z_1 + \gamma_2 X_1 Z_2 \qquad [23]$$
$$+ \gamma_3 X_2 Z_3 + \gamma_4 X_2 Z_2 + \epsilon$$

In short, the models presented thus far are easily extended to include any number of multiple interactions.

Higher order interactions, that is, where more than two variables interact, are more difficult to conceptualize in terms of substantive theory. Using once again the example of stress and social support, and focusing only on the buffering effects of informal social support (Z_1), suppose that the effect of recent stressful events—which by hypothesis is conditioned on levels of support—itself changes or is conditioned by levels of early stress (X_2). We then have

$$\partial(\partial Y / \partial X_1) / \partial Z_1 = \gamma_2 + \delta X_2 \qquad [24]$$

This equation should be understood as saying the effect of Z_1 on the effect of X_1 on Y depends on X_2, or the buffering effect of social support is in turn moderated by early levels of stress.

To get to the estimating equation, we must integrate equation 24 twice. We have first,

$$\partial Y / \partial X_1 = \alpha_1 + \gamma_2 Z_1 + \delta X_2 Z_1 \qquad [25]$$

and then,

$$Y = \alpha_0 + \alpha_1 X_1 + \gamma_2 X_1 Z_1 + \delta X_1 X_2 Z_1 + \epsilon \qquad [26]$$

The estimating equation contains the triple product $X_1 X_2 Z_1$ to represent the two-way interaction of X_2 and Z_1.

If one were representing the three variables X_1, X_2, and Z_1 as mutually interacting, or if separate regression equations were needed to represent the effect of X_1 on Y—that is, if a type II or type III specification were used—then the estimating equation would also include terms for X_2, Z_1, X_1X_2, and X_2Z_1. Substantive theories rarely specify higher order mutual interactions, but, just as with first-order interactions, separate regression equation models (type III specification) are likely to be specified when the interacting variables are categorical or because of measurement considerations. The complexity of higher order interactions requires one to take special care in specifying models to include them.

ESTIMATION

The examples began with the specification of a structural equation, for example equation 2, that shows how the *effect* of one variable depends on another variable. The dependent variable in this equation is not Y, but the *effect* of X on Y. This "effect" equation is integrated to arrive at a regression equation that relates Y to X and the interacting variable, Z. In some cases, equation 11 is an example; this equation must be transformed to arrive at a linear regression equation. We have called this final equation the *estimating* equation, because its purpose is to enable us to estimate the parameters needed to describe the "structural" relationships in the model.

THE NEED FOR A SEPARATE
ESTIMATING EQUATION

The reasons for making such a division will be illustrated using equations 1-3 from our first example. The parameters of the structural equations 1 and 2 are not amenable to regression analysis. If OLS were applied to equation 1, the estimates of β would be incorrect, because β is not a constant, but a variable that depends on Z. But *for a given value of Z*, β is a parameter in the model, representing the effect of stress. An estimate of the value of β for a specified value of Z is obtained from equation 2, but OLS estimation cannot be applied to equation 2, because it is an identity. On the other hand, the parameters of equation 3 *can* be estimated using OLS, even though equation 3 does not explicitly describe the relationship between X and Y. The effect of X on Y is not δ, and the variable XZ is not included in the model of

equations 1 and 2. Still, OLS yields efficient and unbiased estimates of α, δ, and γ, because equation 3 is implied by equations
1 and 2.

ASSUMPTIONS ABOUT ERROR TERMS

The models presented in this chapter assume that the independent variables in the estimating equation are measured without error. Measurement error in product variables requires the
application of complex and not yet fully developed estimating
procedures. A procedure for obtaining estimates of regression
coefficients when one or more of the product terms are measured
with error is given by Heise (1986).

The models presented also assume that the effect of X is completely specified as some function of the facilitating or moderating
variable Z, as shown in equation 2. That is, there is no error term,
say u, in equation 2 to indicate that other, unmeasured variables
condition the effect of X. Consideration of such models requires
advanced methods. A detailed treatment of this problem is found
in Mason et al. (1983).

MULTICOLLINEARITY

Multicollinearity can pose a problem when product variables
are used to estimate interaction effects. If the estimating equation
contains the terms X and Z, as well as the product XZ, X and Z
may be highly correlated with the product term, leading to multicollinearity and imprecise estimation of certain parameters in the
model. If multicollinearity does not occur, it can easily be engen-
dered simply by adding a constant to X and Z.

The threat of multicollinearity, either immediate or easily in-
vocable, lead Althauser (1971) to question the appropriateness of
the use of product variables in regression equations. Others suggested that the terms of the product be transformed into standard
"z score" form (Belsley et al., 1980), or that specially derived constants be added to them to minimize multicollinearity (Smith and
Sasaki, 1979). It often occurs, however, that matrices showing a
correlation between Z and XZ even as high as .9 are not so ill
conditioned that the coefficients of the model cannot be accurately estimated (see Southwood, 1978: 1167). In other words, the
computational advantages of X and Z are seldom needed.

ESTIMATING NONLINEAR INTERACTIONS

Models of interaction involving product variables can take on many different forms. The most common form of interaction is the linear interaction. In this model the effect of X on Y (or the parameters relating X to Y in a type III specification) is a *linear* function of Z, as in equation 2. Sometimes, however, the effect of X on Y may be modeled as a nonlinear function of Z as in equations 4 and 10. In these cases OLS can be used to estimate the parameters of the model only if a linear estimating equation can be derived from the equation(s) for the effect of X. We saw in equation 12 that the nonlinear equation relating X to Y could be made linear if both sides were squared, yielding the estimating equation 13. On the other hand, in the first example of the effect of social support on the effect of stress, we saw that a nonlinear interaction (equation 4) does not yield a linear estimating equation.

Nonlinear estimating equations pose special problems for parameter estimation that are beyond the scope of this chapter. But linear estimating equations can be derived for a large number of nonlinear interaction models. The two that occur most commonly are presented here. In the first, the effect of X is a multiplicative function of itself, Z, and an error term.

$$\partial Y / \partial X = \alpha X^{\beta} Z^{\gamma} \epsilon \qquad [27]$$

is integrated to form

$$Y = \alpha^* X^{\beta^*} Z^{\gamma} \epsilon \qquad [28]$$

where $\alpha^* = \alpha / (\beta + 1)$ and $\beta^* = \beta + 1$. Taking the natural logarithm of both sides, one obtains the linear estimating equation

$$\ln(Y) = \ln(\alpha^*) + \beta^* \ln(X) + \gamma \ln(Z) + \ln(\epsilon) \qquad [29]$$

If one specifies a mutual interaction between X and Z, the system of equations has the same form, but α, β, and γ are different in each equation.

$$\partial Y / \partial X = \alpha_1 X^{\beta} Z^{\gamma^*} \epsilon \qquad [30]$$

$$\partial Y / \partial Z = \alpha_2 X^{\beta*} Z^{\gamma} \epsilon \qquad [31]$$

$$Y = \alpha * X^{\beta*} Z^{\gamma*} \epsilon \qquad [32]$$

where $\alpha* = (\alpha_1 \alpha_2 / \alpha)$, $\beta* = \beta + 1$, and $\gamma* = \gamma + 1$. The estimating equation is the same as equation 29, except $\gamma*$ replaces γ, and $\alpha*$ is defined differently:

$$\ln(Y) = \ln(\alpha*) + \beta* \ln(X) + \gamma* \ln(Z) + \ln(\epsilon) \qquad [33]$$

Note that the estimate of γ (but not β) changes when the model is specified as a mutual interaction.

Another common form of nonlinear interaction model makes the effect of X on Y an exponential function of X, Z, and ϵ.

$$\partial Y / \partial X = \alpha_0 \exp(\alpha_1 + \beta X + \gamma Z + \epsilon) \qquad [34]$$

which is integrated to form

$$Y = \alpha_0^* \exp(\alpha_1 + \beta X + \gamma Z + \epsilon) \qquad [35]$$

where $\alpha_0^* = \alpha_0 / \beta$. Taking the logarithm of both sides yields a linear estimating equation:

$$\ln(Y) = \ln(\alpha_0^*) + \alpha_1 + \beta X + \gamma Zs + \epsilon \qquad [36]$$

Mutual interactions imply the same estimating equation as equation 36, except for a different intercept term, $\alpha_0^* = \alpha_0 / \beta\gamma$.

One advantage of these two models of nonlinear interaction is that if a mutual interaction is specified, the separate contributions of each term in the interaction (β and γ) can be assessed. In linear interaction models with mutual interaction, the coefficients of each term in the interaction must be equal (for an example, see equations 7-9).

STATISTICAL TESTING

Models of interaction involving product variables usually give rise to two kinds of questions that statistical tests can help to answer. Consider the example shown in equations 1-3. First, we usually want to know whether there *is* an interaction, in the sense that the effect of X on Y depends on Z. Second, if an interaction is present, we want to test whether the effect of X on Y is different from zero (or some other theoretically important value) for certain meaningful values of Z. These tests are called tests of the interaction and of the direct effect of X on Y, respectively.

TESTING FOR INTERACTION

The estimating equation forms the basis of tests of significance. The F-ratio is used to test for interaction, but the computation of F will depend on the way the interaction model was specified. The general formula for the F-test is

$$F = \frac{(R_1^2 - R_2^2)(N - k_1)}{(1 - R_1^2)(k_1 - k_2)} \qquad [37]$$

where R_1^2 is the coefficient of determination of the estimating equation; k_1 is the number of parameters in the estimating equation; R_2^2 is the coefficient of determination of a restricted form of the estimating equation (i.e., certain coefficients in the estimating equation are set to zero); and k_2 is the number of coefficients set to zero. R_2^2 and k_2 vary according to the number of product terms in the model, the type of interaction model (linear versus nonlinear), and the type of specification used. Linear interaction models are considered first.

Type I and II specifications. In a type I specification of linear interaction, the effect of X on Y, but not the entire relationship of X to Y, depends on Z; in a type II specification, the effect of X depends on Z and the effect of Z depends on X, but again, not the entire relationship of X to Y. With type I and type II specifications, the null hypothesis is that the coefficient of the product term is 0. Take equation 3 as an example of a type I specification. If the null hypothesis, H_0: $\gamma = 0$, fails to be rejected, equation 2 is tentatively set aside as a specification of the effect of X on Y. Using equation 9 as an example of a type II specification, the null hypothesis is also $\gamma = 0$.

In the F-test for type I and type II specifications, R_1^2 in equation 37 is the coefficient of determination for the estimating equation; R_2^2 is the coefficient of determination for the estimating equation without the product variables; k_1 is the number of parameters in the estimating equation; and k_2 is the number of product variables.

In models with only one product variable, F in equation 37 is the square of t used in the convention t-test of the significance of a regression coefficient. But the F-test in equation 37 is more general in that it can be used to test the significance of several product terms simultaneously. In equation 19, for example, the effect of X on Y depends on Z_1 and Z_2. The estimating equation 20 has product terms XZ_1 and XZ_2 with coefficients γ_1 and γ_2. To test the interaction model as specified, the coefficient of determination from equation 20 is used as R_1^2 in equation 37 and the coefficient of determination from the following equation is used as R_2^2:

$$Y + \alpha_0 + \alpha_1 X + \epsilon \qquad [38]$$

Equation 38 is equation 20 with the product terms dropped. In computing the F-test for this model, k_1 is 4 and k_2 is 2.

Only the joint hypothesis, $H_0: \gamma_1 = \gamma_2 = 0$, is considered here, because two interactions were specified in the model. One may test the significance of the individual coefficients, γ_1 and γ_2, if each interaction were based on a separate theoretical argument, and if the joint hypothesis were not rejected. For the latter condition, see Cohen and Cohen (1975: 162-165).

Type III specification. If one has specified a model in which the entire regression of Y on X depends on particular values of Z, as exemplified in equations 14-17, a different F-test should be used. Recall that in a type III model, both the slope and the intercept of the regression equation relating Y to X are a function of Z. As a result, a term for Z appears in the estimating equation. Consequently, the null hypothesis is $\gamma_2 = \delta_2 = 0$, where γ_2 is the coefficient of Z in equation 17 and δ_2 is the coefficient of the product term, XZ. It is necessary to test both coefficients, jointly because, theoretically, Z is expected to have no effect on Y apart from its effects on α and β in equation 14.

The F-test has the same formula as 37, but k_2 is the number of product terms plus the number of interacting variables, and R_2^2 is the coefficient of determination of the estimating equation with all Z terms and their products dropped. If equations 14-17 are used as an example, R_1^2 in equation 37 is the coefficient of determination in equation 17 and R_2^2 is the coefficient of determination in

$$Y = \gamma_1 + \delta_1 X + u \qquad [39]$$

k_2 is 2 because two parameters γ_2 and δ_2 have been restricted to zero.

Nonlinear interaction models. Nonlinear models of interaction typically yield linear estimating equations in which product variables do not apear (see equations 29 and 36), because of a logarithmic transformation, or estimating equations that may contain the terms X^2 and Z^2, but not products of X and Z (see equation 13). In these models the test for interaction is a test of the coefficient of the Z, ln(Z), or Z_2 terms. If only a single interaction is posited (i.e., the effect of X depends on Z, not several Zs, and there is no mutual interaction between X and Z), the test of the interaction amounts to a simple t-test of the coefficient of Z, ln(Z), or Z^2.

If multiple interactions are specified, such that the estimating equation contains $Z_1, Z_2, \ldots, Z_k$, or $Z_1^2, Z_2^2, \ldots, Z_k^2$, a joint test of the significance of all the interaction terms is done using equation 37 where R_1^2 is the coefficient of determination of the estimating equation; R_2^2 is the coefficient of determination for the estimating equation less $Z_1, Z_2, \ldots, Z_k$ or $Z_1^2, Z_2^2, \ldots, Z_k^2$; k_1 = the number of parameters in the estimating equation; and $k_2 = k$, the number of interaction terms.

Mutual interactions in most nonlinear models are tested in the same way as one-way interactions, because the coefficients in the equations specifying the effect of X on Y and Z on Y (i.e., β and γ) are the same as the coefficients in the estimating equation. If a multiplicative mutual interaction model is used, however (see equations 30-32), the estimating equation yields estimates of $\beta + 1$ and $\gamma + 1$. Hence, one should test the null hypothesis: H_0: $\gamma^* = \beta^* = 1$, instead of the usual hypothesis, H_0: $\beta^* = \gamma^* = 0$, because if $\beta = 0$, $\beta^* = 1$, and if $\gamma = 0$, $\gamma^* = 1$.

For mutual multiplicative interactions, the F-test given by equation 37 is used to test H_0, but R_2^2 is not calculated from a regression equation. Instead, one respecifies equation 33 so that β^* and γ^* are 1:

$$Y' = \ln(Y) = \ln(\alpha^*) + \ln(X) + \ln(Z) + \ln(\epsilon) \qquad \text{[33a]}$$

To estimate the variance of the error term, $\ln(\epsilon)$, in this model, rewrite equation to obtain

$$Y'' = \ln(Y) - \ln(X) - \ln(Z) = \ln(\alpha^*) + \ln(\epsilon) \qquad \text{[33b]}$$

In this form, the estimating equation (with β^* and γ^* restricted to 1) is no longer a regression equation. The variance of $\ln(\epsilon)$ is simply the variance of Y', so that R_2^2, the coefficient of determination of equation 33a, is one minus the variance of Y'' divided by the variance of Y' (i.e., the variance of $\ln[y]$).

$$R_2^2 = 1 - s_{Y''}^2 / s_{Y'}^2 \qquad \text{[40]}$$

F is computed using equation 37 where R_1^2 is the coefficient of determination of equation 33; k_1 is the number of parameters in equation 33; R_2^2 is given by equation 40; and k_2 is 1.

To test a multiplicative interaction model with multiple mutual interaction terms, the same procedure is followed, but Y'' will be computed by subtracting the logarithms of all the independent variables in the estimating equation from $\ln(Y)$. The F-test is then used with R_2^2 obtained from equation 40 above and $k_2 = 1$.

Testing alternative models. The above tests of significance presuppose that a single theory of the interrelationships of three or more variables is being tested. Frequently two or more theories may suggest alternative models to be tested. For example a "main" effects model may be opposed to an interactive effects model. One theory may imply that X and Z both have direct effects on Y, specified as,

$$Y = \beta_0 + \beta_1 X + \beta_2 Z + \epsilon \qquad \text{[41]}$$

while another will suggest that the effect of X is conditioned on Z, as in equations 3. Each alterative may be tested separately. To test the model suggested by equations 1-3, one would test the significance of the interactive term XZ in equation 3 in the manner indicated above. If the test fails, one would then test the significance of β_2 in equation 41 as a test of that model. Alternatively, one could test for the effect of Z in equation 41 first, and if that test fails, test the significance of δ in equation 3. It is quite possible that neither test will fail, indicating that both models are compatible with the data. Because the two models are not nested, the rejection of one does not lead to an acceptance of the alternative.

To obtain a more conclusive test, it is usually recommended that one should test only the coefficient of product term in the equation, $Y = \beta_0 + \beta_1 X + \beta_2 Z + \delta XZ + \epsilon$ (β's = "main effects"; δ = "interaction"). If this test fails, the main effects model is accepted; and if this test succeeds, the main effects model is rejected. In this way, with only one test, only one model is accepted. This procedure is appropriate if a *mutual* interaction (type II) is specified, as in equations 7-9, but it should *not* be used for type I and type III interactions, because it does not test the interaction models that were specified.[3]

It often happens that neither the coefficient of Z nor the coefficient of XZ are statistically significant if tested individually by their respective t-ratios, but if *both* variables are dropped from the regression equation, the R^2 is significantly reduced. When one is dropped, the other becomes significant, and vice versa. If the conventional procedure were adopted, the main effects model would be selected. But a type 1 interaction, which implies that the coefficient of Z is nonsignificant, and a type III interaction, which implies that Z and XZ jointly define the interaction, are compatible with the data in this instance.

TESTING FOR DIRECT EFFECTS

When an interaction is present, the effect of X is not a constant, because it depends on the interacting variable, Z. Tests of the magnitude of X are predicated on specified values of the variables with which it interacts. Past research has singled out two particular values of Z for special testing of the effect of X, Z = 0, and $Z = \overline{Z}$. Consider equation 2. The effect of X when Z is zero is δ. Testing the significance of δ in equation 2 is a way of testing the significance of β when Z is zero. The effect of X when Z is at its expected value (estimated by $\overline{Z}$) is the expected value of β, or the *average* effect of X, that is, the effect of X averaged over all values of Z.

In multiplicative interaction models, the hypothesis that, for a particular value of Z, the effect of X on Y is zero makes no sense. First, in such models, the effect of X on Y depends not only on Z, but on X and ϵ as well (see equations 27-29). Second, the effect of X on Y, given X, Z, and ϵ, is either never zero (see equation 34), or zero only when X, Z, or ϵ are zero. Consequently, the significance of the direct effect of X is tested only for models of linear interactions.

The general procedure for testing the significance of the effect of X for a given value of Z is the t-test, or $\hat{\beta}/\hat{\sigma}_\beta$, where $\hat{\beta}$ is the estimate of the effect of X on Y given Z obtained from one of the equations specifying the interaction model (e.g., equation 2 and $\hat{\sigma}_\beta$ is the standard error of the estimate. The latter is computed using information from the estimating equation, as will be shown below.

$\hat{\beta}$ is computed as a function of Z (or of several Zs, if multiple interactions have been specified). The coefficient of Z in the computation is $\hat{\gamma}$, the regression coefficient of XZ in the estimating equation. The standard error of $\hat{\beta}$, as a function of Z, can be computed from the covariance matrix of the regression coefficients in the estimation equation. This matrix is usually supplied in computational programs. For example, it is requested by BCOV in SPSSX's REGRESSION and by COVB in SAS's REGRESSION command. Selected cells from this matrix are used to compute the estimate of the standard error of $\hat{\beta}$. Where there is only one interacting variable, as in equations 1-3,

$$s_\beta = \{\text{Var}(\delta) + Z^2\text{Var}(\gamma) + 2Z\text{Cov}(\delta, \gamma)\}^{1/2} \qquad [42]$$

When several Z variables interact with an X variable, as in equation 20, the standard error of the effect of X is given by

$$s_\beta = \{\text{Var}(\alpha_1) + Z_1^2\text{Var}(\gamma_1) + Z_2^2\text{Var}(\gamma_2) \qquad [43]$$
$$+ 2Z_1\text{Cov}(\alpha_1\gamma_1) + 2Z_2\text{Cov}(\alpha_1\gamma_2)$$
$$+ 2Z_1Z_2\text{Cov}(\gamma_1, \gamma_2)\}^{1/2}$$

The formula is easily extended to include any number of interacting terms.

Note that the standard error of the estimated effect of X is *not* the standard error of the coefficient of X in the estimating equation. This standard error, s_δ, enters into the formula for s_β, but it becomes the standard error of $\hat{\beta}$ only when $Z = 0$. Computer programs routinely report the standard errors of the coefficients in the regression equation. The standard error of X reported by the program should be interpreted as the standard error of the effect of X when the Z terms on which the effect depends are zero.

It can be shown that adding a constant to Z does not change the standard error of $\hat{\beta}$. If one is interested in the significance of the effect of X evaluated at a substantively meaningful value of Z, say μ, one can obtain the standard error needed for the test simply by subtracting the value of interest from Z and taking the significance reported for the coefficient of X as the significance of the effect of X for $Z = \mu$. To illustrate this procedure, let $Z^* = Z - \mu$. This implies that $Z = Z^* + \mu$. Replace Z in equation 2 with $Z^* + \mu$ to obtain

$$\beta = \delta + \gamma(Z^* + \mu) = (\delta + \gamma\mu) + \gamma Z^* \qquad [2a]$$

Substituting equation 2a into equation 3 yields

$$Y = \alpha + (\delta + \gamma\mu)X + \gamma XZ^* \qquad [3b]$$

an estimating equation with a different product term, XZ^*, and a different coefficient for X, $(\delta + \gamma\mu)$. The significance of this coefficient is the significance of $\hat{\beta}$ when $Z^* = 0$, or equivalently, when $Z = \mu$.

Very often, the effect of X is evaluated at $Z - \bar{Z}$ to estimate the average or *expected* effect of X. To accomplish this, add $-\bar{Z}$ to Z, and compute the product of $Z - \bar{Z}$ and X. If several Zs interact with X, compute the product of each Z minus its mean with X. Regress Y on X and $X(Z - \bar{Z})$. The coefficient of X in this equation estimates the average effect of X, and the standard error of the coefficient of X reported for this equation tests the significance of the average effect X.

In some models, the distribution of Z is highly skewed. In this case, one may want to evaluate β at the median of Z, or if Z has a meaningful zero point, at $Z = $ zero. If Z is a dummy variable indicating class membership, such as $1 = $ nonwhite, $0 = $ white, one should assess the significance of the effect of X on Y for both values of Z.

CONCLUSIONS

Interactive models involving product variables frequently occur in social science research. Often, the specification of the interaction model will lead to an estimation equation that can be treated as a conventional regression equation to obtain estimates of the parameters of the interactive model. But one should not treat this estimation equation as if *it* were the model. The model consists of the equations from which the estimating equation was derived. In many regression analyses, the researcher is confronted with several contending theories, none very strong, but each suggesting that different variables are importantly related to the dependent variable of interest. Accordingly, several variables may be included in a single regression equation in an effort to sift out the merits of the contending theories. If theoretical considerations suggest an interaction may be present, one may also "throw in" a product term when doing the regression, but before doing so, one should give the matter careful thought.

The theory should be queried for directions on how to specify the interaction. As we have seen, there are many possibilities. Is the interaction a *one-way* interaction or a *two-way* interaction? Is only the *effect* of X on Y conditioned by the interacting term, Z, or does the *entire relationship* between X and Y depend on Z? If the interaction is mutual, do each of terms contribute *equally* to the interaction, or should provision be made to estimate the separate contributions of each term? Can the interaction be represented by linear equations relating the effect of X on Y to Z, or is a nonlinear model of the interaction needed? Without answers to these questions, one will not know how to specify the estimation equation, and if a regression equation is used simply because it contains a product term, one will not know which tests of significance are appropriate. In sum, *prior theoretical specification is needed to interpret regression equations with product terms.*

The distinctions among interactive models of the *effect* of X on Y (type I specification), interactive models of *mutual* interaction (type II specification), and interactive models of the *relationship* between X and Y (type III specification) are crucial, because each approach yields its own set of specification equations and tests of hypotheses. Although the interactive model that conditions the relationship between X and Y on values of Z is commonly used, theoretical specifications leading to this model are rarely seen when Z is a continuous variable. One should, therefore, be quite sure that the model of interaction one chooses has a substantive interpretation *before* adopting it.

Finally, interactive models can be quite complex. The parameters of some models cannot be estimated with ordinary regression techniques. Should tests for interaction using simple product variables fail to reach significance, one option is to settle for the less complex linear regression model. But another option (see Wheaton, 1985, for an example) is to *go back to the theory for more insight* and hopefully, a more accurate specification of the interaction.

NOTES

1. Not every interactional model implies the presence of product variables. Southwood (1978) provides examples of models in which the interaction is expressed in terms of *differences* rather than products between two variables.

2. See Cohen and Cohen (1975: 313) for an elaboration of the approach, and Finney et al. (1984) for an empirical example.

3. Allison (1977) considers this procedure too stringent when Z is measured on a ratio scale, but essential when Z is measured on an interval scale, because in the latter case, Z can alway be transformed by a constant, thereby introducing a term for Z in the estimating equation. We have seen, however, that transforming Z in this way leads to a type III specification, which should be tested by deleting the terms Z and XZ from the estimating equation. That is, the test of a type III specification of interaction is not simultaneously a test of an additive model containing only the terms Z and X. Whether Z is measured on a ratio or an interval scale, tests of main effect and interactive models are exclusive only if a mutual linear interaction model is specified.

5

The Statistical
Comparison of Groups

J. SCOTT LONG
TERANCE D. MIETHE

Social scientists are often concerned with comparisons across groups. Political scientists compare Democrats to Republicans to Independents. Demographers examine differences among countries. Psychologists compare treatment and control groups. Sociologists ask questions about the similarities and differences across classes. Economists compare processes across firms and industries. In most fields, researchers are interested in whether processes differ across region, among age groups, over time or birth cohort, by gender, and by other demographic groupings. Regardless of how the groups are defined or the substantive area of research, the basic question is the same: *Does membership in a group affect the process being studied?*

Statistical analyses that attempt to answer this question commonly make two errors. First, the effect of group membership is inadequately incorporated into the statistical model being estimated. This may occur when the group differences suggested by substantive theory are incorrectly translated into the statistical model. Or, it may occur when the substantive theory motivating the research is inadequate or ambiguous in its description of how group membership affects the process. In either case, the result is biased estimates of the effects of the independent variables in the

AUTHORS' NOTE: *We would like to thank Robert M. Hauser for his suggestion of the topic for this chapter. Helpful comments were provided by Carol Bailey, Gene Fisher, and Lowell L. Hargens. Data were provided by the Minnesota Sentencing Guidelines Commission.*

model and incorrect assessments of the effects of group membership. Second, even when the nature of group differences is adequately understood, comparisons across groups are commonly based on ad hoc procedures rather than being based on well-established statistical procedures. At best, valuable information is lost; at worst, incorrect conclusions are drawn.

This chapter demonstrates how group membership can be incorporated into regression models, using an example from criminology to illustrate the techniques. The models presented are found in statistics books under such titles as analysis of covariance, ANACOVA, models for structural change, or models of group differences.

SPECIFYING DIFFERENCES IN MEAN LEVELS

The statement that membership in a group influences some outcome is ambiguous because the way in which membership affects the outcome is unspecified. To illustrate this ambiguity, a series of increasingly complex regression models will be developed, each in turn allowing a more complicated and generally more realistic specification of the influence of group membership.

The simplest interpretation of the statement that group membership influences some outcome variable is that the expected value of the dependent variable differs by group. Readers familiar with analysis of variance will recognize the model as a one-way ANOVA (see Kmenta, 1971: 413-418). Let Y be the dependent variable. Assume that there are two groups, defined by the dummy variable G equal to one if an observation is in the first group, zero if it is not.[1] Within a regression framework the effect of group can be estimated by the equation

$$Y = \alpha + \delta G + \epsilon \qquad [1]$$

ϵ is the error term with the usual regression assumptions that $E(\epsilon) = 0$ and $VAR(\epsilon) = \sigma^2$ for all observations, where E is the expectation operator and VAR indicates the variance. The parameter δ is the difference between the two groups in their expected value of Y. This can be seen by taking the expected value of equation 1 conditional upon group membership.[2] The expected value of Y for those with G equal to zero is $E(Y|G = 0) = \alpha$, because $E(\delta G|G = 0) = 0$ and $E(\epsilon) = 0$. The expected value for those with G equal to one is $E(Y|G = 1) = \alpha + \delta$, because $E(\delta G|G = 1) = \delta$ and $E(\epsilon) = 0$. Thus the expected value of Y for the two groups differs by the amount δ, for all values of X. If δ equals zero, then $\mu_{(G=1)}$ equals $\mu_{(G=0)}$, where $\mu_{(G=1)}$ is the population mean of Y for those in group one and $\mu_{(G=0)}$ is the population mean of Y for those in group zero. This allows a test of the equality of the population means of the two groups, H_0: $\mu_{(G=1)} = \mu_{(G=0)}$, by using the standard t-test of H_0: $\delta = 0$.

To illustrate this model, consider an example from criminology. Numerous studies have examined racial differences in criminal court sentencing practices. Some researchers have found support for the claim of disparate treatment against ethnic/racial minorities, while others report little evidence of racial bias once controls are introduced for the severity of the offense, the number of charges that result in convictions, the offender's prior criminal record, and other legal factors that should influence sentencing decisions (see Miethe and Moore, 1986, for details). Our example considers this claim using a sample of 2312 felons convicted in district courts from July 1977 to June 1978 in the state of Minnesota. The dependent variable L is the length of sentence in years given to a sample member for conviction of a crime. Initially, race is coded with the variable W equal to one for white felons and equal to zero for nonwhite felons.

To determine if there are racial differences in the mean length of sentences, the model $L = \alpha + \delta W + \epsilon$ is estimated. The ordinary least squares (OLS) estimates of α and δ are designated $\hat{\alpha}$ and $\hat{\delta}$. Model 1 in Table 1 presents the results of this regression. $\hat{\alpha}$ equals 4.92 indicating that $E(L|W = 0)$ is 4.92 years; that is, nonwhites have an expected sentence of 4.92 years. $\hat{\delta}$ equals $-.40$ indicating that being white as opposed to nonwhites ($W = 1$ versus $W = 0$) decreases the expected length of sentence by four-tenths of a year. Combining $\hat{\alpha}$ and $\hat{\delta}$, we find that $E(L|W = 1) = 4.92 + (-.40) = 4.52$, which is the expected length of sentence for whites. The t-value for H_0: $\delta = 0$) is 2.00 indicating that the difference is significant at the .05 level for a one-tailed test. A one-tailed test is used because there are substantive reasons to expect nonwhites to receive harsher sentences than whites.

TABLE 1
Regressions on Length of Sentence

Variable		Model 1	Model 2	Model 3	Model 4	
Intercept	α	4.9193	0.2560	0.2034	−2.2120	
	t	26.84	1.06	0.67	3.98	
W	δ	−0.4016	0.3144	0.8365	2.7855	
	t	2.00	0.18	0.33	4.71	
B	δ			0.0888		
	t			0.28		
S	β		0.9453	0.9457	0.9949	
	β^s		0.4921	0.4923	0.5179	S
	t		27.47	27.46	13.27	E
C	β		0.8587	0.8586	2.8109	T
	β^s		0.1209	0.1209	0.3959	
	t		6.79	6.78	6.38	1
P	β		0.1554	0.1548	0.2901	
	β^s		0.0593	0.0591	0.1107	
	t		3.33	3.31	2.70	
S × W	β				−0.0665	
	β^s				−0.0843	
	t				0.79	S
C × W	β				−2.1252	E
	β^s				−0.4599	T
	t				4.62	
P × W	β				−0.1743	2
	β^s				−0.1192	
	t				1.46	
For W = 1						
S	β				0.9284	
	β^s				0.4833	
	t				24.12	S
C	β				0.6858	E
	β^s				0.0966	T
	t				5.21	
P	β				0.1158	3
	β^s				0.4419	
	t				2.25	
	R^2	0.0416	0.2764	0.2764	0.2846	

NOTE: Sample size is 2312. $\hat{\beta}$ is the unstandardized OLS estimate; $\hat{\beta}^s$ is the standardized OLS estimate; t is the t-value; R^2 is the coefficient of determination; df is degrees of freedom. W = 1 if white, else 0; B = 1 if black, else 0; S is severity of crime; C is current charges; P is number of prior convictions; S × W is formed by multiplying S times W; C × W is formed by multiplying C times W; P × W is formed by multiplying P times W.

The major limitation of equation 1 is that it does not include causal variables that might explain why the mean level of the dependent variable differs by group. While average sentences are longer for nonwhites than whites, these differences could result from one group having higher levels on other independent variables that affect the length of sentence. For example, non-whites may commit more serious crimes, which would positively affect the length of sentence. Stated more generally, controls for other causally relevant variables must be included in the model if group differences are to be assessed accurately.

Consider an independent variable X, which is assumed to affect Y. Our original regression model can be extended to incorporate this variable:

$$Y = \alpha + \delta G + \beta X + \epsilon \qquad [2]$$

where β is the expected change in Y for a unit increase in X. Taking conditional expectations we find: $E(Y \mid X, G = 0) = \alpha + \beta X$ and $E(Y \mid X, G = 1) = \alpha + \delta + \beta X$. δ is the expected difference between groups in the level of Y for a given level of X. This can be seen most readily in Figure 1, where for any given level of X the expected difference in the level of Y for those in group one compared to group zero is equal to δ, as indicated by the vertical arrows.

Standard t-tests for regression coefficients can be applied to equation 2. The hypothesis that X does not affect Y is equivalent to H_0: $\beta = 0$. The hypothesis that for a given level of X the expected value of Y does not differ by group is equivalent to H_0: $\delta = 0$.

To understand the relationship between equations 1 and 2 better, assume that the same data were used to estimate both equations. It would be possible for $\hat{\delta}$ in equation 2 to be statistically different from zero, while $\hat{\delta}$ in equation 1 was not statistically different from zero. For example, assume that $\hat{\delta}$ in equation 2 is greater than zero, indicating that for a given level of X those in group one have higher expected values of Y than those in group zero, and that $\hat{\beta}$ is positive. Also assume that those in group one have lower levels of X than those in group zero. In such a case the univariate distribution of Y for both groups could be identical, as reflected by $\hat{\delta}$ being zero in equation 1. Conversely, if $\hat{\delta}$ was statistically different from zero in equation 1, it might not be

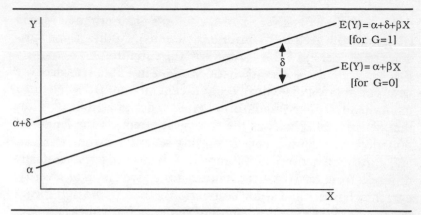

Figure 1: Differences in Mean Levels by Group

statistically different from zero in equation 2 where controls for X are introduced. For example, assume the $\hat{\delta}$ is positive in equation 1, indicating that the average level of Y is greater for group one than group zero. Further assume that $\hat{\delta}$ is zero and $\hat{\beta}$ is positive in equation 2. Let members of group one have larger values of X than members of group zero. This would result in members of group one having larger values of Y than members of group zero (because $\hat{\beta}$ is positive), or equivalently, $\hat{\delta}$ being positive in equation 1. The reader who does not see this should try drawing in sample observations in Figure 1.

Additional independent variables can be added to equation 2. Assume that there are K independent variables, X_1 through X_K, that affect Y. The regression equation becomes

$$Y = \alpha + \delta G + \beta_1 X_1 + \beta_2 X_2 + \ldots + \beta_K X_K + \epsilon \qquad [3]$$

δ is the expected difference in Y for those in group one as opposed to those in group zero for given levels of X_1 through X_K. β_j (for $j = 1$ to K) is the expected increase in Y for a unit increase in X_j, controlling for all $X_{i \neq j}$.

Our substantive example can be extended in this way to include three independent variables that should affect length of sentence: the variable S defined as the severity of the most serious convicted offense (ranging from one to ten); the variable C defined as the number of current charges against the felon that resulted in convictions (ranging from one to eight); and the variable P defined as the extensiveness of the felon's prior criminal record (ranging from zero to six prior convictions). Adding these variables to Model 1 in Table 1, results in the equation: $L = \alpha + \delta_W W + \beta_S S + \beta_C C + \beta_P P + \epsilon$. As shown for Model 2 in Table 1, each of the new variables is statistically significant at the .01 level for a one-tailed test. The standardized effects, designated as β^s, show that severity of crime has the strongest effect on the length of sentence. As a consequence of adding severity, current charges, and prior convictions to the model, $\hat{\delta}$ is no longer statistically different from zero ($t = 0.18$). That is, for a given level of severity, current charges, and prior convictions, there is no significant difference in the expected length of sentence for whites and non-whites. The overall racial difference in mean length of sentence observed in Model 1 disappears when whites and nonwhites are compared at identical levels of the theoretically relevant independent variables. This illustrates that failure to include important causal variables can result in biased estimates of the effects of group membership.

Our model can be further extended to include more than two groups. Suppose there are M groups numbered 1 through M. These groups can be defined by $M - 1$ dummy variables G_2, $G_3, \ldots, G_M$, where G_j equals one if an observation is in group j, or else zero. A dummy variable G_1 is not needed because a sample member in group one is uniquely defined by $G_2 = G_3 = \ldots = G_M = 0$. This is comparable to the two groups in equation 3 being defined by one dummy variable. Considering all M groups, our model becomes

$$Y = \alpha + \delta_2 G_2 + \delta_3 G_3 + \ldots + \delta_M G_M + \beta_1 X_1 + \beta_2 X_2 + \ldots + \beta_K X_K + \epsilon \quad [4]$$

Using summation notation, equation 4 can be rewritten as

$$Y = \alpha + \sum_{m=2}^{M} \delta_m G_m + \sum_{k=1}^{K} \beta_k X_k + \epsilon \quad [4']$$

Additional groups can be added to our criminology example by splitting the sample into three racial/ethnic groups. Let variable W equal one if a felon is white, else zero; and let the dummy variable B equal one if a felon is black, else zero. The excluded group includes felons of other racial and ethnic identities. Our model becomes

$$L = \alpha + \delta_W W + \delta_B B + \beta_S S + \beta_C C + \beta_P P + \epsilon \qquad [5]$$

Model 3 in Table 3 presents the OLS estimates of this equation. The unstandardized estimate for W, $\hat{\delta}_W$, indicates that for a given level of severity, current charges, and prior criminal convictions, the expected length of sentence for whites is .837 years greater than for the excluded group of other racial and ethic groups. A similar interpretation can be given for $\hat{\delta}_B$. The coefficients for S, C, and P can be interpreted as before. For example, $\hat{\beta}_S$ indicates that for a unit increase in severity the expected length of sentence increases by .95 years. $\hat{\beta}_S^s$ indicates that for a standard deviation increase in severity the expected length of sentence increases by .49 standard deviations.

For there to be no differences among races in equation 5, δ_W and δ_B must be *simultaneously* equal to zero. This requires a test of the composite hypothesis H_0: $\delta_W = \delta_B = 0$. This hypothesis cannot be tested with a t-test, because t-tests are limited to tests of a single coefficient (e.g., H_0: $\delta_W = 0$) or to tests of the equality of two coefficients (e.g., H_0: $\delta_B = \delta_W$). Rather, an F-test is required. This test can be computed by comparing the coefficients of determination (R^2) from a *full* and a *restricted* model. The full model contains all of the parameters of interest. In our example, this would be equation 5. The restricted model imposes upon the full model the restrictions implied by the null hypothesis. Imposing the hypothesized restrictions that $\delta_W = 0$ and $\delta_B = 0$ on equation 5 results in

$$L = \alpha + \beta_S S + \beta_C C + \beta_P P + \epsilon \qquad [6]$$

which can also be estimated with OLS. Defining the coefficient of determination in the full model (equation 5) as R_F^2 and in the restricted model (equation 6) as R_R^2, an F-test of the joint hypothesis is defined as (Kmenta, 1971: 371)

$$F = \frac{(R_F^2 - R_R^2)/(k_F - k_R)}{(1 - R_F^2)/(n - k_F)} \qquad [7]$$

where n is the sample size, k_F is the number of parameters in the full model (including the intercept), and k_R is the number of parameters in the restricted model (including the intercept). The

F-statistic with $k_F - k_R$ and $n - k_F$ degrees of freedom tests the hypothesis that the parameters excluded from the full model to create the restricted model are equal to zero. Alternatively, it tests the hypothesis that the parameters in the full model that are not in the restricted model do not explain any variation in the dependent variable. In our example, Model 3 is the full model, with $R_F^2 = 0.27638$ and $k_F = 6$; the restricted model corresponding to equation 6 (not shown in Table 1) has $R_R^2 = .27634$ and $k_R = 4$. With $n = 2312$, the F-statistic equals 0.0637 with 2 and 2306 degrees of freedom, indicating that the hypothesis cannot be rejected. Because this F-test is not directly available on standard printout, the reader should attempt to compute the correct F-value from the information that has been provided.

The F-test is extremely general and can be used to compare any full and restricted regression models. Additional applications of the test are given below.

SPECIFYING DIFFERENCES IN EFFECTS OF INDEPENDENT VARIABLES

Equations 3 and 4 extend equation 1 by allowing differences between groups in the expected value of Y for a given level of the independent variables. The model is limited by not allowing the effect of an independent variable on Y to differ by group. For example, the model requires that the effect of severity on the length of sentence be equal for all races. Yet there are theoretical reasons to believe that nonwhites receive a greater increase in sentence length than whites for the same increase in the severity of the crime. This is not simply the result of a different expected sentence for whites than nonwhites for a given severity of crime (although this may be true), but indicates that the way in which severity of crime is translated into years of imprisonment differs between whites and nonwhites. The extension of our model to allow differences in effects between groups will make this point clearer.

Consider two groups defined by the variable G, and a single independent variable X. Equation 2 can be extended to

$$Y = \alpha + \delta G + \beta X + \beta_G(X \times G) + \epsilon \qquad [8]$$

$(X \times G)$ is defined as X times G, and is often referred to as the interaction between X and G. Notice that if G equals one, then $(X \times G)$ equals X; if G equals zero then $(X \times G)$ equals zero. Taking expectations of equation 8 conditional upon group membership shows that $E(Y|X, G = 0) = \alpha + \beta X$ and $E(Y|X, G = 1) = (\alpha + \delta) + (\beta + \beta_G)X$. Thus, in effect, equation 8 provides separate regressions for each group.

The model in equation 8 is most readily understood by examining Figure 2.[3] For X equal to zero, those in group one have an average of δ more units of Y than those in group zero simply because they are in group one. This is not to say that the difference between the expected values of Y for the two groups will equal δ for all levels of X, because there is a second source of difference. Those in group one receive $\beta + \beta_G$ units of Y for every unit increase in X, compared to an increase of β units of Y for every unit increase in X for those in group zero. For example, at X equal to ten, those in group zero will have $E(Y|X = 10, G = 0) = \alpha + \beta 10$; those in group one will have $E(Y|X = 10, G = 1) = (\alpha + \delta) + (\beta + \beta_G)10$; and the groups will differ by $\delta + \beta_G 10$. In general, the difference in expected values across groups for a given value of X will be $E(Y|X, G = 1) - E(Y|X, G = 0) = \delta + \beta_G X$, as indicated by vertical arrows in Figure 2.

Equation 8 can be generalized to include K independent variables and G groups. With variables defined as in equation 4, we have

$$Y = \alpha + \sum_{m=2}^{M} \delta_m G_m + \sum_{k=1}^{K} \left[\beta_k X_k + \sum_{m=2}^{M} \beta_{k,m}(X_k \times G_m) \right] + \epsilon \quad [9]$$

The intercept for group $m \neq 1$ is $\alpha + \delta_m$ and the effect of X_k for group $m \neq 1$ is $\beta_k + \beta_{k,m}$; the intercept for group one is α and the effect of X_k is β_k.

It is not necessary for the effects of all independent variables to differ by group. For example, variable Z could be added to equation 8 such that its effect did not differ by group. The model becomes

$$Y = \alpha + \delta G + \gamma Z + \beta X + \beta_G(X \times G) + \epsilon \quad [10]$$

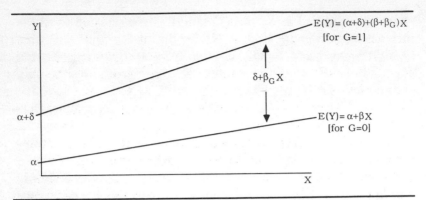

Figure 2: Differences in Effects by Group

γ indicates the expected change in Y for a unit change in Z controlling for all other variables. The interpretations of the other variables change only by adding that the effects are conditional upon Z.

Equation 10 can be generalized to include more groups and more independent variables. Suppose there are M groups defined by M − 1 dummy variables $G_2, G_3, \ldots, G_M$, where G_m equals one if an observation is in group m, else zero. There are K independent variables X_1 through X_K whose effects vary by group membership. There are J independent variables Z_1 through Z_J whose effects do not vary by group membership. Our model becomes

$$Y = \alpha + \sum_{m=2}^{M} \delta_m G_m + \sum_{j=1}^{J} \gamma_j Z_j + \sum_{k=1}^{K} \left[\beta_k X_k + \sum_{m=2}^{M} \beta_{k,m}(X_k \times G_m) \right] + \epsilon \quad [11]$$

This equation is less complicated than it appears. The reader who has trouble following it should expand the summation notation for j = 3, K = 2, and M = 2.

As with the comparison of equations 1 and 2, it is important to understand how using equation 4 when equation 9 is the more accurate substantive model can lead to biased estimates of the effects of the independent variables. In equation 4, group differences are determined by the parameters δ_m. For a given level of the independent variable, the expected value of the dependent variable differs from group one to group m by δ_m. While groups can differ in their average *level* of the independent variable, the *way* in which the independent variable affects the dependent variable is the same for both groups. In contrast, equation 9 allows groups to differ both in the level of the independent variable and in the way in which the independent variable affects the dependent variable. Our example illustrates this point.

When severity of the offense, current charges, and prior convictions are excluded from the regression as in Model 1 of Table 1, whites were estimated to have shorter sentences than nonwhites (i.e., $\hat{\delta} = -.40$). Model 2 of Table 1 added three independent variables. No significant racial differences in the expected length of sentence were found for a given level of severity, current charges, and prior convictions; that is, $\hat{\delta}$ was not significantly different from zero. The change in $\hat{\delta}$ from Model 1 to Model 2 resulted from whites having lower average *levels* of severity and prior convictions, with both of these variables having positive effects on length of sentence. Model 2 specifies that for a given *change* in an independent variable, however, both whites and nonwhites received the same increase in length of sentence. For example, both races received an expected increase of $0.155 (= \hat{\beta}_P)$ in length of sentence for each additional prior conviction, holding severity and current charges constant. Yet, if criminal justice officials perceive nonwhites with longer criminal records to be especially dangerous and consequently give them longer sentences than comparable white felons (see Miethe and Moore, 1986), Model 2 would give an incorrect estimate of the effect of prior convictions for both whites and nonwhites. The estimate of the effect of prior convictions in the misspecified model would be a weighted average of the effects for each group. In general, a model that does not allow differences by group in the effects of the independent variables provides biased estimates if the effects do differ by group. If the effects do not differ by group, no bias would be introduced.

Model 4 in Table 1 allows the effects of the independent variables to differ by group. This model is

$$L = \alpha + \delta W + \beta_S S + \beta_C C + \beta_P P + \beta_{S,w}(S \times W) \qquad [12]$$
$$+ \beta_{C,w}(C \times W) + \beta_{P,w}(P \times W) + \epsilon$$

There are now two types of significant differences between whites and nonwhites. First, beyond the effects of all other independent variables, being white increases the expected length of sentence by

2.79 (= $\hat{\delta}$) years. Second, the effect of current charges differs by race as shown by the significance of $\hat{\beta}_{C,W}$. To understand how the effects differ by race, it is useful to consider equation 12 for nonwhites, that is, when W = 0. All of the interaction variables that are defined as an independent variable times the dummy variable W will drop out because zero, the value of W, times anything is zero. Hence the equation for nonwhite felons is

$$L = \alpha + \beta_S S + \beta_C C + \beta_P P + \epsilon \qquad [13]$$

The estimates of the βs in equation 13 for nonwhites are labeled Set 1 in Table 1. Thus for nonwhites, a unit increase in the current charges increases the expected length of sentence by 2.81 (= $\hat{\beta}_C$) years, holding severity and prior convictions constant. The coefficient is significantly different from zero as indicated by the t-value of 6.38. Similar interpretations are possible for the other variables.

To determine the effects for whites, equation 12 is considered for W equal to one. In this case, all of the product terms reduce to the nongroup variable. For example, P × W equals P, because W equals one. Equation 12 becomes

$$L = (\alpha + \delta) + (\beta_S + \beta_{S,w})S + (\beta_C + \beta_{C,w})C + (\beta_P + \beta_{P,w})P + \epsilon \qquad [14]$$

Each effect for whites in equation 14 is a combination of two coeffients from equation 12. In Table 1 these effects are the sum of the coefficients in Set 1 and Set 2; these sums are presented in Set 3. For example, for whites a unit increase in the number of current convictions increases the expected length of sentence by 0.68 (=2.81 + –2.13 = $\hat{\beta}_C + \hat{\beta}_{C,w}$) years, holding severity and prior convictions constant. Similar interpretations are possible for the other variables. To test the significance of the effects for whites requires a test of the sum of two coefficients. How this is done is discussed below.

The coefficients associated with interaction variables or product terms (e.g., $\beta_{P,w}$) are used to determine the differences between the groups. For example, $\hat{\beta}_{C,W}$ = –2.13 means that for each additional current charge whites received an average increase in sentence that is 2.13 years shorter than the average increase in sentence received by nonwhites, holding other variables constant. The t-value of 4.62 associated with this coefficient indicates that the difference is statistically significant. In Model 4 of Table 1, only the effect of current charges is found to be significantly different between nonwhites and whites.

Our example could also be extended to allow differences among three groups: whites, blacks and others. Once again, two dummy variables are used: W equals one for whites, else zero; and B equals one for blacks, else zero. The model is

$$L = \alpha + \delta_W W + \delta_B B + \beta_S S + \beta_C C + \beta_P P + \beta_{S,W}(S \times W) \qquad [15]$$

$$+ \beta_{S,B}(S \times B) + \beta_{C,W}(C \times W) + \beta_{C,B}(C \times B)$$

$$+ \beta_{P,W}(P \times W) + \beta_{P,B}(P \times B) + \epsilon$$

β_S, β_C, and β_P are the effects for the other group (W = 0 and B = 0). The effects for whites (W = 1 and B = 0) are $\beta_S + \beta_{S,W}$, $\beta_C + \beta_{C,W}$, and $\beta_P + \beta_{P,W}$; the effects for blacks (W = 0 and B = 1) are $\beta_S + \beta_{S,B}$, $\beta_C + \beta_{C,B}$, and $\beta_P + \beta_{P,B}$. To test differences between whites (W = 1 and B = 0) and others (W = 0 and B = 0) requires tests of the parameters $\beta_{S,W}$, $\beta_{C,W}$, and $\beta_{P,W}$. To test differences between blacks (W = 0 and B = 1) and others (W = 0 and B = 0) requires tests of the parameters $\beta_{S,B}$, $\beta_{C,B}$, and $\beta_{P,B}$.

The coefficients and tests described so far can be read directly from the output of such programs as SAS's PROC REG and SPSS-X's REGRESSION. There are two additional tests that are useful in comparing groups that require special options on the programs or the running of additional regressions. First, a test is necessary to determine if the sum or difference of two coefficients is significantly different from zero. For example, consider the hypothesis that the effect of severity for blacks is equal to the effect of severity for whites. The effect of severity for blacks is $\beta_S + \beta_{S,B}$ and the effect for whites is $\beta_S + \beta_{S,W}$. If the effects are equal, then $\beta_{S,B}$ equals $\beta_{S,W}$, requiring a test of the hypothesis H_0: $\beta_{S,B} - \beta_{S,W} = 0$. Second, a test is necessary to evaluate whether all of the coefficients that differentiate the groups are simultaneously equal to zero. These tests are now considered.

TESTING SUM AND DIFFERENCES OF COEFFICIENTS

Consider models in which the effects of independent variables are allowed to differ by group. There are two basic reasons why sums or differences of coefficients need to be tested. First, to test the effect of an independent variable for the group coded one on a dummy variable requires a test of the sum of two coefficients. For example, in equation 14 the effect of P for whites (W = 1) is $\beta_P + \beta_{P,W}$. The hypothesis H_0: $\beta_P + \beta_{P,W} = 0$ can be tested with the t-test defined by $t = (\hat{\beta}_P + \hat{\beta}_{P,W}) / SD(\hat{\beta}_P + \hat{\beta}_{P,W})$, where $SD(\hat{\beta}_P + \hat{\beta}_{P,W})$ is the sample estimate of the standard deviation of $\hat{\beta}_P + \hat{\beta}_{P,W}$. Second, to test whether the effects of an independent variable are equal for two groups both coded as one with differing group variables requires the test of the difference between the effects for each group. For example, comparing the effects of severity for blacks (B = 1) and whites (W = 1) in equation 12 involves testing whether $(\beta_S + \beta_{S,B})$ equals $(\beta_S + \beta_{S,W})$. Because $(\beta_S + \beta_{S,B}) - (\beta_S + \beta_{S,W}) = \beta_{S,B} - \beta_{S,W}$, to determine if the effect of severity differs for blacks and whites requires a test of H_0: $\beta_{S,B} - \beta_{S,W} = 0$, which can be tested with $t = (\hat{\beta}_{S,B} - \hat{\beta}_{S,W}) / SD(\hat{\beta}_{S,B} - \hat{\beta}_{S,W})$.

To make either of these tests requires knowing the standard deviation of a sum or difference of estimated coefficients. In many programs for regression it is possible to request the variances and covariances among the parameter estimates. In SAS's REG this is done with the COVB option and in SPSS-X's REGRESSION the BCOV option is used. With these variances and covariances, it is possible to apply the formulas

$$SD(x + y) = SQRT[VAR(x) + VAR(y) + 2 \times COV(x, y)] \qquad [16]$$

and

$$SD(x - y) = SQRT[VAR(x) + VAR(y) - 2 \times COV(x, y)] \qquad [17]$$

where x and y are random variables. For example, the effect of severity for whites in Model 4 of Table 1 equals $\hat{\beta}_S + \hat{\beta}_{S,W} = 0.995 + -0.067 = 0.928$. The standard deviation of this sum equals $SD(\hat{\beta}_S + \hat{\beta}_{S,W}) = SQRT[VAR(\hat{\beta}_S) + VAR(\hat{\beta}_{S,W}) + 2 \times COV(\hat{\beta}_S, \hat{\beta}_{S,W})] = 0.00148$. The resulting t-value is 25.04, indicating that the effect of severity is significant for whites.

In programs that do not have the covariance option or for those who do not wish to do hand calculations, a recoding of the group variable(s) can be used to obtain the required tests. Consider a modification to equation 8. Let G* be defined as 1 − G. Then if G equals one, G* equals zero; if G equals zero, G* equals one. Using G* instead of G results in

$$Y = \alpha^* + \delta^*G^* + \beta^*X + \beta_G^*(X \times G^*) + \epsilon \qquad [18]$$

When G* equals zero, equation 18 becomes $Y = \alpha^* + \beta^*X + \epsilon$, which is equivalent to $Y = (\alpha + \delta) + (\beta + \beta_G)X + \epsilon$ for G equal to one in equation 8. Thus $\beta^* = \beta + \beta_G$. The statistical testing of the sum $\beta + \beta_G$ can be accomplished with a t-test of β^*, which is standard output from most regression programs.

Some computer packages allow the user to restrict the intercept to equal zero. In such cases the test for both groups can be accomplished in a single regression. For example, equation 8 could be replaced by

$$Y = \alpha_G G + \alpha_{G^*}G^* + \beta_G(G \times X) + \beta_{G^*}(G^* \times X) + \epsilon$$

α_G equals $\alpha + \delta$ from equation 8; α_{G^*} equals α from equation 8; β_G equals $\beta + \beta_G$ from equation 8; and β_{G^*} equals β from equation 8. While this seems easier than running the two regressions suggested above, it does not allow a direct test of whether there is a difference between the groups. To do so involves a test of the difference between the two slopes, which requires either the covariance between the two slopes or a second regression.

Readers should try to set up equation 12 using a dummy variable defined as $W^* = 1 - W$ to be certain they understand how reverse dummy coding can be used to accomplish statistical testing. In addition, readers should experiment with recoding the dummies when there are more than two groups.

COMPOSITE HYPOTHESIS TESTS

Given the importance of testing differences across groups, it is useful to consider tests that all coefficients for one group are equal to the corresponding coefficients from the other group or groups. This requires the F-test defined in equation 7. For the two groups to be equivalent in equation 12 requires that the composite hypothesis $H_0: \delta_W = \beta_{S,W} = \beta_{P,W} = 0$ is true. The restricted model required to test this hypothesis is

$$L = \alpha + \beta_S S + \beta_C C + \beta_P P + \epsilon \qquad [19]$$

Plugging the coefficients of determination from the full model (equation 12) and the restricted model (equation 19) into equation 7 results in an F-score of 6.68 with 4 and 2304 degrees of freedom, which is significant beyond the .01 level. Thus allowing racial differences in the effects of the independent variables significantly improves the fit of the model.

More generally, if the full model includes M groups, K variables X_k whose effects differ by group, and J variables Z_j whose effects do not differ by group, the full model would be equation 11. The null hypothesis would be H_0: $\delta_m = \beta_{k,m} = 0$ for m = 2, M and k = 1, K. All parameters that allow differences between groups are hypothesized to equal zero. The restricted model imposes these hypothesized constraints on equation 11:

$$Y = \alpha + \sum_{j=1}^{J} \gamma_j Z_j + \sum_{k=1}^{K} \beta_k X_k + \epsilon$$

Another useful composite hypothesis is that the effects of the independent variables do not differ by group, but the expected value of Y for a given combination of the independent variable differs by groups. If equation 11 were considered the full model, the null hypothesis would be H_0: $\beta_{k,m} = 0$ for k = 1, K and m = 2, M. The restricted model is

$$Y = \alpha + \sum_{m=2}^{M} \delta_m G_m + \sum_{j=1}^{J} \gamma_j Z_j + \sum_{k=1}^{K} \beta_k X_k + \epsilon$$

It is also possible to test that some, but not all, of the effects differ by group. For example, let equation 11 be the full model. It is hypothesized that the effects of $X_1, X_2, \ldots, X_{k'}$, for k' less than K do not differ by group. That is, H_0: $\beta_{1,m} = \beta_{2,m} = \ldots = \beta_{k',m} = 0$ for m = 2, M. The restricted model is

$$Y = \alpha + \sum_{m=2}^{M} \delta_m G_m + \sum_{j=1}^{J} \gamma_j Z_j + \sum_{k=1}^{k'} \beta_k X_k$$

$$+ \sum_{k=k'+1}^{K} \left[\beta_k X_k + \sum_{m=2}^{M} \beta_{k,m}(X_k \times G_m) \right] + \epsilon$$

These examples illustrate that the F-test can be used to test that any subset of coefficients from a full model can be tested to equal zero. A restricted model is formed by imposing the hypothesized constraints, and the F-statistics in equation 7 is used.

STANDARDIZED REGRESSION COEFFICIENTS

An additional advantage of the recoding discussed in the section "Testing Sums and Differences of Coefficients" is that it provides estimates of the standardized coefficients for the group originally coded one with the group variable. Consider Model 4 in Table 1. The standardized coefficients in Set 1 are for nonwhites (W = 0). For example, the standardized coefficient for severity indicates that for nonwhites a standard deviation increase in severity results in a 0.52 standard deviation increase in length of sentence, holding other variables constant. The standardized coefficient can be obtained directly from most regression programs. For whites (W = 1) the standardized value cannot be obtained directly from standard program output, nor can it be obtained by adding the standardized coefficients from Set 1 and Set 2. For example, while the unstandardized effect of severity for whites can be obtained by adding $\hat{\beta}_S$ and $\hat{\beta}_{S,W}$, the standardized effect for severity cannot be obtained by adding $\hat{\beta}_S^s$ and $\hat{\beta}_{S,W}^s$. To see why this is the case, consider the formulas for the standardized coefficients for S and (S $\times$ W) in equation 12: $\hat{\beta}_S^s = (s_S/s_L)\hat{\beta}_S$ and $\hat{\beta}_{S,W}^s = (s_{(S\times W)}/s_L)\hat{\beta}_{S,W}$, where s_L, s_S, and $s_{(S\times W)}$ are standard deviations. The formula for the standardized effect of severity for whites would be $(s_S/s_L)(\hat{\beta}_S + \hat{\beta}_{S,W})$, which does not equal $\hat{\beta}_S^s + \hat{\beta}_{S,W}^s$. While the correct value could be computed by hand, it can be read directly from the printout when the group variables are recoded.

This discussion should not be taken to imply that it is always appropriate to compare standardized coefficients across groups. For a discussion of this problem, see Alwin (this volume).

RUNNING SEPARATE REGRESSIONS

It may seem that an easier solution to determining the effects within different groups is to run separate regressions for each group, rather than running a single regression using dummy variables. While this approach can be used to obtain correct results, in practice it often leads either to incorrect statistical tests or to the absence of statistical tests for the comparison of groups. This section considers how results from separate regressions should be pooled to obtain results that are identical to those obtained in earlier sections. While pooled tests involve more effort to compute, they are necessary when separate regressions need to be compared but the data from the separate regressions cannot be included in the same regression. This occurs commonly when comparing the results of current research to those of prior published studies. Even if the raw data from the prior study are not available, by using the prior parameter estimates, their variances, and their covariances, it is possible to compare the results statistically across equations.[4] Such tests are now presented.

Assume that there are two groups, group one of size n_1 indicated by G equal to one and group zero of size n_0 indicated by G equal to zero. There are $K - 1$ nongroup variables, X_2 through X_K, whose effects differ by group. We are assuming $K - 1$ independent variables, rather than K as in prior sections, in order to simplify the formulas. Using a single regression, our model is

$$Y = \alpha + \delta G + \sum_{k=2}^{K} [\beta_k X_k + \beta_{k,G}(X_k \times G)] + \epsilon \qquad [20]$$

For group zero the effect of X_k is β_k; for group one the effect of X_k is $\beta_k^* \equiv \beta_k + \beta_{k,G}$. The OLS estimates are $\hat{\beta}_k$ and $\hat{\beta}_k^*$, with standard errors estimated as $\hat{\sigma}_{\beta_k}$ and $\hat{\sigma}_{\beta_k^*}$. σ is the standard error of the regression, estimated as $\hat{\sigma}$.

If separate regressions were run, there would be two equations:

$$Y = \alpha_0 + \sum_{k=2}^{K} \beta_{0k} X_k + \epsilon \qquad \text{for group zero, and} \qquad [21]$$

$$Y = \alpha_1 + \sum_{k=2}^{K} \beta_{1k} X_k + \epsilon \qquad \text{for group one.} \qquad [22]$$

In these regressions, the effect of X_k for group m is β_{mk}, with a sample estimate of $\hat{\beta}_{mk}$. The standard error of $\hat{\beta}_{mk}$ is estimated by $\hat{\sigma}_{\beta_{mk}}$. The estimate of the standard error of the regression for group m is $\hat{\sigma}_m$.

The estimates of the unstandardized parameters obtained from the separate regressions in equations 21 and 22 equal those obtained from the combined equation 20. Thus $\hat{\beta}_k = \hat{\beta}_{0k}$ and $\hat{\beta}_k^* = \hat{\beta}_{1k}$. Estimates of standardized coefficients will differ because the values of the standard devations of the variables used in equations 21 and 22 will differ from those used in equation 20. Further, t-values will differ because in separate regressions only part of the sample (i.e., only those in one of the groups) is used to estimate σ. If it is assumed that the variance of the errors is equal in all groups, an issue discussed below, then the estimate of standard error based on the combined observations from all groups will be efficient, while those based on the separate groups will not (Kmenta, 1971: 421). If the information from the separate regression equations 21 and 22 is pooled, however, results identical to those from equation 20 can be obtained, as shown below.

To test whether the effect of a given variable, say X_k, is identical in both groups, it is necessary to test the hypothesis H_0: $\beta_{0k} = \beta_{1k}$ or equivalently H_0: $\beta_{0k} - \beta_{1k} = 0$. Using the results from separate regressions, $\beta_{0k} - \beta_{1k}$ can be estimated as $\hat{\beta}_{0k} - \hat{\beta}_{1k}$. To compute the test statistic, an estimate of the variance of $\hat{\beta}_{0k} - \hat{\beta}_{1k}$ is needed. Using equation 17,

$$\sigma^2_{\hat{\beta}_{0k} - \hat{\beta}_{1k}} = \sigma^2_{\hat{\beta}_{0k}} + \sigma^2_{\hat{\beta}_{1k}} - 2\sigma_{\hat{\beta}_{0k}, \hat{\beta}_{1k}}$$

Because the estimates of β_{0k} and β_{1k} are uncorrelated, $\sigma_{\hat{\beta}_{0k}, \hat{\beta}_{1k}}$ equals zero. Thus it appears that $\sigma^2_{\hat{\beta}_{0k} - \hat{\beta}_{1k}}$ could be estimated as $\hat{\sigma}^2_{\hat{\beta}_{0k}} + \hat{\sigma}^2_{\hat{\beta}_{1k}}$. The estimates of the two variances are based on separate estimates of the standard error, $\hat{\sigma}_0$ and $\hat{\sigma}_1$, however, each using only part of the data.

For the appropriate test, it is necessary to pool the information from the separate regressions. Under the homoscedasticity assumption that $\sigma_0^2 = \sigma_1^2$, the pooled estimate of the standard error is

$$\hat{\sigma}_p^2 = \frac{(n_0 - K)\hat{\sigma}_0^2 + (n_1 - K)\hat{\sigma}_1^2}{n_0 + n_1 - 2K}$$

$\hat{\sigma}_p^2$ will be identical to the value of $\hat{\sigma}^2$ obtained from equation 20. In computing the variances of $\hat{\beta}_{0k}$ and $\hat{\beta}_{1k}$, $\hat{\sigma}_p^2$ needs to be substituted for $\hat{\sigma}_0^2$ and $\hat{\sigma}_1^2$. The resulting test statistic is

$$t = \frac{\hat{\beta}_{0k} - \hat{\beta}_{1k}}{\hat{\sigma}_p \left[\dfrac{\hat{\sigma}^2_{\hat{\beta}_{0k}}}{\hat{\sigma}^2_0} + \dfrac{\hat{\sigma}^2_{\hat{\beta}_{1k}}}{\hat{\sigma}^2_1} \right]^{1/2}}$$

with $n_0 + n_1 - 2K$ degrees of freedom. This test provides an identical value to that obtained from equation 20. Note, however, that an incorrect test would be obtained if the results of the separate equations were used without computing a pooled estimate of the standard errors (see Cohen, 1983, for examples of this and other errors in simple regression).

It is also possible to test the hypothesis that all of the coefficients in the first equation are equal to all of the coefficients in the second equation. To define this test requires elementary matrix algebra. Let $\hat{\beta}_0 = (\alpha_0 \beta_{02} \ldots \beta_{0K})'$ be a $K \times 1$ vector of estimates from the equation for group zero; let $\hat{\beta}_1 = (\hat{\alpha}_1 \hat{\beta}_{12} \ldots \hat{\beta}_{1K})'$ be the estimates from the equation for group one. In addition to the information required for testing pairs of coefficients, this test requires the $K \times K$ covariance matrix for all estimates in each equation. For group zero, this matrix is defined as

$$\mathbf{V}_0 = \begin{bmatrix} \hat{\sigma}^2_{\hat{\alpha}_0} & \hat{\sigma}_{\hat{\alpha}_0, \hat{\beta}_{02}} & \hat{\sigma}_{\hat{\alpha}_0, \hat{\beta}_{03}} & \cdots & \hat{\sigma}_{\hat{\alpha}_0, \hat{\beta}_{0K}} \\ \hat{\sigma}_{\hat{\beta}_{02}, \hat{\alpha}_0} & \hat{\sigma}^2_{\hat{\beta}_{02}} & \hat{\sigma}_{\hat{\beta}_{02}, \hat{\beta}_{03}} & \cdots & \hat{\sigma}_{\hat{\beta}_{02}, \hat{\beta}_{0K}} \\ \hat{\sigma}_{\hat{\beta}_{03}, \hat{\alpha}_0} & \hat{\sigma}_{\hat{\beta}_{03}, \hat{\beta}_{02}} & \hat{\sigma}^2_{\hat{\beta}_{03}} & \cdots & \hat{\sigma}_{\hat{\beta}_{03}, \hat{\beta}_{0K}} \\ \cdot & \cdot & \cdot & & \cdot \\ \cdot & \cdot & \cdot & & \cdot \\ \hat{\sigma}_{\hat{\beta}_{0K}, \hat{\alpha}_0} & \hat{\sigma}_{\hat{\beta}_{0K}, \hat{\beta}_{02}} & \hat{\sigma}_{\hat{\beta}_{0K}, \hat{\beta}_{03}} & \cdots & \hat{\sigma}^2_{\hat{\beta}_{0K}} \end{bmatrix}$$

$\mathbf{V}_1$ is defined similarly. The F-test for H_0: $\beta_0 = \beta_1$ can be computed as

$$F = \frac{(\hat{\beta}_0 - \hat{\beta}_1)' \left[\hat{\sigma}_0^{-2} \mathbf{V}_0 + \hat{\sigma}_1^{-2} \mathbf{V}_1 \right]^{-1} (\hat{\beta}_0 - \hat{\beta}_1)}{K \hat{\sigma}^2_p}$$

which is distributed as F with K and $n_0 + n_1 - 2K$ degrees of freedom.

The formulas in this section are adaptations of standard formulas for testing structural change (e.g., Amemiya, 1986: 31-35). In most texts these formulas are stated to be consistent with analyzing all groups in a single regression, similar to what was shown in earlier sections of this chapter. The adaptations presented here show that information across equations can be pooled to obtain equivalent tests. Thus even if the raw data are not available for each group, it is possible to make correct statistical comparisons. Errors are introduced if pooled estimates are not computed, if no tests are performed, or if ad hoc tests are made.

THE HOMOSCEDASTICITY ASSUMPTIONS

Throughout this chapter it has been assumed that the variances of the errors around the regression plane are equal for all groups. In terms of the last section, this is the assumption that $\sigma_0^2 = \sigma_1^2$. If the homoscedasticity assumption is not made, significant complications are added to the analyses. Amemiya (1986: 35-38) presents a test for H_0: $\sigma_0^2 = \sigma_1^2$, and reviews various methods for dealing with cases when the variances are not equal. Details are beyond the scope of this chapter.

CONCLUSIONS

Numerous research questions in the social sciences involve the comparison of groups. While statements about how group membership affects some outcome may be ambiguous, either because the underlying theory is not well developed or the research is exploratory, group comparisons are fundamental in all social sciences. As examples, consider two substantive areas in which the authors are working. In criminal justice the notion of a uniform system of criminal justice has been challenged by showing that blacks are victims of disparate treatment and that several legal factors that should influence sentencing decisions are differentially evaluated on the basis of race (see Miethe and Moore, 1986). Similarly, researchers have examined the nature of gender differences in the academic reward system. Questions focus on whether the rewards of salary, citations, and promotion are affected by the sex of the scientist (see Reskin and Hargens, 1979). Reviews of research in these areas show that errors are all too frequently made in specifying and testing group differences. The application of the techniques of this chapter can eliminate such errors.

While this chapter has focused on regression methods for studying group differences, similar methods are available with other techniques. Log-linear models allow tests of whether two or more multiway tables are similar. Indeed, a significant impetus to the development of log-linear models was the comparison of mobility tables across time and countries. In the covariance structure model, recent developments allow the simultaneous estimation of models across groups (Jöreskog and Sörbom, 1984). Other statistical methods have comparable abilities.

Regardless of the method used, there are two common mistakes that are found in studying group differences. First, the specification of the nature of group differences may be inadequate. If group differences are considered only as differences in the mean level of the dependent variable for a given combination of independent variables, important variation in the effects of independent variables across groups may be masked. Not only will information be lost, but biased estimates of the effects of variables that do not differ by group will be obtained. Second, if analyses are applied separately to each group, incorrect statistical tests are often made. Using the standard statistical methods described in this chapter and standard options on common statistical packages, it is possible to avoid these problems.

While the methods of this chapter are quite general, they are limited. In the next chapter Mare and Winship present an important extension by considering models that allow the group variable itself to be causally determined.

NOTES

1. Throughout this chapter we will use dummy coding to specify groups. Other methods of coding, such as effect coding, could also be used. For a discussion of alternative methods of coding, see Kerlinger and Pedhazur (1973: 141-150).

2. Conditional expectations will be used to demonstrate the properties of many of the models being presented. Conditional expectation is designated as $E(.|.)$, where the variable whose expectation is being taken is to the left of the modulus and the condition on the expectation is to the right of the modulus. For example, $E(Y|X)$ indicates the expected value of Y for a specific value of X. Or, $E(Y|X, G = 1)$ indicates the expected value of Y for those with G equal to one for some given value of X.

3. Figure 2 has been drawn such that δ and β_G are greater than zero; with different values of the parameters, the lines could cross.

4. If the covariance matrix, the means, and the sample size are available, it is possible to pool the data from separate studies to estimate all of the models discussed earlier in this chapter. For a detailed presentation of this approach, see Specht and Warren (1976).

6

Endogenous Switching Regression Models for the Causes and Effects of Discrete Variables

ROBERT D. MARE
CHRISTOPHER WINSHIP

Acommon research problem is to assess the consequences for individuals of their social roles, statuses, or group membership. For example, labor market analyses assess the effects on individuals' earnings of their occupations, labor market sectors, social classes, or educational credentials. Education research examines the effects of students' placement in tracks on their academic achievement. Evaluation studies estimate the effects of participation in social programs on social policy outcomes. These analyses attempt either to establish the effects of positions or statuses on outcomes or to see whether other variables differ in their effects on the outcomes across positions. This chapter describes some models for these kinds of analyses that improve upon more commonly used models.

A typical approach to data on social positions and their outcomes is the analysis of covariance (ANACOVA) (e.g., Long and Miethe, this volume). This approach assumes that, once other

AUTHORS' NOTE: *Grants from the National Institute of Aging to Robert D. Mare and Christopher Winship and from the National Institute of Child Health and Human Development (HD 05876) to the Center for Demography and Ecology, University of Wisconsin—Madison, supported the preparation of this chapter. The authors are grateful to Meichu D. Chen for expert research assistance and comments on an earlier draft, to Adam Gamoran for advice and the use of his extract of the High School and Beyond data, and to J. Scott Long and Judith A. Seltzer for helpful comments.*

measured variables that affect the outcome (dependent) variable are taken into account, the process by which individuals are sorted into positions is independent of factors influencing the outcome variable itself. That is, no unmeasured variables affect both the dependent variable and the variables that indicate an individual's position. Such strong assumptions are often untenable. Individuals may choose (or be assigned to) positions based on the expected consequences of those positions for the outcome of interest. For example, school administrators or parents may assign children to school tracks according to the academic benefit that the children will derive from one track versus another. Individuals may decide whether or not to attend college on the basis of the perceived benefit of college relative to that of not attending college. Individuals may self-select themselves into social programs in part because of the benefits of program participation.

In these examples, positions occupied affect outcomes and the outcomes associated with positions affect the assignment of persons to positions. Thus outcomes and positions are simultaneously related. The simultaneity creates a selection bias in that the assignment of persons to positions is not random, even controlling for measured independent variables, but instead is a function of the outcome variable. Omitted variable and simultaneity problems imply that ANACOVA models estimated by OLS yield inconsistent estimates of the effects of social positions and of other independent variables in the models.

This chapter describes models for the joint determination of a discrete outcome, which denotes individuals' statuses or positions, and another outcome—either discrete or continuous—that may be affected by the status or position. These models, sometimes called "endogenous switching models," relax the assumptions of ANACOVA by allowing for the *joint* determination of the discrete variables and the outcomes that they affect. The models enable one to (1) model both the allocation of persons to positions and the effects of positions on other outcomes; (2) estimate the degree to which common, unmeasured variables affect both the outcome and the classification variables; (3) obtain estimates of the effects of other variables *within* levels of the classification variables that take account of potential selection biases; and (4) estimate the impact of the classification regime (e.g., tracking, market segmentation, program treatments) by stimulating how individuals would fare had they entered different positions from those that they in fact occupy.

Much of the material discussed in this chapter is covered in more technical form by Maddala (1983: 257-290), Amemiya (1986: 360-411), and the literature reviewed by them. The endogenous switching model is closely related to two classes of models, namely sample selection (e.g., Berk, 1983) and dummy endogenous variable models (Heckman, 1978). Although the goal of this chapter is to provide a didactic account of endogenous switching models, some of the structural forms of the model are presented here for the first time.

This chapter is restricted to a discussion of problems where the assignment of observations to categories, as well as the realized outcomes for those categories, are both *observed* endogenous variables. Another class of models, not discussed here, assumes an *exogenous* but *un*observed classification. These latter models, also called switching regressions, rely on within-sample heterogeneity in the functional forms that relate observed exogenous and outcome variables (see, e.g., Goldfeld and Quandt [1973], Johnston [1984: 407-409], and Maddala [1977: 394-396]).

ENDOGENOUS SWITCHING MODELS FOR POSITIONS AND THEIR OUTCOMES

We begin with a general model of the sorting of persons to positions and of the effects of position on outcomes. Then we show the general model can be restricted to incorporate assumptions about the rules that govern the assignment of persons to positions. We consider three specific cases. One case, the "Ascription Model," assumes that individuals are assigned to positions solely on the basis of their observed characteristics and not on the basis of their expected outcomes. A second, the "Maximization Model," assumes that persons are optimally assigned, that is they enter the positions where their expected outcomes are most favorable. The final case, the "Quota Model," assumes that one of the positions is "dominant" in the sense that persons are assigned according to how well they would be expected to do if they entered that position, and their expected outcomes in other positions are irrelevant to the assignment decision.

"POSITIONS" AND "OUTCOMES"

In the following discussion *positions* denote a classification of two or more roles, statuses, or other categories into which persons are sorted. *Outcomes* denote the rewards, achievements, or consequences associated with alternative positions. We treat these outcomes as continuous variables, but similar models are available for discrete outcomes. In most applications the outcomes may be regarded as both the *ex post* rewards that depend on entry into positions, and also *ex ante* incentives for persons to choose one position over others. Position and outcome, therefore, may be *jointly* determined.

DECISION MAKING AND RATIONALITY

In many applications of these models, the allocation of persons to positions can be viewed as the decisions of individual actors. Some of our discussion applies this view. The *models*, however, do not depend on the assumption of rational decision making that one might find in applications of the models that derive explicitly from economic or other behavioral theories. Rather, the models are consistent with the view that the sorting of persons to positions is the outcome of the simultaneous actions of *many* persons, such as employers, workers, relatives, and so on. Alternatively, the models may be viewed as altogether independent of the concepts of decision making and choice. Some decision-making processes can be formalized and empirically tested against more flexible versions of the model. Thus assumptions about decision making are testable hypotheses rather than assumptions inherent in the general model.

THE GENERAL MODEL

Denote persons by i (i = 1, ..., I) and positions by j (j = 1, 2). Let d_i be a dichotomous variable that equals 1 for persons entering position 1 and 0 for persons entering position 2. For the i*th* person let Y_i denote the outcome for the i*th* person and X_{ki} denote the value on the k*th* measured independent variable (k = 1, ..., K) that may affect position assignment or outcome within positions. Assume that the X_k are predetermined with respect to both the allocation of persons to positions and the outcome within the position. Assume further that $X_{1i} = 1$ for all individuals so that it enters the model as a constant. Under these assumptions, the usual ANACOVA model is

$$Y_i = \alpha_0 d_i + \sum_k \alpha_k X_{ki} + \epsilon_i \qquad [1]$$

where ϵ_i denotes a stochastic disturbance and the α_k ($k = 0, \ldots, K$) denote parameters to be estimated. Under suitable assumptions about ϵ_i, this model can be estimated by OLS. It can, moreover, be generalized to allow the effects of the X_k to depend on d. This generalization can be written with interaction terms added to equation 1 or as two separate equations, say

$$Y_{1i} = \sum_k \beta_{1k} X_{ki} + \epsilon_{1i}, \qquad [2]$$

$$Y_{2i} = \sum_k \beta_{2k} X_{ki} + \epsilon_{2i}, \qquad [3]$$

where Y_1 and Y_2 denote outcomes in positions 1 and 2, respectively, ϵ_1 and ϵ_2 denote stochastic disturbances, and the β_{1k} and β_{2k} denote parameters to be estimated. Under this formulation the outcome becomes two variables for each individual. Of course, one typically observes only the outcome associated with the position that each individual in fact holds. As discussed below, however, we consider the possibility that both the observed outcomes and the hypothetical outcomes that persons would experience had they entered different positions affect their assignments to positions.

In restricted forms of the model, some of the X_k may be excluded from one or both of equations 2 and 3. In addition, some variables may have the same effect on the outcome in position 1 as in position 2, that is $\beta_{1k} = \beta_{2k}$ for some k. If the effects of the independent variables are identical in the two positions for all independent variables except the constant, that is, $\beta_{1k} = \beta_{2k}$ for $k > 1$, then the net effect of position on outcome is $\beta_{11} - \beta_{21}$. If, on the other hand, the effects of the X_k vary across positions, there is no single position effect. Rather the position effect is conditional upon the values of the X_k. Thus the model allows for the additive or interactive effects of position on outcome that are represented in common ANACOVA models.

Now consider an extension of the model, which represent the process by which persons are allocated to positions. Let persons have latent scores Z_i that index their likelihood of assignment to position 1. The probability of assignment to position 1 is $P(Z_i > 0)$. Let the relative chances that a person is assigned to position 1 or 2 be a function of both the same predetermined factors X_k that affect outcomes in positions, and also the (expected) outcomes of the positions themselves. This extension of the model can be written:

$$Z_i = \sum_k \gamma_k X_{ki} + \eta_1 Y_{1i} + \eta_2 Y_{2i} + \zeta_i, \qquad [4]$$

where η_1, η_2, and the γ_k denote parameters and ζ denotes a stochastic disturbance. Throughout, we assume that ζ is uncorrelated with ϵ_1 and ϵ_2 in equations 2 and 3.

For estimating and interpreting the general model and its restricted forms, it is useful to put equation 4 into its reduced form, that is

$$Z_i = \sum_k \pi_k X_{ki} + \epsilon_{3i}, \qquad [5]$$

where, from equations 2 and 3, $\pi_k = \eta_1 \beta_{1k} + \eta_2 \beta_{2k} + \gamma_k$ and $\epsilon_{3i} = \eta_1 \epsilon_{1i} + \eta_2 \epsilon_{2i} + \zeta_i$. Thus equations 2, 3, and 4 describe the structural form of a model for the allocation of persons to positions and the effects of positions on outcomes; and equations 2, 3, and 5 describe the corresponding reduced form of the model.

To complete the model, it remains to specify the structure of the reduced form disturbances. Assume that ϵ_1, ϵ_2, and ϵ_3 follow a trivariate normal distribution with $\mathrm{Var}(\epsilon_1) = \sigma_1^2$, $\mathrm{Var}(\epsilon_2) = \sigma_2^2$, $\mathrm{Var}(\epsilon_3) = \sigma_3^2$, $\mathrm{Cov}(\epsilon_1, \epsilon_2) = \sigma_{12}$, $\mathrm{Cov}(\epsilon_1, \epsilon_3) = \sigma_{13}$, and $\mathrm{Cov}(\epsilon_2, \epsilon_3) = \sigma_{23}$. The disturbance in the structural equation for allocating persons to positions, ζ, is uncorrelated with the disturbances in the outcome equations, ϵ_1 and ϵ_2. The reduced form disturbance ϵ_3, however, is generally correlated with ϵ_1 and ϵ_2. Equations 2 and 3 define regression models, albeit models that must be estimated in a way that takes account of the correlated disturbances. Because ϵ_3 is normally distributed, equation 5 is a probit model (e.g., Aldrich and Nelson, 1984). The normality assumption makes estimation of the full model feasible and enables us to make useful calculations on the basis of estimates from the model.

Note again that the distributions of not only Z but also Y_1 and Y_2 are defined for the *entire population*, not just for persons who in fact enter position 1 or position 2. For example, if $\overline{X}_k$ is the population mean of X_k, then $\Sigma\beta_{1k}\overline{X}_k$ is the expected level of outcome for a *random* sample of the entire population when placed in position 1. Of the parameters that we have mentioned, however, all except σ_{12} and σ_3 can be estimated from data on the X_{ki}, on d_i, and on one measure on either Y_1 *or* Y_2 for each person. To estimate σ_{12} and σ_3 requires additional information, and, in practice, we assume values for these parameters (see discussion of identification and estimation below).

As written, all of the X_k affect each of the three endogenous variables, but some of the X_k may be excluded from some of the equations. For example, some variables may affect outcome but not position or vice versa. Alternatively, some variables may affect the outcome in one position but not in the other. When it is substantively plausible to exclude some of the X_k from some of the equations, the resulting reduction in possible multicollinearity may make it easier to obtain stable estimates of parameters than when all X_k appear in all three equations.

Unlike the ANACOVA model, however, the endogenous switching regression model includes the effects of nonrandom selection into positions. The ANACOVA model assumes that unmeasured determinants of position placement, ϵ_3, are uncorrelated with unmeasured determinants of outcome within positions, ϵ_1 and ϵ_2. If this assumption holds, then ordinary least squares (OLS) estimates of position effects and of within-position effects of the other X_k on outcome are consistent. If, however, the assumption is false then OLS estimates of the β_{jk} in equations 2 and 3 are *in*consistent because of the nonrandom selection of persons into positions (even conditional upon the observed X_k). In the model discussed here, the covariances between the disturbances in the equation predicting allocation of persons to positions, ϵ_3, and in the outcome equations, ϵ_1 and ϵ_2, adjust for this potential inconsistency. The covariances σ_{13} and σ_{23}, moreover, show the degree and direction of nonrandom selection of persons to positions. This model, therefore, represents the "structural" or population-level effects of position on outcome, rather than just a description of differences in outcomes between observed position 1 and position 2 samples.

SELECTION OF PERSONS INTO POSITIONS

Using the endogenous switching model, we can investigate the direction and degree of nonrandom selection of persons to positions and the selection biases that are implicit in OLS estimates of position effects. We can also simulate how persons would fare if placed in alternative positions. These analyses use formulas for the means of censored normal distributions (e.g., Maddala, 1983: 365-367).

Assume that we have the model defined by equations 2-5. Let $\dot{Z}_i$ denote the predicted value of Z from the X_k for the $i th$ individual, that is, $\dot{Z}_i = \Sigma \pi_k X_{ki}$. The expected outcome for the $i th$ person if they enter position 1, that is, persons for whom $Z_i > 0$, is

$$E(Y_{1i} | Z_i > 0) = \sum_k \beta_{1k} X_{ki} + E(\epsilon_{1i} | Z_i > 0; X_{1i}, \ldots, X_{iK}) \qquad [6]$$

$$= \sum_k \beta_{1k} X_{ki} + (\sigma_{13}/\sigma_3) \left\{ [\phi(\dot{Z}_i)] / [\Phi(\dot{Z}_i)] \right\},$$

where ϕ denotes the normal probability density function and Φ denotes the cumulative normal probability function. This expression implies that the expected outcome of persons who are placed in position 1 is a function of both their measured independent variables, $\Sigma \beta_{ik} X_{ki}$, and also the expected value of their unmeasured characteristics. The latter quantity is a function of the covariance between outcome in position 1 and the chances of assignment to position 1 (σ_{13}) and (a function of) the probability of assignment to position 1 $\{ [\Phi(\dot{Z}_i)] / [\Phi(\dot{Z}_i)] \}$. Thus the outcome of persons *observed* in position 1, $E(Y_{1i} | Z_i > 0)$, is a biased estimate of their expected outcome for position 1 where the bias is equal to the second term on the right side of equation 6. To estimate the expected outcome for an individual in position 1, we need to know both $\Sigma \beta_{ik} X_k$ and also information about the probability of selection into position 1 as well. This is an application of well-known ideas about "sample selection bias" (e.g., Berk, 1983). The expected outcome for a person observed in position 2 is

$$E(Y_{2i} | Z_i < 0) = \sum_k \beta_{2k} X_{ki} + E(\epsilon_{2i} | Z_i < 0; X_{1i}, \ldots, X_{Ki}) \qquad [7]$$

$$= \sum_k \beta_{2k} X_{ki} - (\sigma_{23}/\sigma_3) \left\{ [\phi(\dot{Z}_i)] / [1 - \Phi(\dot{Z}_i)] \right\}.$$

The disturbance covariances, σ_{13} and σ_{23}, measure the direction and degree of nonrandom selection into positions. In particular, equation 6 shows that if $\sigma_{13} > 0$, then there is positive selection of persons to position 1; that is, net of the effects of the X_k, Y_1 is higher for persons who enter position 1 than it would be for the average person in the population. Conversely, $\sigma_{13} < 0$ indicates negative selection into position 1. Equation 7 shows that $\sigma_{23} < 0$ indicates positive selection of persons to position 2, whereas $\sigma_{23} > 0$ implies negative selection.

As pointed out by Willis and Rosen (1979) and Maddala (1983: 258), two combinations of signs of σ_{13} and σ_{23} are of particular interest. First, suppose $\sigma_{13} > 0$ and $\sigma_{23} < 0$. This is the case of positive selection in both positions. That is, net of the effects of the X_k, persons who enter position 1 do better than the population average for position 1 and persons who enter position 2 do better than the population average for position 2. Conversely, were persons who enter position 1 placed in position 2 instead, they would do *worse* than the persons who in fact enter position 2. This accords with a notion of two dimensions along which persons can be assessed, each of which is best suited to one of the positions.

Second, suppose $\sigma_{13} > 0$ and $\sigma_{23} > 0$. In this case, persons who enter position 1 do better than the population average for that position, but persons who enter position 2 do worse than the population averge for that position. Conversely, were persons who enter position 1 to be placed in position 2 instead, they would do better than the persons who in fact entered position 2. This case implies a single dimension on which persons who enter position 1 are more advantaged than persons who enter position 2.

Note that σ_{13} and σ_{23} are parameters to be estimated rather than assumed quantities. Thus under the assumptions of the model, we can assess which of the two cases is closer to the truth. (A third case, where $\sigma_{13} < 0$ and $\sigma_{23} < 0$, mirrors the second case, that is, a single latent dimension on which persons who enter position 2 are more advantaged than persons who enter position 1. Finally, there is the logically possible, but perverse, case where $\sigma_{13} < 0$ and $\sigma_{23} > 0$, which implies negative selection to both positions.)

ALTERNATIVE POSITION ASSIGNMENTS

In addition to illustrating the relationship between population and observed outcome levels for the two positions, the endogenous switching regression model provides a way of calculating the expected level of outcome if persons are assigned to positions other than the ones they in fact entered. The expected outcome of position 1 persons had they been placed in position 2 instead is

$$E(Y_{2i}|Z_i > 0) = \sum_k \beta_{2k} X_{ki} + (\sigma_{23}/\sigma_3) \{ [\phi(\hat{Z}_i)] / [\Phi(\hat{Z}_i)] \}. \qquad [8]$$

The expected outcome of position 2 persons had they been placed in position 1 is

$$E(Y_{1i}|Z_i < 0) = \sum_k \beta_{1k} X_{ki} - (\sigma_{13}/\sigma_3) \{ [\phi(\hat{Z}_i)] / [1 - \Phi(\hat{Z}_i)] \}. \qquad [9]$$

These ideas and formulas can be illustrated with numerical examples. Consider two persons, one observed in position 1, the other in position 2, who have identical values on X_k. Let $\sigma_3 = 1$. First, suppose $\sum \beta_{1k} X_k = 2$, $\sum \beta_{2k} X_k = 1$, $Z = 1$, $\sigma_{13} = 0.5$, and $\sigma_{23} = -0.5$. Given the signs of the covariances, we expect that both persons, if placed in the position in which they are *not* observed, would fare worse than the persons in fact do. Applying equations 6-9, we see that that is indeed the case:

$$E(Y_1 | Z > 0) = E(\text{Pos 1} | \text{Observed in Pos 1}) = 2.14,$$
$$E(Y_2 | Z < 0) = E(\text{Pos 2} | \text{Observed in Pos 2}) = 1.76,$$
$$E(Y_2 | Z > 0) = E(\text{Pos 2} | \text{Observed in Pos 1}) = 0.86,$$
$$E(Y_1 | Z < 0) = E(\text{Pos 1} | \text{Observed in Pos 2}) = 1.24.$$

In a second example, $\sum \beta_{1k} X_k = 2$, $\sum \beta_{2k} X_k = 1$, $Z = 1.41$, $\sigma_{13} = 1.06$, and $\sigma_{23} = 0.35$. This illustrates the case where $\sigma_{13} > 0$ and $\sigma_{23} > 0$. Thus the person observed in position 1 would achieve a higher outcome than the one observed in position 2 irrespective of which position he or she were placed in. From equations 6-9, we compute the following:

$$E(Y_1 | Z > 0) = E(\text{Pos 1} | \text{Observed in Pos 1}) = 2.17,$$
$$E(Y_2 | Z < 0) = E(\text{Pos 2} | \text{Observed in Pos 2}) = 0.35,$$
$$E(Y_2 | Z > 0) = E(\text{Pos 2} | \text{Observed in Pos 1}) = 1.06,$$
$$E(Y_1 | Z < 0) = E(\text{Pos 1} | \text{Observed in Pos 2}) = 0.03.$$

These examples show some alternative assessments of the effects of the sorting of persons to positions. In both examples, persons fare better in the positions where they are observed than in the alternative position, implying that sorting is "optimal" in the sense of placing persons where they will do the best. This result, however, is empirical and is *not* required by the model.

The switching model also allows for a benign or critical judgment of the impact of sorting on group differences. In the first example, the observed difference in outcome between the two positions (2.14 – 1.76 = 0.38) is less than the population difference (2 – 1 = 1), but in the second example, the observed difference (2.17 – 0.35 = 1.82) is larger. Relative to random allocation of persons to positions, therefore, the first example suggests that the observed system of allocation reduces group differences whereas the second shows that it enhances them. These results show the potential richness of the model for understanding the effects of the process of sorting persons to positions on levels and differentials in outcome.

These models can show the potential impact on *marginal* individuals were they to move from one position to another. In the aggregate, they suggest how average levels of the outcome variable would change in their levels and distribution for groups under alternative assignments to the ones observed in the sample. One must be cautious, however, in making such extrapolations from the models to hypothetical systems of assignments. In large populations, movements by small numbers of individuals are unlikely to affect the structure of assignment and outcome for the population as a whole. If, however, substantial portions of the population were reassigned, the overall system and the appropriate model could change, thereby invalidating inference from the original model. These models, therefore, can suggest the impact of a system of sorting persons to positions and outcomes, but they are not a substitute for historical or comparative data on alternative systems.

STRUCTURAL MODELS:
I. ASCRIPTION MODEL

We can now further specify the process by which persons are allocated to positions, and the implications of that process. In the following discussion we consider three models, the Ascription

Model, the Maximization Model, and the Quota Model. In all three models, one or several decision makers assign persons to positions. These models differ in the principle that governs decision making. Each hypothesizes a *structural form* of the switching regression model that implies restrictions on the general model.

Consider first the case where persons are assigned to positions solely on the basis of their observed (predetermined) characteristics. That is, their expected outcomes Y_1 and Y_2 do not affect their assignment to positions, once their measured characteristics X_k are taken into account. This model, which we term the Ascription Model, amounts to placing the restriction $\eta_1 = \eta_2 = 0$ in equation 4. Thus $\epsilon_3 = \zeta$, which is uncorrelated with ϵ_1 and ϵ_2. To test the validity of this model it suffices to estimate the reduced form of the general model (equations 2, 3, and 5) and a restricted model in which $\sigma_{13} = \sigma_{23} = 0$. If these models are estimated by maximum likelihood (see below), then, because the latter model is nested within the former, the restriction can be tested using a likelihood ratio test (using a χ^2 statistic with two degrees of freedom). If the Ascription Model holds, then equations 2 and 3 can be estimated by OLS.

STRUCTURAL MODELS:
II. MAXIMIZATION MODEL

In the Maximization Model, persons are allocated to the positions where their expected outcome is highest. That is, the ith person enters position 1 if $Y_{1i} > Y_{2i}$ and position 2 if $Y_{2i} > Y_{1i}$. This model assumes that persons could not fare any better were they assigned to an alternative position to the one they in fact entered. It does not dictate, however, whether *differences* between groups of persons would be larger or smaller under alternative position assignments than those that occur.

This model is also a special case of the general model and can be written as a set of mathematical restrictions. In particular, in equation 4, let $\eta_1 = -\eta_2 = \eta$ and $\gamma_k = 0$ for $k > 1$, yielding

$$Z_i = \gamma_1 + \eta(Y_{1i} - Y_{2i}) + \zeta_i \qquad [10]$$

$$= \gamma_1 + \eta[(\textstyle\sum_k \beta_{1k} X_{ki} + \epsilon_{1i}) - (\textstyle\sum_k \beta_{2k} X_{ki} + \epsilon_{2i})] + \zeta_i$$

$$= \textstyle\sum_k \pi_k X_{ki} + \epsilon_{3i}$$

where $\pi_k = \eta(\beta_{1k} - \beta_{2k})$ for $k > 1$, $\pi_1 = \gamma_1 + \eta(\beta_{11} - \beta_{21})$, and $\epsilon_{3i} = \eta(\epsilon_{1i} - \epsilon_{2i}) + \zeta_i$. The parameter η in this model is the effect of the difference in expected outcomes between positions 1 and 2 on the chances that a person will be assigned to position 1. The π_k parameters in equation 10, unlike the corresponding parameters in equation 5, are proportional to the differences between the corresponding β_k parameters for outcome in positions 1 and 2. The model also implies restrictions on the covariance matrix of disturbances in equations 2, 3, and 5. That is $\sigma_{13} = \eta(\sigma_1^2 - \sigma_{12})$, and $\sigma_{23} = \eta(\sigma_{12} - \sigma_2^2)$. These restrictions imply that it is possible to estimate σ_{12}, a parameter that is unidentified in the general model. The restrictions also require that $\sigma_{13} - \sigma_{23} > 0$, which, provided $\eta > 0$, eliminates the perverse outcome that persons are negatively selected into both positions. Conversely, it agrees with the key assumption of the Maximization Model, that persons enter the position where they get the best reward.

If the constraints of the Maximization Model hold, then one can make similar interpretations of the σ_{13} and σ_{23} parameters and calculations of expected outcomes under alternative position assignments to those discussed above.

STRUCTURAL MODELS:
III. QUOTA MODEL

In the Quota Model, persons are allocated to positions according to the availability of vacancies in position 1 and to their expected qualifications for the position. Suppose that decision makers seek to fill position 1 with the *top* of the population as defined by its expected outcome in position 1. Conversely, they assign to position 2 persons who are expected to fall in the bottom of the outcome distribution if they enter position 1. Unlike in the Maximization Model, persons' expected outcomes in position 2 are irrelevant to the allocation of persons to positions.

The Quota Model can be specified as a set of restrictions on equation 4, namely $\eta_2 = \gamma_k = 0$ for $k > 1$, that is

$$Z_i = \gamma_1 + \eta_1 Y_{1i} + \zeta_i,$$

which implies a reduced form of

$$Z_i = \gamma_1 + \sum_k \eta_1 \beta_{1k} X_{ki} + \eta_1 \epsilon_{1i} + \zeta_i$$

$$= \sum_k \pi_k X_{ki} + \epsilon_3,$$

where $\pi_1 = \eta_1 \beta_{11} + \gamma_1$, $\pi_k = \eta_1 \beta_{1k}$ for $k > 1$, and $\epsilon_{3i} = \eta_1 \epsilon_{1i} + \zeta_i$. This model implies that all coefficients in equations 2 and 5 except for the constant term should be proportional to each other and that $\sigma_{13} = \eta_1 \sigma_1^2$. As for the other two restricted models, the validity of the restrictions implied by the Quota Model can be tested by computing the loss of fit of the general model when the restrictions are imposed. But the Quota Model is not nested within the Maximization Model because the latter imposes restrictions upon the parameters of the position 2 outcome equation that are not imposed in the former.

PARTIAL FORESIGHT

Our discussion of the Maximization and Quota Models has assumed that the assignment of persons to positions is based on complete knowledge of Y_1 and Y_2, an assumption that may often be unrealistic. For example, in deciding whether or not to continue in school, individuals may know only roughly the benefit that they will derive from staying in school. In evaluating the consequences of possible actions, therefore, they rely on predicted, rather than actual, values of the outcomes.

One way to model this is to assume that persons are assigned to positions on the basis of values of Y_1 and Y_2 predicted from the X_k's for those persons. That is, the person(s) carrying out the assignment know as much as the social researcher, but no more. Then the structural equation for position assignment under the general model (equation 4) becomes

$$Z_i = \gamma_1 + \eta_1 \hat{Y}_{1i} + \eta_2 \hat{Y}_{2i} + \zeta_i \qquad [11]$$

where $\hat{Y}_{1i} = \Sigma \beta_{1k} X_{ki}$ and $\hat{Y}_{2i} = \Sigma \beta_{2k} X_{ki}$. The reduced form is

$$Z_i = \sum_k (\eta_1 \beta_{1k} + \eta_2 \beta_{2k}) X_{ki} + \zeta_i \qquad [12]$$

$$= \sum_k \pi_k X_{ki} + \epsilon_{3i}$$

In this specification, ϵ_3 is uncorrelated within ϵ_1 and ϵ_2 in equations 2 and 3. If statistical tests indicate that $\sigma_{13} = \sigma_{23} = 0$, then the outcome equations can be estimated by OLS. When the restrictions on the π_k implied by the Maximization or Quota Models hold, however, it is better to estimate equations 2, 3, and 11 simultaneously (see below).

MORE THAN TWO POSITIONS

One can extend the models to include more positions. For three positions, for example, a third outcome equation, parallel to equations 2 and 3, can be added. The sorting equation 5 becomes a trinomial probit equation instead of a binary probit. Then two latent variables, say Z_1 and Z_2, index individuals' relative suitability for the three positions. A special case of the multiposition model occurs when the positions are ordered. For example one can model decisions to continue in school and the rewards associated with alternative amounts of schooling as a choice equation and a set of outcome equations associated with each level of schooling (Willis and Rosen, 1979). For two schooling levels, equations 2-5 are such a model. For three or more levels, additional outcome equations are required for additional schooling levels, as in the case of the general polytomous model (Garen, 1984). The sorting equation 5, however, is then a single *ordered* probit equation (e.g., Winship and Mare, 1984), which predicts schooling as an ordered variable that indexes a single latent variable Z. Although standard computer packages do not readily estimate this model, it is easier to estimate than the general polytomous model.

ESTIMATION

This section first discusses identification issues raised by the endogenous switching model. Then it reviews methods of estimation, including multistage consistent estimation and maximum likelihood estimation. Finally, it discusses special estimation issues that are raised by restricted forms of the general model.

IDENTIFICATION

Under the assumption for trivariate normality, the general model defined by equations 2-5 and its associated covariance matrix requires two restrictions to be identified. Because only one of Y_1 or Y_2 is observed, no sample information is available to identify the covariance between the disturbances in the two outcome, σ_{12}. Because the latent variable Z is only indicated by the binary outcome of whether individuals are in position 1 or position 2, its scale, which is determined by the disturbance variance σ_3, is also unidentified. With regard to σ_{12}, it is necessary to assume a value for this parameter or to impose additional restrictions such as those of the Maximization Model (see above). In the general model, however, estimates of the other parameters in the model do not depend on σ_{12}.

Identifying σ_3 is the usual problem of scale identification in binary regression models (e.g., Winship and Mare, 1983: 73-75; 1984: 517). To identify σ_3 in the general model, one must adopt a normalization rule, such as $\sigma_3 = 1.0$ or Var(Z) = 1.0. These rules affect the estimated parameters for equation 3 and σ_{13} and σ_{23} by a factor of proportionality but do not affect the remaining parameters or the fit of the model.

Apart from the restrictions just discussed, no additional assumptions are needed to identify the β and π parameters. In practice, however, the precision with which the βs are identified may considerably improve if some of the X_k do not appear in some of the equations. When no such exclusion restrictions are available, the identification of σ_{13} and σ_{23} depends on the nonlinearity implicit in the normality assumption. Under this circumstance, the correlations and standard errors of the estimates of σ_{13}, σ_{23}, β_{1k}, β_{2k}, and π_k may be large. Of course, the exclusion restrictions should derive from substantive reasoning rather than *ex post* inspection of empirical results.

MULTISTAGE CONSISTENT ESTIMATION

Multistage estimators are valuable because they can be implemented with standard programs that perform regression and probit analysis, and they, unlike many maximum likelihood estimators, intuitively demonstrate the workings of the model. In this section we describe one multistage estimation routine for the general endogenous switching regression model. Depending on the special features of the model, other routines may also be feasible. Maddala (1983: chap. 8) discusses multistage estimators for related models.

Equations 2, 3, and 5 are two linear regression equations and a dichotomous response equation predicting the probability of entering position 1. Assume that we have a random sample of persons, some of whom are in position 1, the remainder of whom are in position 2. Y_1 is observed only for persons in position 1 and Y_2 is observed only for persons in position 2. Which position an individual has entered is known for the entire sample. The model can be estimated as follows:

(A) Assuming that $\sigma_3 = 1$, estimate the π_k parameters in equation 5 by probit analysis.

(B) Use the estimated parameters to calculate predicted values $\dot{Z}_i$ and the quantities $\phi(\dot{Z}_i)$ and $\Phi(\dot{Z}_i)$ for each individual.

(C) With the estimates from step B in hand, compute the following two ratios:

$$\lambda_{1i} = \phi(\dot{Z}_i)/\Phi(\dot{Z}_i); \quad \lambda_{2i} = -\phi(\dot{Z}_i)/[1 - \Phi(\dot{Z}_i)].$$

(D) Modify equations 2 and 3 by including λ_1 and λ_2, respectively, as regressors, that is

$$Y_{1i} = \sum_k \beta_{1k} X_{ki} + \sigma_{13}\lambda_{1i} + \nu_{1i}, \qquad [2^*]$$

and

$$Y_{2i} = \sum_k \beta_{2k} X_{ki} + \sigma_{23}\lambda_{2i} + \nu_{2i}, \qquad [3^*]$$

where ν_{1i} and ν_{2i} are stochastic disturbances that are uncorrelated with the X_k, λ_1, and λ_2. Estimate equations 2* and 3* by OLS over the subsamples for which Y_1 or Y_2 are observed.

Step D yields consistent estimates of not only β_{1k} and β_{2k}, but also σ_{13} and σ_{23}, which are the coefficients on λ_1 and λ_2, respectively. This procedure is tantamount to the commonly applied two-stage procedure for correcting regressions for sample selection bias (e.g., Berk, 1983), except that it adjusts for nonrandom selection into two samples instead of one. It shows that the potential inconsistency in OLS estimation of equations 2 and 3 is a function of the degree of correlation between (functions of) the probability that an individual is selected into position 1 or position 2 (λ_1 or λ_2) and the X_k.

Because λ_1 and λ_2 are functions of $\dot{Z}$, which is a function of the X_k, the above discussion implies that collinearity between λ_1, λ_2, and X_k may be a serious problem in obtaining precise estimates of the parameters. Thus when substantive reasoning implies that some of the X_k can be excluded from some of the equations, collinearity may be substantially reduced.

Steps A-D consistently estimate the parameters but not the standard errors of the β_{ik} and β_{2k}, a result of heteroscedasticity in equations 2* and 3*. To obtain consistent estimates of the standard errors, these equations must be estimated by weighted least squares instead of OLS. Maddala (1983: 225-227, 252-256) provides guidelines for constructing the weights.

MAXIMUM LIKELIHOOD ESTIMATION

Equations 2, 3, and 5, their disturbance covariance matrix, and restricted forms of this model can also be estimated by maximum likelihood. Maximum likelihood is usually the preferred method for these models because it is feasible with available software, provides efficient estimates, allows restrictions to be applied, and permits the construction of likelihood ratio tests of the restrictions.

Maximum likelihood estimation consists of specifying the probability of obtaining the observed data in terms of the parameters to be estimated and picking parameter values that make the probability as large as possible. Again assume a random sample of individuals, some of whom are in position 1 and the rest of whom are in position 2. The likelihood is

$$L(Y_1, Y_2, d_i) = \prod_i \left\{ (d_i) [f(Y_1 \mid d_i = 1)] + (1 - d_i) [f(Y_2 \mid d_i = 0)] \right\} \quad [13]$$

where f denotes the conditional normal density function for Y_1 or Y_2 given d_i. The conditional densities are functions of the parameters β_{1k}, β_{2k}, π_k, σ_1, σ_2, σ_{13}, and σ_{23}. Maddala (1983: 284) provides explicit formulas for the densities.

Maximum likelihood estimation consists of employing a numerical procedure to pick values of the parameters that make L as large as possible. Estimates can be obtained using the program HOTZTRAN (Avery and Hotz, 1983), which is used in the numerical example discussed below. As for maximum likelihood estimation generally, one can assess the *relative* fit of two models when one of the two models contains all of the parameters contained in the other model plus additional parameters. If L_1 denotes the likelihood of the simpler model and L_2 denotes the likelihood of the model in which the simpler model is nested, then the statistic $\chi^2 = -2\log(L_1/L_2)$ follows an asymptotic chi-square distribution with degrees of freedom equal to the difference in the number of estimated parameters between the two models. Likelihood ratio tests enable one to test simple restrictions that sets of parameters are insignificant or the more complex restrictions implied by the Maximization and Quota Models. Maximum likelihood estimation also yields an estimate of the asymptotic standard errors of parameters. Ratios of estimated parameters to their standard errors follow an asymptotic normal distribution and thus can be interpreted as Z-scores.

ESTIMATION OF RESTRICTED MODELS

The Maximization Model is estimated by imposing nonlinear restrictions on the general model. Although it can be estimated by either multistage or maximum likelihood methods, the latter are greatly preferred. When more than a single regressor appears in equations 2 and 3, the model is overidentified. Multistage estimation provides no easy way to impose all of the overidentifying restrictions simultaneously. Typically, therefore, multiple solutions are available for the model. To yield a unique best solution for the model, it is necessary to impose all of the restrictions simultaneously, which is straightforwardly carried out by maximum likelihood.

The Quota Model is also a restricted form of the general model and can, in principle, be estimated as a three-equation model. The trivariate normal distribution of the disturbances, however, reduces to bivariate normal because the latent selection variable Z and the expected outcome in position 1, Y_1, are perfectly correlated. One can, therefore, reformulate the model as a two-equation model; that is, a censored regression (tobit) equation (e.g., Maddala, 1983: 151-161; Tobin, 1958) with unknown censoring point for Y_1 and a linear regression equation subject to selection for Y_2 with disturbances correlated to estimate σ_{23}. Another modification is to assume a known censoring point, and estimate the model as a tobit equation for Y_1 and a linear regression subject to selection for Y_2.

EMPIRICAL EXAMPLE:
ACADEMIC TRACKING AND ACHIEVEMENT

We illustrate endogenous switching models with analyses of the causes and effects of allocating students to college and noncollege tracks within secondary schools. We model the processes by which students are assigned to tracks and tracks affect mathematics achievement. Gamoran and Mare (1987) discuss this research in more detail.

THREE VIEWS OF TRACKING

A rationale for tracking is that students differ in their academic goals and in the environments where they learn best. Ideally, a system of tracking matches students' aptitudes to learning environments. According to this view, student achievement is higher in a tracked high school than in one where tracking is nonexistent or in one where tracks exist but student aptitudes are not matched to track programs. A further goal of tracking is to raise the achievement of students of low academic promise and thus to reduce inequalities in achievement among students.

Critics of academic tracking stress the potential of tracking systems to widen differences between students. Tracks produce larger academic and postschooling inequalities among students than would exist in the absence of tracking. Moreover, because of the potential stigma and uneven quality of instruction attached to noncollege tracks, some students may learn *less* or be less likely to realize their academic or vocational goals when assigned to a noncollege track than they could in a different track or than they could achieve in an untracked high school system.

A third view is that tracking is neutral. That is, tracking systems affect neither inequalities among groups of students nor students' average levels of achievement, competency, or posthigh school success.

Many quantitative studies of tracking incorporate the effects of tracking into linear ANACOVA models of academic achievement and social stratification. Typically, such studies classify students by track and treat track as a variable that "intervenes" between family, school, and early achievement on the one hand and later achievement on the other. While informative, these analyses are ill suited to show whether (1) apparent achievement differences between tracks are due to participation in the tracks themselves or to unmeasured differences between students that are correlated with track placement, (2) the system of tracking widens or narrows achievement differences between groups that would occur under alternative track assignments or in the absence of tracking, and (3) students are optimally (for their aptitudes) assigned to tracks or could potentially perform better if they were assigned to different tracks. These questions are at the heart of an appraisal of the value and cost of tracking.

MODELS OF TRACKING EFFECTS

We apply the models discussed above to the study of track placement and track effects in order to answer important analytic questions more fully than in past research. These models enable one to estimate the effects of school, family, and ability factors on track placement and on schooling outcomes, taking into account that students are assigned to tracks on a nonrandom basis. According to the models, students are systematically selected into tracks on the basis of their known characteristics and the largely unobservable beliefs of teachers, administrators, parents, and students themselves about their "suitability" to a particular track. Both measured and unmeasured factors have *common* effects both on achievement and on track placement. Effectively, therefore, these models control for unmeasured factors that potentially distort estimates of track effects in models used in previous work on tracking. These models also allow for *distinct* latent variables to affect achievement in each track. The unmeasured aptitudes that may govern track placement and subsequent achievement may differ across tracks. This allows for explicit estimation and testing of the presumed beneficial or harmful effects of tracking discussed above.

DATA AND MEASURES

The data for this analysis are from the High School and Beyond Survey (HSB) of students who were sophomores in 1980. Family, school, and achievement measures were obtained in this survey for sophomores and achievement measures were obtained again in 1982 when most of these students were seniors (Jones et al., 1983). Our analyses are for public school students who were interviewed and tested in both waves of the survey, including dropouts, but excluding students who graduated or transferred before the 1982 interview. We use the following measures: mathematics achievement scores in 1980 and 1982; sophomore achievement scores in 1980 and 1982; sophomore achievement scores on science, reading, vocabulary, writing, and civics; socioeconomic status, which is an unweighted linear composite of father's occupational prestige score, father's and mother's grades of school completed, family income, and a home artifacts scale; dichotomous variables that equal one for females, blacks, and Hispanics, and zero otherwise; mean socioeconomic status of school attended; percentage of blacks in school attended; percentage of Hispanics in school attended; number of advanced mathematics courses offered in school attended; and a dichotomous variable that equals one if the student reported being in a college preparatory (academic) track in sophomore year and zero otherwise. Gamoran (1987) and Jones et al. describe these measures in more detail. We retained only students for whom data are present for all variables listed above. To speed computations, we used a 25% random subsample of observations, resulting in a sample of 3377 persons. Table 1 reports means and standard deviations of the variables for the total and track-specific samples.

EMPIRICAL MODELS

We formulate models for senior year mathematics achievement. The models include equations for (1) mathematics achievement within the college track, (2) mathematics achievement within the noncollege track, and (3) the probability of assignment to the college track in sophomore year. These models represent the effects of family, school, and achievement factors as of sophomore year on track placement and subsequent achievement. The models allow common unmeasured variables to affect both track placement and achievement in a track.

In the *structural* versions of the models, senior mathematics achievement is a function of track placement and sophomore

TABLE 1
**Means and Standard Deviations of Variables in Tracking Analysis
for Total, and Track-Specific Samples**

Variable	Total Mean	Total S.D.	College Track Mean	College Track S.D.	Noncollege Track Mean	Noncollege Track S.D.
Senior math achievement	19.97	8.22	24.72	7.81	17.72	7.42
College track (versus other)	0.32	0.47	1.00	0.00	0.00	0.00
Sophomore achievement						
mathematics	18.79	7.41	22.82	7.16	16.88	6.72
science	11.13	3.74	12.63	3.59	10.42	3.59
reading	9.11	3.92	11.01	3.94	8.21	3.57
vocabulary	10.97	4.32	12.95	4.15	10.03	4.08
writing	10.29	3.92	12.20	3.41	9.38	3.92
civics	5.88	2.04	6.67	1.89	5.50	2.00
Female (versus male)	0.48	0.50	0.53	0.50	0.46	0.50
Socioeconomic status	−0.09	0.73	0.19	0.73	−0.22	0.69
Black (versus nonblack)	0.12	0.32	0.11	0.31	0.12	0.33
Hispanic (versus non-Hisp.)	0.13	0.34	0.08	0.28	0.15	0.36
School SES	−0.09	0.36	−0.01	0.37	−0.12	0.35
School % black	13.34	22.13	12.72	21.33	13.63	22.49
School % Hispanic	4.57	25.12	4.26	11.51	4.72	12.90
School math courses	3.42	0.73	3.53	0.67	3.37	0.75

NOTE: Observations are weighted. See text for discussion of variables and samples.

achievement in mathematics, science, reading, vocabulary, writing, and civics; and track placement is a function of expected achievement in college and uncollege tracks, sophomore achievement, and sociodemographic and school variables listed above. This model corresponds to equations 2, 3, and 4, where Y_1 and Y_2 denote senior achievement in the college and noncollege tracks respectively; the X_k in equations 2 and 3 denote sophomore achievement scores and, in equation 4, denote sociodemographic and school factors as well as sophomore achievement; and Z indexes the chances of assignment to the college track. Sociodemographic and school factors do not affect achievement directly, but these variables do affect achievement through their effects both on sophomore achievement and on track assignment.

We estimate several versions of this model, including (1) a general model that allows for nonzero covariances between the reduced form disturbances (σ_{13} and σ_{23}) and no restrictions on the slope parameter; (2) an Ascription Model that does not restrict the slope parameters, but constrains σ_{13} and σ_{23} to be zero; (3) a Maximization Model that constrains both slopes and σ_{13} and

σ_{23}; (4) a Quota Model that imposes alternative slope and covariance restrictions. In these examples the slope parameters are free to vary across the college and noncollege track equations for mathematics achievement. All models are estimated by maximum likelihood, implemented by HOTZTRAN.

Table 2 presents -2 log likelihood statistics and numbers of parameters for each of the four models. The absolute values of these statistics have no interpretation, but their relative values indicate relative fit. Models 2, 3, and 4 are nested within Model 1, but none of the restricted models is nested within any of the other two. The χ^2 statistics show that the general model fits significantly better than both the Quota and the Maximization Models, implying that the restrictions on the latter two models are not consistent with the data. In contrast, the Ascription Model, which assumes that track assignment is based on measured characteristics alone, fits as well as the general model. These results suggest that simple views of how students are allocated to tracks—such as that students are matched to the tracks where they are expected to perform best; or that a "quota" of the most promising students is chosen for the college track—are not adequate to describe the data. They also suggest that, at least for the specification used here, common, unmeasured determinants of track placement and achievement do not seriously distort estimates of the effects of measured variables.

THE EFFECTS OF MEASURED VARIABLES

Although the general model with correlated disturbances does not fit the data significantly better than the Ascription Model, we discuss the general model in further detail to illustrate the interpretation of the disturbance covariances. Table 3 reports the *reduced form* parameter estimates for the general model.

The slope coefficients mainly reflect well-known effects of social factors on achievement and track placement. Sophomore achievement in all subjects except civics affects senior mathematics achievement, and sophomore mathematics achievement has by far the strongest effect. These factors explain approximately 73% and 66% of the variance in mathematics achievement in the college and noncollege tracks, respectively. Except for science, all sophomore achievement scores positively affect the

TABLE 2
Likelihood Statistics and X^2 Tests for Selected Models
of Mathematics Achievement and Track Assignment

Model	General	Ascription	Maximization	Quota
−2 Log likelihood	46074	46076	46724	46180
Number of parameters	33	31	26	26
Likelihood ratio test versus general model				
X^2		2	650	1062
D.F.		2	7	7
p		$.3 < p < .5$	$p < .001$	$p < .001$

chances of assignment to the college track. Socioeconomic status also positively affects college track placement. The effects for blacks and Hispanics on track placement suggest that minorities who have *equivalent* sophomore achievement levels to those of white non-Hispanics are more likely to enter the college track. Achievement levels of these groups, however, are significantly lower than average (e.g., Gamoran, 1986) and, as Table 1 shows, Hispanics are substantially *under*represented in the college track.

THE EFFECTS OF UNMEASURED FACTORS

The disturbance covariances, σ_{13} and σ_{23}, provide information about unobserved influences on tracking and achievement. As Table 2 shows, these parameters are not statistically significant when considered together. Their Z-scores, however, indicate that whereas σ_{13} is insignificant, σ_{23} is significantly less than zero. For the college track, this suggests that students who actually enter the track score no higher on senior mathematics than would a random sample from all sophomores *who have equal sophomore achievement levels* if they were placed in that track. In other words, OLS estimates of the achievement equation for the college track have no selection bias.

For the noncollege track, the selection bias is again small, but larger than for the college track. (The estimates for σ_{13} and σ_{23} imply *correlations* of $-.051/4.094 = -.012$ and $-.334/4.343 = -.077$, respectively.) That σ_{23} is negative indicates that students who in fact enter the noncollege track do somewhat *better* on senior mathematics than would a random sample of all sophomores *who have equal sophomore achievement levels* if they were placed

TABLE 3
**Reduced Form Parameters for Model of Track Assignment
and Mathematics Achievement in Senior Year**

Independent Variable	College Track Assignment		Achievement in College Track		Achievement in Noncollege Track	
	π	Z*	β	Z*	β	Z*
Constant	−2.815	−22.7	1.355	3.5	0.816	3.5
Sophomore achievement						
math	0.040	11.0	0.725	39.6	0.709	49.5
science	−0.001	−0.2	0.177	4.8	0.220	8.3
reading	0.024	3.3	0.130	3.5	0.055	2.0
vocabulary	0.020	3.2	0.079	2.5	0.103	4.4
writing	0.033	4.7	0.137	3.9	0.139	5.8
civics	0.029	2.6	0.076	1.3	−0.010	−0.2
Female	0.141	3.7				
SES	0.269	9.3				
Black	0.281	4.1				
Hispanic	0.078	1.3				
School SES**	−0.103	−1.7				
% black**	0.006	6.0				
% Hispanic**	0.004	3.5				
Math courses**	0.124	4.9				
R^2			0.725		0.657	
σ	1.000		4.094	68.2	4.343	94.3
σ_{13}, σ_{23}			−0.051	−0.8	−0.334	−4.0

*Z denotes ratio of estimated coefficient to its asymptotic standard error.
**Characteristics of high school that respondent attended in 1980.

in that track. Selection into the noncollege track, therefore, is biased in favor of students who can perform well in that track compared to other students with the same attributes. Thus OLS potentially *overestimates* achievement within the noncollege track because it ignores positive selection into that track.

THE EFFECTS OF TRACKING ON ACHIEVEMENT

The results discussed thus far suggest that observed net differences in achievement between tracks understate actual differences due to tracks because of the positive selection of students into the noncollege track. It remains to be shown, however, whether students who enter the noncollege track score higher on senior mathematics than they would were they assigned to the *college* track.

To investigate tracking effects more fully, we calculate expected levels of achievement that students would attain under alternative track assignments. We use the parameter estimates for college and noncollege achievement reported in Table 3 and apply equations 6-9 for a hypothetical individual who has the average values of the total sample on the sophomore achievement tests and a probability of assignment to the college track equal to the sample proportion of persons in the college track (see Table 1). Table 4 summarizes the calculations. The columns of the table compare tracks and the rows denote alternate groups of persons: actual college track students, actual noncollege track students, and all students combined.

The final row of the table provides estimates of achievement that would be observed if students were *randomly* assigned to tracks. That is, these estimates are free from selection biases and their difference denotes the structural track effect. The "College-College" and "Noncollege-Noncollege" cells of the table denote the conditions that the students actually experienced. The "College-Noncollege" and "Noncollege-College" cells denote hypothetical levels of achievement that students would experience were they assigned to a different track from the one that they in fact experienced.

All the contrasts in Table 4 are very small—a fraction of a standard deviation of senior mathematics achievement and much smaller than the observed difference between tracks on senior achievement (see Table 1). This, of course, results from our adjustment of all effects to the sample averages for sophomore level achievement. The following discussion, therefore, is useful for illustrating the model, but it is based on contrasts of limited substantive importance. The main results in Table 4 are as follows:

(1) The college track produces higher mathematics achievement than the noncollege track for the population as a whole and, hypothetically, within the populations defined by persons who in fact entered one track or the other. For the total population, the advantage of the college track is 20.86 – 19.59 = 1.27, an estimate of the difference in achievement that would be observed were students with equal sophomore achievement levels randomly assigned to tracks.

(2) This effect of tracking is *larger* than the actual contrast between college and noncollege students (20.80 – 19.76 = 1.04).

TABLE 4
Summary of Hypothetical Effects of Assignment
to Alternative Tracks on Senior Mathematics Achievement

| | Track | |
	College	Noncollege
Population:		
college	20.80	19.22
noncollege	20.88	19.76
all	20.86	19.59

NOTE: Effects are estimated holding constant levels of sophomore achievement on all academic subjects at total sample means and assuming a probability of assignment to college track of .32.

Relative to a system in which students are randomly assigned to tracks, the actual system has smaller achievement differentials between the tracks. This results because noncollege students are positively selected into the noncollege track, but selectivity is negligible for the college track.

(3) The existing tracking regime slightly increases the average *level* of achievement in the population. Assuming that the proportion of students in the college track is fixed at .32, actual achievement is 20.09 (that is [.32] [20.80] + [.68] [19.76]); whereas under random assignment it is 20.00 (that is [.32] [20.86] + [.68] [19.59]). This is also a result of positive selection into the noncollege track.

(4) Paradoxically, the actual noncollege track students would do at least as well as the actual college track students if they competed in the same track. *Within* both college and noncollege tracks, the actual noncollege students have slightly higher levels of achievement (a difference of 20.88 − 20.80 = 0.08 in the college track and of 19.76 − 19.22 = 0.54 in the noncollege track). Because the *between*-track difference is so strong, however, the noncollege track students do not actually fare as well as the college track students.

(5) Although the relative standing of the noncollege students is most favorable in the noncollege track (an advantage of 0.54 in the noncollege track versus 0.08 in the college track), their absolute standing is greatest in the college track (20.88 versus 19.76).

In summary, the existing system of tracking narrows the achievement gap between the actual college and noncollege students and produces higher achievement than under random tracking; but noncollege students could increase their achievement if more of them enrolled in the college track.

The results presented have been simplified for didactic purposes. A fuller study of tracking effects requires the investigation of other models and outcomes of tracking. An important extension of our models is the analysis of more than one outcome. A regime of tracking may, for example, have different effects on mathematics or other types of achievement than on rates of high school graduation. Decision makers may explicitly choose a track for students that does not maximize their achievement but rather yields an optimal combination of expected achievement and expected graduation probabilities. The combined effects of tracking on achievement and high school graduation can be assessed using extensions of the models discussed here.

CONCLUSION

Sociological investigations commonly assume that whereas the structure of social positions is relatively immune to the types of individuals who occupy the positions, positions have substantial effects on individuals. Although this assumption is often valid, many investigators erroneously infer that the characteristics of positions are exogenous variables in empirical models that predict individual outcomes. When social actors have discretion over how persons and positions are matched, then the characteristics of the positions and of the individuals that occupy them are *jointly* determined.

This chapter has described models that can be used to study the consequences of social positions when both allocation to the positions and their consequences have common causes. These models are likely to have their greatest value when investigators wish to assess explicit hypotheses about the linkage of social positions and their occupants. When the goals of the analyst are more exploratory and descriptive, then models such as ANACOVA, which make simpler assumptions about unobserved variables, may be more useful.

7

Practical Issues in Structural Modeling

P. M. BENTLER
CHIH-PING CHOU

The methodology of theory testing via structural equation models, which is accepted today as a major component of applied multivariate analysis, is historically relatively new, having been developed in a general and widely accessible form only during the past decade (see Bentler, 1986a, for a review). The process has several basic steps that are probably well known: A model containing random vectors and parameters is developed on the basis of substantive theory, the assumptions underlying the model are used to develop the covariance or moment structure implications of the data, the fixed and free parameters of the model as well as any constraints are imposed, and a statistical method, such as maximum likelihood (ML) or generalized least squares (GLS), is used to estimate the unknown parameters based on a nonlinear optimization method, thus permitting the empirical adequacy of the model to be assessed on the basis of the degree

AUTHORS' NOTE: *Supported in part by grants DA01070 and DA00017 from the National Institute on Drug Abuse. Address reprint requests to P. M. Bentler, Department of Psychology, Franz Hall, University of California, Los Angeles, CA 90024-1563* of fit of the model to appropriate sample data. In practice, of course, path diagrams are used to make developing and specifying the model relatively easy, and a general computer program, such as LISREL (Jöreskog, 1977; Jöreskog and Sörbom, 1984) or EQS (Bentler, 1985), which permits a wide range of models and estimation methods to be applied to one's particular model and data, is used to generate the parameter estimates and tests of fit.

Many conceptual elaborations are needed to be able to implement smoothly and appropriately the approach to model building and evaluation summarized above. These important details include not only issues surrounding the translation of substantive theory into a form that can be tested by structural modeling, but also technical details such as mathematical and statistical topics relevant to algebraic model structures, concepts in multivariate analysis, the requirements of a particular computerized procedure, and so on. The first goal of this article is to review the basic assumptions that are needed to assure the appropriate use of structural modeling. Some difficulties that occur, and possible solutions, are discussed. The second goal of this article is to address some further issues that arise in practice, and give suggestions on how to handle these problems. We shall assume that the reader has a general familiarity with structural modeling. See Bentler (1987a) or Long (1983b) for introductory presentations.

REVIEW OF BASIC ASSUMPTIONS

Although structural models can be quite easy to set up, estimate, and evaluate with modern computer programs, their output should always be viewed with a certain amount of skepticism: there are many ways in which the methods can fail to reach the lofty goal of evaluating a causal hypothesis. We shall discuss three types of difficulties: conceptual, statistical, and practical.

CONCEPTUAL REQUIREMENTS

It is quite easy to get carried away with the beautiful simplicity with which path diagrams can capture a theory, and with the awesome stacks of computer printouts that epitomize alternative theory-guided views of one's data, thereby losing sight of the fundamental issue of whether some basic conditions for structural modeling have been met. Even the best possible model fit may not protect one from meaningless results.

Obviously, any model will be tested against data obtained from some sample of subjects. An important question that should be answered affirmatively prior to engaging in structural modeling is whether the sample at hand comes from a population that is relevant to the theoretical ideas being evaluated. If the sample cannot be defended as coming from a relevant population, any obtained results may be uninformative about a theory. Thus it is important to know whether the theory one is evaluating should hold for males as well as females, only for a given ethnic group, or only with adolescents. For example, theories of cognitive growth may be relevant only to children or adolescents, but not to young adults. An example of a questionable choice of sample is given in the study of models of female orgasm by Bentler and Peeler (1979). A surprisingly large part of their sample had never had sexual intercourse, and thus did not have a good experiential basis for responding about orgasmic feelings. Luckily, their key findings were validated in a more mature sample (Newcomb and Bentler, 1983).

A closely related issue, easily forgotten in the details of the modeling process itself, is whether the data that might be obtained are gathered under appropriate conditions of measurement (appropriate in relation to the theory under investigation). In the case of opinion surveys, for example, confidentiality of responses may be a requisite to having valid responses to sensitive questions. When evaluating physiological functioning, certain conditions may be called for, such as obtaining urine samples after an appropriate fasting period. When evaluating intelligence in children, appropriately standardized conditions of testing have been recognized as important for many years. However, the fairness of a particular type of test to the ethnic sample being tested, for example, to youngsters who are not native English speakers, may be a question to ponder.

Another important issue involves whether a structural theory is attempting to describe cause-effect sequences that occur over time. The lag required for an antecedent variable to have an effect must be considered. For example, in a model designed to assess the maximum effect of aspirin on relief of pressure headaches, if an antecedent variable is the taking of aspirin, and the consequent variable is relief from headache pain, a contemporaneous measure of relief from pain must be obtained at the causal lag that is appropriate to the maximum expected effect of aspirin: An immediate measure, or one delayed by 24 hours, is likely to show no effect even if one exists at, say, 30 minutes. Whether "instantaneous" causation, with simultaneous mutual influences of variables on each other, makes sense in a model will depend on one's philosophy (e.g., Strotz and Wold, 1960) as well as statistical considerations (e.g., Bentler and Freeman, 1983). A related general point is that longitudinal, or panel, studies may be required to evaluate certain causal sequences. Although some exogenous variables (such as age, sex, race, and so on) may be able to be measured at any time point and still be appropriately incorporated into a model that assumes these variables occur "prior" to others, as causal sequence may not be unambiguously able to be established in many models without incorporating across-time measurement (e.g., Baumrind, 1983). Gollob and Reichardt (1987) have gone so far as to state that cross-sectional models, based on data at one time point only, will virtually always yield biased results on causal effects that are presumed to operate across time. In essence, they argue that a prior measure of the consequent variable is necessary in order to interpret effects of other variables on this consequent variable. A related question is whether a more dynamic, differential-equation type of model is more appropriate to the concepts at hand than the standard model (Arminger, 1986).

An additional conceptual requirement for valid evaluation of theories via structural modeling lies in having theoretically appropriate operationalizations of variables. A given task designed to measure intelligence may not, for example, be appropriate as a variable in a model designed to evaluate Piaget's theory of intellectual functioning. His theory requires specialized assessments, perhaps of such constructs as conservation (Goldschmid and Bentler, 1968), in which equal quantities of water are poured into a narrow and a wide glass, and children are asked whether the narrow and wide glasses have the same amount of water in them (they look unequal).

A final requirement relates to the previous issue, particularly in relation to the use of measured variables as indicators of latent variables. Does a latent variable make sense in a given domain—whether or not a latent variable model fits statistically? In general, a latent variable makes sense when its indicators are logical (theoretical) consequences of the latent variable, not causally related to each other, and correlated sufficiently highly to suggest a common core concept. For example, education, income, and housing quality are from one perspective indicators of a single latent construct. That is, it is easy to conceive of a dimension of social class that has the "haves" at one end, and the "have-nots" at the other end. Increases in the cost of gold, increases in the cost of housing, and increases in the cost of goods over a particular time span would seem to be obvious candidates to be indicators of a latent construct of inflation. However, theory must support the existence of a latent variable for such a construct to make sense in a given model. Thus for some purposes education and income may best not be considered as indicators of social class, since education may be causally related to income. And then, if the construct is meaningful, the particular variables chosen as operationalizations of the construct may be lousy, casting doubt on whether the meaning of the construct has been captured in the operationalizations. Thus a verbal report measure of perceived pressure on the job may, or may not, adequately capture a key idea in a particular theory of stress. And even if it does, the way the respondent's reply is coded into a score may destroy its meaningfulness. In addition, it may well be that the latent space is properly thought of as multidimensional, and a rationale for choosing only a given aspect of such a space may be needed in particular applications. For example, the concept of a single common factor latent variable was introduced by Spearman (1904) in his theory of general intelligence, but recent theory emphasizes a multidimensional construct. Thus performance on college or graduate school entrance examinations will usually contain measures of quantitative as well as verbal skills. The use of a single summary score, the total across both measures, may be justified primarily for practical predictive purposes (see Thorndike, 1985). However, in the prediction of engineering skills, the quantitative score may be more critical. And in developing a structural model with latent variables, a wide enough range of indicators of quantitative skills—say, geometric reasoning, algebraic manipulation, and computational skills (depending on one's theory)—would be desired to assure that the broad construct is well represented. Having an adequate number of indicators also minimizes computational problems (e.g., Anderson and Gerbing, 1984; Boomsma, 1983, 1985).

STATISTICAL REQUIREMENTS

In addition to conceptual requirements associated with structural modeling, there are technical conditions that must be met for the results to be meaningful. Violation of these conditions may make the statistics involved, such as chi-square tests or standard errors, be of questionable quality or possibly downright misleading.

Independence of observations. Current statistical theory used in structural modeling is based on the assumption that data have been gathered from independent observations (cases, subjects, sampling units). It is assumed that responses given by one person will not in any way influence the responses given by another person. In many surveys or telephone interviews, this condition is easy to meet. However, it may also be easy to violate: For example, one may obtain data from a single subject across time, with "observations" referring to repeated measures on the individual. In that case, serial correlation among the responses are quite likely. For example, a mood state that may influence a response at a given time may also influence the response 15 minutes later; however, dependence due to mood fluctuation may not be a problem if the measures are a week apart. Lack of independence may also crop up in innocuous situations: scores from twins may be analyzed, or data may be taken from best friends. It has been argued (e.g., Freedman, 1985) that such a data-gathering design makes the statistical results doubtful since the basic assumption of independence may be violated. Currently, except for specialized regression models, no methods exist for appropriately taking such dependence into account, or of evaluating the assumption by statistical means. Logical arguments must be used.

Identical distributions. The basic theory of structural modeling holds that the same process that describes influences of variables on each other is operating in each and every individual observation or case. (Typically, this condition is described simultaneously with the previous one, under the heading of "i.i.d." assumptions: independent and identically distributed observations.) Stated differently, it is assumed that the path diagram accurately reflects a process that is homogenous across all observations. If such an assumption is false, it is likely that other assumptions— such as a normality assumption—may be violated, which, in turn, may show up in a model not fitting the data. Deviations from a normality assumption can be tested by several means, including Mardia's (1970) test based on multivariate kurtosis that is available in the EQS program. EQS also calculates case contributions to Mardia's test, and these contributions can be used to locate outlying individuals regardless of the distribution. A few extreme outliers are unlikely to be described by a structural model that describes all the remaining observations. Outliers can also be detected by other means (e.g., Comrey, 1985).

If it is suspected that the process theory is different for identifiable subpopulations, such as males or females, it would be appropriate to perform the analysis separately in these populations, based, perhaps, on different models. Actually, the homogeneity assumption can be evaluated in part by a multiple-group or multiple-population model (Bentler, Lee, and Weng, 1987; Lee and Tsui, 1982; Sörbom, 1982), in which key features that differentiate models for different groups can be evaluated.

Simple random sampling. Existing methods in structural modeling are based on the assumption that each of the units or cases in the population has an equal probability of being included in the sample to be studied. In particular, the statistics such as standard errors are appropriate estimators of population parameters only under this assumption. The reason that this is so involves the fact that unadjusted means, variances, and covariances are treated as data to be structurally modeled, and these must be consistent estimators of the corresponding population parameters. When more complex sampling designs are used, the usual covariances as inputs to structural modeling are inappropriate, and the sample means, variances, and covariances must be adjusted to estimate appropriately and consistently the population parameters. This can be accomplished by procedures that give cases differential weight in computations. When such adjustments are needed but not implemented, one must be certain that one understands that the results of modeling will generalize to a population similar to that observed in the sample, but not necessarily to the general population. In some circumstances this drawback may not be crucial, since there is no intent to generalize results to a given population. For example, if the population itself cannot be well defined, then drawing a sample from the population is very difficult if not impossible. To illustrate, the population of cocaine users is easy to conceive, but it is virtually impossible to draw a random sample from the population since most users go to great lengths not to be publicly identified due to legal consequences.

The random sample assumption is usually a reasonable one in practice, although certain data bases are obtained using other methods of sampling. For example, some studies oversample subgroups (such as high-risk subgroups, or subgroups of special interest) that might be critical for a given purpose. More typically, nonrandom samples may occur due to relatively uncontrollable conditions such as the almost inevitable volunteer bias. Thus females are frequently more available and/or cooperative as research subjects, as compared to males, leading to differential representation of the sexes unless special efforts are undertaken. When such differential representation of different groups is encountered, it may be desirable to evaluate the extent to which the grouping accounts for variance in the responses. If this percentage is trivial, analyzing all subjects together is not a significant problem. When variables behave quite differently in different groups, it may be necessary to run a multiple-groups structural model to see the similarities and differences of results across groups. Although recent research has been directed toward developing methods to adjust for biased sample selection (e.g., Bowden, 1986), some controversy exists about whether it is possible to adjust for selection bias (e.g., Little, 1985).

Functional form. The structural models emphasized in this review assume that all relations among variables are linear. This assumption must not only be conceptually appropriate to the theoretical questions being addressed, it should be true empirically as well. It is probably a reasonable assumption when the variables are multivariate normally distributed, or are approximately so distributed after some normalizing transformations. The assumption may be less reasonable if the variables are arbitrarily distributed. In contrast to the case of regression, where numerous diagnostics exist to evaluate assumptions of the model (e.g., Chatterjee and Hadi, 1986), structural modeling diagnostics are virtually nonexistent. Regression diagnostics can, of course, be used equation-at-a-time in multiple-equation path or simultaneous equation models. However, these diagnostics cannot be applied to latent variable models since case scores for the latent variables cannot be determined precisely.

One way to approach the validity of the linearity assumption would be to embed strictly linear models in more complete models that permit nonlinearities, for example, polynomial relations among variables, or interactions between latent variables. If the nonlinear components do not add appreciably to model fit, these could be ignored and the linearity assumption could be accepted. However, while a general theory for such methods has been developed (Bentler, 1983), existing implementations have been quite specialized (e.g., Etezadi-Amoli and McDonald, 1983; Heise, 1986; Kenny and Judd, 1984; Mooijaart and Bentler, 1986a), and no general computer program is available for use. Thus the use of linear relations is currently based largely on implementability, supported more by successful experience with such models than with evidence that linearity is usually well-justified in social research. Two practical reasons that may be cited for not worrying unduly about linearity is that nonlinear models often do not hold up well in new samples (e.g., Wiggins, 1972), and that nonlinear relations may be approximated by more complex linear models.

The place where nonlinearity is most likely to occur in a predictable manner, and where some progress has been made toward developing methods, has been in models employing categorical variables. Categorical variables raise not only the linearity issue, but also a question about the continuous nature of variables. Continuity will, of course, never be observed in sample data, because the largest number of different scores that could be obtained is the number of subjects in the study. But many variables, such as income, can be seen to be continuous, at least in theory. In practice, they may be categorical because only a few levels of a variable are scored: Individuals may be asked whether they earn less than $5,000, between $5,000 and $15,000, and so on. Other variables, on the other hand, such as sex, may be intrinsically categorical. The methods reviewed in this article are based on the assumption of continuity of dependent variables. Independent observed variables, however, may be categorical.

Olsson (1979), Muthen and Kaplan (1985), and others have argued that the use of categorical variables with methods based on the assumption of linearity and continuity yields distortion of results. One approach to rectifying the problem is to nonlinearly map a categorical variable into a latent continuous variable, and then to develop linear structures for the continuous variables. For instance, tetrachoric, polychoric, or polyserial correlations (e.g., Lee, 1985c; Lee and Poon, 1986) can be used to describe the relations between two underlying continuous variables that, in turn, nonlinearly generate the categorical variables. These indexes of association may be used in structural modeling (e.g., Muthen, 1984; Lee, Poon, and Bentler, 1987). Other approaches are also being developed (e.g., Aitkin and Rubin, 1985; Arminger and Kusters, 1986; Bock and Aitkin, 1981; Bye et al., 1985). However, it has not been verified that these theoretically more appropriate methods generally work better in practice. For example, Collins et al. (1986) found that tetrachorics could yield quite misleading results when compared to the use of technically less appropriate ordinary correlation coefficients with binary variables.

We suggest adopting the following practices for the near future. Continuous methods can be used with little worry when a variable has four or more categories, but with three or fewer categories one should probably consider the use of alternative procedures. If the categorization induces marked nonnormality in variables, a distribution-free method of estimation is called for (see next section). Of course, one should recognize that some distortion will occur in a purely linear model as a result of using categorical variables, yielding a degradation in fit. But this disadvantage must be weighed against the difficulties associated with categorical variable methodology, especially, the restricted number of variables that one will be limited to (this is an even worse problem than with distribution-free procedures), and the necessity, with many of today's methods, of having to make the strong assumption of multivariate normality of the latent continuous variables. (Nonparametric approaches are being developed, however; see, for example, Bye et al., 1985.) Thus categorical variable methodology itself has drawbacks, including a lack of software, that may outweigh the drawbacks of its theoretically less appropriate competitors. Of course, in some situations it may also not make any sense to believe that a continuous variable lies behind a categorical variable. In that case other methods, such as log-linear or latent-class methods, are more appropriate. See Clogg and Eliason's (this volume) or Bonett et al. (1985).

Distribution of variables. Within methodologies for continuous variables, a decision must be made about the distributional form of the variables. Distribution-free methods (Browne, 1982, 1984; Chamberlain, 1982; Bentler, 1983; Bentler and Dijkstra, 1985), of course, do not require such a choice, but they become computationally impractical with models having more than 20-30 variables. Furthermore, their statistics tend to be questionable in small samples, say with less than 200 subjects (Harlow, 1985; Tanaka, 1984). Distributions that are not normal, but in which the variables have a symmetric shape but tails that are heavier or lighter as compared to the normal, are called elliptical if the variables have homogeneous shape or kurtosis (see, e.g., Bentler and Berkane, 1985; Berkane and Bentler, 1987a, 1987b). Then the theory of Browne (1982, 1984), Tyler (1983), Bentler (1983), and Bentler and Dijkstra (1985) can be used to correct the normal theory statistics to lead to appropriate test statistics and standard errors. Distribution-free and elliptical estimators are built into the EQS program (Bentler, 1985). Recent results imply that with some specialized models, such as exploratory factor analysis, the observed variables may in fact not need to be normally distributed and yet, normal theory estimators, standard errors of loadings, and the test statistic may remain correct. This occurs provided that the errors are normally distributed (Amemiya, 1985; Browne, 1985; Mooijaart and Bentler, 1986b; Satorra and Bentler, 1986). These results generalize to a wider class of linear structures when factors are normal and errors are independently distributed (Satorra and Bentler, 1986). Unfortunately, diagnostics to evaluate the relevance of these theories to robustness of statistics in particular applications remain to be developed. Bentler et al. (1986) have made a start in this direction by providing a means for evaluating the distribution of latent variables. However, no diagnostic tests are currently computerized. In the meantime, one can be reassured by simulation evidence that indicates that normal theory ML estimators are almost always acceptable even when data are nonnormally distributed (Harlow, 1985; Muthen and Kaplan, 1985; Tanaka and Bentler, 1985). It is the χ^2 and standard errors that become untrustworthy under violation of distributional assumptions. If one utilizes fit indexes (e.g., Bentler and Bonett, 1980) in addition to statistical criteria for evaluating fit, one's conclusions ought to be reliable.

The use of higher-moment data, such as skewness or kurtosis, to be modeled is a new development (Bentler, 1983). Such methods promise more efficient (lower variance) statistical estimators. However, only sporadic applications of such a theory have been made so far (e.g., Kenny and Judd, 1984; Mooijaart, 1985; Mooijaart and Bentler, 1986a; Heise, 1986).

Covariance structures. Current implementations of structural modeling are based on a statistical theory derived from the distribution of sample means and covariances, and not the distribution of sample-standardized variables having unit variance. Thus the practice of substituting correlation for covariance matrices in analysis is only rarely justified, since the associated statistics will usually be inappropriate (e.g., Bentler and Lee, 1983). While methods have been developed for the structural analysis of correlation matrices (Bentler and Lee, 1983; Lee, 1985a), they are not available in current publicly distributed computer programs.

Large sample size. The exact distribution of estimators and test statistics used in structural modeling is not known. The statistical theory is based on "asymptotic" theory, that is, the theory that describes the behavior of statistics as the sample size becomes arbitrarily large (goes to infinity). In practice, samples can be small to moderate in size, and the question arises whether large sample statistical theory is appropriate in such situations. Even this problem has proven to be hard to study analytically or theoretically, and empirical evidence based on studies with artificial data and models—so-called Monte Carlo studies—have had to be used instead. This research is relatively recent (e.g., Anderson and Gerbing, 1984; Bearden et al., 1982; Boomsma, 1983, 1985; Gerbing and Anderson, 1985; Geweke and Singleton, 1980; Harlow, 1985; Muthen and Kaplan, 1985; Tanaka, 1984; Velicer and Fava, 1987) and has involved only a few types of models, sample sizes, and estimators. Definitive recommendations are not available.

An oversimplified guideline that might serve as a rule of thumb regarding the trustworthiness of solutions and parameter estimates is the following. The ratio of sample size to number of free parameters may be able to go as low as 5:1 under normal and elliptical theory, especially when there are many indicators of latent variables and the associated factor loadings are large. Although there is even less experience on which to base a recommendation, a ratio of at least 10:1 may be more appropriate for arbitrary distributions. These ratios need to be larger to obtain trustworthy z-tests on the significance of parameters, and still larger to yield correct model evaluation chi-square probabilities.

It should also be noted that computational problems during optimization are an inverse function of sample size (e.g., Anderson and Gerbing, 1984; Boomsma, 1983; Gerbing and Anderson, 1987; MacCallum, 1986). While estimating a given model in a large sample may pose no problem, the same model estimated in a small sample may yield such problems as inadequate convergence behavior, boundary or Heywood solutions in which parameters go outside of the permissible range (the classical example being negative variance estimates), inability to impose constraints among parameters, and problems with estimation of standard errors (which may become inappropriately large or very small).

Identified model. Although a recent general statistical theory has been developed for models containing parameters that are not "identified" (Shapiro, 1986), essentially all implementations of structural modeling assume that a model has been specified such that, if the model were true, a single set of parameters θ can reproduce the population covariance matrix. That is, $\Sigma = \Sigma(\theta)$. In contrast, an "underidentified" model will have many different sets of parameters that can equally well reproduce the population covariance matrix. Thus $\Sigma = \Sigma(\theta_1) = \Sigma(\theta_2)$, where θ_1 and θ_2 are different vectors. Parameter identification is a very complex topic, but it can help to think of the uniqueness of parameters as synonymous with identification: A model that does not have identified parameters may have many sets of parameters that can equivalently well account for the data. An example of the complexity of identification was recently given by Bollen and Jöreskog (1985), who showed that previous authors were incorrect to conclude that a factor model is identified if it has factor loadings that are unique with respect to rotation of factors. Such a model may still not be identified, that is, have unique parameters.

The issue of identification can be readily understood in the context of setting the metric in models with latent variables.

Suppose one has a model that includes equations of the form $V1 = .5*F1 + .2*V2 + E1$, where $V1$ and $V2$ are observable variables and $F1$ and $E1$ are hypothetical variables. Although the scale or variance of every measured variable such as $V2$ is known in the population (in a sample, it may have to be estimated), this is not true of hypothetical constructs such as factors or errors in variables. The previous equation can be equivalently written as $V1 = (10 \times .5)*(.1F1) + (10 \times .2)*(.1V2) + 10(.1E1)$, where we have multiplied each coefficient by 10 but then compensated by multiplying each variable by .1. Are we permitted to make such a transformation? When we examine $V2$ first, it becomes apparent that we would be creating a new measured variable $V2$ whose variance is $.1 \times .1 = .01$ times as large as the variable we actually have (rescaling by a constant has the effect that the variance is changed by the square of the constant). But $V2$ has a certain variance and the revised equation would imply that it has a different variance: We are not permitted to make such a transformation. Thus measured variables by themselves create no problem of identification, whereas the situation is quite different for constructs. Since $F1$ and $E1$ are hypothetical, with no fixed scale, we could never detect if we replaced the constructs by constructs that are .1 as big (have .01 as much variance). This problem is solved by adopting an arbitrary identification condition that would not permit the rescaling we have illustrated. The best single way of identifying the scale of a latent variable is to fix a path from that variable to another variable at, say, 1.0. When a variable is an independent variable, another way is to fix the variance of the variable at some known value. This is usually done in factor analysis, where factors are fixed to have unit variance. So, we might fix the variance of $F1$ at 1.0: Then we could not rescale $F1$ since it would then have a different variance that we do not permit. And we might fix the path from $E1$ to $V1$ at 1.0: Then we could not change the implicit 1.0 coefficient in the equation either. Forgetting to fix the scale of unmeasured variables is perhaps the single most frequently made error in applications of structural modeling.

The second most frequently made identification error also involves latent variables. In particular, every latent factor that is meant to account for correlations among some indicators must not only have its scale fixed, but in general it must have effects on (paths to) three or more indicators of that factor. Models with one indicator for a factor will never work (except when a factor is synonymous with a measured variable, that is, the factor is not really a factor). Models with only two indicators will usually run into trouble. While there are exceptions to this rule, particularly when the factor also has nonzero covariances with other factors or variables, such situations must be evaluated quite carefully. Residual variables, such as the E1 variable above, do not need multiple indicators.

Parameter identification may require substantially more care than simply fixing the scale of unmeasured variables or having enough indicators of a factor. Some models require careful attention to particular equations, which may be problematic for additional reasons, or to sets of equations, which may permit several rather than a single solution, or to sets of constraints, which may be redundant (they are not permitted to be so). The most widely known problem involves a "nonrecursive" model, in which two (or more) variables are involved in two-way causation, where a variable is not only an antecedent of other variables, but also a consequent of those same variables. Such models are generally underidentified unless there also exist additional variables that influence, or are influenced by, one but not the other of the variables involved in two-way causation.

A phrase that will frequently be found in discussions of identification involves "overidentification." This is almost always a desirable state of affairs, and refers to a situation where there are fewer parameters in the model than data points. The data to be analyzed are usually $p^* = p(p + 1)/2$ variances and covariances of p variables, and any interesting (testable) model will have fewer than p^* free parameters to be estimated. This difference between p^* and the number of parameters yields the degrees of freedom associated with the model fit. If a model has more than p^* parameters, it will be underidentified and cannot be tested. A model that has exactly p^* parameters will usually be "just-identified," meaning that the parameters are simply transformations of the data, and, hence, the model cannot be tested or rejected. Since there may exist several different sets of parameters that are transformations of the data, just-identified models may not be unique (see, e.g., Bollen and Jöreskog, 1985). Furthermore, a model with less than p^* parameters, which is thus nominally overidentified, may nonetheless in particular parts of the model be underidentified (e.g., by an absence of a fixed scale for factors) and hence be not routinely testable until the problem is eliminated.

The theory of identification primarily deals with local, rather than global, uniqueness of parameters. That is, there may exist conceptually quite different parameterizations that reproduce the population covariances equally well. For example, in some models, the direction of certain paths can be completely turned around without affecting the goodness of fit of the model. This topic has hardly been studied. Some interesting examples of this phenomenon, along with a set of rules for generating equivalent path models, are given by Steltzl (1986).

Underidentified models will generally yield statistics that are not strictly correct. While the chi-square value may be trustworthy if an optimum function value was attained, the degrees of freedom may well be understated and thus the p-value (probability) of the model may be too low. If an optimum function value (usually, a minimum) was attained, the computed estimates can be relied upon to reproduce Σ appropriately, but only the identified parameters and their standard errors, or identified functions of all parameters, should be interpreted.

Nested model comparisons. There is little agreement on methods for evaluating the relative merits of two models that are not "nested" or hierarchically related (see Leamer, 1978). Thus an evaluation of the statistical necessity of sets of parameters is limited, under current statistical theory, to a comparison of models in which one model is a subset of the other model, for example, some free parameters in the model are set to zero in a second model. Although current practice is based on the chi-square difference test for making model comparisons, two other equally correct methods exist. Buse (1982) provides an introduction to the key ideas involved in the use of three statistics appropriate to such a purpose: Wald, Lagrange Multiplier, and likelihood ratio tests. Bentler and Chou (1986) and Bentler (1986b) develop these theories for structural modeling.

Increasing the constraints in the more general model will result in a decrease in the number of free parameters, an increase in the number of degrees of freedom, and a consequent increase in the goodness-of-fit χ^2 value. The impact of increasing constraints can be investigated through the Wald (1943) test (Bentler and Dijkstra, 1985; Lee, 1985b), in which only the more general model needs to be estimated. The second approach is to release constraints in the more restricted model, thus increasing the number of free parameters and decreasing the degrees of freedom. Adding new parameters will decrease the goodness-of-fit χ^2 test. The statistical theory for this method is known as the Lagrange Multiplier (LM) theory and has been discussed by Aitchison and Silvey (1958), Silvey (1959), and Lee and Bentler (1980). The application of LM theory requires estimation of only the more restricted model. The third approach is the likelihood ratio approach, or its equivalent. In this approach, both the restricted and less-restricted models are estimated, and the significance of the model-differentiating parameters is investigated by a chi-square difference test. Then χ^2 and degrees of freedom are obtained by calculating the difference between the two goodness-of-fit χ^2 tests, as well as their degrees of freedom. This is currently the standard approach to model comparison.

A priori structural hypotheses. The statistical theory used in structural modeling is based on the fundamental premise that the model itself has been specified completely prior to any analysis of data, that is, the model represents an a priori set of hypotheses. Although one may not know the values of the free parameters of the model (and hence may estimate them in a sample), the entire structure (the particular equations, and variances and covariances of independent variables) should be theoretically derived. If the data are examined, and structural hypotheses are formed after such data snooping, the statistical theory may become incorrect because one may then be capitalizing on chance associations in the data. The effects of capitalizing on chance are particularly acute in small samples, as shown by MacCallum (1986). Adding parameters to an incomplete model on the basis of data snooping can lead to accepting an incorrect true model.

A less serious situation occurs when dropping nonsignificant parameters on the basis of the data, as in backward stepping in regression. It appears that the Wald test for dropping parameters will be more robust than the Lagrange Multiplier test for adding parameters when these tests are data-driven rather than a priori. This is because the Wald test is asymptotically independent of the fit of the more complete model (Steiger et al., 1985). The comparable situation does not occur for the LM test: It depends upon the restricted model.

No parameters on boundary. The statistics of structural modeling assume also that the true parameters are, in the population, in the "interior" of the legitimate parameter space. This assumption is unimportant when dealing with parameters such as regression coefficients that could, theoretically, take on any value. The assumption becomes important when dealing with variances, which must be assumed to be nonnegative. While this is a perfectly natural assumption, estimated variance parameters are sometimes on the boundary (zero) or even in improper regions of the space (negative) and hence not in the interior of the parameter space (e.g., Gerbing and Anderson, 1987). If the population value of the variance is also zero, the model fit tests will be wrong. In that case, a correction to the test statistic as proposed by Shapiro (1985) must be made. However, because it is difficult to know when a population rather than the estimated variance is precisely zero, Shapiro's theory is hard to apply. Thus the researcher must recognize that an assumption is being made, and be prepared to reexamine the assumption when confronted with problematic results.

PRACTICAL REQUIREMENTS

The above conceptual and statistical issues create a number of demands for careful design, data gathering, and analysis in structural modeling. In implementing such requirements, additional practical matters immediately arise. We can review a few of these.

It is easy to become too grandiose when executing a structural model. Most valuable substantive theories are quite complex, and it is easy to hope that most of the complexity can be studied in the context of a single structural model. Rarely is this possible: the data are almost always far more complex than even the best theory, and it is easy to become frustrated in not being able to fit one's model to data. Although one's theory may capture a substantial amount of variation in the data (say, by nonstatistical fit indexes, see Bentler and Bonett, 1980, and Wheaton, this volume), statistical tests can lead to model rejection when only a few effects in the data have been overlooked. In large samples, in particular, even the best model may not fit, since the sample-size multiplier that transforms the fit function into a χ^2 variate will multiply a small lack of fit into a large statistic. To avoid such frustration, without a great deal of knowledge about the variables under study, it is wisest to analyze relatively small data sets, say, 20 variables at most.

On the other hand, it must be recognized that one of the greatest weaknesses in structural modeling lies in excluding key variables that may influence a system. When important control or causal variables are omitted from a model, the parameter estimates of the model will be biased and misleading conclusions can be drawn from an analysis (e.g., Reichardt and Gollob, 1986). Thus one is, in principle, always subject to the criticism of having omitted a key variable. One can only do one's best at ensuring that plausible causal variables are included in a model. But every attempt to include such variables in a model yields a larger model. In turn, this leads to the practical inability to fit models to data noted above. The researcher will have to balance practicality with the ideal of a single, comprehensive model.

Analyzing models with latent variables is an especially demanding problem, since models often do not fit only because a poor measurement structure has been hypothesized for the data. Bentler and Bonett (1980) developed a specification test that evaluates the fundamental adequacy of the measurement model, but it has rarely been used. Ideally, the basic factor structure of the data—how many factors, which variables are good indicators of which factors, the factor intercorrelations—should already be well-known, based on exploratory factor analyses on similar data bases. In that case, generating a complete model that includes a reasonable measurement structure is much easier. Determining the factor structure using structural modeling is a rather difficult and unattractive procedure. It frequently requires so much data snooping to lead one to worry about the quality of any final results.

In the ideal situation, the researcher has in mind not only a single, large structural model, but also a series of submodels that would shed light on key features of the large model. As noted above, nested models can be compared: If the fit of the more restricted model is about as good as that of the more general model, the restrictions can probably be accepted (i.e., the simpler model is chosen and the more complex, rejected). Since there are many possible sequences of submodels that might be entertained, comparing models is an art and requires a good deal of thought.

ISSUES ENCOUNTERED IN PRACTICE

When utilizing structural modeling methods, one will frequently find some problems emanating from the statistical results. These problems may make the results difficult to interpret or even misleading, and hence an awareness of alternative actions that might be taken is valuable. In addition to the problems that are basically created by the estimation procedure, we will also discuss the issues of model improvement.

PROBLEMS IN ESTIMATION

Incomplete data. Although there is no requirement in theory that data used for covariance structure analysis should be complete, that is, that every case should have a score on every variable, current methods were really designed to deal with complete data only. In theory, all that is needed for structural modeling to be appropriate is that the sample covariance matrix S be a consistent estimator of the population matrix and have an asymptotically normal distribution with a known or estimable sampling covariance matrix. Alternatives to the standard matrix can be used. Direct calculation of the sample covariance matrix in fact becomes problematic with missing data, so that programs from general packages such as BMDP may need to be used as preprocessors prior to submitting a job to the current version of EQS. LISREL does have an option for dealing with missing data. Its missing data option may, however, create a problematic sample covariance matrix, as noted below.

A number of recent developments promise better ways of dealing with missing data. For example, Little (1986) has developed a procedure for estimating a sample covariance matrix that is likely to be more robust to outliers than standard methods. Lee (1986) and Van Praag et al. (1985) have provided methods that optimally use all available information during estimation. These methods, however, are not currently available in canned programs.

Covariance matrix not positive definite. Given that a sample covariance matrix to be used in EQS or LISREL exists, one of the first actions of the programs could be to reject the input matrix for analysis. Often this occurs because the input matrix is not positive definite. This can occur for two major reasons. First, there may be linear dependencies among the input variables, in which case the matrix will be singular. Second, the matrix may not be a covariance matrix of real numbers, in which case the matrix will have one or more negative eigenvalues.

Linear dependencies reflect redundancies among variables. Although it may be possible to use an estimation method such as least squares that will accept a singular input matrix, it would generally be desirable to find those variables that are a linear combination of other variables, say, by regression or principal components analysis, and remove them from the input. The reduced matrix then should be acceptable for analysis. Negative eigenvalues tend to occur if the covariance matrix is not computed from raw scores, for example, if tetrachoric correlations are used. They may also occur because a pairwise-delete option was used in generating the covariance matrix (listwise deletion does not have this problem, though it may reduce sample size excessively). There is no generally accepted solution for this difficulty. With missing data, it may be worthwhile to search for outliers in the data, since they may create the problem. Otherwise, it may be necessary to modify the offending entries in the matrix. This can be done by smoothing procedures, for example, by changing negative eigenvalues to a small positive value, or by using special estimators (Theil and Laitinen, 1980). However, the optimality properties of such procedures are not known.

Nonconvergence. This is a common problem that is easy to observe because most computer programs will provide a warning to the user if this has occurred. In covariance structure analysis, parameters are estimated through an iterative process. In other words, the estimates are improved and changed from one iteration to the next until they have stabilized, indicating that they can no longer be improved to obtain a smaller function value. Iterative procedures have a built-in convergence criterion to determine if the change in estimates is so trivial that the iterative process can be terminated. The iterative process can be said to have converged when the change in estimates is smaller than the convergence criterion, and if appropriate derivatives of the fit function are equal to zero. The values updated at the final iteration are the parameter estimates at the solution. However, an infinite or arbitrarily lengthy iterative process may occur if the change in parameter estimates is always large compared to the convergence criterion. This may occur if the model is very nonlinear (e.g., a nonrecursive model), if the model is extremely bad for the data to be modeled (i.e., there are large residuals $s_{ij} - \sigma_{ij}$ even with optimal estimates), if the start values for the parameters are very poor, if unreasonable equality constraints are being imposed, or if critical parameters are underidentified. Corrections for these problems have been mentioned above, or are obvious (e.g., attempt to use good start values, and fix identification problems). The simplest solution, increasing the number of iterations, sometimes yields a convergent solution.

In theory, it may be possible to converge to different solutions, that is, to different local minima rather than a unique global minimum of the function being optimized. In such a case, the model should probably be suspect. However, in spite of the theoretical possibility of local minima, they are very rarely observed. In one case for which multiple solutions were claimed (Rubin and Thayer, 1982), more careful analysis verified that only one minimum actually existed (Bentler and Tanaka, 1983).

Verification that the model specified is the one desired is also a good practice when convergence problems occur. It is easy to make errors that affect estimation, for example, more parameters are fixed at nonzero values than are needed for identification, or inconsistent constraints are imposed. It is valuable to know how the estimates should look at the solution (e.g., small, medium, or large; positive or negative), because a theoretical view of the model can highlight not only problems in job set-up, but also in peculiarities of results. Even LISREL's automatic start values may occasionally yield nonsensical results for nonstandard models, and these can cause nonconvergence. If Σ is singular based on initial estimates, further iteration may not be possible. This can occur because error variances are too small (initially, the variance of an error variable should be as large as possible, but less than that of the corresponding measured variable) or the factor loadings, paths, or variances are too large. In general, the scale of observed variables should be considered when determining the appropriate size of parameters.

Empirical underidentification. Lack of parameter identification will certainly contribute to failures of convergence, but there is no 1:1 relation. Identified models may not converge, and under-identified models may converge. A more difficult problem to spot is that of empirical underidentification, in which a model is actually theoretically identified under most conditions but some special data-related problem occurs that makes the model under-identified (Kenny, 1979; Rindskopf, 1984). This may show up as a nonconvergence problem, as a problem with the information matrix (see below), or a problem with some parameter estimates.

In general, a latent variable model that has only two indicators of a factor will be underidentified since three indicators (another factor may serve as an indicator of the factor as well) are needed at a minimum. So if a factor has three indicators, one may be tempted to conclude that there can be no problem. However, as noted by Kenny (1979) and McDonald and Krane (1979), if one factor loading is identically equal to zero the model will not be identified. Although one may assume that one's estimates will not be zero precisely, in fact some estimates may approach zero and the consequences of underidentification will be felt. These conse-quences include, for example, "Heywood" cases in which an error variance goes negative (in LISREL) or is held to the boundary (in EQS), and cases in which parameter estimates become very unstable, that is, have very large standard error estimates. Inade-quacy of indicators may arise in many guises: It is possible that other paths from a factor, or covariances with the factor, serve the role as a third indicator to identify a factor. For example, a two factor model with two indicators of each factor (and no complex loadings) will be identified as long as the covariance or correla-tion between the factors is nonzero. But in practice it may approach zero, creating serious difficulties. It is always important to have as many indicators of a factor as possible, subject to practicality, especially indicators having high loadings on their factors (e.g., Gerbing and Anderson, 1985, 1987; Velicer and Fava, 1987). In the context of questionnaire studies, additional indica-tors can often be created by breaking down a composite measured variable (say, a total score across many items) into a number of subscores. Since such subscores will tend to be less reliable than the composite, this procedure is most beneficial when the sub-scores are also reliable.

Singular information matrix. The covariance matrix of the parameter estimates is given by the inverse of a particular matrix that is called, in maximum likelihood theory, the information matrix. A similar matrix is used in all methods. Thus, to obtain standard errors, this matrix must be positive definite, and invertible. When this matrix is close to singular, some of the standard error estimates may be meaningless (very small, or arbitrarily large) because they are generated from a numerically unstable matrix. A singular information matrix may also affect iterations, since the updated parameter estimates hinge upon the matrix as well. If the function is appropriately minimized, the χ^2 value and possibly nonunique estimates can be acceptable even if the standard errors are questionable.

Singularity is often caused by dependence among parameter estimates, and EQS and LISREL will flag such dependencies. These dependencies may arise: from model underidentification, in which case the redundant parameters must be removed; from a poor iterative path, in which case different start values must be used; from inappropriateness of one's model, in which case model modifications must be made; or, possibly, from a poorly conditioned set of input variables, in which the input variables must be rescaled to have more similar variances or, more extremely, one or more variables will have to be removed from the model. It may also be caused by sheer numerical problems associated with inadequate computer precision, which may happen to crop up in a special model but not others due to some unknown combination of events. In that case, little can be done by the user.

The above discussion has focused on the case of no equality constraints among parameters. When constraints are also imposed, the covariance matrix of the parameter estimates must of necessity be singular. The information matrix itself need not be invertible, but a modified or augmented information matrix will still need to be invertible. When a problem exists, EQS will give a similar message in this situation, and the same action should be taken to resolve the problem as noted above.

Inability to impose a constraint. When imposing a constraint has the effect that a model will provide a very poor fit to data, it may not prove possible to impose the constraint. EQS will print a message to that effect if this happens. In that case, the constraint must be relaxed and the model reestimated. The iterative process in EQS also needs start values for parameters that meet the constraint. While EQS will adjust the user's start values to meet this condition, in unusual cases this may not be possible and the user will have to make the correction.

PROBLEMS WITH RESULTS

If it appears that an analysis has yielded an appropriate, converged solution, and no condition codes to warn the user about existing difficulties, it is still desirable to analyze the computer output in some detail to determine whether or not more subtle difficulties with the solution can be observed. These subtle problems, if encountered, suggest problems with the model in relation to the data, rather than problems with the estimation method itself.

Improper variances. The most frequently encountered problem involves variances that are estimated as negative or zero. In LISREL, there are no constraints on variances, and they can be estimated as negative. Such estimates are not only meaningless, they are also inappropriate since, for example, true ML or GLS solutions do not allow negative variances. In LISREL, one may accept the solution as is, rerun the job with negative variances set to zero, or reparameterize to yield nonnegativity (Rindskopf, 1983). Setting a negative variance to zero has the effect of changing the degrees of freedom inappropriately and alters the interpretation of the results. In the EQS program, variances cannot go negative unless the user has changed the program's defaults. Thus zero or boundary variances can occur. In both LISREL and EQS the user must evaluate whether such a zero variance estimate causes problems for the conceptual design of the study. A zero error variance may imply that the measured variable is synonymous with a factor, which may or may not make sense. A zero residual in a prediction equation implies that a dependent variable is perfectly explained by its predictors. If results such as these do not make sense, it may be necessary to modify the design of the study, for example, by adding variables to the input data so that more indicators of a factor are created. If it can be assumed that the zero variance observed in a sample represents the population accurately, Shapiro's (1985) theory indicates that the goodness-of-fit chi-square test is not accurate. No alternative or more accurate test value is, unfortunately, currently available in standard computer programs. On the other hand, if the results do make sense and these "Heywood" cases are isolated occurrences, one need not worry too much, especially in large samples. Boundary solutions can be conceived as indicators that the sample size may be too small for an adequate reliance on large sample theory in the given application, since boundary solutions become much less likely with large samples (e.g., Boomsma, 1985; MacCallum, 1986). However, there may be no alternative to accepting the results since a larger sample may not be available.

Improper solutions may also be a clue that a model has been fundamentally misspecified, so it may be worthwhile to evaluate this hypothesis by considering some quite different models, for example, models with a radically different measurement structure. In some cases, improper solutions can arise from outliers in the data, and deleting the offending cases may eliminate the problem (e.g., Bollen, 1987). EQS provides methods for locating and eliminating outliers. If none of these actions solves the problem, we suggest that the model be accepted with the offending estimate held to the boundary. Usually it does not make sense to eliminate the parameter corresponding to a negative or boundary variance. It is true that fit will usually not be degraded significantly by this practice, since negative estimates are usually not significantly different from zero by z-test (Gerbing and Anderson, 1987). Completely aside from the issue of doing data-based model modification, eliminating a boundary parameter may change a model's form into an undesirable one. For example, in a factor analysis model it usually does not make sense to assume that a variable will be perfectly predictable from the factors, and in a predictive equation it seems a priori unlikely that one should be able to predict a given dependent variable perfectly.

Improper correlations. Covariance or correlation parameters may also go outside the legitimate boundary. Correlations, obviously, must lie in the interval of +1 to –1. Covariances, after being transformed into correlations by dividing by standard deviations, must have the same property; EQS forces this on the solution when the variances are fixed, and correlations greater than one do not then occur. Out-of-bounds correlations can be obtained otherwise, as they can in LISREL where there are no constraints at all. Potential problems can be located as follows: EQS prints out a standardized solution in which all covariances have been transformed into correlations, while LISREL transforms only some of its variables so that some hand calculation may be necessary to determine whether any estimated covariances or correlations are outside the legitimate range.

Correlations at the boundary as well as outside the legitimate range imply that two variables are behaving as if they are identical. Even if other features of the solution are adequate, this implies a problem with the model specification. A very high or improper correlation between factors may occur if more than a few variables have loadings on both factors. Adding indicators that are affected by one but not another factor may help. Changing the causes and consequences of the factor may also help.

More generally, the covariance matrix of the independent variables should be positive definite. No program is currently able to impose this feature on the estimates.

Problem path coefficients. In a completely standardized path analysis solution (provided in EQS), path coefficients can be interpreted as standardized regression coefficients (Wright, 1934). Such coefficients should, generally, lie in the interval +1 to –1. When a coefficient in an equation becomes very large, a specification problem should be suspected. Large coefficients may signal linear dependencies among the predictor variables in the equation, for example. It may be necessary to redefine the variables in the equation, possibly by changing the predictor set. If some of the predictors are factors, it may be desirable to alter their indicators. More generally, causes or consequents of the affected variables may need to be changed.

Although there is no reason that the sign of a beta coefficient must be the same sign as the correlation between predictor and criterion variables, differing signs are usually taken as an indication of a "suppressor" effect. For example, when predicting college GPA from high school grades and SAT scores, since all correlations are positive one would hesitate to see a significant negative beta. Such effects can be located by checking the implied correlation. They may arise due to multicollinearities, in which case they will probably be uninterpretable. Suppressor effects are often not only hard to interpret, but in the area where they were first studied, they were hard to replicate (Wiggins, 1972), and the same appears to be true in structural models. Modifications in model structure may make these paradoxical effects disappear.

Statistical discrepancies. Statistical functions and estimators that have the same large sample distribution should yield chi-square tests and estimates that are roughly similar. Thus normal theory ML and GLS methods should yield equivalent results. When large discrepancies are observed, one should be suspicious about the adequacy of the structural model or the distributional assumption. In EQS, several estimators are easily available in the same run and can be compared, and when ML estimation is obtained, a corresponding GLS (called RLS in the program) chi-square statistic is printed out as well. Unfortunately, it is sometimes hard to make changes that eliminate the discrepancies. They should, at least, be reported.

PROBLEMS WITH MODEL FIT

Even when there are no problems with estimation, or unusual features to the results, a specified model may simply not fit sample data. The next step then is to improve the model. In general, there are two ways to do this. One way is through adding constraints and making the model more restricted. The other is through releasing constraints and making the model less restricted, or more general. In either approach, the proper constraints need to be identified. It is essential that the constraints to be added or dropped should be based on theory.

Typical problems. Perhaps the major problem that leads to the need for model modification is lack of a priori knowledge about the measurement structure of the variables. If at all possible, this should be obtained from prior studies with different data. The measurement structure can be wrong for several reasons: an insufficient number of latent variables is hypothesized; a factor is hypothesized for variables that do not correlate well among themselves; or an extremely restricted cluster-type of loading structure is used, in which a factor directly influences only one measured variable. A highly restricted loading structure will usually result in a relatively complex path structure for the latent variables; in contrast, a less restricted loading structure may permit a simpler path structure. A related problem that frequently occurs, not only in measurement models but path models as well, is that predictor independent variables, or criterion dependent variable residuals, are not allowed to covary. A measurement model with a highly restricted loading structure that forces the factors to be uncorrelated will rarely be appropriate for real data. A similar problem occurs when residuals in factors are forced to be uncorrelated. Even if one has strong theory that predicts lack of correlation, one should be immediately prepared to evaluate the theory against data if the strong model does not fit.

Model modification. Bentler and Chou (1986) proposed two statistical methods to obtain information concerning model improvement. When imposing constraints, both the fit function and the degrees of freedom will increase, but it is hoped that the loss of fit is minimal. When releasing constraints, on the other hand, both the fit function, and degrees of freedom will decrease. Here, it is hoped that the gain in fit is maximal. It is hoped, therefore, that the χ^2 can drop significantly with only a slight decrease in degrees of freedom. The two theories for these methods have been mentioned previously. The Wald (W) theory provides a multivariate test for dropping a set of free parameters, and the Lagrange Multiplier (LM) theory yields comparable information for releasing a set of constraints on parameters, or adding free parameters. In both ML or GLS estimation procedures, the Wald and Lagrange Multiplier theories yield statistics with chi-square distributions, but Bentler and Chou also provided nonstatistical equivalents for least-squares estimates. These tests have been implemented in the EQS program (Bentler, 1986b), as described next.

In the W test, only a multivariate test procedure is executed since the univariate W test is the same as the square of the z-test for each parameter estimate at the solution. Both univariate and multivariate LM tests are performed in the EQS program. The univariate LM test is a special case of the multivariate LM test. It offers a χ^2 value for each fixed parameter in a set to be tested multivariately. The concept behind this univariate test is the same as that of model modification indices in LISREL. However, the univariate test usually provides incomplete information. The univariate statistics are obtained under the assumption that there is no relationship between the various constraints. This is seldom the case. A statistically significant LM test for freeing one fixed parameter may not necessarily remain significant in the multivariate test. Therefore, the information generated by the univariate test can be misleading when several fixed parameters need to be freed to get a well fitting model. We strongly recommend the multivariate test for more adequate and efficient model improvement. Of course, in the selection of constrained parameters to be released in the multivariate LM test, a researcher should carefully examine the theoretical basis for each parameter. In addition to the specification of a parameter set, the theoretical importance of each parameter, or parameter group, compared to others, might also be considered.

The EQS program has been developed to allow parameters to be added or dropped in a stepwise process. Free parameters are dropped from the model one at a time in the W test, while fixed parameters are freed one by one in the LM test. Statistically, the W test is designed to drop the least important free parameters in sequence, and the LM test adds parameters in order of multivariate significance. These procedures can be recognized as variants of the backward and forward stepwise approaches in multiple regression analysis. The complete multivariate tests are obtained at the last step.

Several options on parameter set selections and testing procedures have been implemented in EQS, using the Bentler-Weeks (1980) model matrices Φ, γ, and β. Each matrix is composed of several submatrices, depending on the type of variable combinations involved. For example, in the covariance matrix of independent variables Φ we may be interested in correlations between factors, or in correlations between errors (or even in such unusual correlations as between errors in variables and disturbances in equations). Or, we may be interested in specific subparts of the regression coefficient matrices γ (dependent on independent variables) or β (dependent on dependent variables). A parameter, free or fixed, can be from any of these submatrices. Three types of LM testing procedure are available: sequential, simultaneous, and separate. After the set of fixed parameters is specified, these parameter matrices may be grouped in a predetermined order. The sequential procedure will use this order to prioritize parameters in the test. All the parameters in a submatrix (e.g., factor correlations) that are significant (at a previously assigned level) will be included in the test before the next matrix (e.g., correlated errors) can be considered. The significance of a parameter is defined in terms of the increment of χ^2 contributed by that parameter. Since these groups of parameters are tested sequentially, a more significant parameter from a group with lower priority may not get into the test process earlier than a less significant parameter from a higher priority group. The sequential procedure is especially useful when some groups of parameters are theoretically more important than others. In the simultaneous procedure, all parameters are considered for inclusion on an equal basis. In the separate procedure, separate LM tests are provided for each group of parameters. These results must then be combined subjectively by the researcher. These options are not available in the W test, in which all free parameters are automatically included and parameters are dropped on a simultaneous basis, that is, the least statistically significant parameter will be excluded from the model first. The multivariate LM and W tests can be specified to include or exclude parameters in a sequence that is wholly given by the researcher, or in a sequence that is determined by the empirical size of the increment.

From a theoretical point of view, of course, some parameters might need to remain fixed or freed, no matter what a W test or LM test might find. The user can specify which free parameters should not be considered in the W test and which fixed parameters should be excluded from the LM test. One example is that causal paths involving variables ordered in time have only one direction. A path from a variable at time two to a variable at time one would always be undesirable.

Model modification based on theory yields appropriate statistical tests under typical assumptions usually associated with chi-square tests (e.g., Lee and Bentler, 1980; Bentler and Dijkstra, 1985; Lee, 1985b; Satorra, 1986). If empirical model modification is done using a search procedure to locate the best changes, on the other hand, the probability values given for the statistics may be incorrect and the "true" model may not be found (see, e.g., MacCallum, 1986). One way to establish some validity to the resulting model is to compare the final adjusted model with the originally specified model, for example, by correlating parameter estimates for common parameters across solutions, as is done in most research in our laboratory. This does not address the question of whether newly added parameters are inadequate, but can provide some reassurance regarding the stability of the original parameterization across alternate specifications. Thus if the correlation is in the high .9s, the final solution at least contains most of the same information as the initial solution. Thus the initial solution was basically incomplete. On the other hand, if the correlation is lower, the added parameters also destroy the adequacy of the initial parameterization, suggesting greater problems than simple incompleteness of the initial model. Ideally, of course, one would cross-validate any final model (Cliff, 1983; Cudeck and Browne, 1983).

CONCLUSION

This article has provided a summary of various practical issues in structural modeling. These were addressed from the viewpoint of workers engaged in the theory as well as applications of structural modeling. Evidently, we believe the method to be valuable in social research. However, we would be remiss in not pointing out that some individuals are highly skeptical about the value of structural models. Cliff (1983), for example, has a favorable view toward the theory, but feels that the theory is easily misused when researchers forget basic principles of research. Freedman (1985, 1987) is more extreme in his evaluation. He considers the assumptions underlying the method to be inherently implausible, and the entire field to have essentially no value. As might be expected on the basis of our previous discussion, Freedman's arguments have, in our opinion, no solid foundation (Bentler, 1987b).

8

Assessment of Fit in Overidentified Models with Latent Variables

BLAIR WHEATON

An overidentified model presents the researcher with a relative luxury: more than sufficient information to identify some parameters, plus the ability to use the extra restrictions to evaluate the plausibility of the model as specified. If the extra restrictions are consistent with the pattern of covariances in the data, then the difference between input covariances among variables and the covariances implied by the model estimates will be minimal, that is, the fit of the model to the data will be good. But there is a cost to this luxury. Most of the available overidentified models will not fit the data clearly, and among the better candidates, the issue is when good fit becomes sufficient fit. Researchers using these models thus face a commonly shared and ubiquitous problem: Which model from a set of many possible overidentified models is the "best" one for interpretation. To help in choosing one model over others, summary measures of goodness of fit are usually applied.

The covariance structure model is a popular form of overidentified model for which the fit problem is particularly acute. This model is an amalgamation of a measurement submodel, relating

AUTHOR'S NOTE: *I am indebted to Peter Bentler, Mike Sobel, Scott Long, and Carol Bailey for their useful comments on an earlier draft. Of course, all viewpoints, conclusions, derivations, and calculations are the responsibility of the author.*

observed measures to a set of unobserved latent variables, as in a factor analysis, and a structural submodel that specifies a set of causal relations among the latent variables. Expository discussions can be found in Jöreskog and Sörbom (1979), Bentler (1980), and Long (1983a, 1983b); for a general discussion of problems in applying the model, see Bentler (this volume). Compared to overidentified models employing only observed variables, covariance structure models often incorporate many more overidentifying restrictions (in part as an expression of relatively strong theories relating measures to latent variables). One consequence of this, however, is that there are also more opportunities for fit to deteriorate.

In the last decade, a number of measures of fit have been proposed for these models (Wheaton et al., 1977; Bentler and Bonett, 1980; Hoelter, 1983; Jöreskog and Sörbom, 1984; Sobel and Bohrnstedt, 1984; Bollen, 1986), leaving researchers not only with the problem of choosing a model but also with the prior problem of choosing a fit criterion to help in choosing a model. The multiplicity of available measures for assessing the fit of a model leads to an unfortunate situation. Researchers do not use the same fit measures, reducing comparability of chosen final models, the fit measures themselves vary in what is intended and what is achieved, and because researchers can use a measure of choice with impunity, there is some added room for arbitrary decisions about a "best model."

This article has two purposes: (1) to make clear the decision-making context of the fit problem, with emphasis on the fact that assessment of fit is grounded in other model issues, and (2) to investigate the operational behavior of a set of goodness-of-fit measures in models that vary in function and sample size, with the emphasis on states of model development under which various measures agree or disagree regarding lack of fit or converge in restrictions, with the accompanying probability of the null hypothesis of perfect fit (stated more precisely, that the model as specified does not differ significantly from a completely unrestricted model); (2) the χ^2/df ratio for the model (Wheaton et al., 1977), included here primarily for historical interest; (3) Hoelter's (1983) "Critical N" measure; (4) the Jöreskog and Sörbom Goodness-of-Fit Index (1984); (5) the Bentler and Bonett (1980) nonnormed and normed incremental fit indices relative to a null model that assumes no relations among variables; and (6) the Sobel and Bohrnstedt (1984) modification of Bentler and Bonett based on a substantively determined null model baseline.[1]

A DISCLAIMER

Practically every paper written on the subject of fit indices contains an appropriately strong caution about the exclusive dependence on global indices in deciding the adequacy of a model. The reason should be obvious: a fit index can communicate only one aspect of the interpretability of parameter estimates in a model. Sobel and Bohrnstedt (1984: 158) put the issue emphatically:

> Scientific progress could be impeded if fit coefficients . . . are used as the primary criterion for judging the adequacy of a model.

I can only echo and endorse this warning. This article is about overall fit indices, but that should not imply that global measures can capture all that is important in deciding the worth of a model. suggesting acceptable fit. Six different measures will be compared: (1) the χ^2 goodness-of-fit test of the set of overidentifying There are many other aspects of a model to consider, and there are a number of clues that something basic may be wrong with a model, even when the fit is very good (see Bentler, this volume,for further discussion and specific examples).

THE FIT PROBLEM

EVALUATION LOGIC

A model becomes identified by virtue of assumptions. When there are more assumptions than necessary for identification, the plausibility of the extra assumptions versus *a model with no extra assumptions* can be assessed. This evaluation cannot test for the exclusivity of a set of assumptions in producing a model that fits. When we find that a particular model fits, it is important to remember that among the various ways of arriving at an over-identified model, there may not be one but many specifications that could produce an equally satisfactory fit.

At the same time, the starting point assumptions used in identifying a model tend to determine the set of restrictions considered in testing a series of hierarchically defined nested models. The effect of the initial model often goes unrecognized. The problem of model inertia, whether it is due to personal commitment or the legitimation of certain specifications in previously published research, is the sense of uniqueness attached to a model that fits. But citing the fit of a model as *prima facie* proof of its plausibility will usually be misleading.

The fact that multiple models may fit the data points to one inescapable conclusion: Other criteria must be considered in conjunction with fit in deciding on a final or "best" model. These other criteria could involve, for example: (1) restrictions on the range of specifications considered, based on theoretical guidance or previous research; (2) invocation of parsimony; (3) differences in the generality of latent variables across models; (4) the relative plausibility of distinguishing assumptions necessary to identify alternative models; and (5) precedence of explicit over implicit specifications of relationships (e.g., a methods factor rather than correlated errors between affected measures).

THE RANGE OF SPECIFICATIONS

Restricting the range of specifications means essentially the definition of boundaries for a set of models one is willing or must be ready to interpret. Presumably, every model in this set expresses a realistic and interpretable possibility. Other models outside this range may be used for comparison or testing purposes, but the subset of substantively interesting models constitutes the set from which a final model will be chosen.[2]

There are various forms of "specification abuse" that suggest the need for boundaries and for guidelines in setting boundaries. A common form of abuse is the inappropriate fitting of correlated errors. This can take on a number of forms, but the two most important are the excessive use of such terms in a model and the masking of alternative specifications of a model. Correlated error terms stand for additional factors (latent variables) in a measurement model, and explicit representation of these factors is generally preferred (Alwin and Jackson, 1979).[3]

The problem caused by correlated errors in the assessment of a model is illustrated by the following example. Suppose that researcher A believes that a single general factor expresses the common content in a set of items while researcher B believes there are two factors. "A" fits a one-factor model, finds it does not fit, and proceeds to free sequentially a set of correlated errors among the items until the model fits. "B" will also be able to fit a two-factor model the same way, so that we will have two quite different conclusions about the best model based on the citation of satisfactory fit as a criterion. If the correlated errors fit by Researcher A correspond to the second factor hypothesized by Researcher B, the two-factor specification is to be preferred.

Another quite common form of specification abuse occurs when either arbitrary or poorly informed restrictions are used to identify or overidentify the structural (causal) part of the model. Arbitrary restrictions result either from a lack of knowledge of the research area or the claim that all sets of restrictions have equal plausibility. The latter will most often be a result of the former. What at first glance may appear to be a choice between equally weak theories often proves upon experience with a particular research question to be a much clearer choice. Put another way, the specifications to be considered can often be limited by judicious use of a priori information.

A less common form of specification abuse involves the estimation of a measurement relation between an observed and a latent variable that has no clear interpretation. We would not think, for instance, of saying that an indicator of social integration, such as the number of social roles occupied, is a *measure* of psychological well-being, but we might argue that the latent variable social integration is causally related to well-being.[4] A related and also uncommon problem occurs when a latent variable, by virtue of the measures it is specified to cause, has no meaningful substantive interpretation. The problem can arise subtly from the application of a general model to inappropriate combinations of variables. For example, the synchronous common-factor model can be applied as an alternative in a cross-lagged panel model, thereby stating that the measures at each time point really measure one underlying concept. But if the two sets of measures considered involve locus of control items and social class indicators, the idea of a common factor will usually be considered unacceptable.

These examples are certainly not exhaustive, but they do suggest the importance of restrictions on the range of alternative models considered for interpretation. In essence, specification abuse can trivialize the fit issue.

UNDERFITTING AND OVERFITTING

Restricting specification alternatives is one way to reduce the complexity of the fit problem. There are other areas of uncertainty in assessing fit. One of the most insidious problems in terms of its consequences is knowing "when to stop," that is, how much fit is enough fit without being too much fit. I refer here to the issues of underfitting and overfitting a model.

There are few guidelines as to sufficient fit that can be easily rationalized. Some suggested thresholds exist for selected measures (Bentler and Bonett, 1980; Hoelter, 1983), but it is clear even to those making the suggestions that the *idea* of thresholds is problematic. This necessarily leads to some arbitrariness in the decision to stop fitting a model. If the criteria for sufficiency are arguable, then the researcher can stop at a model of choice, within a broad range of possibly acceptable models, without threat of serious sanction.

The problem of underfitting is that important parameters are excluded, which means in turn that the estimates of other parameters will be biased—the classic case of specification error due to omitted effects. Since fitting a model can be quite complex, there is little doubt that there are a number of underfit models reported in the literature that do not appear to be so, and that there are many fewer overfit models. The worst possible consequence of this is the proliferation of published models that, by virtue of model inertia, become assumed truths even though they exclude essential parameters that may change the interpretation of results.

While underfitting is almost always a problem, whether or not overfitting is a problem depends on the situation. Overfitting involves the inclusion of extra parameters in a model after reaching some threshold that stands for minimally sufficient fit. If these extra parameters are predicted a priori, by theory or by previous findings, then standard practice dictates that overfitting may not only be acceptable, but necessary. If the extra parameters are fit as part of a post hoc exploration, then there can be a problem, for example, if the extra parameters are "fragile" in the sense of replicability because they stand for weak effects, or they lead to significant inflation of standard errors, or they affect essential parameters but have no clear substantive meaning themselves.[5]

Whether the parameters are predicted a priori or not, overfitting may present certain strategical advantages in evaluating a model. An obvious example is when important parameters remain stable across models as we go from borderline to overfit models. There are at least two advantages here: the "when to stop" problem is resolved, and we create the possibility of knowing more rather than knowing less. Overfitting does not mean we have to take the extra parameters seriously, but it will invariably mean we can compare essential parameters across models that fit increasingly well.

The conditions under which overfitting may be useful involve one or more of the following: (1) when the extra parameters fit do not affect the important parameters of interest, whether or not the extra parameters have specific a priori interpretations; (2) when the extra parameters fit either indicate strong relationships with a plausible interpretation or serendipitous possibilities that should be considered in future research; (3) when the sample size is large and stopping points for acceptable fit are especially unclear; and (4) the fewer the number of modifications necessary beyond a basic confirmatory model.

A MULTIPLE-MEASURE APPROACH

The fact that a number of measures of fit are available, and no one predominates, complicates the problem of assessing fit further. For one thing, it is common practice to report only one measure. But different measures have different intentions, and a model that fits according to one measure may not fit according to others. Although many measures use similar sources of information from an estimated model, the manipulation of this information differs markedly. We need to know in each case what is being fit to what.

On the one hand, this creates a problem in comparing measures directly. On the other hand, the differences among measures could be used to advantage, namely, the weaknesses of one measure may be compensated by others. Given the uncertainty about thresholds of sufficiency, about differences in purpose across measures, and the varying sensitivity of different measures to sample size, a prudent approach would be to use several measures of fit and estimate models to a point of consensus among measures about the issue of adequate fit. The question is which measures should be used, and under what circumstances.

SIX MEASURES

To understand what fit measures are designed to do, as well as their similarities and differences, the definition and interpretation of six measures will be reviewed. All of these measures depend indirectly on the minimum value of the (ML) fitting function for a model, and almost all depend directly on a goodness-of-fit statistic based on the fitting function. Some measures, by virtue of how they are constructed, are sensitive to sample size; others are not. Because this is a major problem in the application of fit indices, often meaning indications of poorer fit in large samples compared to small samples, dependence on sample size will be discussed for each distinct case.

THE χ^2 GOODNESS-OF-FIT TEST

Given that S is the input covariance matrix for a set of observed measures, that $\hat{\Sigma}$ is the reproduced covariance matrix for these measures implied by the parameter values from an estimated model, and that p is the total number of measures (variables), the maximum likelihood fitting function is:

$$F = \log|\hat{\Sigma}| - \log|S| + \text{tr}(S\hat{\Sigma}^{-1}) - p$$

This is the usual form of the ML function, but there are variants (see for example Jöreskog, 1971). What is going on in this function is a kind of "double" minimization task that considers the difference between the log of the determinant of the input and reproduced covariance matrices plus the difference between the diagonal sum of a matrix (the trace), formed by multiplying S times the inverse of $\hat{\Sigma}$, and the number of variables. The logic of this second component is seen by noting that as $\hat{\Sigma}$ approaches S, this diagonal sum approaches a sum of ones, and therefore p.

When F is defined as above, the goodness-of-fit test of the proposed model is (Bentler and Bonett, 1980; Jöreskog and Sörbom, 1984):

$$\chi^2 = (N - 1)F$$

where N is the sample size and F is taken at its minimum value. The degrees of freedom (df) for the test are $(p(p + 1))/2 - t$, where t is the number of independent parameters estimated. The logic of this test, and its problems, can be seen from the components of χ^2. When a model fits very well, F is small, thus χ^2 is small. The null hypothesis here is that the proposed model does not differ significantly from an unconstrained model that fits the data exactly. The probability of the χ^2 for a model under the null can be taken as a measure of fit, so values in excess of .05, for instance, are desirable. Poor fit leads to larger values of F, larger χ^2, and rejection of the model.

The well-known problem with this is that χ^2 depends directly on the sample size, leading to almost certain rejection of models in large samples even when they differ trivially from perfect fit. Long (1983b) has shown how χ^2 is affected by N exactly. For any given constant value of F, the χ^2 in a larger sample (N_2) compared to a smaller sample (N_1) is $(N_2 - 1)/(N_1 - 1)$ times the χ^2 for the model in the smaller sample. The fit of the model has not changed, but the χ^2 value has. The implication is obvious: the χ^2 test will not be very useful in large samples, and we know that, at least in this case, other measures will have to be used.

THE χ^2/df RATIO

If we divide the model χ^2 by the degrees of freedom, we have an indication of the fit of the model per degree of freedom used, or in other words, per overidentifying restriction. This measure was first proposed, somewhat in passing, in a relatively early application of LISREL modeling (Wheaton et al., 1977). It has the virtues of simplicity and intuitive sense, but in actual applications it tends to favor underfit models—at least when using the suggested thresholds of 5 (Wheaton et al., 1977) or even 2 (Carmines and MacIver, 1981).

It is unfortunate that this measure has gained such widespread use when even in the 1977 article it was not taken as the primary criterion for fit. The following sentences seem to be the source of the trouble (emphasis added):

> We will want to assess varying χ^2/df ratios across models in order to get a rough indication of fit per degree of freedom. *For our sample size,* we judge a ratio of around 5 or less as *beginning to be reasonable,* based on our experience in inspecting the sizes of residuals that accompany varying χ^2 values [1977: 99].

The qualifiers in this statement seem to have been lost in practical applications. In the article, we used two other measures to evaluate the fit of models while reporting this ratio as well. These measures were a matrix of residuals divided by the S matrix, a measure of proportion of input covariances explained, and the probability of the model produced by the χ^2 test. Using a sample of 932, we continued to consider models until they fit with probability = .1507 under the null, not when the χ^2/df ratio reached some threshold.

I do not advocate use of the χ^2/df ratio at this stage, for three reasons. First, the measure is just as dependent on sample size as the χ^2 test. For two models with the same minimum F value and df, sample size will have the same effect as it has on the χ^2 test itself. Second, this direct dependence on N makes it impossible to suggest general thresholds as guidelines, so definition of satisfactory fit is unclear. Finally, because the problems of the χ^2/df ratio are inherited directly from the χ^2 test, there is no reason to replace the χ^2 test with this ratio—other than to state something descriptively about the "efficiency" of the model in achieving whatever fit it achieves.

HOELTER'S CRITICAL N

Hoelter (1983) has proposed a simple and interesting measure of fit that is quite different from the others included here. Instead of attempting to free the measure of sample size effects, this approach uses sample size as a measure of fit. "Critical N" (CN) is the maximum sample size up to which a particular model cannot be rejected under the null for the χ^2 test. If, for instance, a model does not fit in a large sample, the question would be at what sample size the model would fit with probability .05 or .01? The better the model, the larger the sample size. Or, if a model fits in a small sample according to the χ^2 test, Critical N will tell us how much larger the sample could be before rejection of the model.

Hoelter gives a definition of CN based on the minimum value of F for a model, but the formula he uses is not consistent with the ML fitting function as defined above. Since the particular form of CN will vary depending on how the fitting function is defined, I recommend the form of the measure expressed in terms of the χ^2 and N used in estimating the model. The reason is that differences in definition of F are absorbed by the transformation to χ^2. When $\chi^2 = (N - 1)F$, the definition of CN is:

$$CN = \frac{(z_c + \sqrt{2df - 1})^2}{2\chi^2/N - 1} + 1$$

where z_c is the critical value of z at a chosen significance level. This formula is derived from the expression for the normal approximation to χ^2, by substituting for χ^2 with $(N-1)F$ and then solving for N.[6] Hoelter suggests, with some care, a threshold level of 200 (times the number of groups in a multisample analysis) for this measure. This means that a model that has an acceptable fit should have a CN of at least 200 (per sample).

THE JÖRESKOG AND SÖRBOM GOODNESS-OF-FIT INDEX

Jöreskog and Sörbom (1984) suggest the following goodness of fit index (GFI) for descriptive fit purposes:

$$GFI = 1 - \frac{tr(\hat{\Sigma}^{-1}S - I)^2}{tr(\hat{\Sigma}^{-1}S)^2}$$

This measure is defined by Jöreskog and Sörbom as a "measure of the relative amount of variances and covariances jointly accounted for by the model" (1984:I.41). For those unfamiliar with matrix algebra, however, it may not be clear what this measure actually does.

Recall that S is the input covariance matrix and $\hat{\Sigma}$ is the covariance matrix as reproduced by a particular model. Obviously, the closer that $\hat{\Sigma}$ approximates S, the better. $\hat{\Sigma}^{-1}S$ denotes taking the inverse of $\hat{\Sigma}$ and multiplying by S. The inverse of $\hat{\Sigma}$ is a matrix that when multiplied by $\hat{\Sigma}$ equals an identity matrix, I, with one's in the diagonal and zeros in the off-diagonal (i.e., $\hat{\Sigma}^{-1}\hat{\Sigma} = I$). As $\hat{\Sigma}$ approaches S, the value $\hat{\Sigma}^{-1}S$ is thus approaching an identity matrix. This means that as fit improves an identity matrix is subtracted from an increasingly similar matrix. Because of this, squaring of this difference will result in smaller and smaller entries in the resulting matrix, and the trace will approach zero. In the denominator, $\hat{\Sigma}^{-1}S$ will also approach an identity matrix. After this matrix is squared, and the trace is taken, the target value is a sum of ones, or p, the number of variables in the model. Since the numerator is approaching zero while the denominator is approaching p, progressively smaller numbers are subtracted from 1 as fit improves.

This measure is based on the fitted values in $\hat{\Sigma}$ and the given values of S and thus does not depend on N. Given the definition, the theoretical limits are zero and one, although some results can cause negative values. One issue in considering any descriptive measure is the range of values it takes on in actual applications. The theoretical limits may not reflect the operational limits of the measure in most models. These operational limits may be a large subset of the theoretical limits or a small subset. Since a larger subset is desirable, indicating more sensitivity to differences among models, differences in the operational range of measures represent an important point of comparison.

BENTLER AND BONETT INCREMENTAL FIT INDICES ρ_{hf} AND Δ_{hf}

Bentler and Bonett (1980) proposed two fit indices, one a nonnormed and the other a normed increment fit index. The nonnormed index is defined as:

$$\rho_{hf} = \frac{(\chi_h^2/df_h) - (\chi_f^2/df_f)}{(\chi_o^2/df_o - 1)}$$

where, in general, the subscript o stands for a null model that specifies no relations among variables, subscript h stands for a substantive model of interest, and subscript f stands for a "fitted" model developed from model h. In the present application, model h is the basic confirmatory model we are interested in testing, and f is any exploratory model developed by removing selected restrictions from model h.[7] This means that model h will always be "nested" in model f, in the sense that model h contains restrictions on free parameters in model f but is otherwise the same.

Following Bentler and Bonett, the null model specifies no common factors (latent variables) for the set of input measures as well as no covariances among these measures. The usual way of specifying this model is to set to zero all of the covariances among measures while allowing their variances to be estimated as free parameters. I will refer to this class of null models as complete null models, since there are other less restrictive nulls that can be used.

The analytical issue addressed by this index is whether model f should be retained over model h. Given that the point of comparison is "all the fit there is to fit," as reflected by the χ^2 per degree of freedom for the null model, the measure asks this question: Is the improvement resulting from model f as opposed to model h substantial or notable relative to the total amount of fitting to be done?

The incremental form of the index is only one form; an overall fit version ρ_{of} can also be calculated by replacing the χ^2/df ratio for model h in the numerator with the χ^2/df ratio for model o. Note these two versions have somewhat different intentions: The former is for evaluating the necessity of a less restricted substantive model relative to a more restricted substantive model, and the latter is for evaluation of the overall sufficiency of any fitted model. The index is "nonnormed" because it is possible to get negative values and values above one in actual applications. Finally, note that the fit ρ_{oh} and ρ_{hf} add up to the overall fit ρ_{of}.

Bollen (1986) has shown that this index does depend on N, although not in any simple way. Following Bollen, the index can be written in this equivalent form:

$$\rho_{hf} = \frac{F_h/df_h - F_f/df_f}{F_o/df_o - 1/(N-1)}$$

As a result of the $1/(N-1)$ term in the denominator, Bollen notes that ρ_{hf} will be attenuated in larger compared to small samples, and that differences in the size of ρ_{hf} will be smaller when comparing larger samples to each other. The exact relationship between $\rho_{hf(2)}$ in a larger sample and $\rho_{hf(1)}$ in a smaller sample can be shown to be:

$$\rho_{hf(2)} = \rho_{hf(1)} \frac{(N_2 - 1)}{(N_1 - 1)} \frac{(\chi^2_{o(1)} - df_o)}{(\chi^2_{o(2)} - df_o)}$$

Remembering that $\chi^2_{o(1)}$ could be replaced by $(N_1 - 1)F_o$ and $\chi^2_{o(2)}$ could be replaced by $(N_2 - 1)F_o$, we see that ρ_{hf} depends not only on N, but on the F and df for the null model as well. Values of the right hand expression in the equation above can be calculated for varying combinations of F_o, df_o, N_1, and N_2. The result is an attenuation factor that, when multiplied by $\rho_{hf(1)}$, produces $\rho_{hf(2)}$.

Varying F_o between a typical value for a relatively weak set of covariances and a strong set of covariances, df_o between 28 and 210—standing for models with from 8 to 21 variables, and considering increases in N based on $N_1 = 100, 200$, and 500, I find that the attenuation effect is larger the smaller the base N, the weaker the given set of covariances, and the more variables in the model (results not shown). But the effect of these three factors together is definitely not additive. In fact, it appears to be multiplicative, so that the attenuation effect is considerable only under specific combinations of model conditions. For instance, when there are 15 or more variables, attenuation falls below .80 only when N_1 is as low as 100. When there are about 20 or more variables, the attenuation factor falls below .80 for $N_1 = 200$ as well. But for all model comparisons based on larger base N, or for fewer than 15 variables if the base N is 200 or less, the attenuation of ρ varies from nonfatal to very minor. This fact suggests that ρ may be more immune to sample size changes than χ^2 under most model conditions.

The effect of attenuation does have different implications for ρ_{hf} and ρ_{of}. Applied to ρ_{of}, it means that satisfactory fit will be more difficult to achieve in larger samples. Applied to ρ_{hf}, it means that initial hypothesized models will be favored relative to fitted models. Note that this means that as N increases, ρ_{of} may suggest further fitting is in order while ρ_{hf} may suggest that improvements in fit are very difficult to achieve.

The normed index suggested by Bentler and Bonett is bounded by a 0 to 1 range for all nested models and is not affected by N. As given by Bentler and Bonett, this index has the form:

$$\Delta_{hf} = \frac{F_h - F_f}{F_o}$$

This expression can be transformed into one that shows the relation of this measure to others by replacing F with $\chi^2/N - 1$ for each model. The N – 1 terms cancel, resulting in:

$$\Delta_{hf} = \frac{\chi^2_h - \chi^2_f}{\chi^2_o}$$

This index can also be stated in an overall fit version Δ_{of}. It would appear that this measure has a number of advantages over the nonnormed measure, but it should be remembered that the non-normed measure includes the idea that improvements in fit should be considered relative to the degrees of freedom used in achieving acceptable fit.

The question arises as to when fit is sufficient for these measures, since they are both descriptive in nature and have no known sampling distribution. For the overall measures ρ_{of} and Δ_{of}, Bentler and Bonett (1980) suggest .9 as a threshold, but for the incremental versions ρ_{hf} and Δ_{hf}, no precise guidelines are given.

SOBEL AND BOHRNSTEDT'S
INFORMED NULL BASELINE INDICES

While retaining the basic structure of Bentler and Bonett's fit measures, Sobel and Bohrnstedt (1984) have proposed a new approach to defining the null model used in the denominator. They argue that the null model in the Bentler/Bonett indices represents an extreme that does not take into account the previous accumulated knowledge in an area. Thus the complete null amounts to a "know nothing" assumption that does not correspond to actual research situations.

Of course, the null model approach of Bentler and Bonett is designed to capture all of the fitting to be done as the baseline. Sobel and Bohrnstedt point out that this creates such unrealistically large denominators in real applications that the measure is biased toward lower values of ρ_{hf} and Δ_{hf} and thus acceptance of intermediate models. In effect, it becomes more difficult for improvements in fit to look important. The Sobel and Bohrnstedt position is that the null model used should reflect the accumulated state of knowledge in an area. In general, this "informed" null model should be a realistically possible, substantively meaningful, but restrictive, model, given current theory and/or empirical evidence.

We should keep in mind the difference in interpretation between what I am calling the incremental and overall fit versions of ρ and Δ. It is not necessarily the case that the logic of defining a null model for one applies equally to the other, even if it is desirable to have the same null model in both cases. Applying the Sobel and Bohrnstedt approach to the incremental fit issue, it is clear that given improvements in fit will look better relative to an informed baseline (there are fewer χ^2 to be explained). Applied to the overall fit issue, however, use of an informed null will produce smaller fit values, making sufficient fit more difficult to achieve.

There could be a potential problem with use of a floating null model baseline across applications and over time. The definition of sufficient fit is shifting, and as more knowledge accumulates, we see that we are really getting a relative measure of sufficient fit only. The meaning of the incremental version will also shift with progress. At each stage, the informed null model approach will produce a measure of fit that represents improvement relative to the distance in fitting left to go, not all of the fitting that can be achieved as in the original version. While the Bentler and Bonett measures and the Sobel and Bohrnstedt modification of these measures appear to be in competition, it would make more sense to see them as complementary, since they answer different questions about a particular model.

Sobel and Bohrnstedt suggest some guidelines for specifying informed null models that will apply to many situations. These guidelines differ most from a complete null model approach at the measurement level, where most of the degrees of freedom in many models occur. A large class of null measurement models will involve fixing to zero loadings of measures on all factors except one, assuming zero autocorrelation among error terms, specifying parallel measurement for all measures of the same factor, and using the fewest number of factors possible in a range of articulated alternatives in the literature.

I refer the reader to Alwin and Jackson (1979) for a more complete discussion of the specification of measurement models, but for present purposes it is important to note that a parallel measures model implies that measures of each factor have loadings fixed at one (or equal to each other if the variance of the factor is fixed at one), and error variances set equal. This is obviously the strongest possible measurement model, stating a full definition of equivalence of measures. Two other less restrictive measurement models may be appropriate for some kinds of measures. Tau-equivalent measures imply factor loadings fixed at one as well, but the error variances are free to vary. Here the true score is "the same" but each measure has a different reliability. Finally, a congeneric model implies only that each measure loads on one factor only and not necessarily equally (given the constraint that at least one loading on each factor must be fixed to one).[8] These are, of course, nested models that can be tested in sequence.

At the structural level of a model, Sobel and Bohrnstedt (1984) suggest a null causal model as a baseline, as do Bentler and Bonett (1980) for use as an intermediate null model incorporating tau-equivalent assumptions at the measurement level. Sobel and Bohrnstedt also suggest modified versions of this baseline, which can include the existence of correlations between errors for endogenous latent variables and correlations among exogenous latent variables that are not at issue in the model.

To distinguish between the Bentler/Bonett and Sobel/Bohrnstedt versions, I will use ρ^* and Δ^* to stand for the informed null version. Note that the dependence on N noted for ρ must also apply here, since the measures have the same structure. However, the null models for ρ^* will generally have fewer degrees of freedom for a given set of variables, and thus attenuation factors will be somewhat smaller than for the original measure.

A COMPARISON OF THE OPERATIONAL BEHAVIOR OF FIT MEASURES

In this section I will present two empirical examples of fitting a model. The two fitting situations are chosen to be quite different, one a measurement model in a small sample, and the other a full covariance structure model in a moderately small sample compared to the same model in a large sample. The approach is purposely exploratory, since our interest is in how fit measures change across models.

A MEASUREMENT MODEL

The first example is a factor model for sixteen personality measures estimated in a random community sample of a midsized city in Texas with N = 132. This is a small sample, but this will allow us to find a model that fits in probability terms under the χ^2 test quite easily and then continue to fit the model to see how other fit measures behave under such conditions.

The particular issue in this model is the number of factors necessary to represent the covariances among the sixteen measures. I chose these items because there are competing available theories about their factor structure. The items (see Table 1) are all measures of locus of control, personal flexibility, or trustfulness. Kohn and Schooler (1982) might use a single-factor representation for such items, arguing that the overarching theme in these items is the issue of self-directedness versus conformity to external authority. Wheaton (1985) argues that these items suggest three distinct factors, one a fatalism factor (all of the locus of control items included are ones worded in the external direction), another an inflexibility factor, indicated by endorsing items that represent the self as needing exactness, perfection, and strict adherence to rules and standards, and the third a mistrust factor, indicated by initial suspiciousness of others, mistrust of others' motives, and so on. The initial factor structure for a three-factor model is shown in Table 1.[9]

Table 2 shows the calculated fit values of all indices for a series of models.[10] Models are designated using a subscript system that indicates the specification, for example, M_{1c} is a one-factor congeneric model, and M_{33} is a three-factor model with 3 correlated error terms.

The complete null model in this case, specifying zero covariances among all 16 items, produces a χ^2 of 345.72 with 120 df. Three versions of a one-factor model were estimated, the most restrictive being a parallel measures model.[11] The χ^2 in this model

TABLE 1
Factor Pattern Matrix for Three-Factor Model

Item	F_1	F_2	F_3
Will always be wars	λ_{11}	0.	0.
Often things unavoidable	λ_{21}	0.	0.
Decide by flipping a coin	λ_{31}	0.	0.
Victim of world forces	λ_{41}	0.	0.
No control over politicians	λ_{51}	0.	0.
Little influence	λ_{61}	0.	0.
Need breaks	λ_{71}	0.	0.
Good job depends on luck	λ_{81}	0.	0.
Safer to trust no one	0.	λ_{92}	0.
Honest when could get caught	0.	$\lambda_{10,2}$	0.
Suspicious	0.	$\lambda_{11,2}$	0.
On guard with people	0.	$\lambda_{12,2}$	0.
Need perfection	0.	0.	$\lambda_{13,3}$
Do things exactly my way	0.	0.	$\lambda_{14,3}$
Stick to rigid standards	0.	0.	$\lambda_{15,3}$
Like places neat and clean	0.	0.	$\lambda_{16,3}$

is very close to the null model χ^2. The tau-equivalent one-factor model shows a sharp reduction in χ^2, reflecting the importance of allowing for unequal error variances, and the congeneric model causes a modest further improvement in fit, although it is significant according to a difference of χ^2 test, which can be applied to successive nested models. The one-factor congeneric model is already in a maximally unrestricted form, and it does not fit. However, the three-factor unrestricted model does fit with probability = .08 under the null. This model is specified by setting to zero just $k - 1$ entries in each column of the factor matrix, where k equals the number of factors, and fixing the factor variances to one (Alwin and Jackson, 1979). This result tells us only that some three-factor model fits. We are interested, of course, in a more restricted version.

The same sequence of measurement-restricted models was estimated for the three-factor specification as for the one-factor specification. At each stage the fit improved, and the three-factor congeneric model produced the first sign of a nonzero probability under the null $(Pr(M_{3c}) = .004)$. However, in a sample this small this is not acceptable fit; thus further modifications were necessary. In this case, this involved the estimation of correlated error terms between selected measures, as indicated by the modifica-

TABLE 2

Overall Fit of Measurement Models for 16 Personality Items

Model		χ^2	df	Pr	$\dfrac{\chi^2}{df}$	GFI	CN	ρ_{of}	ρ_{hf}	ρ^*_{of}	ρ^*_{hf}	Δ_{of}	Δ_{hf}	Δ^*_{of}	Δ^*_{hf}
M_o	: Complete Null	345.72	120	.000	2.88	.717	56								
M_{1p}	: 1 factor., parallel	342.76	132	.000	2.60	.748	62	.151				.009			.035
M_{1t}	: 1 factor., tau-equiv.	239.76	118	.000	2.03	.802	80	.451				.306			.097
M_{1c}	: 1 factor., congeneric	223.27	104	.000	2.15	.813	76	.390		−.111		.354		.069	.117
M_{3u}	: 3 factors., unrestricted	92.85	75	.080	1.24	.920	136	.873		.769		.731		.613	.173
M_{3p}	: 3 factors., parallel	269.13	127	.000	2.12	.806	76	.405		−.085		.222		.289	.225
M_{3t}	: 3 factors., tau-equiv.	170.58	114	.000	1.50	.858	108	.736		.519		.507		.406	.268
M_{3c}	: 3 factors., congeneric	142.52	101	.004	1.41	.883	116	.781		.602		.588			
M_{31}	: 3 factors., 1 corr. error	134.18	100	.013	1.34	.891	122	.818	.037	.669	.067	.612	.024	.440	
M_{33}	: 3 factors., 3 corr. errors	119.15	98	.072	1.22	.904	135	.885	.104	.791	.189	.655	.068	.503	
M_{34}	: 3 factors., 4 corr. errors	114.48	97	.109	1.18	.907	139	.904	.123	.825	.224	.669	.081	.523	
M_{36}	: 3 factors., 6 corr. errors	101.02	95	.317	1.06	.915	155	.966	.185	.939	.337	.708	.120	.579	
M_{38}	: 3 factors., 8 corr. errors	88.51	93	.612	.95	.924	173	1.026	.244	1.047	.445	.744	.156	.631	
M_{310}	: 3 factors., 10 corr. errors	78.29	91	.826	.86	.932	192	1.074	.293	1.135	.534	.774	.186	.673	

NOTE: See text for description of models and fit measures.

tion indices in LISREL VI (Jöreskog and Sörbom, 1984).

As these correlated errors were estimated, the probability of the model under the null came into the nonsignificant region. By the time three correlated errors were estimated, the probability of the model was .072. I continued to fit the model, however, given this is a borderline figure in a small sample and in order to investigate the effects of overfitting on other fit measures. A model with six correlated errors fits with a probability of .317, and one with ten correlated errors, the final model, produces a probability of .826. The pattern of correlated errors in this model did not point to any plausible fourth factor. Thus the correlated error specification was retained.

It is clear this analysis suggests the necessity of a three-factor model for these items. The question is which should be retained from the variations tried. Should we report the first nonsignificant model M_{33} or a later model? The issue here is not finding a model that fits but knowing which of a set of models that fit is appropriate. Normally, this would not be a question, but in small samples models may fit all too easily. Presumably, the other fit measures will provide further guidance. All we can say at this point is that models with zero probability under the null do not fit adequately and that models that fit with probabilities such as .826 would usually be thought of as overfit.

The χ^2/df ratio at least decreases monotonically with improving fit, although it gives little guidance on when to stop. If, for instance, the threshold of 2 was used as criterion, we would stop at M_{3t}, a model that does not fit according to the χ^2 test. Thus the χ^2/df ratio would be less demanding than the χ^2 test in this case.

The GFI measure does not fare much better. Its lowest value in the complete null model is .717. It increases to .80 by the time a one-factor tau-equivalent model is specified, but takes until M_{33}, many models later, to get to .90. It increases only to .932 by the final model. A measure does not have to increase linearly, but these results suggest that large differences in fit produce rather small changes in GFI.

The CN measure produces some surprising results. Despite the fact that the last five models considered fit according to the χ^2 test, not one produces a CN above 200. The CN for M_{33}, for example, is only 135, and the CN for M_{310}, a model with a very high probability of .826, is 192. Hoelter's own discussion suggests that this measure may not be useful in samples under 200, and these results support that prediction.

We must turn, then, to the Bentler and Bonett family of measures. The rest of Table 2 shows values of ρ and Δ defined in various ways. In each case, I defined the hypothesized model (model h) as the three-factor congeneric model, and then computed improvements for succeeding versions of model f with reference to the same model h. The issue in the column for ρ_{of} is one of overall fit of the sequence of models specified. In fact ρ_{of} seems to work quite well here: It reaches a value of .904 at model M_{34}, which has a probability under the null of .109. We see that improvements in fit beyond the three-factor congeneric model seem minor; for M_{34}, for instance, ρ_{hf} is .123. That may be enough to argue M_{34} is a worthwhile improvement, especially when ρ_{of} for M_{3c} is .781 and points to room for improvement. But we do not have clear standards for judging the size of the incremental fit measure. We could apply a χ^2 difference test, which does have clear standards, but all we can say with that test is that every decrease in χ^2 for nested models in this table is significant. Applied to the improvement in comparing M_{34} with M_{3c}, this χ^2 is $142.52 - 114.98 = 27.54$ with $101 - 97 = 4$ df, which is significant beyond the .001 level.

For application of the Sobel and Bohrnstedt approach, I used the one-factor tau-equivalent model as the informed null baseline. The one-factor model represents, obviously, the fewest possible number of factors in the hypothesized range. I chose the tau-equivalent rather than the more restrictive parallel specification because of the type of measures involved. One way of distinguishing the appropriateness of null models is the type of measure at issue. A parallel measures model may be more generally applicable for ability, test, and achievement measures while a tau-equivalent model may be more generally appropriate for attitude and personality measures, for example.

Values of ρ_{hf}^* and ρ_{of}^* were calculated using M_{1t} as the informed null. Note that the limit problem surfaces here especially: At the extremes, the measure takes on values below zero and greater than one. However, these occur for implausible models. The Sobel and Bohrnstedt approach also works well in this case, with ρ_{of}^* reaching .9 by model M_{36}, one model beyond the stopping point suggested by ρ_{of}. Also, as one would expect, given the smaller denominator used, the incremental fit values are notably higher, with M_{36} showing an incremental fit of .337 relative to the congeneric three-factor model.

The last four columns of Table 2 show results for the normed measures. Another small surprise here is the relatively lower values of Δ compared to the corresponding ρ. This is explained, in this case, by the fact that the null model does not produce very high χ^2 values, and thus the amount of reduction of χ^2 necessary to reach a model that fits according to χ^2 is also smaller. Calculated values of Δ_{of} are around .70 for the two models suggested as adequate by the ρ_{of} and ρ^*_{of} measures. It appears that in this model both Δ and Δ^* do not yield information we can use in deciding on a model.

The conclusion we can reach from these results is an ironic one: In a small sample such as this, the χ^2 test proves to be useful in suggesting at least a minimally acceptable model. The other two measures that are most clearly helpful are ρ_{of}, which varies over a wide range and reaches a rule-of-thumb threshold for a model that also fits under the null hypothesis with a probability = .109, and ρ^*_{hf}, which shows the true relative improvement in choosing M_{34} or M_{36} over M_{3c}. As I indicated in the previous section, it is possible to use either or both of ρ and ρ^* for the purposes for which they are specifically designed, as long as it is clear that their interpretation is relative to different starting points.

A FULL COVARIANCE STRUCTURE MODEL

For this example we will consider a full model, including both a measurement submodel and a structural submodel stating causal relations among the factors. The model is shown in Figure 1. There are two endogenous latent variables, one labelled satisfaction with public life and the other satisfaction with private life. The causal issue is their reciprocal effect on each other. Public life satisfaction, in this initial model, has two indicators: satisfaction with the city or place of residence, and satisfaction with the country as a whole (in the case of this data set, Canada). Private life satisfaction has four indicators: overall life satisfaction, which is interpreted here as primarily tapping assessment of personal life states, satisfaction with leisure time, satisfaction with finances, and satisfaction with the current intimate relationship—includ-

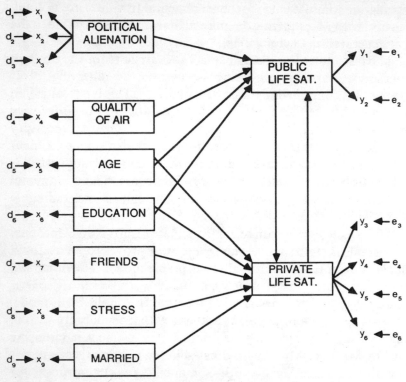

NOTES: x_1 = No control over Parliament; x_2 = Elected officials don't care; x_3 = No say in what politicians do; x_4 = Clean air in local area; x_5 = Age in years; x_6 = Education in years; x_7 = Number of close friends; x_8 = Number of stressors this year; x_9 = Married; y_1 = Satisfaction with city/town; y_2 = Satisfaction with life in Canada; y_3 = Overall life satisfaction; y_4 = Satisfaction with leisure; y_5 =Satisfaction with finances; y_6 = Satisfaction with relationship.

Figure 1: An Initial Model for the Reciprocal Effects of Public and Private Life Satisfaction

ing both those who are married and nonmarrieds with ongoing relationships.

The model has seven exogenous variables. Two of these, political alienation, with three indicators, and quality of the air in the local area, with one indicator, are exclusive causes of public life satisfaction. Three others, the number of reported close friends, the number of life stressors experienced in the last year, and being married, are specified to be exclusive causes of private life satisfaction. This leaves two variables, age and education, as common causes of both kinds of satisfaction. All of the latter five are single-indicator variables. The reader will recognize that this is a model with overidentifying restrictions at the structural level, since there is more than one exclusive instrumental variable for each endogenous variable.[12]

The data used in estimating this model are from a Canadian quality of life survey applied to a national cross-section in 1981. The available sample size for the variables in this model is 2,568. The model will be estimated and fitted both in this larger sample and in a much smaller random subsample of 355.

In this kind of model a number of null models are possible. I estimated four variations of a null model in each sample in order to be able to assess the effect of varying the definition of the null on results. There was a complete null that was modified to allow for covariances among all exogenous measures in the model. This modification takes into account the fact that we are not really interested in these covariances. Three versions of informed null models were used: the first a restrictive informed null that at the measurement level was a parallel measures specification and at the structural level specified no causal effects and only covariances among exogenous variables (covariances among single-indicator variables were fixed to known values), the second a less restrictive informed null that specified tau-equivalent assumptions at the measurement level and the same assumptions at the structural level, and the third a causal-null-only specification that allowed for congeneric measures at the measurement level and specified no causal effects at the structural level while allowing for covariances among exogenous variables and a free covariance between the residuals for the two endogenous variables (as suggested by Sobel and Bohnrstedt, 1984).

The results of fitting the model in both samples are shown in Table 3. The first four rows in each sample show the results for the null models. In both samples, each successive null model leads to a considerable reduction in χ^2, relative to the starting point χ^2 for the complete null. This is especially the case in the larger sample, where the χ^2 starts at 5,388.91 and is only 1,220.96 by the causal-null-only model. Note that Δ_{of} tells us that this represents an increase in fit of .655 in the small sample and .773 in the larger sample. This means that changes in the null model here should have a substantial impact.

In the subsample of 355, the fitting process was fairly simple. The basic causal model (M_h) in Figure 1 was estimated first, and

TABLE 3
Overall Fit of Full Covariance Structure Models for
Reciprocal Effects of Public and Private Life Satisfaction

Model	χ^2	df	Pr	$\dfrac{\chi^2}{df}$	GFI	CN	ρ_{of}	ρ_{hf}	M_{op} ρ^*_{of}	ρ^*_{hf}	M_{ot} ρ^*_{of}	ρ^*_{hf}	M_{oc} ρ^*_{of}	ρ^*_{hf}	Δ_{of}	Δ_{hf}	Δ^*_{of}	Δ^*_{hf}
SAMPLE N: 355:																		
M_o : Complete null	691.29	111	.000	6.23	.764	71												
M_{op} : Restrictive informed null	419.48	108	.000	3.88	.870	113	.448								.393			
M_{ot} : Less restrictive informed null	300.46	102	.000	2.95	.900	150	.628		.325						.565			
M_{oc} : Causal null only	238.51	95	.000	2.51	.920	177	.711		.476		.224				.655		.206	
M_h : Basic causal model	142.10	84	.000	1.69	.950	265	.868		.760		.645		.542		.794		.527	
M_{f1} : + specified marr. effect	102.87	83	.069	1.24	.962	362	.954	.087	.917	.157	.877	.232	.842	.299	.851	.057	.658	.131
M_{f2} : + specified educ. effect	92.45	82	.202	1.13	.966	399	.976	.108	.956	.196	.935	.290	.916	.374	.866	.072	.692	.165
SAMPLE N: 2568:																		
M_o : Complete null	5388.91	111	.000	48.55	.731	66												
M_{op} : Restrictive informed null	2609.91	108	.000	24.17	.878	132	.513								.516			
M_{ot} : Less restrictive informed null	1904.02	102	.000	18.67	.907	171	.628		.237						.647			
M_{oc} : Causal null only	1220.96	95	.000	12.85	.943	250	.751		.488		.329				.773		.359	
M_h : Basic causal model	673.06	84	.000	8.01	.966	406	.853		.697		.603		.408		.875		.647	
M_{f1} : + marr. effect	441.18	83	.000	5.32	.977	612	.909	.057	.814	.116	.756	.153	.636	.228	.918	.043	.768	.122
M_{f2} : + 1 loading, 1 corr. error	305.27	81	.000	3.77	.984	865	.942	.089	.880	.183	.843	.240	.766	.358	.943	.068	.840	.193
M_{f3} : + stress effect	265.34	80	.000	3.32	.986	984	.951	.099	.900	.203	.869	.266	.805	.396	.951	.076	.861	.214
M_{f4} : + 4 corr. errors	195.55	76	.000	2.57	.990	1275	.967	.114	.932	.235	.911	.308	.867	.459	.964	.089	.897	.251

NOTE: See text for description of models.

the first modification led to a model that fit with probability = .069. The extra parameter represents a direct effect of being married on the relationship satisfaction measure of private life satisfaction.[13] A possible interpretation of this parameter is that the underlying latent variable is quite general and the parameter measures a specific substantive effect not captured by this latent variable. Another parameter representing a positive effect of education on satisfaction with finances was included as model M_{f2}. The probability of the model at this point was .202 and no further models were estimated.

The GFI index again is not very helpful in selecting a model. It starts at a value of .764 and reaches .9 for the less restrictive null model. No other measure, not even the χ^2/df ratio, is so kind. Further changes from that point are therefore small and hard to judge. One could not, for example, easily say that model M_{f1} was better than M_h by pointing to the increased GFI of .962 compared to .950.

The CN measure is more useful in this case, however, although also too kind to models that do not fit sufficiently. CN reaches a value of 265 for the basic causal model, which at least means it does not reach this threshold for any of the null models, and increases to 362 for the next model $(Pr(M_{f1}) = .069)$. If we look at the relative change in CN across models, we see it increases by 88 in going from the causal null model to the basic causal model, by 97 in going to model M_{f1} with the marriage effect, and by 37 in going to M_{f2}. This suggests that M_{f1} is more than sufficient in fit terms and still a considerable improvement relative to M_h.

The Bentler and Bonett ρ_{of} and ρ_{hf} perform similarly to the previous example. Note again that ρ_{of} reaches .90 at a model that also begins to fit according to the χ^2 test (M_{f1}). However, ρ_{hf} shows that this model is only a small improvement over M_h (the chosen model h for all comparisons with less restrictive models) relative to the complete null $(\rho_{hf} = .087)$.

The effect of varying the null model is particularly highlighted by the following columns of the table. In each successive column ρ_{of}^* and ρ_{hf}^* are calculated relative to a less restrictive null (the null is designated at the top of each column). While M_{f1} produces an incremental fit value relative to M_h of only .087 when the complete null is used, this value increases to .157, .232, and .299 as the null becomes less restrictive. At the same time, the overall fit of any model measured by ρ_{of}^* decreases, so that the value of .954 for M_{f1} using ρ_{of} becomes .917, .877, and .842 as measured by ρ_{of}^* using increasingly informed baselines for null models.

The same conclusion can be applied here that was suggested by the first example. The Bentler and Bonett index and the Sobel and Bohrnstedt modification seem to function best for different purposes. In this example, we might wonder what null model should be chosen. Given either a primary interest in the structural model and/or a belief that tau-equivalent assumptions are realistically restrictive for these kinds of measures, either M_{ot} or M_{oc} could be used. Both suggest that M_{f1} is an improvement relative to M_h.

Although the normed measures are considerably closer in value to the corresponding ρ and ρ^*, this simply means that they provide little distinguishing information. It is true that Δ and Δ^* suggest the fit of the model could be improved, but χ^2, CN, and ρ all suggest that this is not so.

The fitting process was restarted for the full sample of 2,568. The same marriage effect surfaced as the first parameter to be estimated beyond the basic model (M_{f1}). At this point, the χ^2 still seems to be considerably beyond the realm of the null hypothesis; indeed, the χ^2/df ratio is still 5.32. Model M_{f2} adds two parameters: a loading for satisfaction with finances on the public life satisfaction factor, clearly an interpretable parameter, and a correlated error between two of the political alienation indicators (these parameters were actually added in sequence, as in the case of all models reported here). Model M_{f3} adds a direct effect of stress on satisfaction with finances (negative), and after further modifications we arrive at model M_{f4}, which adds four more correlated errors to model M_{f3} and achieves a χ^2 of 195.55 with 76 df. A great deal of exploratory fitting has transpired by this point; indeed, many would consider the number of extra parameters excessive.

These results show especially that χ^2 and the χ^2/df ratio are very sensitive to sample size. Despite the fact that we began with over 5,000 χ^2 and ended up with under 200 in the final model, this final model is still not acceptable according to the probability. And the χ^2/df ratio never gets below two, although it does easily in smaller samples.

The GFI index varies over a similar range here, reaching .9 again for one of the null models, and then increasing slowly up to

.99 by the final model. These examples both suggest that this measure reaches a relatively high value quite easily, and then changes slowly over a small range across models that range from the quite unacceptable to the clearly acceptable.

The CN measure here reaches a threshold of 200 and a value of 250 for the causal null model. This is unfortunate, since the relationships in this part of the model are anything but weak (to be reported shortly). We would not want to accept the causal null under any circumstances. If the threshold was shifted to 500, we would stop at M_{f1} as before, but CN values in the smaller samples never reached this threshold. It appears, then, based on empirical information only, that the range of CN is affected by N.

At this sample size, we see few differences in results for ρ and Δ. It is to the credit of ρ that it seems to be the least affected by N (as is ρ^*), achieving a value above .9 for the same model as in the smaller subsample. Whether or not M_{f1} is sufficient is not exactly clear from ρ_{of}, since the next model does go up to .942. Perhaps ρ^* can be used to help in choosing M_{f1} or M_{f2}. The incremental fit values for M_{f1} are .116, .153, and .228, depending on the null model, and the corresponding values for M_{f2} are .183, .24, and .358. Each of the increments for M_{f2} is considerably larger. This suggests M_{f2} as the model of choice. Note that this model does contain a set of easily interpretable parameters relative to some of the later models.

One does not need to, nor should, rely solely on fit measures in coming to a final decision. The point of going beyond a minimal point in fitting a model is to see if essential results are affected. There is no point in looking only at fit indices since the difference between results in any two models under consideration may be minimal. Or, on the other hand, if results are different, we can consider the importance and interpretability of parameters in deciding on a model.

Table 4 contains estimates of the causal parameters from three models in the larger sample: the basic causal model M_h, the model of choice M_{f2}, and the "overfitted" model M_{f4}. Comparison of these parameters indeed suggests that there are important differences between estimates in M_h and M_{f2}. For instance, the balance of the reciprocal effects changes considerably. In the basic model, it appears that public life satisfaction has a stronger effect on private life satisfaction than vice versa (their variances are quite

TABLE 4
Changes in Estimates of Causal Parametsrs Across Models

	M_h		M_{f2}		M_{f4}	
	b	β	b	β	b	β
Equation 1: Public life satisfaction:						
Independent variables:						
private life satisfaction	.228	.236	.698	.686	.575	.629
political alienation	−.881	−.329	−.915	−.287	−.868	−.286
clean air	.199	.209	.146	.167	.135	.172
age	.016	.235	.018	.294	.017	.321
education	−.028	−.092	−.004	−.016	.002	.009
Equation 2: Private life satisfaction:						
Independent variables:						
public life satisfaction	.565	.547	.445	.453	.499	.456
close friends	.016	.142	.012	.117	.013	.126
stress	−.134	−.113	−.084	−.082	−.076	−.073
married	.347	.146	.106	.051	.111	.054
age	.000	−.006	−.005	−.078	−.005	−.092
education	.015	.048	−.005	−.020	−.009	−.033

similar), but in M_{f2} this is not the case. If anything, private life satisfaction affects public life satisfaction more strongly. The substantive conclusions we reach would change in this case depending on the model selected. The exclusive effects on both endogenous variables are somewhat weaker in the second model, while age has a stronger positive effect on public life satisfaction and a stronger negative effect on private life satisfaction. The final model, on the other hand, shows few differences of any importance when compared to M_{f2}. Thus these comparisons verify that the selected model does produce different results compared to a model that clearly does not fit as well, and, at the same time, the overfitted model has little effect on the estimates produced by M_{f2}.

DISCUSSION AND CONCLUSIONS

It is more appropriate to recommend a general strategy in fitting a model than the use of particular measures. Caution is in order, since these fit indices may behave quite differently in other applications. On the other hand, narrowing the range of choice of measures of fit is also in order.

It is clear that any fitting strategy must be specific to the sample size involved. While it is impossible to designate hard-and-fast sample size ranges for the application of measures, we can distinguish, based on the Ns used here, between small to moderate samples and clearly large samples. If the sample is in the small to moderate range, and this could include samples in the hundreds and up to a thousand, I advocate, with full awareness of the full circle we have come on this issue, use of the χ^2 test and its associated probability, along with ρ_{of} for a sense of overall fit of any model and ρ_{hf}^* for a sense of the gain in fit of any particular model relative to an informed null stating a minimalist but realistic possibility.

To make use of both ρ and ρ^*, the researcher will want to define two null models: one a complete null, to allow for measurement of all the fitting to be achieved, and the other an informed null, for use of measures of gain in fit relative to previous knowledge. A primary confirmatory model should also be specified for comparison with any exploratory models.

In larger samples, different combinations of fit measures may have to be used. In particular, it is obvious that the χ^2 test became not only difficult but nearly impossible to satisfy in the last example, but ρ_{of} and ρ_{hf}^* were both still useful. Also, the Δ version of these measures was equally, but no more, helpful.

It may be unusual to suggest using one version of ρ for assessing the overall fit and another, ρ^*, for assessing relative gain, but this raises no logical problem as long as it is clear that the two measures are not additive, that they have different baselines, and that they need to be interpreted differently. The Bentler and Bonett ρ_{of} seems remarkably stable across model situations and sample sizes, but at the same time ρ_{hf} rarely reveals much improvement of fit over a basic model that every indicator suggests does not fit. The Sobel and Bohrnstedt ρ_{hf}^* solves this problem by redefining the nature of the baseline to be considered.

There are three components to the fitting strategy I advocate: use of multiple measures, overfitting, and comparison of parameter estimates across a subset of models one is considering. The point of using multiple measures is to search for convergence. In every example, some convergence of measures occurred for a particular model, and convergence will blunt somewhat the effects of the arbitrariness of chosen thresholds.

The purpose of overfitting should not be misunderstood. It should not be used to look mindlessly for desired results. The parameters in an overfit model are less believable than those in earlier models; thus, given a choice, an earlier model should be chosen. As a strategy, however, overfitting simply suggests that it is better to know than not to know what further models look like.

Given a starting point model, a model of choice, and a model fit beyond this point, parameter estimates can be compared across models. The pattern that occurred in the large sample model is an ideal one: Parameter estimates were clearly different in the model of choice compared to the initial model, the extra parameters fit were readily interpretable and not large in number (3), and the difference between this model and a model with five more parameters, some of which were not readily interpretable, was minimal.

Of course, other patterns will occur. Some of these other patterns will result in a more difficult choice. Consider, for example, a case where the parameters in a fitted model are different than an initial model, and the parameters in an overfit model are also different from the fitted model. Because the overfit model is definitely more exploratory, less easily replicable, and vulnerable to Type I error problems, the burden of proof must be on this model.

In the ideal case, we want to avoid both underfit and overfit models, and only report models that contain all of the important and necessary relationships—and no more. Choosing a particular model, finding the middle path, can be a delicate matter. The goal of the approach used in this article is to make it possible for researchers to arrive at the same choice of model across research situations by making this choice as independent as possible of the hypotheses they entertain, differences in sample size, and the weaknesses of particular measures of fit.

NOTES

1. I have restricted the discussion to applications of these measures based on the maximum likelihood fitting function, in part because of the current predominance of this approach to fitting covariance structure models and in part to standardize comparisons across measures. It should be noted that fit indices are being developed for recently developed estimation methods, such as Browne's asymptotically distribution-free (ADF)

generalized least squares estimator (1984). The purpose of this estimator is to achieve maximum likelihood's asymptotic properties with less restrictive distributional assumptions. Tanaka and Huba (1985) have recently suggested a fit measure specifically for the ADF-GLS approach.

2. Of course, the problem of model inertia suggests the importance of not restricting the range under consideration too severely.

3. There are situations where the correlated error specification is appropriate, for example, when the pattern of these errors does not point to an interpretable ρ factor, or when the factors indicated are much more specific in content than the factors already specified.

4. There will be times when it makes sense to allow causation of measures by multiple factors, such as when a measure is imprecise or more general in content than other measures, or when a sociodemographic factor, such as sex, age, or income, exhibits a specific causal effect on one of the indicators of a multiple-indicator latent variable. Johnson and Meile (1981) discuss a case in which such effects can be interpreted as a response tendency, since they can be interpreted as an effect net of the content represented by the latent variable.

5. These problems are not caused by the overfitting per se, and can occur in underfit models as well.

6. Hoelter also discusses a general multisample version of CN, in which case $2\chi^2$ should be divided by N - G, the number of groups, in the denominator, and +1 should be replaced by +G.

7. This is a slightly less general interpretation than the original scheme used by Bentler and Bonett, in which model h could be any intermediate model and f any model that is less restrictive than h.

8. Parallel measures have the same underlying true score or true scores that differ by only a constant and equal error variances. Tau-equivalent measures are one step less restrictive in that they have the same or constant-adjusted true scores but unequal error variances, and congeneric measures require only that the true scores be a perfect linear function of one another, which includes the possibility of a proportional, rather than unit, translation from one to the other.

9. Note that the issue at hand restricts the range of models considered to a one- versus a three-factor specification.

10. I also considered Bollen's (1986) correction of the Bentler and Bonett ρ to achieve independence of N. These results are not included, but they can be described straightforwardly. In small samples, the corrected version never achieved levels of sufficient fit, even in presumably overfit models, and in larger samples, results were essentially the same as for the Bentler and Bonett index.

11. Actually, this was a modified version of parallel measurement that took into account the fact that the first eight items had one response format while the next eight had another response format. Thus equality assumptions held only within these two sets; in each set, factor loadings were set equal (factor variances were fixed to one), and error variances were set equal.

12. The assumptions involved in specifying the model are relatively plausible. We would not expect political alienation to affect private life satisfaction directly except by virtue of its effect on public life satisfaction, for example. And we would not expect stress, or close friends, or being married to affect public life satisfaction directly other than because of their effects first on satisfaction with private life.

13. The fact that this parameter is identified is suggested by the proof given by Johnson and Meile (1981) for an essentially similar case.

9

Some Common Problems in Log-Linear Analysis

CLIFFORD C. CLOGG
SCOTT R. ELIASON

In this article, several problems in log-linear analysis are discussed and strategies for dealing with them are outlined. We assume that readers have been exposed to contingency-table methods as presented in Goodman (1978), Haberman (1978, 1979), Fienberg (1980), Knoke and Burke (1980), or books similar to these. We also assume that readers have analyzed data using procedures for log-linear or logit models. Our goal is to augment the standard sources with some practical solutions to problems often encountered in the analysis of categorical variables.

The following terminology will be used. A cross-classification of discrete variables produces a *contingency table* or simply *cross-table*. The *dimension* of the crosstable, called M below, corresponds to the number of cells in the crosstable. If there are q variables, the table is said to be "q-way." For example, a 3-way crosstable with variables A, B, and C produces *observed frequencies* f_{ijk}, $i = 1, \ldots, I$; $j = 1, \ldots, J$; $k = 1, \ldots, K$, where I, J, and K refer to the number of *levels* or categories of variables A, B, and C, respectively. The number of cells in the table (the dimension) is

AUTHORS' NOTE: *The research in this article was supported in part by grants SES-8303838 and SES-8421179 from the National Science Foundation. We are indebted to Rebecca Burt for assistance with some of the calculations and to Richard Alba, Leo A. Goodman, J. Scott Long, Michael P. Massagli, and an anonymous reviewer for helpful comments.*

226

$M = IJK$. Corresponding to the observed frequencies are *expected frequencies* F_{ijk}. The F_{ijk} are expected values of f_{ijk} *under some model or hypothesis*, $F_{ijk} = E_H\{f_{ijk}\}$, where the expectation refers to the model (H) assumed for the data. We reserve the term $\hat{F}_{ijk}$ for the *maximum likelihood estimates* of the F_{ijk}. The expected frequencies F_{ijk} can be arranged into a vector $\mathbf{F}$ of length M. Let $\nu_{ijk} = \log(F_{ijk})$ denote the corresponding *log-expected frequency*; the vector (of length M) collecting all of these is ν.

The log-linear model decomposes the ν_{ijk} into additive components that reflect the *interactions* of various orders. For example, the model of no 3-factor interaction initially considered in Bartlett (1935) and Birch (1963),

$$\nu_{ijk} = \lambda + \lambda_i^A + \lambda_j^B + \lambda_k^C + \lambda_{ij}^{AB} + \lambda_{ik}^{AC} + \lambda_{jk}^{BC}, \qquad [1]$$

has 1-factor and 2-factor terms but the 3-factor term (λ_{ijk}^{ABC}) is excluded. This model says that the association between any two of the variables does not depend on the levels of the third variable. After deleting redundant parameter values—values that can be retrieved from knowledge of the other parameter values—the model in equation 1 or any log-linear model can be represented as

$$\nu = \mathbf{X}\,\lambda, \qquad [2]$$

where ν is of order M, the *model matrix* or design matrix $\mathbf{X}$ is of order $M \times p$, and λ is of order p; p is the number of nonredundant parameters included in the model.

In regular situations, the *degrees of freedom* for the model will be computed as $DF = M - p$. The primary use of the concept of degrees of freedom arises in *chi-squared tests* for goodness-of-fit. The *Pearson statistic* will be denoted X^2 (H) and the *likelihood-ratio statistic* will be denoted $L^2(H)$. These should be thought of as functions of the model under consideration. When model H is true in the population, sample values of X^2 (H) and L^2 (H) will follow the chi-squared distribution with DF degrees of freedom when the samples are large. Goodness-of-fit statistics play a prominent role in log-linear analysis of contingency tables. It is important to note that goodness-of-fit is assessed in terms of the actual data (i.e., the cell frequencies in the contingency table) rather than statistics calculated from the data (e.g., means, correlations, and variances). Of course, we need to have the correct value of DF in order to make proper use of the fit statistics.

DEGREES OF FREEDOM

THE PROBLEM

In the situations covered for the most part in standard references, the degrees of freedom for a model are obtained from the formula,

$$DF = M - p, \qquad [3]$$

where M is the number of cells in the crosstable and p is the number of nonredundant parameter values. There are two major complications that can arise in using formula 3. First, there can be *structural zeroes* or *blanked-out cells* that are not an explicit part of the model. For example, the model in equation 1 could be defined for all cells in a $4 \times 4 \times 4$ table except cells (1, 1, 1) and (4, 4, 4), which would be ignored. Such models are called *quasi-log-linear models*. Second, there can be *fitted zeroes*, cells with estimated expected frequencies of zero. Either condition reduces the effective dimension of the crosstable in an obvious way. What is not so obvious is how many parameters are actually needed to represent the model for the crosstable of reduced dimension.

Table 1 gives some examples that can be used to diagnose computer programs used for log-linear analysis. Table 1a has a total of 12 structural zeroes that would be "blanked out" through the use of a "start table" in computer programs using the iterative-proportional-fitting (IPF) algorithm. If we tested the independence model for the 5×5 crosstable without taking account of the structural zeroes, the model would have $4 \times 4 = 16$ degrees of freedom. It seems natural to subtract the number of cells that are blanked out from this total to find the degrees of freedom for the quasi-independence model; this gives $16 - 12 = 4$, which is incorrect. The model of quasi-independence in this case implies row-column independence in the 2×2 subtable in the upper left and row-column independence in the 3×3 subtable in the lower right. The two subtables are said to be *separable* (they share no rows or columns), so the overall model can be partitioned into two separate models. The correct number of degrees of freedom is $1 + 4 = 5$. Many of the IPF-based programs give the wrong answer (DF = 4) for this elementary case. It is interesting to note that examples involving separable subtables were used in the early work on quasi-independence (Goodman, 1968; Clogg, 1986).

Tables 1b and 1c can also be used to diagnose programs. The zeroes in these tables should be regarded as *sampling zeroes*. Imagine that with repeated sampling at least some of the samples would have positive frequencies in these cells. Table 1b has two sampling zeroes situated in such a way that guarantees that the model of no 3-factor interaction will have fitted zeroes for the corresponding cells (i.e., $f_{111} = f_{222} = 0$ implies $\hat{F}_{111} = \hat{F}_{222} = 0$). The model of no 3-factor interaction has one degree of freedom for a $2 \times 2 \times 2$ table when all fitted values are positive. When there are fitted zeroes it will have zero degrees of freedom and actually correspond to a *saturated model* (with $L^2 = X^2 = 0$). Most programs give the incorrect degrees of freedom for this model, some have difficulty calculating the correct estimates of expected frequencies, and practically none provide useful diagnostic messages.

Table 1c has two sampling zeroes that produce a zero marginal total ($f_{111} = f_{112} = f_{11+} = 0$). If we fit the model of no 3-factor interaction, the model is again saturated with zero degrees of freedom. Many programs give incorrect answers for this case. (This situation is slightly different from that of Table 1b; here the value of a "fitted marginal" or sufficient statistic is zero.)

The simple examples in Table 1 cause problems in using many software packages for log-linear analysis. For such simple cases, correct rules for calculating degrees of freedom for chi-squared statistics can be found in sources such as Bishop et al. (1975), Goodman (1968, 1984), or Haberman (1979). The problem is that these formulas cannot be easily applied to more complex situations, such as crosstables of high dimension involving many variables or models other than independence models.

THE SOLUTION

First we obtain the model matrix **X** for the full crosstable, including the structurally empty cells, the blanked-out cells, and

TABLE 1
Three Crosstables for Diagnosing Computer Programs
Used for Log-Linear Analysis

a.   A 5 x 5 Table with Structural Zeroes[a]

		Variable B				
		1	2	3	4	5
	1	X	X	0	0	0
	2	X	X	0	0	0
Variable A	3	0	0	X	X	X
	4	0	0	X	X	X
	5	0	0	X	X.	X

b.   A 2 x 2 x 2 Table with Sampling Zeroes[b]

A	B	C = 1	C = 2
1	1	0	X
1	2	X	X
2	1	X	X
2	2	X	0

c.   A 2 x 2 x 2 Table with a Zero Marginal[b]

A	B	C = 1	C = 2
1	1	0	0
1	2	X	X
2	1	X	X
2	2	X	X

a. "0" refers to structural zero or blanked-out cells, "X" to a positve frequency.
b. "0" refers to a sampling zero, "X" to a positive frequency.

cells with zero fitted values. Second, create the working model matrix $\mathbf{X}^*$ formed by deleting rows that correspond to structural zeroes, blanked-out cells, or fitted zeroes. Let the number of cells with *positive fitted values* be denoted as M^*. Note that the matrix $\mathbf{X}^*$ has M^* rows and p columns. The problem is to calculate the "column rank" of $\mathbf{X}^*$ or, equivalently, the rank of the matrix $\mathbf{X}^{*T}\mathbf{X}^*$, which is a square, symmetric matrix. Let p^* denote the column rank of $\mathbf{X}^*$, which is the same as the rank of $\mathbf{X}^{*T}\mathbf{X}^*$; p^* is the number of nonredundant (linearly independent) parameter values in the model. The degrees of freedom for the model implied by $\mathbf{X}^*$ is

$$DF = M^* - p^*,\qquad\qquad [4]$$

that should be thought of as the difference between the *effective* dimension of the crosstable and the *actual* number of independent parameters estimated.

Programs that are based on IPF algorithms seldom calculate the model matrix explicitly and are thus particularly prone to erroneous calculation of degrees of freedom. (Indeed, some IPF-based programs do not report degrees of freedom when there are zero fitted values or structurally empty cells.) With iterative weighted least squares (or Newton-Raphson, NR hereafter) algorithms, on the other hand, the matrix X^* is checked and updated if necessary from cycle to cycle. Unfortunately, some NR programs use automatic "fixups" for sampling zeroes, such as replacing them with .01 or some function of sample size. Such a "fixup" has disastrous consequences for degrees of freedom, since it effectively rules out the possibility of having fitted zeroes. To check these programs, it is recommended that sampling zeroes be replaced by $.1 \times 10^{-8}$, or even a smaller number, and then results should be checked against those obtained without such an adjustment. (If results differ, with respect to reported DF or other quantities, researchers interested in using strict maximum-likelihood methods should override the "fixup" implicit in the program by replacing sampling zeroes with a very small number.)

We illustrate the calculations for the first crosstable in Table 1 under the model of *quasi-independence*. This model says that $\nu_{ij} = \lambda + \lambda_i^A + \lambda_j^B$ for cells that are not structurally empty. In total, 12 of the 25 cells in the 5×5 crosstable are structurally empty. Deleting the corresponding rows of the model matrix produces the matrix X^* displayed in Table 2. This matrix has 13 rows, corresponding to the number of nonempty cells, and 9 columns, corresponding to the nonredundant λ values ordinarily included in the independence model for a 5×5 table. The DF for the model is $13 - p^*$ where p^* is the column rank of X^*. Using any standard matrix routine (we used LIMDEP), one can verify that $p^* = 8$ (not 9); equivalently, the rank of $X^{*T}X^*$ is 8. Hence DF $= 13 - 8 = 5$, which is the correct answer.

The above procedure should be used for cases where it is not so easy to inspect the data to determine the correct DF, which is almost always the case for crosstables with many variables and/or for models different from the independence model. Note that the values of frequencies in the nonempty cells are irrelevant

TABLE 2

**The Effective Model Matrix for the Quasi-Independence
Model Applied to Data in the Form of Crosstable 1a**

Row (cell)		λ	λ_1^A	λ_2^A	λ_3^A	λ_4^A	λ_1^B	λ_2^B	λ_3^B	λ_4^B
					Column (parameter value)					
1	(1, 1)	1	1	0	0	0	1	0	0	0
2	(1, 2)	1	1	0	0	0	0	1	0	0
3	(2, 1)	1	0	1	0	0	1	0	0	0
4	(2, 2)	1	0	1	0	0	0	1	0	0
5	(3, 3)	1	0	0	1	0	0	0	1	0
6	(3, 4)	1	0	0	1	0	0	0	0	1
7	(3, 5)	1	0	0	1	0	−1	−1	−1	−1
8	(4, 3)	1	0	0	0	1	0	0	1	0
9	(4, 4)	1	0	0	0	1	0	0	0	1
10	(4, 5)	1	0	0	0	1	−1	−1	−1	−1
11	(5, 3)	1	−1	−1	−1	−1	0	0	1	0
12	(5, 4)	1	−1	−1	−1	−1	0	0	0	1
13	(5, 5)	1	−1	−1	−1	−1	−1	−1	−1	−1

NOTES: Rows correspond to nonempty cells in Table 1a. Columns pertain to parameters included in the model without taking account of possible identifiability problems. The column rank of this matrix is eight (= rank of $X^{*T}X$), so there are only eight nonredundant parameter values (instead of nine). DF = 13 − 8 = 5.

for the calculations. Also note that fitted zeroes are dealt with in exactly the same way.

SPARSE DATA

THE PROBLEM

When the sample size (n) is not large relative to the dimension (M), observed frequencies tend to be sparsely distributed throughout the crosstable. Sampling zeroes become frequent; and small, nonzero frequencies (1s, 2s, 3s) arise. Table 3 is an example of sparse data in a $3 \times 3 \times 2 \times 2$ contingency table: there are n = 154 observations spread across M = 36 cells, including 28 counts less than or equal to 5 and seven sampling zeroes (producing a zero "group total" in one instance). Practically all of the statistical theory on which log-linear analysis rests is asymptotic (or large sample) theory; exact theory for contingency table models is not well developed at the present time. What should be done with data such as that in Table 3? We have already dealt with one problem that can arise in modeling sparse data: calculation of

TABLE 3
Survival of Breast Cancer Patients by Diagnostic Center,
Age, and a Histologic Criterion
(patients with "greater inflammation")

| Center (C) | Age (A) | Malignant Appearance | Three-Year Survival (S) | | Total |
			No	Yes	
Tokyo	< 50	Yes	4	25	29
	50-69	No	3	9	12
	50-69	Yes	11	18	29
		No	2	5	7
	> 70	Yes	1	5	6
		No	0	1	1
Boston	< 50	Yes	6	4	10
		No	0	0	0*
	50-69	Yes	3	10	13
		No	2	3	5
	> 70	Yes	3	1	4
		No	0	1	1
Glamorgan	< 50	Yes	3	8	11
		No	0	1	1
	50-69	Yes	3	10	13
		No	0	4	4
	> 70	Yes	3	4	7
		No	0	1	1
		Total	44	110	154

SOURCE: Fienberg (1980: 117). Cases with "minimal inflammation" omitted. The asterisk (*) denotes a zero "group total" in the logit model.

degrees of freedom for models that have fitted zeroes. (Fitted zeroes become more likely as the number of sampling zeroes increase, depending on the model being considered.) The other main problems associated with sparse data are as follows.

First, the goodness-of-fit statistics may not possess the desired null distributions, even after using the theoretically "correct" number of degrees of freedom. Thus the ability actually to test a model is jeopardized.

Second, sparse data often create *existence problems*. This means that estimates of the λ parameters originally postulated for the model cannot be calculated because one or more of them take on the value of plus or minus infinity. An equivalent description is that estimated expected frequencies take on the *boundary value* of zero; this is the problem of fitted zeroes alluded to in the previous section. Numerical stability is a problem in either IPF or NR algorithms when data are sparse. Smart programs will detect the nonexistence and effectively delete columns of the model matrix or recalculate only a subset of the λ's originally posited. The problem is that the model matrix obtained from the numerical procedure might be quite different from the one originally entertained for the data; that is, the λ parameters actually calculated can be quite different from the set requested. The parameters calculated in such instances are an arbitrary set and have to be interpreted differently than if there had been no numerical problems.

Third, inferences about parameter estimates are jeopardized. The key result justifying statistical inferences is that $(\hat{\lambda} - \lambda)/s(\hat{\lambda})$ follows a standard unit normal distribution for any particular λ value, *in large samples*. (This statement does not apply for the constant term or for other terms required to fit marginals fixed by sampling design. Essentially, for λ values other than these the statistics $z = \hat{\lambda}/s(\hat{\lambda})$ can be used to test the null hypothesis that $\lambda = 0$.) With sparse data the sampling distribution of $\hat{\lambda}$ might be far from normal, and because of this conventional inferential procedures based on standardized parameter estimates can be misleading.

SOME SOLUTIONS—GOODNESS-OF-FIT

Goodman (1978, 1984) always presents both the Pearson and the likelihood-ratio statistics for the models he considers. Although both statistics have the same distribution when the model is true and the sample size is large, they have different distributions when the sample size is small—or when the data are sparsely distributed among the cells in the crosstable. When the two statistics lead to different conclusions, the sample is simply not large enough to make a decision about the model. (Examples where the two statistics lead to different conclusions appear in Goodman, 1978.) When the two statistics lead to the same conclusion (either to reject a model or to accept it), we have some assurance that the sample size may be adequate for the given model. Inspecting both X^2 and L^2 values, or even other chi-square statistics related to these (Cressie and Read, 1984) is thus sensible whenever sparse data are encountered.

There is much recent research on adjusting chi-squared statistics applied to sparse data; see McCullagh (1985), Cressie and Read (1984), Koehler (1986), and Zelterman (1987) for various practical alternatives. But there is a sense in which goodness-of-fit is the wrong question to ask when sparse data are analyzed. It is simply unreasonable to expect to be able to test a model where there are many degrees of freedom relative to the sample size. For example, suppose that one had a contingency table with M = 200 cells, a sample size of 100, and a model H with DF = 100. This means that the model H tests 100 restrictions simultaneously, with an average of one observation per restriction. A test based on exact theory could not have much power in such a situation. In other words, when the data are so sparse that conventional goodness-of-fit tests are questionable, the data are also so sparse that even an exact test would be nearly useless.

SOME SOLUTIONS: PARAMETER ESTIMATION AND INFERENCE

Existence problems created by sparse data were partly responsible for the development of the log-linear model. We illustrate with the data in Table 3. Most analysts would view these data in an asymmetric way, with survivorship (S) playing the role of a specified dependent variable and the other variables C, A, and M playing the role of specified independent variables. Various *logit models* would normally be considered for these data. These models all have the property that $\hat{F}_{ijk+} = f_{ijk+}$. Logit models fit the marginal distribution of the set of predictors taken as a joint variable, in this case the 3-way marginal CAM. Sometimes this marginal table is referred to as the set of group totals. We see from Table 3 that one group total (C = 2, A = 1, M = 2) is zero. For some logit models that might be considered, this zero group total will create existence problems. We can remedy the problem by considering log-linear models that do not fit the CAM marginal.

First consider model H_1, which fits all two-way marginals, or, equivalently, the model where only 1-factor and 2-factor λ terms are used to model the ν_{ijke}. We are interested in only the λ terms that involve the dependent variable S. The other λ terms are included only to place restrictions on the $\hat{F}_{ijk+}$. Model H_1 fits the data well with $L^2(H_1) = 22.23$ on 16 DF, but with such sparse data we should not pay too much attention to overall fit. The goal should be to analyze whether variable C, A, and/or M have effects on S. Model H_1 is the model that includes all main effects. If the constraints used to obtain H_1 from the corresponding logit model are true, the parameter values under H_1 will be asymptotically unbiased estimates of the corresponding parameter values in the logit model.

The implication is that we can overcome existence problems in many cases by applying restrictions of various kinds, such as modifying logit models to produce various models that do not actually fit the observed group totals. Carrying this further produces model H_2, the model obtained from H_1 by noting that the categories of age are equally spaced (approximately) and restricting interactions with age to follow a linear trend. For example, the estimated values of λ_{ij}^{SA}, j = 1, 2, 3, are -.092, -.016, and .108 (= .092 + .016), which suggests approximate linearity of the S-A association over levels of A. Applying all such restrictions leads to an increase in 4 degrees of freedom and only a negligible increase in chi-squared values. As Table 4 shows, the parameter values are essentially the same.

The logit model with main effects of the factors (linear effect for age) is model H_3. There are 18 possible response patterns and 5 estimated parameters, which appears to give DF = 18 - 5 = 13. In fact, some programs will give DF = 13 for this model. However, there is one zero group total so the correct number of degrees of freedom is DF = 17 - 5 = 12. The estimated model is actually the same whether the offending response pattern has structural or sampling zeroes. Notice how close the parameter values of this logit model are to the parameter values of the previous two models. Inferences about the relationships in the data can be based on the estimated interactions for H_1, H_2, or H_3. As mentioned earlier, however, the sparseness of the data should lead us to consider the robustness of the inferences so obtained.

Rubin and Schenker (1987) consider the role of adding constants to cell frequencies, and Clogg et al. (1986) consider generalizations for logistic regression. Adding constants to cell counts has a long history in both frequentist and Bayesian theories of

TABLE 4
Chi-Squared Values and Parameter Estimates
for Some Models Applied to the Data in Table 3

| | Model | | | | |
	H_1	H_2	H_3	H_4	H_4^*
DF	16	20	12	13	13
L^2	22.23	23.31	14.90	10.49	13.12
X^2	19.01	19.71	12.91	10.10	12.10
Parameter Estimates:					
λ_1^S	−.466	−.472	−.472	−.375	−.470 (.122)
λ_{11}^{SC}	−.101	−.101	−.101	−.117	−.100 (.121)
λ_{12}^{SC}	.265	.264	.264	.235	.254 (.138)
λ_{11}^{SA} $[\lambda_{1L}^{SA}]$	−.092	.094*	.096*	.100*	.092* (.132)
λ_{12}^{SA}	−.016	—	—	—	—
λ_{11}^{SM}	.105	.106	.107	.044	.102 (.115)

NOTE: Only parameter estimates involving the specified dependent variable (S) are reported; standard errors in parentheses for H_4^*; for models H_2 through H_4^*, the interaction between S and A (survivorship and age) is restricted to linear-by-linear form.

inference. Two methods will be illustrated.

A common recommendation in computer manuals, as well as in some standard references, is to add one-half to each cell when analyzing sparse data. Goodman (1978) recommends such a practice, however, *only* when estimating the saturated model, not for unsaturated models. Nevertheless, many analysts add one-half to each cell when analyzing unsaturated models applied to sparse data. This practice is misleading in many ways, some of which can be illustrated with our example. Model H_4 is model H_3 with .5 added to each cell prior to the estimation. The constant term is estimated poorly under H_4, as is the interaction between S and M. A perverse result of adding .5 to each cell is that the "sample size" has been increased by 18 (154 to 172), a 12% increase.

A different approach taken from Clogg et al. (1986) is to shrink the data toward the marginal distribution of the dependent variable adding only p observations (p is here the number of parameters to be estimated disregarding λ parameters included to fit group totals). The conventional approach (add one-half to all cells) shrinks the data toward equiprobability and adds $M/2$ observations regardless of which model is estimated. From Table 3 we find that the marginal distribution of S is $(.2857, .7143)$. The logit model of interest has $p = 5$ parameters so 5 observations must be distributed across 18 response patterns (36 cells). For cells with $S = 1$, the flattening constant is $c_1 = .2857 \times (5/18) = .0794$; for cells with $S = 2$, the constant is $c_2 = .7143 \times (5/18) = .1984$. The result is called model H_4^* in Table 4. Note that the estimated parameter values are very close to those for the logit model H_3 and also close to those for the log-linear model H_2. They are quite different from the parameter values of H_4 where .5 was added to all cells. Note that each interaction parameter has been shrunk slightly toward zero. One advantage of shrinking the data in this fashion is that the ratios $\lambda/s(\lambda)$ are much more likely to follow the normal distribution. The coefficients and standard errors reported for H_4^* are better for inferential purposes than those for the other logit models. When logit models are considered for sparse data, adding constants in proportion to the marginal distribution of the dependent variable, and to an extent that varies directly with the number of parameters to be estimated (rather than the dimension of the table), is a route that can always be followed with little extra effort. For further details, see Clogg et al. (1986).

WEIGHTED DATA

Many data sets analyzed in the social sciences are *weighted* on a case by case basis. Stratified sampling ordinarily results in a disproportionate sampling of specific groups selected as strata; to obtain unbiased inferences about the population, weights that reflect the sampling proportions must be used. Often social surveys, especially panel surveys, are reweighted to reflect attrition from the sample, missing data, or nonrepresentativeness of other kinds. This is done by matching distributions in the sample with distributions assumed to be more representative of the population. It is common for data sets to have weighting systems that reflect both stratified sampling and post hoc reweighting to achieve certain goals. The Current Population Survey, for example, stratifies by states (fixes the total to be sampled within each state) and adjusts the data to match age distributions derived from census enumerations. Most such data sets have a "case-weight" variable that inflates or deflates observations to reflect built-in features of the sample. Procedures for analyzing linear models in software packages often include a "weight" option.

THE PROBLEM

Most social researchers, to our knowledge, use one of the two following strategies when analyzing weighted data: (1) analyze the unweighted data, or unweighted frequencies, by simply ignoring the weighting feature altogether, or (2) analyze weighted frequencies *as if* they were obtained from a data set without any weighting features. Both strategies are incorrect. Using the unweighted counts can lead to incorrect inferences, particularly when one or more of the variables studied is related to the stratifying variables. Parameter estimates can be biased, fit statistics can be misleading, and standard errors can be incorrect. When simple stratification is the only complication, including the "stratifying variable" as one of the dimensions of the contingency table solves the problem. This is the case because the standard methods for analyzing log-linear models apply with almost no modification when "product-multinominal" sampling designs are considered. These designs merely require that margins of stratifying variables be fitted by the models used for making inferences about population relationships. (When predictor variables are stratifiers, there are no special problems at all; when specified dependent variables are stratifiers, as in retrospective case-control studies or in "choice-based" sampling, the main complication is that the one-factor λ for the dependent variable requires adjustment. See Fienberg [1980: 135-137] for discussion and references.) However, when many strata are considered it is not feasible to include the stratifying variable in the contingency table. When case weights that reflect post hoc adjustments are present, the solution of adding a variable to the contingency table is simply not an option.

Perhaps the most common way of dealing with weighted data is to analyze weighted frequencies. Consider the $I \times J$ contingency table for a sample of size n and let (i, j) represent a typical cell. Let $\delta_{ij(h)} = 1$ if the h-th observation falls in cell (i, j), and $\delta_{ij(h)} = 0$ otherwise. The unweighted frequency in cell (i, j) is obtained as $f_{ij} = \Sigma_h \delta_{ij(h)}$. Let w_h denote the weight assigned to the h-th case on the basis of stratification, post hoc reweighting, and so on. The weighted frequency in cell (i, j) is obtained from the formula:

$$f_{ij}^w = \sum_{h=1}^{n} \delta_{ij(h)} \, w_h. \qquad [5]$$

The conventional approach is to rescale the weights so that $\Sigma_h w_h = n$ (to "preserve" the sample size) and then analyze the weighted frequencies as if they were obtained from a sample without weighting features.

Using the weighted and the unweighted counts, we can define the *average cell weight* as

$$w_{ij} = f_{ij}^w / f_{ij}, \qquad [6]$$

so that w_h in equation 5 could be replaced by w_{ij}. The weighted frequencies can be written as $f_{ij}^w = f_{ij} w_{ij}$. Some interesting cases include: (a) the w_{ij} are constant ($= w$, say)—weighted and unweighted frequencies are equivalent; (b) $w_{ij} = w_{i.}$ (or $w_{ij} = w_{.j}$)—weights depend on only the row variable (or column variable), which is equivalent to stratified sampling where the stratifying variable is used in the crosstable; (c) $w_{ij} = w_{i.}w_{.j}$—weights depend on both rows and columns; (d) w_{ij} cannot be expressed in terms of row and/or column factors used in the contingency table. Case a is trivial: The unweighted counts suffice. For case b the unweighted counts can be used if the row (or column) marginal distribution is fitted. For case c the unweighted counts can be used if both rows and columns are fitted. For case d, however, which will be applicable except in cases of simple stratification where the stratifier is included in the crosstable, unweighted and weighted frequencies will differ. If the weighted frequencies are analyzed as if they were obtained from a sample without weighting, estimates of the parameters will be unbiased, but estimates of the standard errors will be biased; interval estimates, hypothesis tests, and fit statistics will also be biased. These remarks generalize in straightforward ways to multidimensional crosstables.

A GENERAL SOLUTION

Analyzing unweighted data can lead to bias; analyzing the weighted data (as is conventional) removes the bias but can produce the wrong impression about sampling variability. To see the latter point, note that the f_{ij} are the *sampled frequencies*, not the weighted frequencies f_{ij}^w. In a 2×2 table, for example, we might be interested in the logarithm of the odds ratio $(= 4 \lambda_{11}^{AB})$. If the cell weights w_{ij} cannot be factored into row- and/or column-specific factors, the weights have to be taken into account somehow. The correct estimate of the log-odds-ratio is

$$\log(f_{11}w_{11}f_{22}w_{22}/f_{12}w_{12}f_{21}w_{21}) = \log(f_{11}^w f_{22}^w / f_{12}^w f_{21}^w),$$

but it would be incorrect to use the ordinary estimate of variance,

$$\hat{V}(.) = \sum_{i,j} (f_{ij}^w)^{-1},$$

to assess the precision of the estimated log-odds-ratio.

A procedure that conditions on the observed values of the cell weights produces both unbiased estimation of parameters and consistent estimation of variability. Let cell u in a crosstable with M cells in all have average cell weight w_u (see equation 6). Let $z_u = 1/w_u$. The weighted log-linear model of interest is

$$\{\log(F_u/z_u)\} = X\lambda, \qquad [7]$$

where the term on the left is understood as a vector of log-weighted frequencies. Note that F_u is the expected value of f_u, the *unweighted* frequency in cell u, and that F_u/z_u is merely $F_u w_u = F_u^w$, the weighted frequency. Estimates of λ parameters will be identical to the case where weighted counts were used; but $V(\hat{\lambda})$ will be assessed in an appropriate way by conditioning on the average cell weights. In programs based on Newton-Raphson calculations, such as the LOGLINEAR program in SPSS^x, the z_u values would be entered as "cell weights." In programs based on the IPF algorithm, the z_u values correspond to the "start table." In other programs, the z_u might be called "exposures." In GLIM they would be used as "offsets." But all program can deal with the weighted model in equation 7 although the documentation for them might not make this obvious.

An example will illustrate the application of the weighted log-linear model. Table 5 gives a cross-classification of sex, color (white, black, other), and labor force category (unemployed,

TABLE 5
Cross-Classification of Labor Force
(unemployed, part-time unemployed, other)
by Color and Sex: Weighted and Unweighted Counts

Sex (S)	Color (C)	Labor Force Category (L)		
		Unemployed	Part-time	Other
Male:				
	white	3511	4227	31467
		3530	4183	31131
		[1431]	[1408]	[1408]
	black	604	356	2245
		815	462	2783
		[1921]	[1849]	[1764]
	other	165	157	924
		119	124	797
		[1029]	[1124]	[1228]
Female:				
	white	2281	7833	18945
		2234	7559	18704
		[1394]	[1373]	[1405]
	black	545	563	2132
		653	644	2498
		[1705]	[1627]	[1668]
	other	89	216	725
		64	162	574
		[1029]	[1070]	[1127]

NOTE: First entry is unweighted count, second entry is weighted count, third entry is average weight for observations in cell. Total unweighted n = 76,985; total of weighted counts = 77,036. The two totals do not agree because of accumulated effects of round-off.

part-time, other) for the March 1982 civilian labor force. The unweighted frequencies (f_{ijk}), the weighted frequencies (f_{ijk}^w), and average cell weights (w_{ijk}) are given. (These cell weights differ from those obtained from equation 6 only by a constant of proportionality.) It is difficult to know whether the weights affect inferences without analyzing the w_{ijk}. We can let $z_{ijk} = w_{ijk}^{-1}$ and analyze the weighted model to obtain correct inferences regardless of the patterns in the w_{ijk}. Note that the weights depend on states, on age, and other factors not included as variables in the crosstable.

The model of no 3-factor interaction was considered for this crosstable for illustrative purposes. Some results for the unweighted data, for the weighted data (analyzed with an unweighted

TABLE 6
Chi-Squared Values and Some Parameter Estimates for Model of No Three-Factor Interaction Applied to Data in Table 5

Statistic	1 Unweighted Data	2 Weighted Data	3 Observed Frequencies and Cell Weights	
L^2	86.54	100.27	89.46	
X^2	89.80	104.05	93.39	
Standardized values, $\hat{\lambda}/s(\hat{\lambda})$				$\hat{\lambda}$ values from columns 2 and 3
λ_1^L	−38.6	−35.2	−39.2	−.69
λ_2^L	−26.2	−24.2	−25.8	−.44
λ_1^S	−2.0	1.4	1.4	.01
λ_1^C	162.3	149.0	163.0	1.86
λ_2^C	−25.7	−9.1	−9.6	−.14
λ_{11}^{LS}	18.5	19.0	19.0	.17
λ_{21}^{LS}	−46.8	−46.0	−47.3	−.34
λ_{11}^{LC}	−15.4	−13.0	−14.4	−.26
λ_{12}^{LC}	15.4	16.8	17.5	.39
λ_{21}^{LC}	11.3	10.1	11.2	.19
λ_{22}^{LC}	−10.5	−10.5	−10.9	−.24
λ_{11}^{SC}	9.2	6.4	6.7	.06
λ_{12}^{SC}	−8.7	−7.4	−7.6	−.08

model), and for the weighted log-linear model appear in Table 6. Parameter estimates for the last two methods agree to within .01. (Round off in producing the weighted frequencies accounts for slight discrepancies.) These differ from results obtained from the unweighted data. The main differences are with fit statistics (the correct value of $L^2(H)$ is 89.5, whereas the value obtained from the weighted data is 100.3) and standard errors, the latter of which can be assessed by considering the standardized values $\lambda / s(\lambda)$ given for all nonredundant λ values in the model. If we had analyzed cross-classifications with variables more closely associated with the weights, more substantial differences would have been observed. Conversely, if we had analyzed cross-classifications with variables that are practically independent of the weights, then there would be no discrepancies among the three schemes of analysis.

LOG-LINEAR MODELS FOR RATES

THE PROBLEM

Many researchers have failed to appreciate the relationship between *rates* and *odds* and hence between models for rates and models for odds. Unfortunately, few of the standard references on log-linear analysis tie the two together; Allison (1984), Fleiss (1981), and Laird and Olivier (1981) are important exceptions. There is a very close connection between analysis of rates and conventional log-linear analysis. One way to understand this connection is to consider the relationship between the binomial and Poisson distributions.

Let π denote the probability of "success" on each of n independent trials, $1 - \pi$ the probability of "failure," so that $n\pi$ is the expected number of successes. (A 2×1 table has expected frequencies $F_1 = n\pi$ for success and $F_2 = n(1 - \pi)$ for failure.) The sampling distribution of the number of successes follows the binomial distribution (see, e.g., Hays, 1981). Standard theory of *exponential families* tells us that $\phi = \log[\pi / (1 - \pi)]$, the log-odds of success, is the natural parameter for the binomial distribution, not the proportion or rate π (see, e.g., Andersen, 1980). When n is large, with $n\pi$ small relative to n, the distribution of the observed number of successes can be approximated by a Poisson distribution (Feller, 1968). The exponential-family property of the Poisson distribution tells us that the log-rate, in this case $\log(\pi)$, is the natural parameter to characterize the distribution. These facts are closely related to the fact that the *odds* $\omega = \pi / (1 - \pi)$ is approximately equal to π (the rate) when π is small, or that the logit $\phi =$

$\log(\omega)$ is approximately equal to $\log(\pi)$ when π is small. How small does π have to be? Rates and odds are virtually indistinguishable for rates in the range $[0, .10]$; for $\pi = .10$ we get $\omega = .11$, while for $\pi = .15$ we get $\omega = .18$, a rather large discrepancy.

To summarize, odds and rates are approximately equal when the Poisson approximation to the binomial can be used, that is, whenever rare events are considered. When analyzing rare events, logit models for a dichotomous dependent variable will be virtually identical to log-linear models for rates. How can we analyze log-linear models for rates in a direct way, for rare or not-so-rare events, without using a logit or logit-model approximation?

THE SOLUTION

Any conventional program for log-linear analysis can be used to analyze *log-rate models* in essentially the same way that logit models are analyzed. The procedure will be illustrated with a contingency table setup such as that typically used to motivate the ordinary logit model.

Let F_{ijk} denote the expected frequency in cell (i, j, k) of an $I \times J \times 2$ crosstable, where the third variable (which is dichotomous) is viewed as a dependent variable. The *log-frequency* model of no 3-factor interaction in equation 1 is equivalent to the logit model,

$$\Omega_{ij}^{ABC} = \log(F_{ij1}/F_{ij2}) = 2\lambda_1^C + 2\lambda_{i1}^{AC} + 2\lambda_{j1}^{BC} \qquad [8]$$

$$= \beta^{\bar{C}} + \beta_i^{A\bar{C}} + \beta_j^{B\bar{C}},$$

which is a model with additive effects of the factors on the log-odds of success (see Goodman [1978] or Knoke and Burke [1980] for details). A characteristic of the logit model is that it fits the "group totals" f_{ij+}, the marginal distribution of the joint variable composed of all predictors. This means that $f_{ij+} = \hat{F}_{ij+}$ for all i and j. The logit model is usually viewed as a model for a set of IJ binomial distributions with fixed "sample size" f_{ij+} for the ij-th binomial. Note that the parameters in the logit model are obtained by multiplying the corresponding λ parameters by two (assuming that the λ parameters are defined as in the analysis of variance).

Now define the expected rate of success as

$$R_{ij}^{AB} = F_{ij1}/F_{ij+},$$ [9]

and note that R_{ij}^{AB} will be approximately equal to Ω_{ij}^{ABC} when level 1 of variable C is "rare" as previously defined. If we condition on the observed group totals, f_{ij+}, the following *log-rate model* can be used:

$$\log(R_{ij}^{AB}) = \log(F_{ij1}/f_{ij+}) = \delta + \delta_i^A + \delta_j^B.$$ [10]

The δ parameters in this model approximate the β parameters in the logit model when the IJ responses pertain to rare events. When some or many of the events are not rare (π values greater than .10), the two models differ more substantially, and in such cases the log-rate model provides an alternative to the ordinary logit model. Note that the model in equation 10 is simply a weighted log-linear model, as presented in the previous section, where the group totals f_{ij+} correspond to the weights. This means that the log-rate model can be estimated and tested with IPF-based programs, with the f_{ij+} forming the "start table," or for NR-based programs, with the f_{ij+} serving as the "cell weights" or "exposures."

Table 7 gives a $2 \times 5 \times 2$ cross table involving the variables industry, age, and lung functioning (abnormal versus normal). The rate of abnormal lung functioning is a rare event; observed rates are below .10 for all age-industry combinations. The data have been displayed to emphasize the group totals, f_{ij+}, which play a key role in both logit and log-rate models. As indicated above, both models condition on these values in an explicit way. To analyze the logit model, we would use the counts in the contingency table (20 cells); to analyze the log-rate model, we would use the 10 "success" counts (in this case, abnormal lung functioning is a success), and the marginal totals displayed in Table 7 would be entered as cell weights. Results from both models are presented in Table 8. Note that the parameter estimates, their standardized values, and the fit statistics from one model provide good approximations for the corresponding quantities from the other model. Because abnormal lung functioning is a rare event, the models are the same in all important respects. Had we analyzed events that

TABLE 7
Lung Functioning (abnormal versus normal)
by Age and Industry

Predictor Variables		Dependent Variable (lung functioning)		
Industry	Age Group	Abnormal	Normal	Total
Manufacturing	20-29	9	394	403
	30-39	22	666	688
	40-49	15	668	683
	50-59	37	502	539
	60+	17	116	133
Service	20-29	12	244	256
	30-39	17	508	525
	40-49	17	582	599
	50-59	30	423	453
	60+	14	141	155

SOURCE: Calculated from percentage tables in Fleiss (1981).

TABLE 8
Log-Odds (Logit) and Log-Rate Models
for the Lung Functioning Data

Parameter	Log-Odds Model $(\hat{\beta} = 2\hat{\lambda})$	$\hat{\beta}/s(\hat{\beta})$	Log-Rate Model $(\hat{\delta}$ values$)$	$\hat{\delta}/s(\hat{\delta})$
Constant	−3.04	−37.98	−3.10	—[a]
Age				
20-29	−.36	−1.92	−.34	−1.84
30-39	−.36	−2.40	−.34	−2.26
40-49	−.62	−3.88	−.59	−3.75
50-59	.42	3.32	.40	3.30
60+	.92	—[a]	.87	—[a]
Industry				
Manufacturing	−.03	.41	−.03	−.40
Service	.03	.41	.03	.40
Chi-squared statistics[b]				
L^2	4.40	—	4.18	—
X^2	4.47	—	4.26	—

a. Standard errors for these parameter estimates were not calculated.
b. Both models have four degrees of freedom.

are not rare, the two models could have differed more substantially. We would then need to use both statistical and substantive criteria to choose between the two.

We next consider an example where exposures are obtained by

following individuals through time and the frequencies studied correspond to event counts over some interval. Table 9 presents death counts among subjects receiving kidney transplants cross-classified by donor status (cadaver or living relative), time, and match grade (number of matched antigens out of a maximum of four). Note that time is included to model "time dependence" (or "duration dependence"); and it has been grouped into intervals based on the exploratory work by Laird and Olivier. The person-months exposed, approximated by using life table methods, appear for each cell in the $2 \times 5 \times 3$ crosstable. Call these exposures E_{ijk} for cell (i, j, k). The first model considered for the data in Table 9 uses the weighted log-frequency model, with $\log (F_{ijk}/ E_{ijk})$ as the set of quantitites to be predicted; notice that this is equivalent to a log-rate model, and it is equivalent to assuming that the event counts in each cell follow a Poisson distribution. A model that fits the data well incorporates main effects of D and T, a linear effect of M, and a D-M interaction linear in levels of M. The estimates for this model appear in Table 10.

A related approach is to note that

$$\log(F_{ijk}/E_{ijk}) = (\delta \text{ terms}) \quad <==> \qquad [11]$$

$$\log(F_{ijk}) = (\delta \text{ terms}) + \gamma [\log (E_{ijk})] .$$

The model in equation 11 can be estimated easily with programs that allow for cellwise covariates. We note that the value of γ should be one; it becomes an exponent of the exposure when terms are rearranged. Testing whether $\gamma = 1$ can be an important check on the model; in Table 10 we find $\hat{\gamma} = .88$ and $s(\hat{\gamma})$ (not shown) is .28, which indicates that the estimate of γ is well within the range anticipated. Better diagnostic checks can be had by considering interactions of functions of the exposures (e.g., $\log(E_{ijk})$) with levels of the predictor variables. No 2-factor interaction of this kind was significant when added to the model considered in Table 10. The reader will note that while coefficient estimates are similar between the two models (they would be identical if $\hat{\gamma}$ were 1.0), standard errors and standardized parameter estimates are greatly affected by using exposures as a "cell covariate" rather than as a "cell weight." In this case, the first

TABLE 9
Graft Failures Following Kidney Transplants: Death and Exposures by Donor Relationship, Match Grade, and Time

Donor	Time	Deaths: Match Grade			Exposures: Match Grade		
		0-2	3	4	0-2	3	4
Cadaver	0-1 months	204	30	1	27390.5	3471	521
	1-3 months	170	16	4	43470	5340	930
	3-6 months	94	10	2	54000	7110	1080
	6-12 months	54	6	0	94860	12600	1980
	> 1 year	91	10	3	351090	48600	6570
Living relative	0-1 month	35	19	5	13677	4665.5	4839
	1-3 months	64	9	6	24510	8325	9300
	3-6 months	31	8	4	32715	11880	13590
	6-12 months	26	4	3	60210	22590	26595
	> 1 year	34	5	6	242100	104940	115380

NOTE: Calculated from entries in the larger table provided in Laird and Olivier (1981: 237-238). Calculations supplied by Rebecca Burt.

TABLE 10
Two Log-Rate Models for the Kidney Transplant Data in Table 9

Predictor	Log-Rate Model			
	Cell Weight[a]		Cell Covariate[b]	
	$\hat{\delta}$	$\hat{\delta}/s(\hat{\delta})$	$\hat{\delta}$	$\hat{\delta}/s(\hat{\delta})$
Donor cadaver	.53	8.19	.48	3.61
Time				
0-1	1.56	27.22	1.44	4.90
1-3	.98	16.63	.92	5.60
3-6	.14	1.99	.11	.97
6-12	−.91	−10.34	−.88	−7.52
Match grade (linear)	−.32	−4.62	−.47	−1.27
Donor X grade (linear)	.22	3.24	.14	.67
Log (exposure)	−	−	.88	3.19
L^2	28.61		28.44	
X^2	28.07		27.50	

a. Exposures used as cell weights in weighted log-linear model.
b. Log (exposures) used as a cell covariate in log-frequency model.

model provides the correct solution if we condition on the observed values of the exposures and assume that $\gamma = 1$ in the population.

The models of survival analysis developed in statistics are closely related to so-called duration models in sociology or economics. Many of them can be recast as log-linear models for rates of the kind suggested above whenever the predictor variables are discrete. Allison (1984) and Laird and Olivier (1981) provide valuable introductions to the subject.

INTERPRETING RESULTS

Several papers on log-linear analysis deal with the problem of interpreting results. The objective in most of these sources is to convert the estimated parameter values and/or the estimated expected frequencies into quantities that summarize the main features of the data in ways that are analogous to regression results or even simple percentage tables. Papers by Kaufman and Schervish (1986), Amemiya (1981), and Alba (this volume) provide many references to literature on such problems and also propose convincing models for summarizing results. The material in this section is intended as a supplement to this literature and to the suggestions of Kaufman, Schervish, Alba, and others.

PROBLEM ONE: TOO MANY PARAMETERS

A common complaint is that log-linear analysis produces *too many parameters* to interpret. In most cases this is a blessing rather than a curse, because the point of log-linear analysis is that relationships among a set of discrete variables should not always be reduced to a set of pairwise correlations among the variables.

Often the solution to the problem of too many parameters is merely to focus on only those parameter values of substantive interest for the problem at hand. In other cases, researchers should simply consider models with various restrictions that reduce the number of effective parameters that need to be interpreted. The analysis of Table 3 reported in Table 4 is a case in point. The original crosstable had 36 cells; the saturated model would have 36 λ terms. But we are interested only in the relationships between the specified predictor variables (center, age, and malignant appearance) and the dependent variable (survival); this eliminates 18 of the 36 λ automatically. It was found that a model with only 2-factor interactions involving the dependent variable was necessary to describe the data; further restrictions for the age-survival interaction that took account of the spacing of age levels were imposed. A set of results was produced that had only four key parameter values, which could hardly be thought of as too many parameters.

Much recent work in the contingency-table area deals with devising restricted models that are sensible for polytomous (ordered and unordered) variables considered in multiway cross-classifications. See, for example, Agresti (1984), Clogg (1982), and Goodman (1984). It is beyond the scope of the present article to cover these models, but many of them can be considered with existing software.

PROBLEM TWO: RETRIEVING ODDS-RATIOS

Alba's splendid treatment in this volume covers the problem of retrieving odds-ratios and partial odds-ratios from the parameter values. It is important to realize that the λ values included in a fitted model are rarely the quantities that should be used to summarize the data. It can be perilous to compare λ values from one study with those in another study, for example. The λ values are not the fundamental parameters of interest, even though they are closely related to them. Some useful guidelines are as follows.

For two-way $I \times J$ tables, the log-odds-ratio for the *subtable* formed from rows i and i' and columns j and j' is

$$\log(\Theta_{ij(i'j')}) = \log(F_{ij} F_{i'j'} / F_{i'j} F_{ij'}) \qquad [12]$$

$$= \nu_{ij} + \nu_{i'j'} - \nu_{i'j} - \nu_{ij'}$$

$$= \lambda_{ij}^{AB} + \lambda_{i'j'}^{AB} - \lambda_{i'j}^{AB} - \lambda_{ij'}^{AB}$$

In other words, to retrieve the log-odds-ratio for any 2×2 table in the $I \times J$ table, take a linear contrast of the 2-factor λ values. This contrast is the same as the contrast of the ν's that defines the log-odds-ratio. For the 2×2 table, the usual constraints on the λ's imply that $\lambda_{11}^{AB} = \lambda_{22}^{AB} = -\lambda_{12}^{AB} = -\lambda_{21}^{AB}$, so the log-odds-ratio in the 2×2 table is $4\lambda_{11}^{AB}$ using equation 12. In many cases, the researcher will wish to convert log-odds-ratios to odds-ratios, which is done by taking antilogs ($\exp(4\lambda_{11}^{AB})$ in the 2×2 case). It should be noted that interval estimates for odds-ratios can be created from information on the estimated λ's. For example, if $\hat{\lambda}_{11}^{AB} \pm z_{\alpha/2} s(\hat{\lambda}_{11}^{AB}$ is the $(1 - \alpha)$ level confidence interval for λ_{11}^{AB} in a 2×2 table, multiplying the limits by four gives the corresponding interval estimate for the log-odds-ratio, and taking antilogs of these limits gives the appropriate interval estimate for the odds-ratio. For general $I \times J$ tables, interval estimates will be less straightforward. The approximate variance of the estimated log-odds-ratio, say $s^2(\log(\hat{\theta}_{ij(i'j')})$, can be obtained by calculating the variance of the contrast of estimated λ values implied by equation 12. Fortunately, the required covariances between respective λ terms are provided as an option by most of the available software packages.

For 3-way tables, some algebra shows that equation 12 is the correct formula for the *partial* log-odds-ratio between variables A and B when there is no 3-factor interaction. Analogous expressions can be used to retrieve the partial log-odds-ratios between A and C and between B and C (when there is no 3-factor interaction). Of course, in situations where one of the variables is a dependent variable and the other two are specified predictor variables, there might be little interest in one set of partial log-odds-ratios.

For multiway tables, partial log-odds-ratios between, say, variables A and B, can be calculated as above if the model considered excludes higher-order interactions (3-factor, 4-factor, and so on) involving both A and B. When 3-factor interaction is present, one needs to calculate 2-factor interactions at each level of the third variable involved. These may then be converted to log-odds-ratios and/or odds-ratios.

PROBLEM THREE:
HIGHER-ORDER INTERACTIONS

Because the emphasis of log-linear analysis is on goodness-of-fit of a model, it is not surprising that researchers have had to include higher-order interactions of various kinds to provide good agreement between the model and the data. Models with 3-factor and even 4-factor interactions involving some specified dependent variables are common in substantive applications, if not in the standard references on log-linear analysis.

One response to this problem has been to sidestep the issue by considering only models that exclude higher-order interactions. This sort of strategy usually downplays the importance of goodness-of-fit; chi-squared statistics for testing the agreement between the model and the data are often ignored. A case in point is Model D in Winship and Mare (1983: Table 2), a certain type of main-effects-only model applied to a contingency table where goodness-of-fit tests are feasible. This model turns out to have an L^2 value of 142.98 on 86 degrees of freedom. (This was calculated by using the reported value of the log-likelihoods in the source and the log-likelihood obtained from the relevant unrestricted model.) The parameter values, the standard errors, and indeed the model itself cannot be defended as a plausible description of the data. Higher-order interactions should be taken into account if they are present in the data.

PROBLEM FOUR: CHOICE OF SCALE

Regardless of the type of log-linear model considered, a natural byproduct of the analysis will be parameter values that are expressed in metrics involving logarithmic and exponential functions. This statement applies to log-linear models for frequencies, odds (logit models), odds-ratios (association models in Goodman, 1984), rates, and hazards. Taking antilogs of parameter values is helpful, but there are times when this does not go far enough. Although we appreciate the importance of the issue, we do not believe that any universally valid solution is available. We illustrate with some *strategies* for interpretation that amount to changing the scale.

SOME SOLUTIONS

A simple method that can always be utilized is based on the following observation. The odds-ratio $\theta = F_{11}F_{22}/F_{12}F_{21}$ in a 2×2 table can be converted to Yule's Q according to the formula, $Q = (\theta - 1)/(\theta + 1)$. This gives $Q = 0$ for $\theta = 1$, $Q = +1$ for $\theta = +$ infinity, $Q = -1$ for $\theta = 0$; Q is a normed measure of association based on the odds-ratio. The more general formula,

$$Q^* = (\theta^f - 1)/(\theta^f + 1), \qquad [13]$$

will also produce a normed measure of association based on the odds-ratio, for any positive constant f. Digby (1983) finds that f = .75 does a good job in reproducing the tetrachoric correlation that arises from normal theory applied to the 2×2 table. Becker and Clogg (1987) let f depend on the marginal distributions of the two variables giving even better agreement between Q^* and the tetrachoric correlation. Because results from log-linear analysis can always be recast in terms of fundamental sets of odds-ratios or partial odds-ratios or related quantities, the above approach can be generally applied if a correlation-type interpretation of the data is sought. See, for example, Clogg (1979a: Appendix E) for some related comments on "normed effects."

An alternative approach is based on the *purging method* presented in Clogg (1978) and generalized in Clogg et al. (1986). We illustrate purging by considering a 3-way table. For simplicity, denote the parameters in the multiplicative model as τ's (e.g., τ_i^A = exp (λ_i^A), and so on). Suppose that variable C (with K levels) is the dependent variable and that variables A and B are predictors. A natural way to summarize the relationship between A and C is to calculate rates (or proportions) of the levels of C by the levels of A. If we use the *marginal* table cross-classifying A and C (F_{i+k}, say), we merely reproduce the "crude rates" or unadjusted percentages. These rates are determined from the expression

$$r_{i.(k)} = F_{i+k}/F_{i++}, \qquad [14]$$

where a "+" denotes summation over the subscript it replaces. The idea of purging is based on the fact that marginal relationships (i.e., relationships in the 2-way crosstable) will be identical to partial relationships (i.e., relationships between A and C in the 3-way table) when there is no 2-factor interaction between the predictors A and B. This suggests creating a table of adjusted frequencies where the A–B interaction in the data has been purged, that is,

$$F_{ijk}^* = F_{ijk}/\tau_{ij}^{AB}. \qquad [15]$$

An adjusted cross-classification of A and C is calculated by taking F_{i+k}^*, and adjusted rates are obtained from these quantities. When there is 3-factor interaction in the data, one can calculate purged frequencies according to the formula,

$$F_{ijk}^{**} = F_{ijk} / (\tau_{ij}^{AB} \, \tau_{ijk}^{ABC}).$$ [16]

Rates calculated from the F_{ijk}^{**} (by collapsing over levels of B) can be compared to the rates calculated from the F_{ijk}^{*} to examine the effect of 3-factor interaction on the inference.

To illustrate the purging method as a strategy for interpretation, consider the data in Table 11. This $5 \times 4 \times 2$ table would ordinarily be studied in terms of a logit model, with desire for children the dependent variable and age and parity the predictors. The logit model with main effects of age and parity (equivalent to the log-linear model of no 3-factor interaction) does not fit the data; the L^2 value is 30.82 on 12 degrees of freedom (p – value = .002). Various restricted models given in Clogg (1982) do not fit the data well. The problem is that there is a substantial 3-factor interaction that should be taken into account. The saturated logit model actually has 20 nonredundant parameters. In Table 12, purging methods were used to characterize the association between parity (a predictor) and desire for children (the dependent variable). The crude percentages are obtained directly from the 2-way table, parity by desire, and show, for example, that over 70% of mothers with one child want an additional child, that there are steep declines in desire as parity increases, and that all differences among adjacent parities are significant when compared to standard errors. Adjusting for the interaction between age and parity greatly reduces the parity differentials, and we find that the differences between parities 2 and 3 and between parities 3 and 4+

TABLE 11
Desire for More Children (yes or no)
by Maternal Age and Parity, for Women
with at Least One Child in 1970

| | Parity | | | | | | | |
| | 1 | | 2 | | 3 | | 4+ | |
Age	Yes	No	Yes	No	Yes	No	Yes	No
20-24	327	36	133	138	22	46	10	17
25-29	160	48	118	228	58	156	29	129
30-34	54	42	43	219	29	165	34	190
35-39	12	47	14	158	12	156	12	227
40-44	5	43	4	142	7	128	13	198

SOURCE: Rindfuss and Bumpass (1978: 49). The data are from the 1970 National Fertility Survey.

TABLE 12
Crude and Adjusted Percentage of Desiring More Children,
by Parity Group, Based on the Purging Method

Type of Purging[a]	Parity Levels				Differences Among Parities			
	1	2	3	4+	1-2	2-3	3-4+	1-4+
None (crude percentages)	72.1%	26.1	16.4	11.5	46.0 (2.1)[b]	9.6 (1.8)	4.9 (1.7)	60.9 (1.9)
Adjusted for λ_{ij}^{AP}	60.0	20.6	17.5	15.6	39.4 (3.3)	3.0 (2.3)	2.0 (2.2)	44.4 (3.2)
Adjusted for λ_{ij}^{AP} & λ_{ijk}^{APD}	57.7	20.1	18.2	16.9	37.6 (4.1)	1.9 (2.9)	1.2 (2.6)	40.8 (3.8)

a. Variables are A (age), P (parity), D (desire for more children).
b. Standard errors (in parentheses) calculated by the jackknife method.

are not significant. If we use the difference between parity 1 and parity 4+ as an overall measure, we see that adjusting for the age-parity interaction brings about a reduction from 61% to 44%. When 3-factor interaction is taken into account, the latter difference is 41%, so 44% – 41% = 3% is the effect of 3-factor interaction in the data. This procedure could be repeated to study the age differentials in desire for children, adjusting for age-parity interaction. Indeed the procedure is fully multivariate (since each of the variables can represent crossed combinations of other variables) and the roles of dependent and independent variables can be interchanged depending on the substantive context. The simplicity of results in Table 12 recommends the approach for at least some situations where summarization in terms of percentage distributions is important. This approach is related to but different from the approach considered in Kaufman and Schervish (1986).

CONCLUSION

From our experience, the problems discussed above seem to be ones faced often in log-linear analysis of discrete variables. We hasten to add that the same or similar problems are encountered with any modern statistical model applied to discrete data. The solutions offered here can be modified easily in many cases where models other than those of the log-linear variety are used. As with any problem in data analysis, there are both practical and theoretical or mathematical issues that have to be addressed in order to acquire a full appreciation of the subtleties involved. This review has emphasized common problems and practical solutions that for the most part are not featured either in the standard references on the methodology or in the documentation for software used for its application. The solutions proposed can be applied with a little extra effort using only existing programs for log-linear or logit analysis. References to current literature on the technical aspects of these problems have also been provided along with some background on the inferential issues that arise. We hope that researchers will be able to use these solutions to perform more valid analyses of categorical variables and to avoid some of the obstacles that have plagued log-linear analysis for the last decade.

10

Interpreting the Parameters of Log-Linear Models

RICHARD D. ALBA

Although log-linear models have become widely accepted as a tool for analyzing complex relationships among discrete variables, their full power is still not always exploited by researchers. The most cumbersome aspect of their use remains the interpretation of parameters. Many applications of log-linear models make little interpretative use of parameter values or use them inappropriately, even though the fact that log-linear methodology is a parametric technique should be one of its greatest strengths. The confusion that still envelops parameter interpretation is attested to by the frequency of articles on the topic (e.g., Long, 1984; Kaufman and Schervish: 1986). Noteworthy is that these articles frequently devote considerable space to correcting the errors of their predecessors.

The persisting confusion is regrettable because the parameters should occupy a central place in any interpretation based on log-linear analysis. In the case where the analysis involves a dependent variable, it is only through them that one can understand the magnitudes of the effects of the independent variables. Just as the coefficients of variables in regression analysis must play a major role in any interpretation of results, so must the parameters of a log-linear model.

The confusion is also regrettable because, in fact, these

AUTHOR'S NOTE: *I am grateful for the comments of Clifford Clogg, Scott Long, Scott South, and an anonymous reviewer to an earlier draft.*

parameters are not as difficult to interpret as is frequently believed. In this article, I will present a straightforward approach to the interpretation of parameters for models involving dependent variables. I depart from many previous presentations by using the conventions of regression analysis for representing variables. Since these conventions are well understood by researchers, they allow a clear exposition of the mathematics relating parameter values to changes in a dependent quantity.[1] The presentation that follows can be understood by anyone familiar with the representation of categorical variables and interaction effects in regression equations and with the basic properties of logarithms. Although I will confine the discussion to models with just one dependent variable, the interpretive steps I present can be also used for more general log-linear models, involving two or more dependent variables.

SOME PRELIMINARIES

I rely heavily on examples to reveal the critical steps in moving from the output provided by a log-linear computer program to an interpretation of the underlying model. To provide suitably "real-life" examples, I have drawn upon some of my own research investigating changes in indicators of ethnicity across cohorts of white ethnics in the United States (Alba, 1986). In particular, I will use analyses of intermarriage and of childhood exposure to a non-English mother tongue among cohorts of U.S.-born persons with ancestry from south-central-eastern Europe. The measure of exposure to a mother tongue is used as an indicator of the broader concept of exposure to an ethnic culture (Stevens, 1985), while the marriage variable indexes social assimilation (Gordon, 1964). The data are taken from the November 1979 Current Population Survey.

The two dependent variables provide the opportunity for analyzing a dichotomy and a trichotomy. Exposure to a mother tongue is measured in terms of two categories: a non-English mother tongue was spoken in one's childhood home; only English was spoken there. Intermarriage is measured in terms of three categories in order to take into account the growing complexity of ancestry mixtures: the ancestries of husband and wife do not overlap (i.e., they have no ethnic components in common); they overlap partially; they are identical.

Categories of cohort are defined in terms of 15-year intervals that correspond approximately with important periods in immigration and U.S. history. The oldest cohort contains persons born before 1916 (such persons were born during the period of the most intense mass immigration from southern and eastern Europe). The remaining cohorts are the periods 1916-1930, 1931-1945, 1946-1960, and post-1960. Because of its youth, the last cohort is not used in the analysis of intermarriage. Other independent variables include: generation, which measures ancestral distance from immigration (divided between the second generation, that is, the children of the immigrants, and the third and later generations); ancestry type (ancestry from a single group versus ethnically mixed or multiple ancestry); and gender.[2]

ODDS, ODDS RATIOS, AND PERCENTAGES

Log-linear models require a very different way of thinking about relationships among variables from what many social scientists are used to. Percentages are deeply ingrained and intuitively appealing as a way of expressing the frequency of some event or characteristic; and, accordingly, percentage differences, an additive way of comparing relative frequencies, are a well-understood and comfortable method for evaluating a relationship between variables. But log-linear models are nonlinear in terms of percentages, and thus the effects they represent cannot be viewed adequately in terms of percentage differences.

Odds are a way of expressing the frequency of an event that is consistent with the mathematical form of a log-linear model. *Odds* are defined as the frequency (or probability) of one category of a variable compared to the frequency (or probability) of another. As an example, Table 1 presents the relationship between cohort and childhood exposure to a mother tongue in terms of frequencies and odds as well as percentages. The overall odds of exposure to a mother tongue versus only English are 5,709 to 7,767, or .424 to .576 (i.e., $1 - .424$).

Odds are typically expressed as ratios. Thus, in the usual expression, the overall odds of exposure to a mother tongue are

TABLE 1
The Relationship Between Cohort and Exposure to a
Mother Tongue: Frequencies, Percentages, Odds, and Logits

Birth Cohort	Frequencies		% Exposed	Odds Exposure versus Nonexposure	Logit
	Exposed	Not Exposed			
Pre-1916	1272	385	76.8	3.304	1.195
1916-30	1855	788	70.2	2.354	.856
1931-45	1219	1457	45.6	.837	−.178
1946-60	1199	3625	24.9	.331	−1.106
Post-1960	164	1512	9.8	.108	−2.221
Total	5709	7767	42.4	.735	−.308

SOURCE: Current Population Survey (1979, November).
NOTES: The table includes only U.S.-born persons with at least some Southern, Central, or Eastern European ancestry. The frequencies incorporate sampling weights, which have been scaled so that the weighted and unweighted totals of cases in the table are the same.

.74 (i.e., 5,709/7,767). Expressed in this way, odds are unbounded at the upper end; that is, they can take on any value greater than 0.

Conversion between odds and percentages or proportions is straightforward. Given any proportion, P, the corresponding odds, O, are as follows:

$$O = P/(1 - P) \qquad [1]$$

(If a percentage is used, the 1 must be replaced by 100.) A small amount of algebra shows that the proportion corresponding with any given odds is yielded by the formula:

$$P = O/(1 + O) \qquad [2]$$

An odds can be viewed as the dependent variable in a multiplicative version of a log-linear model. But as the very name of this type of model implies, there is also a linear version in the logarithmic scale. The dependent quantity in the linear formulation is the natural logarithm of an odds, or the logit. The results of log-linear models are frequently presented in terms of the parameters for the logit version, since these are relatively easily manipulated to derive odds ratios and other quantities relating to the odds. Table 1 presents logits for the relation between cohort and mother-tongue exposure.

The appropriate way to compare odds is by division, not subtraction (as in a percentage difference), and this leads to the odds ratio, a central concept in log-linear modeling. Thus, the odds ratio for exposure to a mother tongue between the post-1960 and pre-1916 cohorts is .033 (i.e., .108/3.304). Obviously, this odds ratio reveals that the odds of exposure are much less in the post-1960 cohort than in the pre-1916 one, paralleling the conclusion to be drawn from the corresponding percentage difference, −67% (i.e., 9.8% − 76.8%).

One potentially deceptive aspect of odds ratios should be noted: A comparison of ratios above and below one can be misleading. For example, odds ratios of 1.5 and .67 may appear, at first glance, to register effects of different magnitudes, but in fact the magnitudes are the same—it is simply the direction of the comparison that is different. That is, by reversing the direction of comparison, the odds ratio of 1.5 becomes .67, the latter being the reciprocal of the former. For this reason, it is usually wise to express odds ratios as uniformly above 1 or below 1, insofar as this is possible through the choice of an appropriate reference point, and thus to simplify comparisons of their magnitudes.[3]

Odds ratios are perhaps the best way to understand the effects of independent variables in log-linear models. But these ratios are not part of the output of the most widely used programs for log-linear modeling. How, then, are they to be calculated? A consideration of this question carries us into the logit form of a log-linear model.

FROM A LOGIT EQUATION TO ODDS RATIOS

To be able to interpret the parameters of a log-linear model, it is useful to express it first in the form of a logit equation—one where the natural logarithm of the odds of the dependent variable is predicted by a linear function of the independent variables and any interaction effects that may be present. In such an equation, independent variables and interaction effects can be represented by the well-known conventions of regression models—either dummy or effect-coded variables (defined below) to express independent variables, and product terms to express interactions.

Consider as an example an analysis of exposure to a mother tongue in terms of cohort, generational status, and ancestry type. The dependent quantity is the logarithm of the odds of mother-tongue exposure versus English only (recall that the first-named frequency, or probability, is in the numerator of the odds, the second in the denominator). For now, I restrict the discussion to models without interaction effects. The following logit equation[4] represents the results of the log-linear analysis:

$$\text{log odds of exposure} = -.288 + .664x_1^C + .550x_2^C + .336x_3^C$$

$$- .244x_4^C + .810x_1^G + .470x_1^A, \qquad [3]$$

where the x^C's represent the categories of cohort, x_1^G generation, and x_1^A ancestry type (a more complete specification appears in Table 2).

As is very common in log-linear models, all of the independent variables in this equation are based on effect coding, which differs from the more familiar dummy-variable coding only in the treatment of the omitted category. In the case of effect coding, the omitted category is coded with -1's. As a result, the coefficients of the resulting terms can be interpreted as deviations from "average" (the average is across categories, not across individuals). (Effect coding is equivalent to imposing as an identification restriction the condition that the effects of all the categories of any variable sum to 0.) By comparison, in dummy-variable coding, the effect of the excluded category is scored as zero. The distinction between the two codings has also been described in terms of "ANOVA-like constraints," in the case of effect coding, and "regression-like constraints," in the case of dummy variables; see Long (1984) for further details.

The model in equation 3 demonstrates that there are systematic differences in mother-tongue exposure among cohorts even after generation and ancestry type are controlled. For instance, given the effect codings in Table 2, membership in the pre-1916 cohort adds .664 more than average to the log odds of exposure, while membership in the 1946-1960 cohort subtracts .244; membership in the post-1960 cohort, the omitted category, reduces the logit by 1.306 (i.e., .664[-1] + .550[-1] + .336[-1] - .244[-1]). The deriva-

TABLE 2
A Logit Equation for the Odds of Exposure to a
Mother Tongue (versus Nonexposure) and Implied Odds Ratios

	Logit Coefficients		Logit Differences Relative to Reference Category	Odds Ratios Relative to Reference Category
	Effect Coded	Dummy Coded		
Intercept	−.288	−2.874	—	—
Cohort:				
Pre-1916 (x_1^C)	.664	1.970	1.970	7.17
1916-1930 (x_2^C)	.550	1.856	1.856	6.40
1931-1945 (x_3^C)	.336	1.642	1.642	5.17
1946-1960 (x_4^C)	−.244	1.062	1.062	2.89
Post-1960*	(−1.306)	(0)	(0)	(1)
Generation:				
Second (x_1^G)	.810	1.620	1.620	5.05
Third*	(−.810)	(0)	(0)	(1)
Ancestry Type:				
Single (x_1^A)	.470	.940	.940	2.56
Mixed*	(−.470)	(0)	(0)	(1)

NOTE: Coefficients are derived from the model [CGA] [TC] [TG] [TA] (see Table 3).
*Indicates omitted category. Numbers in parentheses are effects for these categories: in effect coding, omitted category effects are evaluated by substituting—1s for x terms; in dummy coding, they are fixed at 0. For odds ratios, omitted category effects are fixed at 1.

tion of logit differences among the categories is obvious: For example, by comparison with the 1946-1960 cohort, members of the pre-1916 cohort have a log odds of exposure that is .908 higher (i.e., .664 − [−.244]). The largest logit difference among the cohorts lies between the oldest and youngest: Members of the pre-1916 cohort have a log odds of exposure to a mother tongue that is 1.970 higher than is the case for members of the post-1960 cohort with the same generational status and ancestry type.

Equivalent statements for an independent variable with just two categories are even simpler to arrive at. For example, having a single ethnic ancestry adds .470 to the logit, while having mixed ancestry subtracts the same value. Thus the logit difference between the ancestry types is .940—persons of single ancestry have a log odds of mother-tongue exposure that is .940 greater than that for persons of mixed ancestry who belong to the same cohort and generation.

Dummy-variable coding can also be used in a logit model, and the translation between effect coding and dummy-variable coding is straightforward. The coefficients of the dummy variables are simply the differences between the categories they represent and the omitted category. Expressed in terms of dummy variables (labeled as d's) and with the same omitted categories as before, the equation for the log odds of exposure to a mother tongue becomes:

$$\text{log odds of exposure} = -2.874 + 1.970d_1^C + 1.856d_2^C + 1.642d_3^C$$
$$+ 1.062d_4^C + 1.620d_1^G + .940d_1^A. \qquad [4]$$

Since the intercept in this equation represents the predicted log odds for individuals in the omitted categories of the three variables (i.e., members of the post-1960 cohort who have mixed ancestry and belong to the third and later generations), it can be calculated from the earlier equation by substituting −1's for all x terms.

Effect and dummy-variable coding are equally valid and ultimately consistent ways of representing the variables in a logit equation. But for most of us, the parameters of a logit model, however it be expressed, are not sufficient to interpret the model, for it is difficult to grasp concretely the magnitudes of effects in a logarithmic scale.[5] For this reason, it is generally preferable to convert the effects derived from the logit form into corresponding multiplicative effects, and particularly to translate logit differences between categories into their multiplicative equivalent, odds ratios.

The effects of variables in the multiplicative version of a model are easily understood by an examination of its mathematical form. Suppose, for instance, that the earlier logit equation with effect-coded variables is converted into its multiplicative equivalent by taking the antilogarithm of both of its sides. The resulting equation is:

$$\text{odds of exposure} = (.75)\,(1.94)^{x_1^C}\,(1.73)^{x_2^C}\,(1.40)^{x_3^C}$$

$$(.78)^{x_4^C}\,(2.25)^{x_1^G}\,(1.60)^{x_1^A} \qquad [5]$$

According to this equation, if the value of any x term is changed by one (e.g., from 0 to 1), the odds are multiplied by the corresponding parameter (because $a^{(x+1)} = a^x a$). Hence the parameters can be interpreted as multiplicative effects, or as odds relative to some "average."[6] For instance, relative to this average, the odds of mother-tongue exposure for members of the pre-1916 cohort ($x_1^C = 1;\ x_2^C = x_3^C = x_4^C = 0$) are 1.94; alternatively, one can say that membership in this cohort raises the odds above the average by a factor of 1.94. On the other hand, relative to the same average, members of the 1946-1960 cohort have an odds of .78. Membership in the post-1960 cohort, the omitted category, reduces the odds by a factor of .27 in relation to the average, since .27 = $(1.94)^{-1}(1.73)^{-1}(1.40)^{-1}(.78)^{-1}$.

The interpretation of the multiplicative equivalent of the dummy-variable form is similar, except that the reference point for the odds is the omitted category. Hence the multiplicative parameters are odds ratios between the various categories explicitly represented in the equation and the omitted category. Conversion of the earlier dummy-variable logit equation to a multiplicative equation predicting the odds of mother-tongue exposure yields:

$$\text{odds of exposure} = (.06)\,(7.17)^{d_1^C}\,(6.40)^{d_2^C}\,(5.17)^{d_3^C}$$

$$(2.89)^{d_4^C}\,(5.05)^{d_1^G}\,(2.56)^{d_1^A} \qquad [6]$$

According to the equation, for example, the odds of exposure are 7.17 times higher for members of the pre-1916 cohort than they are for those in the post-1960 group, with generation and ancestry type controlled. Likewise, the odds of exposure for persons of single ethnic ancestry are 2.56 higher than they are for persons of multiple ancestry who are in the same cohort and generation.

Odds relative to an average or to some category are equally valid and completely consistent ways of viewing the multiplicative effects in a log-linear model. But my preference is to base the interpretation of such a model on the latter odds—odds ratios, in other words—on the grounds that direct contrasts between categories are more compelling than comparisons to an average that is hypothetical in the sense that it does not occur as a data value (on the interpretive value of odds ratios, see also Page, 1977, and Holt, 1979). The odds ratios necessary for interpreting the model of exposure to a mother tongue are presented in Table 2. They are easily calculated: They are simply the antilogarithms of appropriate logit differences between categories of an independent variable, since

$$\log(\text{odds}_1 / \text{odds}_2) = \log \text{odds}_1 - \log \text{odds}_2 \qquad [7]$$

Table 2 also makes clear the derivation of the odds ratios in this case.

No matter which coding is used to present multiplicative parameters for interpretation, one should be careful to investigate thoroughly the odds ratios implied by a model in order to interpret it correctly. For example, a cursory examination of Table 2 may suggest that there are substantial differences among all the cohort categories. But in fact the odds ratio for exposure between the pre-1916 and the 1916-1930 cohorts is only 1.12 (i.e., 7.17/6.40). Somewhat larger is the difference between the 1916-1930 and 1931-1945 cohorts—the odds ratio is 1.24. But the difference between adjacent cohorts grows after 1945. The odds ratio between the 1931-1945 and 1946-1960 cohorts is 1.79, and that between the 1946-1960 and post-1960 cohorts is 2.89.

Often some assistance is needed to get an intuitive grasp of the magnitude of change implied by an odds ratio. A straightforward way of doing this is to convert the odds ratio into one or more percentage differences, keeping in mind, however, that such differences are not a substitute for the odds ratios themselves. Suppose, for example, we consider a member of the post-1960 cohort who has an average chance of childhood exposure to a mother tongue—.424, the proportion found in the sample as a whole (see Table 1).[7] For such a person, the odds of exposure are .736 (i.e., .424/[1 − .424]). Then, a similar member of the pre-1916 cohort—one of the same generation and ancestry type—is expected to have an odds of 5.28 (i.e., .736 × 7.17). The predicted probability of exposure is therefore .841 (i.e., 5.28/6.28, using equation 2). In this instance, cohort makes a difference of more than 40 percentage points (i.e., 84.1% – 42.4%). Clearly, this is a large difference.

The smallness of the difference between the two pre-1931 cohorts is easily shown by this method. Compared to a member of the 1916-1930 cohort with an average chance of mother-tongue exposure and hence an odds of .736, a member of the pre-1916 cohort has a predicted odds of .824 (i.e., .736 × 1.12, the latter being the odds ratio between the two cohorts) and therefore a predicted probability of .452. The difference in this case is less than .03 in probability terms—obviously very small.

This section has demonstrated that once a log-linear model is expressed in the form of a logit equation, all of the values needed to interpret it are readily derived. In particular, odds ratios can be easily calculated—they are just the antilogarithms of logit differences. One can, to be sure, express a model directly in the form of a multiplicative equation for the odds, without going through the intermediate step of the logit equation; some of the most widely used log-linear computer programs—ECTA and BMDP4F—provide the multiplicative parameters that, with a little further calculation, yield the equation for the odds. But my recommendation is to use the logit equation as the basis for further calculations: Its additive nature makes the derivation of such quantities as odds ratios less error prone. The next issue to be tackled is, therefore, the derivation of a logit equation from the output produced by log-linear programs.

CALCULATING THE PARAMETERS OF A LOGIT EQUATION

A confusing aspect of log-linear modeling is that some widely used computer programs (such as ECTA, BMDP4F, and SPSS-X LOGLINEAR) do not calculate directly the parameters necessary for interpreting the effects of the independent variables on a substantive dependent variable, that is, either the additive effects on the logit or the multiplicative effects on the odds. Rather, these programs estimate the parameters in a model for the logarithm of a cell frequency (in the additive form) or the cell frequency itself (in the multiplicative form)—not an appropriate dependent variable in either case. Interpreting a log-linear model therefore requires some translation into a different form of the numbers appearing in the output.

The translation is quite straightforward if one keeps in mind the equation that lies behind the numbers reported in the output. Consider, for example, the logit model considered in detail in the preceding section. Table 3 displays the additive parameters (generally called lambda or u parameters) generated by the BMDP4F program. These parameters are of two sorts: the first pertaining to relationships of the dependent variable to various independent variables; and the second pertaining to relationships among the independent variables (since these relationships must be taken as givens in constructing a logit model; see the Clogg and Eliason contribution in this volume). Note that some log-linear computer programs may not report the second set (for example, SPSS-X LOGLINEAR when set up for a logit model).

(Note also that the L^2 for this model is fairly high: There is room for improvement, and in the next section we will interpret a better fitting model, which includes some interaction terms.)

Making use of the conventions of regression analysis for writing additive equations, we can represent the equation in which the parameters of Table 3 appear in the following way (only a small portion is reproduced here to save space):

$$\log f = 5.109 - .144x_1^T - .177x_1^G + .234x_1^A + .231x_1^G x_1^A$$

$$+ .405x_1^G x_1^T + .235x_1^A x_1^T + \ldots \qquad [8]$$

where f represents the expected frequency in a cell; x_1^T represents the category of exposure to a mother tongue, with nonexposure the omitted category; the other x variables are defined as before; and terms such as $x_1^G x_1^T$ represent interactions. Assume here, as before, that the x variables are effect coded, and note that parameter values in Table 3 pertaining to omitted categories of variables do not appear in the equation (since they are redundant).

To create a logit equation, we need take only the difference between equation 8 when $x_1^T = 1$ and hence the equation predicts the cell frequencies for the category of exposure to a mother tongue; and when $x_1^T = -1$ and the equation predicts the cell

TABLE 3
Derivation of a Logit Equation from Parameters Reported in the Output of Common Log-Linear Programs (BMDP4F, ECTA, or SPSS-X LOGLINEAR)*

Model Terms Relevant to Logit Equation	Lambda Parameters		Logit Equation
	Exposure	Nonexposure	
Mother Tongue (T):	−.144	.144	−.288
Cohort (C) x Mother Tongue (T):			
Pre-1916	.332	−.332	$+.664\ x_1^C$
1916-1930	.275	−.275	$+.550\ x_2^C$
1931-1945	.168	−.168	$+.366\ x_3^C$
1946-1960	−.122	.122	$-.244\ x_4^C$
Post-1960	−.652	.652	−**
Generation (G) x Mother Tongue (T):			
Second	.405	−.405	$+.810\ x_1^G$
Third and later	−.405	.405	−**
Ancestry type (A) x Mother Tongue (T):			
Single	.235	−.235	$+.470\ x_1^A$
Mixed	−.235	.235	−**

Model Terms Not Relevant to Logit Equation	Lambda Parameters	
Grand Mean	5.109	
Generation (G):		
Second	−.177	
Third and later	.177	
Ancestry type (A):		
Single	.234	
Mixed	−.234	
Generation (G) x Ancestry (A):	Single	Mixed
Second	.231	−.231
Third and later	−.231	.231

Continued

TABLE 3   Continued

Other terms not reported
(to conserve space) include:

    Cohort (C)
    Cohort (C) x Generation (G)
    Cohort (C) x Ancestry Type (A)
    Cohort (C) x Ancestry Type (A) x Generation (G)

NOTE: Model is [CGA] [TC] [TG] [TA], L^2 = 93.74, with 13 degrees of freedom, (p < .001).
*The derivation is appropriate for any program that reports parameters for variables expressed in effect-coded form (or alternatively put, reports parameters constrained to sum to 0); see text concerning programs such as GLIM, which report parameters for dummy variables.
**Chosen as omitted category.

frequencies for nonexposure. Under the assumption that the other variables do not change in value, such a difference yields:

$$\log f_{(x_1^T=1)} - \log f_{(x_1^T=-1)} = \log f_{(x_1^T=1)} \Big/ f_{(x_1^T=-1)}. \tag{9}$$

The right-hand side is, of course, the log of odds for exposure to a mother tongue, the logit.

Substituting the appropriate x_1^T values, we find that the subtraction is carried out with the following two equations:

$$\log f_{(x_1^T=1)} = 5.109 - .144 - .177x_1^G + .234x_1^A + .231x_1^G x_1^A$$
$$+ .405x_1^G + .235x_1^A + \ldots \tag{10}$$

$$\log f_{(x_1^T=-1)} = 5.109 + .144 - .177x_1^G + .234x_1^A + .231x_1^G x_1^A$$
$$- .405x_1^G - .235x_1^A - \ldots \tag{11}$$

After cancellations are taken into account, the subtraction produces:

$$\log f_{(x_1^T=1)} - \log f_{(x_1^T=-1)} = (-.144 - .144)$$
$$+ (.405x_1^G - [-.405x_1^G])$$
$$+ (.235x_1^A - [-.235x_1^A]) + \ldots$$
$$= -.288 + .810x_1^G + .470x_1^A + \ldots \tag{12}$$

This is the logit equation that started off the preceding section.

By examining the details of the subtraction, we see that two things occur in converting the parameters in the equation for the logarithm of a cell frequency to the parameters in a logit model:

(1) All terms not involving the dependent variable are canceled and thus do not appear in the logit equation. This occurs because other variables are held constant, and hence these terms are the same in both equations and disappear when one is subtracted from the other.

(2) All terms involving the dependent variable are retained in the logit equation, but their coefficients are doubled. *The doubling of their coefficients occurs when only effect coding is used and the dependent variable is a dichotomy.* In particular, what is doubled is any value pertaining to the category of the dependent variable that appears in the numerator of the odds.

The full derivation of the logit equation (equation 3) is shown in Table 3. Its parameters are twice the values of the parameters from the output that are relevant for predicting the frequencies of exposure. Lambda values relevant to the independent variables only are ignored, as are those for omitted categories.

The rules above, and in particular the doubling rule, cover instances where the model underlying the output has variables in effect-coded form. This is the case for such widely used log-linear computer programs as ECTA, BMDP4F, and SPSS-X LOGLINEAR. But a log-linear model may also be expressed in dummy-variable form; the computer program GLIM produces such output (Breen, 1984: 78-80). In this case, the first rule still applies: Terms relating only to independent variables do not appear in the logit equation. But the second rule must be modified. In particular, since the dependent variable is expressed as a dummy variable, any terms involving it are zero when the frequencies for its omitted category are being predicted. Hence the subtraction that generates the logit equation leaves the coefficients of terms involving the dependent variable unchanged (this assumes the omitted category is in the denominator of the odds; if it is in the numerator, then the signs of these coefficients are reversed).

Given the translation necessary to derive interpretable values from log-linear computer output, it is helpful to have some way of checking the end products of calculations. Here, the expected frequencies, routinely produced by many programs, are of assistance. Since the model for the expected frequencies is the basis for the logit model and quantities derived from it, there is necessarily a match between the predictions from the models. More specifically, since the logit model itself directly predicts the odds expected for specific values of the independent variables, the expected frequencies can be used as a check that the model has been correctly calculated. Table 4 presents the expected frequencies for the log-linear model described in Table 3. From these frequencies, one sees, for example, that the expected odds of exposure to a mother tongue for a second-generation member of the pre-1916 cohort who has single ancestry are 5.23 (i.e., 1,064.8/203.7). Except for a minor rounding error, this matches the value one obtains from the logit equation (equation 3) evaluated for: $x_1^C = x_1^G = x_1^A = 1$; and $x_2^C = x_3^C = x_1^C = 0$ (the predicted value of the logit is 1.656, and hence the predicted odds are 5.24).

In general, one can also directly verify odds ratios from the expected frequencies (except when multiple interaction effects involving the same independent variable are present). In the case of our model, we have already seen that when one independent variable is changed but the others are held constant, the predicted odds ratio is derived solely from the parameters for the altered variable (this follows from the fact that the model contains no interaction effects). The relevant odds ratios are those in Table 2, and it follows that these odds ratios can be verified in Table 4. For example, according to our earlier calculations, the odds ratio for mother-tongue exposure between the pre-1916 and post-1960 cohorts is 7.17. This odds ratio can be checked against the expected frequencies for second-generation persons of single ancestry ([1,064.8/203.7]/[37.4/51.2]), third-generation persons of single ancestry ([52.6/50.8]/[39.8/274.9]), second-generation persons of mixed ancestry ([120.6/59.0]/[18.0/63.1]), and third-generation persons of mixed ancestry ([21.4/52.8]/61.5/1,087.2]). Although the odds involved are different in each case, each odds ratio is within rounding error of 7.17.

INTERPRETING MODELS
WITH INTERACTION EFFECTS[8]

Log-linear models are well-known for their sensitivity to interaction effects, and, accordingly, such effects frequently appear in

TABLE 4
Observed and Expected Frequencies Under
the Model [CGA] [TC] [TG] [TA]

| Ancestry: | | Mother Tongue | | | |
| | | Exposure | | Nonexposure | |
Generation	Cohort	Observed*	Expected	Observed*	Exposure
Single:					
Second	Pre-1916	1083.4	1064.8	185.1	203.7
	1916-1930	1440.2	1411.4	273.8	302.6
	1931-1945	476.2	504.7	162.5	134.0
	1946-1960	209.1	219.8	114.9	104.3
	Post-1960	61.8	37.4	26.8	51.2
Third	Pre-1916	50.3	52.6	53.1	50.8
	1916-1930	138.5	157.1	188.7	170.1
	1931-1945	381.6	376.5	499.8	504.8
	1946-1960	501.9	512.1	1237.0	1226.8
	Post-1960	33.1	39.8	281.6	274.9
Mixed:					
Second	Pre-1916	114.1	120.6	65.5	59.0
	1916-1930	203.1	200.5	107.2	109.8
	1931-1945	103.3	127.4	110.5	86.4
	1946-1960	97.7	102.9	129.9	124.7
	Post 1960	18.4	18.0	62.7	63.1
Third	Pre-1916	11.5	21.4	62.6	52.8
	1916-1930	52.8	65.7	194.5	181.7
	1931-1945	248.4	200.9	641.0	688.5
	1946-1960	367.8	341.7	2066.7	2092.7
	Post-1960	43.4	61.5	1105.3	1087.2

*Fractional observed values occur because of weighting.

a well-fitted model. Needless to say, interaction effects add to the complexity of interpretation, but the difficulties they pose should not be overestimated. The principles already explicated for interpreting models without interactions remain in force when they are present. But one further principle must be added: Odds ratios, or whatever quantities are directly used for interpretation, must be calculated to match the complexity of the interaction effects. (For a formal statement of rules governing the calculation of interpretable quantities when interactions are present, see Long, 1984.)

The interpretation of models with interaction effects can be illustrated by continuing the discussion of models for exposure to a mother tongue. So as not to leap directly into a very complicated model, I will begin with a model to which a single interaction effect has been added. Note, however, that everything I will say about it can be applied to models with multiple interaction effects, as long as these effects have no independent variables in common. My discussion presumes hierarchical models—that is, models in which the presence of higher-order terms implies the presence of all nested, lower-order terms.

As noted in the preceding section, the model containing only main effects does not adequately fit the mother-tongue data. However, one interaction effect, involving cohort and generation, explains most of the remaining L^2. Adding this effect to the model reduces L^2 to 28.48, with 9 degrees of freedom (p $<$ .001). The model can still be improved, but the cohort-generation interaction has made a significant improvement (L^2 difference = 65.26, with 4 degrees of freedom [p $<$ .001]).

Even though an interaction effect is present, the lambda values in the output can be readily converted into the parameters for the logit model by using the principles of the preceding section. If the logit equation is expressed using the conventions of regression equations, then the interaction effect can be represented by a set of product terms between the relevant independent variables. In the case of the cohort-generation interaction, then, there are four product terms, because cohort is represented by four variables and generation by one. The parameters of these product terms are generated from the lambda values in the output by exactly the same rules used for main-effect terms. Thus, if effect coding is used to represent variables, the parameter values are double the corresponding lambda values for the category in the numerator of the odds. Table 5 shows the relationship between lambda values and the logit parameters in the case of the new model for mother-tongue exposure.

The presence of the interaction effect means that the effect of cohort depends upon the value of generation and, likewise, the effect of generation depends upon cohort. Interpreting such contingencies can be straightforward if one starts from an appropriate layout that can show odds changes among the combinations of categories of the variables involved. Such a layout must correspond with the complexity of the interaction effect it represents. A two-variable interaction requires us to interpret the odds ratios between all combinations of the categories of the two variables. In other words, we need to know how the odds change among the cells of a two-variable layout (see Table 6). A three-variable interaction requires consideration of odds changes among the cells of a three-way layout, and so forth.

TABLE 5

Derivation of a Logit Equation from Lambda Parameters
for a Model with an Interaction Effect

Model Terms Relevant to Logit Equation	Lambda Parameters		Logit Equation
	Exposure	Nonexposure	
Mother Tongue (T):	−.160	.160	−.320
Cohort (C) x Mother Tongue (T):			
Pre-1916	.287	−.287	$+.574\ x_1^C$
1916-1930	.254	−.254	$+.508\ x_2^C$
1931-1945	.141	−.141	$+.282\ x_3^C$
1946-1960	−.131	.131	$−.262\ x_4^C$
Post-1960	−.551	.551	—*
Generation (G) x Mother Tongue (T):			
Second	.458	−.458	$+.916\ x_1^G$
Third and later	−.458	.458	—*
Ancestry type (A) x Mother Tongue (T):			
Single	.232	−.232	$+.464\ x_1^A$
Mixed	−.232	.232	—*
Generation (G) x Cohort (C) x Mother Tongue (T):			
Second			
Pre-1916	.038	−.038	$+.076\ x_1^C x_1^G$
1916-1930	.034	−.034	$+.068\ x_2^C x_1^G$
1931-1945	−.166	.166	$−.322\ x_3^C x_1^G$
1946-1960	−.090	.090	$−.180\ x_4^C x_1^G$
Post-1960	.184	−.184	—**
Third			
Pre-1916	−.038	.038	—**
1916-1930	−.034	.034	—**
1931-1945	.166	−.166	—**
1946-1960	.090	−.090	—**
Post-1960	−.184	.184	—**

(continued)

TABLE 5   Continued

Other model terms, not relevant to the logit equation, include:

    Grand mean
    Ancestry (A)
    Cohort (C)
    Generation (G)
    Cohort (C) x Generation (G)
    Cohort (C) x Ancestry Type (A)
    Ancestry Type (A) x Generation (G)
    Cohort (C) x Ancestry Type (A) x Generation (G)

NOTE: Model is [CGA] [TCG] [TA], L^2 = 28.48, with 9 degrees of freedom
($p < .001$).
*Chosen as omitted category.
**Does not appear in logit equation because at least one omitted category is involved.

In order to express the odds changes among the cells of such a layout, one must choose a reference point, which can be either the geometric average across the cells or a particular cell. My preference, as before, is for the latter. For the interaction between cohort and generation, I have chosen the odds for the post-1960 cohort and third generation as the reference point, therefore fixing these odds at 1 and expressing other odds relative to the odds for this cell.

The odds ratios between the reference cell and other cells can be calculated by, first, determining the differences in the logit among the cells and, then, translating these differences from the logarithmic scale. For the interaction involving cohort and generation, the only relevant terms in the logit equation are the main-effect terms for cohort and for generation and the terms for the interaction between these variables ($x_1^C x_1^G$, $x_2^C x_1^G$, $x_3^C X_1^G$, $x_4^C x_1^G$). Thus, calculating the difference in the logit between, say, second-generation members of the 1916-1930 cohort and individuals in the reference cell requires evaluating the relevant terms for the two cells. From Table 5, which shows the logit model's derivation, we can see that the evaluation of these terms leads in the first case to:

$$+ .574(0) + .508(1) + .282(0) - .262(0) + .916(1)$$

$$+ .076(0)(1) + .068(1)(1) - .332(0)(1) - .180(0)(1) = 1.492.$$

Evaluating these terms for the reference cell yields:

$$+ .574(-1) + .508(-1) + .282(-1) - .262(-1) + .916(-1)$$

$$+ .076(-1)(-1) + .068(-1)(-1) - .332(-1)(-1)$$

$$- .180(-1)(-1) = -2.386.$$

Thus the logit difference between the two is 3.878 (i.e., 1.492 – [–2.386]), and the corresponding odds ratio is 48.33 (i.e., exp[3.878]). That is, with ancestry type controlled, the odds of exposure to a mother tongue are approximately 48 times higher for a second-generation member of the 1916-1930 cohort than they are for a third-generation member of the post-1960 cohort. Obviously, the joint effect of cohort and generational status on exposure to a mother tongue is quite large.

Similar calculations fill in the layout for the interaction effect of cohort and generation, which is displayed in Table 6 in completed form, along with the odds ratio for ancestry type. Incidentally, the odds ratios in the table can be verified with expected frequencies. Using these frequencies (which are not shown in order to conserve space), one finds that the odds ratio between second-generation members of the 1916-1930 cohort and third-generation members of the post-1960 cohort is 48.49 for persons of single ancestry and 48.48 for those of mixed ancestry—both

TABLE 6
Odds Ratios for Exposure to a Mother Tongue,
from the Model with an Interaction Effect
Involving Cohort and Generation

Cohort	Generation		Odds Ratios Between Second and Third Generations
	Second	Third	
Pre-1916	52.04	7.16	7.27
1916-1930	48.33	6.75	7.16
1931-1945	25.84	8.04	3.21
1946-1960	17.46	4.01	4.35
Post-1960	13.04	1*	13.04
Odds ratio between pre-1916 and post-1960 cohorts	3.99	7.16	
Ancestry type:			
Single	2.53		
Mixed	1*		

*Arbitrarily chosen reference points for odds ratios.

within rounding error of the ratio above, calculated from the logit model.

Just as with the main-effects model, it is important to examine thoroughly the odds ratios in order to comprehend fully the effects described by the model. It is, for instance, immediately apparent that in both generations the odds of exposure are generally higher in older cohorts; but by calculating the odds ratio between the oldest and youngest cohorts in each generation (see Table 6), we see that the effect of cohort is smaller in the second generation than in the third (and later). Nevertheless, even in the second generation, cohort makes a substantial difference. This is indicated by an illustrative percentage difference: Compared to a second-generation member of the post-1960 cohort who had an average chance of exposure to a mother tongue (42.4%), a second-generation member of the pre-1916 cohort had a 74.6% chance (with ancestry type controlled). (That is, the person in the post-1960 cohort has an odds of .736, and hence a comparable member of the pre-1916 has an odds of 2.94 [i.e., .736 × 3.99], according to the odds ratios implied by the model; an odds of 2.94 is equivalent to a 74.6% chance.)

By a similar examination of the odds ratios between generations in each cohort, one sees that the second generation consistently has a greater odds of exposure to a mother tongue and that this difference is larger for pre-1930 cohorts and for the post-1960 group; the odds ratio is 13.0 for the post-1960 cohort and 7.3 for the pre-1916 cohort, but just 3.2 for the 1931-1945 cohort, for instance. Also noteworthy is that the odds ratios for generation and for cohort are generally higher than the odds ratio for ancestry type. But even this last effect is substantial.

Finally, there is an interesting difference between the generations in the timing of the decline in mother-tongue exposure. For the second generation, the decline sets in for the cohorts born after 1930; there is little difference in the pre-1930 groups. But for the third (and later) generations, mother-tongue exposure does not decline until the post-1945 cohorts.

Everything that has been said so far extends in a straightforward manner to models with interaction effects involving more than two independent variables or to models with multiple interaction effects, as long as these do not share any independent variables in common. But new complexities are introduced when an independent variable appears in more than one interaction effect. These complexities are not inherent in log-linear models, but in the difficulties associated with complex interaction structures. They can be illustrated by continuing the development of a model for mother-tongue exposure, for there is one more interaction effect that can be added—namely, the interaction between cohort and ancestry type. Its addition reduces the model L^2 to 12.35 with 5 degrees of freedom (p $>$ .03); the L^2 difference associated with the interaction is 16.13 with 4 degrees of freedom (p $<$ .01). This is probably the model one would choose for final interpretation. Its logit equation is shown in Table 7.

According to the model, the effect of cohort depends on the values of generation and ancestry type. At first sight, this feature of the model suggests constructing a three-variable layout for odds changes. However, such a layout would not be parsimonious, for the model does not contain anything more complicated than a two-variable interaction. In cases like this, moreover, a three-variable layout for the odds would represent no gain in parsimony over the original table, which contains only three independent variables.[9] Therefore, all the information essential for understanding the interaction effects on the odds can be represented in two-way layouts, but the effects in these layouts no longer correspond in every case with odds ratios that can be found among the expected frequencies.

Two-variable layouts, calculated in a manner similar to that used for Table 6, are shown in Table 7. There is one for the interaction involving cohort and generation and one for the interaction involving cohort and ancestry type. In each layout, one cell has been selected as a reference point—its value is fixed at 1—and the remaining numbers have been calculated to represent effects on the odds relative to this reference point. The calculation of the effects uses a particular set of interactions from the logit equation and the lower-order terms associated with them; the method is the same as that used for Table 6.

To see how these effects can be interpreted, let us consider the most complicated effect, that of cohort. To begin with, the cohort effects in Table 7 do not match the odds ratios found in the expected frequencies, since the odds ratios for cohort depend simultaneously on the values of ancestry type and generation; the effects in either layout can, however, be shown to be geometric

TABLE 7
Logit Equation and Effects on the Odds for the
Model with Two Interaction Effects

log odds of exposure $= \quad -.334 + .504x_1^C + .506x_2^C + .312x_3^C$

$$-.242x_4^C + .908x_1^G + .536x_1^A + .062x_1^Cx_1^G + .074x_2^Cx_1^G$$

$$-.314x_3^Cx_1^G - .170x_4^Cx_1^G + .110x_1^Cx_1^A - .030x_2^Cx_1^A$$

$$-.132x_3^Cx_1^A - .120x_4^Cx_1^A$$

Effects on odds:

Cohort	Generation		Odds Ratios Between Second and Third Generations
	Second	Third	
Pre-1916	45.15	6.49	6.96
1916-1930	45.79	6.42	7.13
1931-1945	25.58	7.80	3.28
1946-1960	16.98	3.88	4.38
Post-1960	12.33	1*	12.33
Ratios between pre-1916 and post-1960 cohorts	3.66	6.49	

Cohort	Ancestry Type		Odds Ratios Between Single and Mixed Ancestry
	Single	Mixed	
Pre-1916	18.88	5.19	3.64
1916-1930	16.44	5.98	2.75
1931-1945	12.23	5.45	2.24
1946-1960	7.11	3.10	2.29
Post-1960	4.12	1*	4.12
Ratios between pre-1916 and post-1960 cohorts	4.58	5.19	

NOTE: Model is [CGA] [TCG] [TCA], $L^2 = 12.35$, with 5 degrees of freedom (p > .03).
*Arbitrarily chosen reference point.

averages of the relevant odds ratios across categories of the third variable. Despite the lack of an isomorphism to the odds ratios, the cohorts effects in Table 7 are readily interpretable. Each layout isolates the interaction between cohort and one of the other variables.

Thus the layout for cohort and ancestry type reveals that the effect of cohort, as indicated by the ratio between the effects for the pre-1916 and post-1960 cohorts, is slightly greater among persons of mixed ancestry than among persons of single ancestry. This difference between ancestry types is notably less than the contrast between generational groups—an indication that the cohort-ancestry type interaction is not of great import. But the cohort effects are substantial for both ancestry types. The cohort-generation interaction is almost identical to the pattern already discussed for Table 6.

POLYTOMOUS DEPENDENT VARIABLES

A powerful feature of log-linear modeling is its ability to handle dependent variables with more than two categories. The analysis of such variables requires some modification of the rules described in previous sections, but the general approach of building from logit equations to multiplicative effects can still be applied.

Two points are essential in understanding the difference between the analysis of a dichotomous dependent variable and the analysis of a polytomous one. First, more than one logit equation is required in the polytomous case, because there is more than one odds. Indeed, there are $[k(k-1)]/2$ distinct odds arising from a dependent variable with k categories; and $k-1$ of the odds are independent. Second, the derivation of these multiple logit equations differs from the derivation of the single logit equation in the dichotomous case. In the latter case, the logit coefficients are double the relevant lambda values found in the log-linear output (if the variables are effect coded). But when the dependent variable has more than two categories, the doubling rule no longer applies. In this case, the logit coefficient for a specific term is found by subtracting the corresponding lambda parameter for the dependent-variable category in the denominator of the odds from the lambda parameter for the category in the numerator.

Consider an analysis of intermarriage, with three categories based on the degree of overlap in the ethnic ancestries of husband and wife (i.e., ancestries are identical, partly overlapping, or nonoverlapping). More specifically, the analysis concerns the marriage patterns of persons of southern, central, and eastern European ancestry, and the independent variables are cohort,

generation, ancestry type, and gender. A model with one interaction effect on the dependent variable, between cohort and
ancestry type, fits extremely well ($L^2 = 33.25$, with 44 degrees of
freedom, $p > .8$). Table 8 shows the lambda parameters for this
model, as calculated by BMDP4F.

In this case, there are three logit equations (although any two of
them imply the third). I have chosen to express each by placing in
the numerator the category of greater difference in the ancestries
of the spouses. (For example, one equation predicts the log of the
odds of a marriage to someone of entirely different ancestry
versus to someone of identical ancestry). Since a logit equation is
derived by subtracting the equation predicting the log of the
frequency in the denominator of the odds from the equation
predicting the log of the frequency in the numerator, the coefficients of its terms can be found by subtracting the lambda values
pertaining to the category in the denominator from those pertaining to the category in the numerator. The resulting logit equations
for the model of intermarriage are also shown in Table 8.

The interpretation of these equations proceeds along the same
lines as before, and therefore I will discuss just one of them: the
equation for the logit of different ancestry versus the same. Since
there is only one interaction effect in the model, the derivation of
odds ratios from the parameters of the logit equation is straightforward; these ratios are presented in Table 9.

The effects of both generation and gender appear to be small in
terms of the odds ratios. The odds of marriage to someone of
different ancestry are only slightly higher for members of the third
generation than for members of the second; and these odds are
also only modestly higher for men than for women.

Much larger effects are associated with cohort and ancestry
type, the two variables involved in the interaction. Persons of
mixed ancestry have much greater odds of marriage to someone
from a different ethnic background than do individuals of single
ancestry, and the effect of ancestry type is greater in the pre-1946
cohorts than for the 1946-1960 group. The difference between the
ancestry types declines because of the effect of cohort, which is
more pronounced among persons of single ancestry than among
those from a mixed ethnic background. Among persons of single
ancestry, the odds of marriage to someone from a different
background rise steadily with each new cohort, revealing a

TABLE 8
Derivation of Logit Equations for a Polytomous
Dependent Variable (Intermarriage)

| | Relevant Lambda Parameters | | | Logit Equation Coefficients | | |
	Different	Part	Same	Odds of Different Versus Same	Odds of Different Versus Part	Odds of Part Versus Same
Marriage type (M):	1.042	−.438	−.603	1.645	1.480	.165
Cohort (C) x Marriage Type (M):						
Pre-1916 (x_1^C)	−.198	−.210	.408	−.606	.012	−.618
1916-1930 (x_2^C)	.009	.016	−.024	.033	−.007	.040
1931-1945 (x_3^C)	.101	.133	−.234	.335	−.032	.367
1946-1960*	.088	.062	−.150	—	—	—
Ancestry Type (A) x Marriage Type (M):						
Single (x_1^A)	.008	−1.066	1.058	−1.050	1.074	−2.124
Mixed**	−.008	1.066	−1.058	—	—	—
Generation (G) x Marriage Type (M):						
Second (x_1^G)	.002	−.066	.064	−.062	.068	−.130
Third**	−.002	.066	−.064	—	—	—
Gender (S) x Marriage Type (M):						
Female (x_1^S)	−.046	−.029	.074	−.120	−.017	−.103
Male**	.046	.029	−.074	—	—	—
Ancestry Type (A) x Cohort (C) x Marriage Type (M):						
Single ancestry (x_1^A):						
Pre-1916 (x_1^C)	.034	−.112	.078	−.044	.146	−.190
1916-1930 (x_2^C)	−.078	−.120	.197	−.275	.042	−.317
1931-1945 (x_3^C)	−.074	.098	−.023	−.051	−.172	.121
1946-1960***	.118	.134	−.252	—	—	—
Mixed ancestry:						
Pre-1916***	−.034	.112	−.078	—	—	—
1916-1930***	.078	.120	−.197	—	—	—
1931-1945***	.074	−.098	.023	—	—	—
1946-1960***	−.118	−.134	.252	—	—	—

NOTE: Model is [CGAS] [MCA] [MG] [MS], L^2 = 33.25, with 44 degrees of freedom (p > .8).
*Omitted category for cohort. (The post-1960 category has been eliminated from the analysis because few of its members were married at the time of the survey.)
**Omitted category.
***Interaction terms that do not appear in the logit equations because they involve one or more omitted categories.

Richard D. Alba   285

TABLE 9
Odds Ratios for Intermarriage
(Different Versus Same Ancestry),
by Ancestry, Cohort, Generation, and Gender

| | Ancestry Type | | Odds Ratios of |
	Single	Mixed	Mixed to Single
Cohort:			
Pre-1916	1*	8.92	8.92
1916-1930	1.50	21.28	14.19
1931-1945	2.54	23.01	9.06
1946-1960	3.52	13.71	3.89
Odds ratio of			
1946-1960 cohort to			
pre-1916 cohort	3.52	1.54	
Generation:			
Second	1*		
Third	1.13		
Gender:			
Female	1*		
Male	1.27		

*Reference points for remaining odds ratios. Note that, in this case, they do not correspond with omitted categories.

secular trend toward greater ethnic intermarriage among persons of European ancestry generally (Alba and Golden, 1986; Lieberson and Waters, 1985). The pattern is less clear among persons of mixed ancestry; after increasing between the pre-1916 and 1916-1930 cohorts, the odds remain steady and then fall in the 1946-1960 cohort. The odds ratio between the oldest and youngest cohorts is just 1.5 among persons of mixed ancestry, while it is 3.5 among those of undivided ethnic heritage. Clearly, the rising trend of intermarriage is having its deepest impact among persons of single ancestry, but individuals of mixed ancestry have a generally greater tendency to out-marry in any event (Alba and Golden, 1986).

CONCLUSION

The interpretation of log-linear models generally has been seen as a distinct topic, presenting special problems. Such treatment in isolation is unfortunate, for in many ways the interpretation of these models proceeds along lines that are familiar to social scientists from regression analysis. In particular, a log-linear model can be viewed as a linear model with categorical variables and a special dependent variable—the natural logarithm of an odds. Once this family resemblance is noted, many manipulations of log-linear models that contribute to their interpretation become readily apparent, and the interpretive step unique to them—namely, translation out of the logarithmic scale to odds ratios or similar quantities—seems much smaller in magnitude. Removing some of the clouds of abstruseness surrounding the interpretation of log-linear parameters will, I hope, contribute to their more frequent use—for they are essential to intelligent use of log-linear models in research.

NOTES

1. I make no claim to originality on behalf of this presentation. Virtually all of what follows can be found in other expositions of log-linear models, although I develop the material in a somewhat different way. For my own knowledge of log-linear interpretation, I am most indebted to Swafford (1980), Knoke and Burke (1980), and Long (1984). These papers, as well as that by Kaufman and Schervish (1986), also provide a more complete bibliography on log-linear models than I do.

2. The analyses that follow are based upon tables that incorporate CPS sampling weights to make the sample more representative; the weights have been scaled so that weighted and unweighted totals of cases are the same.

This analysis situation is discussed in detail by Clogg and Eliason (this volume). For the reader who may wish to replicate my results from the observed data in Table 4, I note that I have not used the conditioning procedure recommended in their article, since analysis of the weighted data leads to unbiased parameter estimates, the primary concern here.

3. This lack of symmetry between odds magnitudes above and below 1 disappears in the logarithmic scale (the logarithms of 1.5 and .67 are .4 and –.4, respectively); and this is one reason why some may prefer the logit coefficients.

4. For the benefit of the reader familiar with the literature on log-linear models, I note that equation 3 is conventionally written:

$$\log F_{ijk1}/F_{ijk2} = 2\lambda + 2\lambda_i^C + 2\lambda_j^G + 2\lambda_k^A,$$

where F_{ijk1} is the expected frequency in the cell for cohort$_i$, generation$_j$, ancestry type$_k$, and mother-tongue exposure$_1$. In this notation, the λ values play the role of the x coefficients in equation 8—for example, $2\lambda = -.288$, and $2\lambda_1^C = .644$.

5. One reader points out that the logit scale is, in fact, commonly used in natural science and engineering literatures.

6. The "average" in this case is the geometric average of the effects of the categories of a given variable: For a variable with n categories, this is defined as the nth root of the product of the effects of its categories. This occurs as the reference point because of the use of effect coding in the logit equation, which is in a logarithmic scale. The reference point for the coefficients of effect-coded variables consists of the arithmetic average of effects across the categories of the variable, and the geometric average results from the antilogarithmic transformation of the arithmetic average.

7. This, it should be underlined, is just a convenient reference point; other reference points (.5, say) may be equally plausible, and would yield somewhat different percentage differences.

Another method of converting odds ratios into percentage differences is developed by Kaufman and Schervish (1986).

8. The term *interaction effect,* as used here, indicates an effect of an independent variable on a substantive dependent variable (e.g., the logit) that is contingent upon the values of one or more other variables. This is the general meaning of interaction in multivariate analysis; the modeling of interaction effects in regression analysis is described by Allison (1977). This is not the same as the meaning found in many log-linear discussions, where an *interaction* refers to any association between two or more variables that is included in a log-linear model. Except for the model of statistical independence, all log-linear models include interactions of the latter sort; fewer include interactions of the kind designated here.

9. The alert reader will notice that, in this case, representing the model with separate interaction effects, as in Table 7, achieves no gain in parsimony over representing the model through the format of the original table (a $5 \times 2 \times 2$ layout here). This results from the fact that two of the variables are dichotomies, and it will not be true in general, as can easily be verified.

11

Latent-Class Analysis

An Introduction to Discrete Data Models with Unobserved Variables

JAMES W. SHOCKEY

Much of the research undertaken in the social sciences focuses on concepts that are not directly observable. A number of techniques have been developed to handle the latent-variable problem, each utilizing observable information in conjunction with a set of assumptions about the underlying constructs. Among this list of methods are covariance-structure analysis (e.g., LISREL models, which include the traditional factor analytic model as a special case), latent-trait analysis (e.g., Rasch models), and latent class analysis. These models differ primarily in the scale of measurement assumed for each variable. The focus of this chapter—latent-class analysis (or LCA)—is appropriate in cases in which all of the observed and latent variables are measured on, at most, an ordinal scale. Factor analysis and latent-trait analysis are both analogous to LCA, where the latent variable is assumed to be continuous and the observed variables are all either continuous or categorical, respectively. (See Muthen, 1984, for extensions of the covariance-structure model with categorical data.)

As with other latent-variable methods, latent-class models are often used to identify a latent variable and describe its relation-

AUTHOR'S NOTE: *I wish to thank Clifford Clogg, Scott Eliason, Roberto Fernandez, Scott Long, and Michael Sobel for helpful comments.*

ship to the observed variables. In addition, it is often desirable to determine a value of the latent variable for each member of the sample. In factor analysis, a linear combination of the observed variables is used to construct an index of each latent factor with factor scores used as weights. Analogously, latent-class models use a probability-based assignment rule to determine the category of the unobserved variable to which a sample member (or response pattern) belongs.

The aim of the present chapter is to describe the latent-class model, showing how it may be more appropriately applied in many circumstances than other latent-variable models. The model is presented first in its simplest form as a function of unrestricted probabilities, and is then extended to cover restricted parameter values and multiple-group hypotheses. Goodman's (1978) formulation of the latent-class model is stressed throughout, although Haberman's (1974, 1979) general log-linear parameterization is also discussed.

The presentation below is made in the context of two examples. First, a model of extrinsic job satisfaction is fit to data obtained from the Quality of Employment Survey 1977 Cross Section (Shockey, 1985). Three items dealing with separate dimensions of work satisfaction (earnings, fringe benefits, and job security) are used as indicators of the true unobserved level of satisfaction with the extrinsic aspects of work. Second, a model of survey response error in three sample rotations of the June 1980 Current Population Survey is presented. In this example, latent-class models are used to adjust the measurement of a respondent's labor force status for errors in response believed to be caused by the nature of the interview (e.g., use of telephone interviews, proxy respondents, and so on). This is an example of a more complex latent-class model incorporating within- and across-group restrictions both on the relationship among observed and latent variables and on latent-class membership.

GENERAL APPROACH TO
LATENT-CLASS ANALYSIS

Suppose a researcher is interested in using observed data on extrinsic job satisfaction to construct an indicator of the underlying level of satisfaction. The usual approach is to compute a weighted sum of the scores on several observed items, with weights often obtained from a factor analysis of the data. Unfortunately, this procedure assumes that all variables are measured as continuous data, whereas items are typically no more than ordinal in nature (e.g., four- or five-category Likert items).

Alternatively, the observed items may be used to define *latent* satisfaction using latent-trait models where satisfaction is assumed continuous or latent-class models where it is defined as categorical (or as discretized continuous). The advantage in using LCA is that only the distributional assumption that the data arise from a multinomial (or product-multinomial) distribution is required. In order to estimate values for the continuous latent variable itself (e.g., the score on a latent continuous attitude scale), latent-trait models are forced to define the latent distribution (e.g., normal or logistic); with LCA, the models are applied with distributional constraints that are much less restrictive.[1] When the latent variable is assumed to be a discretized representation of an underlying continuous variable, a distribution for the latent variable may be advantageously defined after the fact, but this is not a necessary condition (Clogg, 1985).

THE ASSUMPTION OF
CONDITIONAL INDEPENDENCE

To understand the approach used in latent-class analysis more generally it is useful to think in terms of a simple elaboration strategy for survey analysis (Rosenberg, 1968). Consider a set of characteristics observed to have a nonzero level of association. One hypothesis to consider is that this joint association is *not* the result of a direct relationship among the observed variables, but is in fact due completely to the association of each variable with an additional unconsidered variable. For example, there may be a significant association among the three items relating to satisfaction with extrinsic job characteristics in Table 1 although the association may in fact be a realization of an overall level of job satisfaction. If this overall satisfaction is controlled statistically, the observed item association would fall to zero. Where overall satisfaction is directly measurable, tests for zero partial correlations or conditional independence are available; when this additional factor is left unobserved, as is true here, the elaboration approach is not immediately applicable. It is possible, however, to *assume* the existence of an unobserved explanatory variable. A model incorporating the assumption of mutual independence conditional on the latent variable is then used to specify the latent variable as well as its relationship to each observed variable. This is often referred to as the "axiom of local independence" (Clogg, 1985; Lazarsfeld and Henry, 1968). Thus the association among the observed satisfaction items can be used to understand the unobservable degree of satisfaction by using latent-variable models.

MATHEMATICAL REPRESENTATION OF THE LATENT-CLASS MODEL

Based on the above example, we will (1) define a latent variable representing the underlying level of satisfaction with T categories, (2) describe the association between the three observed and one unobserved variable, and (3) use this association to create a single indicator of extrinsic job satisfaction.

The particular parameterization of the latent-class model used here is due to the work of Goodman (1978) and its recent extensions (Clogg and Goodman, 1984, 1985, 1986). Alternative formulations are available, such as those of Haberman (1977, 1979), Formann (1982), and Mooijaart (1982). The Goodman approach is used because it follows directly from our conceptual definition of LCA. While the Goodman model may be thought of as being somewhat less general than these other models, it has advantages in defining and testing certain key hypotheses concerning structural relationships among the variables.

Let π_t^X represent the proportion of the population in an unobserved status t on the latent variable X. If four underlying categories of extrinsic job satisfaction are hypothesized (X: t = 1, 2, 3, 4), then π_1^X denotes the proportion of the population that falls into the least satisfied category, π_4^X the proportion in the most satisfied category, and with π_2^X and π_3^X similarly defined. Now let π_{it}^{PX} represent the conditional probability that a person in the t*th* latent satisfaction category is observed to respond in category i to the PAY item (P: i = 1, 2, 3, 4). Throughout this chapter, a bar

TABLE 1
Data and Class Assignments for Example 1: Extrinsic Job Satisfaction

P =	S =	B = 1			2			3			4		
		Frequency	Assign to Class	Assignment Error[b]	Frequency	Assign to Class	Assignment Error	Frequency	Assign to Class	Assignment Error	Frequency	Assign to Class	Assignment Error
1	1	42	1	.005	7	1	.063	7	1	.087	2	1	.271
2	1	12	1	.071	4	1	.499	5	3	.583	1	3	.533
3	1	13	1	.087	5	1	.524	12	3	.235	2	3	.368
4	1	5	1	.107	1	1	.541	5	3	.409	5	4	.172
1	2	19	1	.150	11	2	.320	4	2	.535	1	4	.670
2	2	15	2	.315	29	2	.066	18	2	.279	7	2	.525
3	2	13	1	.469	10	2	.527	21	3	.198	12	3	.477
4	2	2	1	.582	4	2	.391	10	3	.496	15	4	.109
1	3	24	1	.115	10	2	.503	13	3	.548	3	3	.512
2	3	20	2	.514	28	2	.258	34	3	.334	10	3	.327
3	3	25	3	.399	30	3	.164	108	3	.042	48	3	.174
4	3	3	3	.491	11	3	.271	26	3	.172	28	4	.309
1	4	15	1	.113	7	2	.534	7	3	.640	10	4	.166
2	4	11	2	.550	14	2	.268	24	3	.428	21	4	.262
3	4	14	3	.485	22	3	.200	65	3	.201	84	4	.242
4	4	8	4	.442	6	3	.463	45	4	.291	172	4	.027

a. Pay (P): The pay is good (on present job). (1) not at all true; (2) a little true; (3) somewhat true; (4) very true.
Secure (S): The job security is good. (Categories same as above.)
Benefit (B): The fringe benefits are good. (Categories same as above.)
b. Lambda for the model is 0.6476.

over a factor denotes the variable to be estimated within levels of the variable without a bar, so that the overall parameter represents a *conditional* probability. The quantity π_{24}^{PX} is thus the probability that a respondent in the most satisfied category of the latent variable will respond "a little true" (i = 2) to the probe dealing with the job's level of pay. Conditional probabilities for the items dealing with fringe benefits (π_{jt}^{BX}; B: j = 1, 2, 3, 4) and job security (π_{kt}^{SX}; S: k = 1, 2, 3, 4) are defined in a similar manner. Based upon the assumption of independence among P, B, and S given the level of X, it follows that the joint probability that an individual in the population having unobserved response pattern (i, j, k, t) can be written as

$$\pi_{ijkt}^{PBSX} = \pi_t^X \, \pi_{it}^{\bar{P}X} \, \pi_{jt}^{\bar{B}X} \, \pi_{kt}^{\bar{S}X} \qquad [1]$$

where the probabilities are subject to the usual constraints:

$$\sum_i \pi_{it}^{\bar{P}X} = \sum_j \pi_{jt}^{\bar{B}X} = \sum_k \pi_{kt}^{\bar{S}X} = \sum_t \pi_t^X = 1 \qquad [2]$$

The parameters in equation 1 represent population values; maximum-likelihood estimates (MLEs) are denoted by placing a caret ($\scriptstyle\wedge$) over the corresponding parameter (e.g., $\hat{\pi}_t^X$).

The estimated distribution of the population observed across variables (i.e., the set of $\hat{\pi}_{ijk}$) is obtained by substituting MLEs for population parameters in equation 1 and summing over levels of the latent variable X:

$$\hat{\pi}_{ijk} = \sum_t \hat{\pi}_{ijkt} \qquad [3]$$

The adequacy of a given model can be measured by comparing the observed cell proportions (p_{ijk}) with the MLEs by using the familiar Pearson or Likelihood-Ratio Chi-Square statistics (Bishop et al., 1975). The degrees of freedom associated with these statistics are equal to the number of nonredundant cells in the observed table minus the number of freely estimated parameters. In the present example, there are 64 (= $4 \times 4 \times 4$) cells in the data, but because the sample size is fixed, one of the cells is redundant, leaving 63 nonredundant cells. The model posits 39 estimated parameters. There are four probabilities defined within each of the latent classes, but because these must sum to 1 (by equation 2) there are only three nonredundant parameters in each of the 12 parameter sets (four classes and three variables). In addition, there are four latent-class proportions, only three of which are nonredundant given equation 2. Thus the unrestricted model presented above has $(3 \times 12) + 3$ or 39 nonredundant parameters and 24 $(= 63 - 39)$ degrees of freedom (df).

In addition to L^2 and X^2, the Index of Dissimilarity (D) can also be used as an index of fit. D is computed as

$$D = .5 \sum_i \sum_j \sum_k | p_{ijk} - \hat{\pi}_{ijk} | \qquad [4]$$

and can be interpreted as the proportion of cases in the expected distribution that would require reclassification in order to reproduce the observed distribution perfectly. When $D = 0$, the two distributions are exactly the same, indicating a model that fits the data perfectly; a value of 1 suggests a very poor fit. There is no way to determine precisely what a "good" value of D is, but a value suggesting fewer than 5% of the cases are misspecified is commonly considered acceptable. The index of dissimilarity has the advantage of being independent of sample size, unlike measures based on chi-squared, which tend to increase as a function of N and thus produce an overly pessimistic view of a model's fit as the sample size increases.

An important feature of this class of models is the ability to test specific hypotheses by fixing parameters to known values (e.g., 0 or 1) or constraining a set of parameters to be equal to one another. For example, given the typical upward response bias observed on satisfaction items, we might hypothesize that someone who is very satisfied $(t = 4)$ will not be observed responding to any related item in the category of least satisfaction $(i = j = k = 1)$. In terms of the model, this translates to

$$\pi_{14}^{\bar{P}X} = \pi_{14}^{\bar{B}X} = \pi_{14}^{\bar{S}X} = 0 \qquad [5]$$

Because none of these three parameters will be estimated by the model, the degrees of freedom would correspondingly increase by 3. More generally, we may wish to test some specific hypothesis that assumes a degree of similarity among the observed variables but leaves the actual value to be estimated by the model rather than fixed a priori:

$$\pi_{it}^{\bar{P}X} = \pi_{jt}^{\bar{B}X} = \pi_{kt}^{\bar{S}X} \qquad [6]$$

where the parameters are values either to be estimated under the model or fixed a priori. The hypothesis of equation 5 may be reexpressed in terms of equation 6, where all parameters are set equal to 0 for i = j = k = 1 and t = 4. Another attractive hypothesis says that each observed indicator has the same relationship with the underlying construct. Provided each indicator has an equal number of categories, this can be derived from equation 6 by

$$\pi_{it}^{\bar{P}X} = \pi_{it}^{\bar{B}X} = \pi_{it}^{\bar{S}X} \qquad [7]$$

(for example, $\pi_{11}^{\bar{P}X} = \pi_{11}^{\bar{B}X} = \pi_{11}^{\bar{S}X}$).

Several computer programs are available for estimation of latent-class models. The program MLLSA (Clogg, 1977), and several of those based on it, conforms most closely to the latent class approach as presented in terms of probabilities, and has been used for all results presented in this chapter. The algorithm is based on a method of iterative proportional scaling that is equivalent to the EM algorithm (Dempster et al., 1977; Goodman, 1974a), and is capable of estimating any of the models derived from equation 1.[2]

Standard errors for the parameters obtained from equation 1 can be computed in several ways. The information matrix may be transformed in a standard manner, yielding the estimates directly, but this procedure requires matrix inversion, which can become difficult for large problems. Alternatively, the standard jackknife or the infinitesimal jackknife (or "delta") methods can be employed (Efron, 1982; Henry, 1981; Miller, 1974). The two approaches are asymptotically equivalent and appear to reach parallel conclusions with moderate sample sizes. In general, the standard errors produced under the jackknife should be slightly larger than those from the delta method where a difference exists, thus providing the more conservative estimate.

In general the jackknife variance estimates may be computed as follows. A random sample of n observations is used to estimate the values of a given parameter, say θ. Let $\hat{\theta}_{(h)}$ be the estimate of θ obtained when the h*th* observation has been deleted. By successively removing each of the n observations, a set of n $\hat{\theta}$ values is obtained. The estimated asymptotic standard deviation (EASD) for the overall estimate of θ is defined as the square root of the sample variance of the $\hat{\theta}_{(h)}$:

$$s^2(\hat{\theta}) = [(n-1)/n] \sum_h (\hat{\theta}_{(h)} - \hat{\theta}_{(\cdot)})^2$$

where

$$\hat{\theta}_{(\cdot)} = (\sum_h \hat{\theta}_{(h)})/n$$

In the case of latent-class models, we replace $\hat{\theta}$ by, for example, $\hat{\pi}_{ts}^{\overline{X}G}$. To obtain the EASD for $\hat{\pi}_{11}^{XG}$, its parameter estimate is recomputed N times, each time deleting one of the observations and using the remaining N − 1 observations for the computation. The process is simplified somewhat by noting that the calculations are identical for each observation deleted within a given cell of the observed cross-classification. If there are f_{ijk} (= Np_{ijk}) observations in the ijk*th* cell, the parameters need only be recomputed once, but the new value should be weighted by the cell size f_{ijk}. Let $\theta_{(ijk)}$ represent the latent-class parameters to be estimated (e.g., π_{11}^{XG}), where the parameter is computed by dropping all cases in the (i, j, k)*th* cell. Then

$$\theta_{(\cdot)} = [\sum_i \sum_j \sum_k f_{ijk}\, \theta_{(ijk)}]/N$$

and

$$s^2(\hat{\theta}) = [(N-1)/n] \sum_i \sum_j \sum_k f_{ijk} (\hat{\theta}_{(ijk)} - \hat{\theta}_{(\cdot)})^2$$

For a detailed discussion of the jackknife, see Efron (1982); see Henry (1981) for the jackknife applied to cross-tabulated data.

LOG-LINEAR FORMULATION OF LCA

As mentioned, the model in equation 1 may be reexpressed in several ways. The most general alternative, discussed by Haberman (1977, 1979), is based on the log-linear model. Let F_{ijkt} be the number of respondents expected to have the unobserved (i, j, k, t) response pattern under some model. Given the assumption of conditional independence, the natural log of F_{ijkt} (L_{ijkt}) can be written as (using the notation of Bishop et al., 1975):

$$L_{ijkt} = u + u_{P(i)} + u_{B(j)} + u_{S(k)} + u_{X(t)} + u_{PX(it)} + u_{BX(jt)} + u_{SK(kt)} \qquad [8]$$

for $i = 1, \ldots, (I-1)$; $j = 1, \ldots, (J-1)$; $k = 1, \ldots, (K-1)$; $t = 1, \ldots,$ $(T-1)$; and where the u terms are parameters each constrained to a zero sum over any subscript (as in analysis of variance models).

Haberman (1979) shows that a wide range of hypotheses may be examined by placing constraints on the parameters in equation 8. For example, we might wish to test the notion that job security has no relationship with overall unobserved satisfaction: $u_{SX(it)} = 0$; or that each observed variable relates to latent satisfaction in precisely the same manner:

$$u_{PX(it)} = u_{BX(jt)} = u_{SX(kt)} \qquad [9]$$

Note, however, that these constraints do not correspond to setting $\pi_{it}^{\overline{P}X} = 0$ or those of the latent agreement model expressed in equation 7, respectively. Solving equation 8 in terms of probabilities yields

$$\pi_t^X = \sum_i \exp(u_{P(i)} + u_{PX(it)})$$

and

$$\pi_{it}^{\overline{P}X} = \exp(u_{P(i)} + u_{PX(it)})/\pi_t^X$$

Similar comments apply to variables B and S. The hypothesis of equality in conditional probabilities across variables is, therefore, a more complex hypothesis than that of equal association; the constraints $u_{P(i)} = u_{B(i)} = u_{S(i)}$, in addition to those made in equation 9, are sufficient to define the desired equality hypothesis.

The added flexibility in the model provided by equation 8, however, comes at the expense of computational ease. The program LAT (Haberman, 1979; appendix, vol. 2), based on the Fischer scoring algorithm, requires a design matrix as input as well as initial approximations for either the cell counts or the model parameters. The maximum-likelihood solution produced by LAT is apparently quite sensitive to the initial values used (Haberman, 1979). In our satisfaction example, the $4^4 = 256$ initial unobserved cell counts must be quite close to the final estimates, otherwise the program may not converge to a proper solution. In addition, the input for the data of Table 1 would require a design matrix of 256 rows and 46 columns. For most applications, the program MLLSA is recommended over LAT, but particularly where the latent-class proportions are fixed in some way. Some models that are not estimable with MLLSA will, of course, require the use of LAT or another alternative. This is true, for example, when a scoring system is assumed for any or all variables under study (Clogg, 1985).

EXAMPLE 1:
FORMING AN INDICATOR OF
LATENT SATISFACTION

DETERMINING AN APPROPRIATE MODEL

The first step in producing a categorical indicator of latent satisfaction is to obtain a latent-class model that adequately reproduces the data in Table 1. We start by fitting several un-restricted models with differing numbers of latent categories. In what follows, a model that posits two categories in the latent variable will be referred to as a "two-class model," that with three latent categories, a "three-class model," and that with t classes of the latent variable X, a "t-class" model. Results are displayed in panel A of Table 2. Model M_1 is the unrestricted two-class model, and clearly does not fit the data well ($L^2 = 228.73$ on $63 - 19 = 44$ df). Similar models positing three and four latent classes are labeled M_2 and M_3, respectively. The three-class model performs much better than the two-class model with $L^2 = 66.36$ on 34 df, but not until a fourth latent category is added do we find an adequate model ($L^2 = 15.11$ on 24 df). Note that the index of dissimilarity is only .0302, suggesting that a mere 3% of all cases would require a shift to another cell in order to equate the observed and expected distributions across all observable response patterns. Thus a model that considers four categories of latent satisfaction (M_3),

TABLE 2
Fit Statistics for Latent Class Models
Applied to the Data in Table 1 and Table 4[a]

Model	L^2	X^2	DF	D
A. Latent Class Models of Extrinsic Job Satisfaction (Table 1):				
M1	228.73	271.54	44	.1590
M2	66.36	75.25	34	0.703
M3	15.11	14.31	24	.0302
M4	32.58	36.01	27	.0412
M5	190.59	194.50	48	.1368
B. Latent Class Models of Response Error (Table 4):				
H1 (H1')[b]	73.53	74.47	9	.0085
H2	73.42	74.38	7	.0085
H3	71.78	72.69	5	.0085

a. See test for model descriptions.
b. Model H1' is properly identified with one additional restriction beyond H1; see text for discussion.

equal to the number of categories on each observed item, cannot be rejected.[3]

It may be possible, however, to simplify M_3 by fixing or constraining certain parameters. We might assume that respondents in the most satisfied category of the unobserved variable will not respond in the least satisfied category to any of the three observed items. This hypothesis (M_4), displayed earlier as equation 5, fits the data well ($L^2 = 32.58$ on 27 df, D = .0412). Because M_4 is derived from M_3 by setting the three parameters in equation 5 equal to zero, the difference in L^2 values, itself distributed as a chi-square variate with degrees of freedom equal to the number of parameters fixed, can be used to test the hypothesis implied by equation 5. Here L^2 is 17.42 (= 32.58 − 15.11) with 3 (= 27 − 24) df, which represents a significant deterioration in fit between models M_3 and M_4 and leads to a rejection of the hypothesis. One final hypothesis (M_5) assumes that a form of latent agreement exists between the observed items (see equation 7). While this model has great substantive appeal, it obviously provides a poor fit to the data ($L^2 = 190.59$ on 48 df). As a result, we conclude that M_3, an unrestricted four-class latent structure, is the best model with which to describe the latent structure of extrinsic job satisfaction.

DISCUSSION OF MODEL PARAMETERS—
DESCRIBING THE LATENT STRUCTURE

The MLEs of the conditional probabilities and latent-class proportions are presented in Table 3. Category 3, labeled "high," is the modal latent class, capturing almost 40% of the population. The distribution of satisfaction is in general upwardly skewed, with nearly 70% of the population estimated to be in one of the two highest categories. Next consider the conditional probabilities, which may be thought of as analogues to factor loadings used in describing factor pattern relationships. For example, category 1 always "loads" highest among the four observed categories of each variable given t = 1 of the latent satisfaction variable. Indeed, the highest probability of observed response given a latent class occurs where i = j = k = t. In short, Table 3 reveals a clear relationship between each of the observed items and the latent variable, particularly for the items dealing with pay and fringe benefits.

LATENT CLASS ASSIGNMENTS—
INDICATORS OF UNOBSERVED CONSTRUCTS

Having decided upon an acceptable model of satisfaction for the sample, the next task is to assign response patterns (and thus individuals) to one of the categories of the latent variable. The appropriate assignment rule is to assign all cases with a given response pattern (i, j, k) to the most likely latent class given the observed variables are at levels i, j, and k, respectively; that is

$$\max (\hat{\pi}_{ijkt}^{PBS\overline{X}}), \quad t = 1, \ldots, T \qquad [10]$$

where from equations 1-2:

$$\hat{\pi}_{ijkt}^{PBS\overline{X}} = \hat{\pi}_{ijkt}^{PBSX} / \hat{\pi}_{ijk}^{PBS}$$

with $\hat{\pi}_{ijk}^{PBS}$ equaling the estimated proportion in the (i, j, k)*th* observed response category collapsing (or summing) over the categories of X. The error in making latent-class assignments based on equation 10 can be thought of as 1 minus the probability of a correct assignment (i.e., equation 10), which leads the error to lie between 0.00 and 0.75. The error can become rather larger (in

TABLE 3
Estimated Parameters Under Model M3[a]

Observed Item Category	Very Low (t = 1)	Low (t = 2)	High (t = 3)	Very High (t = 4)
Pay:				
1	.587 (.033)[b]	.158 (.026)	.033 (.007)	.031 (.008)
2	.167 (.025)	.656 (.034)	.149 (.016)	.062 (.012)
3	.197 (.027)	.129 (.024)	.666 (.021)	.247 (.022)
4	.049 (.013)	.057 (.016)	.151 (.016)	.660 (.024)
Secure:				
1	.442 (.034)	.024 (.008)	.046 (.009)	.018 (.006)
2	.174 (.025)	.438 (.036)	.097 (.013)	.068 (.013)
3	.236 (.029)	.347 (.035)	.557 (.022)	.093 (.015)
4	.148 (.023)	.190 (.028)	.300 (.021)	.820 (.019)
Benefit:				
1	.737 (.029)	.210 (.029)	.077 (.012)	.020 (.006)
2	.128 (.022)	.501 (.036)	.155 (.016)	.009 (.004)
3	.118 (.021)	.240 (.031)	.565 (.022)	.156 (.018)
4	.017 (.005)	.048 (.013)	.202 (.018)	.815 (.019)
Unobserved distribution of extrinsic job satisfaction:	.168 (.011)	.146 (.010)	.384 (.014)	.301 (.013)

a. Model L^2 = 15.11, X^2 = 14.31 on 24 df; D = .0302; N = 1265.
b. Standard errors in parentheses.

general between 0 and $[T - 1]/T$), but the error for any other category is by definition greater still. Asymmetric lambda (Blalock, 1972: 302-303; Goodman and Kruskal, 1954) may be used as an indicator of the success in assignment across all observed response patterns. Lambda measures the proportionate reduction in the probability of making an assignment error

TABLE 4
Four-Way Cross-Tabulation of Observed Data[a]

F	R	L	I	VI	VII
	Variable[b]			Rotation Group	
1	1	1	47	1988	2116
2	1	1	2413	544	490
1	2	1	57	2829	3025
2	2	1	3310	725	560
1	1	2	8	372	423
2	1	2	579	131	104
1	2	2	6	225	209
2	2	2	409	100	97
1	1	3	115	4861	5009
2	1	3	5793	1086	847
1	2	3	164	3433	3577
2	2	3	4268	855	676
Total			17169	17149	17133

a. Data are taken from the June 1980 Current Population Survey. Counts are weighted to be representative of the full U.S. working-age population, and are re-weighted downward to correspond with the actual CPS sample size.
b. Variables used are F: Interview Format (1 = telephone, 2 = face-to-face); R: Respondent Type (1 = proxy, 2 = self); L: Observed Labor Force Status (1 = NILF, 2 = unemployed, 3 = employed).

when the rule in equation 10 is used as opposed to placing all cases naively into the unconditional modal latent class (max $\hat{\pi}_t^X$, $t = 1, \ldots, T$). Thus if the probability of assignment error across all cells of the table is

$$E_{cond} = \sum_{i,j,k,t} (1 - \max (\hat{\pi}_{ijkt}^{PBS\bar{X}})) (\hat{\pi}_{ijk}^{PBS})$$

and the error knowing only latent-class membership is

$$E_{uncond} = 1 - \max(\hat{\pi}_t^X)$$

then lambda may be defined as

$$\lambda = (E_{uncond} - E_{cond}) / E_{uncond} \qquad [11]$$

(see Clogg, 1979, 1981). The proportionate-reduction-in-error (PRE) property of lambda is clearly seen in equation 11, with the numerator defining the reduction in error when more information is used to make assignments and the denominator showing the total error in using the single unconditioned rule.

The probabilities of incorrect class assignments for the satisfaction example are found in Table 1, along with the assignments themselves. Out of 64 total response patterns, 16 or 25% have assignment error probabilities above .50 and 2 (or 3%) have probabilities above .60. These last two are response patterns having satisfaction with pay quite low (i = 1) that are being assigned to satisfied latent classes (t = 3 or 4); a great deal of error is accumulated from this pattern over the entire table. On the other hand, the reduction in error obtained in utilizing the conditional assignment rule is very good (λ = .6476); that is, the assignment rule reduces error by nearly two-thirds over the modal class assignment. Given this information, and the general high level of fit for the model overall, we can accept the assignments as providing a reasonable four-category indicator of latent extrinsic job satisfaction.

In the absence of this indicator, integer scores might be assigned to each category of the three observed variables and a new index obtained by summing the three observed scores. This produces a scale with 10 potential values (3, 4, . . ., 12), which is typically treated as a continuous rather than a categorical variable. To see the danger in this, consider a score of 7 obtained by summing the assumed integer scores. When using integer scores, 12 response patterns would be represented by a score of 7 (e.g., the [1, 2, 4], [1, 4, 2], and [4, 2, 1] responses). These 12 cells do not fall, however, into the same latent categories. Indeed, two belong on category 1, five to category 2, four to category 3, and one to category 4. The naively summed scale must be questioned for equating heterogeneous response patterns in this manner. Of course, the summed scale can be informed by deriving variable weights via factor analysis, but it remains true that the distance between observed categories must be known or assumed in order to obtain the factor analytic solution (see extensions, however, by Muthen, 1984). Because the assumption of interval-level measurement is not required, latent-class models are often a more appropriate alternative for indicator construction than either the simple summation of scores or the factor-analytic approach.

This first example is designed to show how latent-class models can be used to examine the unobserved structure that underlies the association observed among a set of variables. In addition, information concerning this structure can be used to construct indexes from the observed variables in order to reduce the amount of data needed in subsequent analyses. A consistent theme has been that the latent-class model is more appropriate in some circumstances than the more often used factor-analytic model. The substance of the example, however, dealt with a variable that most researchers consider to be continuous—satisfaction. In contrast, the next example considers a fairly complex measurement model for a variable that is naturally categorical—an individual's employment status—and shows how the basic approach defined above can be extended when latent structures are posited simultaneously in more than one group.

EXAMPLE 2:
ADJUSTING FOR RESPONSE
ERROR IN SEVERAL GROUPS

ROTATION GROUP BIAS AND RESPONSE ERROR

A common problem in survey research is the phenomenon known as response error or response bias. An individual's response to any given questionnaire item may differ systematically from his or her true response as a result of factors such as the wording and order of questions, the expectations held by the interviewer, or the use of telephones to conduct the interviews (Bradburn, 1984; Schuman and Presser, 1981). Each observed response may consist of a part due to the true, underlying response, plus the influences of random error and systematic error. This last form of error encompasses what we are referring to as response error.

One particularly important example of this kind of systematic bias occurs in the measurement of labor force status using the Current Population Survey (CPS) (Bailar, 1975). Stated briefly, the CPS sample contains eight groups (or rotations) based upon the number of times a respondent's household has been interviewed (i.e., group one contains first-time respondents and group eight contains those interviewed for the eighth time). Based upon the sampling procedure, each group should be a representative sample of the U.S. working-age population. Each of the eight groups, then, should provide an equivalent estimate of any characteristic of the population. In reality, however, the unemployment rate reported in the first rotation group has consistently been higher than that reported for any of the other groups since the late 1950s. This problem, on its surface one of unexpected heterogeneity in labor force status, is potentially a threat to the sampling frame of most panel surveys, and has come to be known as rotation group bias (Bailar, 1975; Shockey, 1986).

Many potential explanations for the existence of rotation group bias have been proposed. The approach taken here is that the true rate of unemployment in each of the eight groups is actually the same. The observed differences arise because each group is exposed to slightly different interviewing conditions—in short, they suffer differentially from the influence of response error. Specifically, initial interviews (i.e., group I) are almost always conducted face-to-face with the interviewer, as are most interviews in groups II and V. Nearly all interviews in the remaining groups (III, IV, VI, VII, VIII), however, are conducted over the telephone. To the extent that face-to-face interviews are more likely to yield biased responses to sensitive questions (such as those concerning unemployment) than are telephone interviews, responses obtained for individuals in groups I, II, and V are likely to differ from those in other groups. This alone could give rise to the unexpected pattern of observed unemployment. In addition, however, some responses are obtained directly from the respondent while others are obtained through "proxy" respondents— a responsible adult who is available to answer questions in lieu of the actual respondent. This form of error is introduced evenly to all groups and should not directly lead to the rotation group problem, but may act to exacerbate it.

A LATENT-CLASS APPROACH TO RESPONSE ERROR

In the event the estimation of a given characteristic is biased, the usual approach is to adjust the data for the bias, thereby obtaining unbiased estimates. Several adjustment strategies may be used. Often the amount of bias is estimated from another source and used to correct the sample data. In other cases, re-interviews are available that can be used to "triangulate" on the true response. In this exercise, we propose the use of latent-class models to obtain estimates of the true but unobserved labor force status variable.

Consider the case with only one group. In theory, labor force status should be independent of the format used to conduct the interview, but we know this is not true. Knowing the true labor force status classification, we could test whether the observed classification is independent of the interview format conditional on the true status. Not knowing the true values, however, but *assuming* that conditional independence holds, the standard latent-class model can be used to estimate the unbiased distribution of labor force status. For any one group this model would be written as

$$\pi_{ijkt}^{FRLX} = \pi_t^X \; \pi_{it}^{\bar{F}X} \; \pi_{jt}^{RX} \; \pi_{kt}^{LX} \qquad [12]$$

with constraints equivalent to those of equation 2. Here π_{ijkt}^{FRLX} is the unobserved proportion of the population with response pattern (i, j, k, t) in the four-way classification of interview format (F: i = 1, 2 for telephone and face-to-face interviews), respondent type (R: j = 1, 2 for proxy and self), observed labor force status (L: k = 1, 2, 3 for not in the labor force [NILF], unemployed, and employed), and true or latent labor force status (X: 1, 2, 3 with categories as defined for L). Again, π_t^X represents the population proportion in category t of the latent variable, where π_2^X is the proportion unemployed, $(\pi_2^X + \pi_3^X)$ the proportion in the active labor force, and $\pi_2^X / (\pi_2^X + \pi_3^X)$ is the true unemployment rate. The π_{kt}^{LX} define the conditional probability that a person with status t on the latent labor force variable is in category k of the observed labor force classification. Thus π_{11}^{LX}, π_{22}^{LX}, and π_{33}^{LX} represent accurate responses among those NILF, unemployed, and employed, respectively, whereas π_{21}^{LX} (for example) is the proportion of the population actually NILF (t = 1) who respond as if they were unemployed (k = 2). These terms can be used to verify the existence of response error as it was hypothesized. In a similar manner the $\pi_{it}^{\bar{F}X}$ and $\pi_{jt}^{\bar{R}X}$ parameters define the nature of the bias introduced into the measurement process by the interview format and type of respondent, respectively.

MULTIPLE-GROUP LATENT-CLASS ANAYLSIS

The main hypothesis concerning this bias, and the corresponding adjustment strategy, is that the nature of the bias is fundamentally different in the first rotation group. As a result we expect the latent structures to differ between the final group and the remaining seven. For simplicity, only groups I, VI, and VII are used (represented by the grouping variable G: s = 1, 2, 3 for the first, sixth, and seventh rotation groups, respectively). In order to examine the latent-class model defined in equation 12 across groups, we could fit the model separately in each of the three rotations groups. The same result can be obtained by fitting all groups simultaneously with one model, utilizing constraints defined below. This multiple-group model is obtained by conditioning each term in equation 12 on the level of G:

$$\pi_{ijkts}^{\overline{FRL}XG} = \pi_{ts}^{\overline{X}G}\ \pi_{its}^{\overline{F}XG}\ \pi_{jts}^{\overline{R}XG}\ \pi_{kts}^{\overline{L}XG} \tag{13}$$

(recalling that the "bar" over a factor indicates that its category is to be estimated conditional on the level of the variable *not* barred). Again the restrictions of equation 2 apply. Here $\pi_{ijkts}^{\overline{FRL}XG}$ represents the probability of obtaining an unobserved (i, j, k, t) response pattern for a member of the *s*th rotation. The $\pi_{ts}^{\overline{X}G}$ parameters denote the proportion of the *s*th group having a true labor force status t, so that $\pi_{21}^{\overline{X}G}$, $\pi_{22}^{\overline{X}G}$, and $\pi_{23}^{\overline{X}G}$ are the proportions unemployed (t = 2) in rotations I, VI, and VII, respectively. Analogous to the interpretation of the single group model, the $\pi_{kts}^{\overline{L}XG}$ indicate the correspondence between observed and latent labor force status classifications in the *s*th group. Thus $\pi_{211}^{\overline{L}XG}$, $\pi_{212}^{\overline{L}XG}$, and $\pi_{213}^{\overline{L}XG}$ are the proportions of rotation groups I, VI, and VII who are actual NILF but are observed in the unemployment response category.

The advantage in formulating the multiple group model as in equation 13 rather than fitting a separate model for each group (as in equation 12) is that the relationship defined by the parameters in equation 12 can be constrained in various ways across groups and tested simultaneously. For example, consider how the $\pi_{ts}^{\overline{X}G}$ parameters might be constrained to fit the hypotheses developed concerning rotation group bias. It may be, as proposed, that the proportions in each category of the true labor force classification are the same in each of the three groups examined here. This hypothesis of *homogeneity* across groups is represented as

$$H_1:\ \pi_{t1}^{\overline{X}G} = \pi_{t2}^{\overline{X}G} = \pi_{t3}^{\overline{X}G}, \quad t = 1, 2, 3 \tag{14}$$

On the other hand, it may be that the proportions are equal in all groups except the first (i.e., *partial homogeneity*):

$$H_2: \; \pi_{t1}^{\bar{X}G} \neq \pi_{t2}^{\bar{X}G} = \pi_{t3}^{\bar{X}G}, \quad t = 1, 2, 3, \qquad [15]$$

or that the latent proportions are completely different in each of the three groups (i.e., heterogeneity):

$$H_3: \; \pi_{t1}^{\bar{X}G} \neq \pi_{t2}^{\bar{X}G} \neq \pi_{t3}^{\bar{X}G}, \quad t = 1, 2, 3 \qquad [16]$$

Note that H_1 requires only one degree of freedom for each of the categories of the latent variable X (or t), while H_2 and H_3 require 2t and 3t df, respectively. The perspective on multiple group models taken here is due to recent work by Clogg and Goodman (1984, 1985, 1986); Haberman (1979: 541ff) considered similar extensions of the latent class model defined in equation 8.

The three hypotheses stated in equations 14-16 are the heart of the issue of rotation group bias, but similar hypotheses could be defined for each of the observed variables (interview format, respondent type, and observed labor force status) conditional on both the group and the latent status. That is, the $\pi_{ts}^{\bar{X}G}$ in equations 14-16 could be replaced by either π_{its}^{FXG}, π_{jts}^{RXG}, or π_{its}^{LXG}, where in the latter case the constraints would be aimed at examining differences in the accuracy of labor force classsifications between the first, sixth, and seventh rotations. In actuality the presence or absence of constraints must be considered for each set of parameters in order to define the latent-class model of equation 13.

While each part is critical to a complete analysis, we will simplify the following discussion by focusing solely on the constraints imposed on the classification of true labor force status across groups. We will assume that the other hypotheses have been considered previously, with the following results: (1) the association between respondent type (R) and the true labor force classification (X) is the same in each of the three groups (i.e., homogeneity); (2) the relationship between interview format (F) and true status (L) is different in each group (i.e., heterogeneity); and (3) as was hypothesized, the association between observed and true labor force classifications is the same in the sixth and seventh rotation groups but differs significantly in the first (i.e., partial homogeneity). See Shockey (1986) for a more complete discussion of these models.

TESTING FOR LATENT-CLASS
HOMOGENEITY ACROSS GROUPS

With the above results as a base, each of the three hypotheses examining differentials in the distribution of latent labor force status across groups is fit to the data displayed in Table 3. The model-fitting results are listed in panel B of Table 2.[4] None of the models fit the data based on the significance of L^2 or X^2. The data set under analysis, however, contains over 51,000 respondents, and recalling the influence of sample size on these indices of fit, the inadequacy of the models may be overstated. In support, note that the index of dissimilarity for each of the three models is .0085—less than 1% of the sample would require shifting into another category in order to equate the observed and expected distributions. If we make the assumption that this error is proportionately spread across statuses and groups, the estimated rate of unemployment will be off by only $1/100th$ of one percentage point (.0085x.0557x.3333). Given the extremely low values for D, we must conclude that models H_1, H_2, and H_3 all fit the data quite well.

These three models together form a nested hierarchy in the distribution of labor force statuses across rotations, ranging from one to less restrictive. This means that the difference in L^2 values computed for two models can be used to test the corresponding relaxing of constraints. The difference in fits between H_1 and H_2, quite small relative to the two degrees of freedom gained ($L^2 = 0.11$ on 2df), indicates that there is no advantage in freeing the latent distribution of the first group. The same is true for allowing all groups to have different distributions [$L^2(H_2) - L^2(H_3) = 1.64$ on 2df], and we conclude that H_1 is the best model examined. This provides strong support for the hypothesis that the actual distribution of employment statuses differs among the CPS rotations primarily due to a lack of uniformity in the interviewing circumstances.

MODEL IDENTIFICATION IN
LATENT-CLASS MODELS

When fitting latent structure models in general, including those commonly known as LISREL models, it may turn out that the amount of information available in the data is not sufficient to derive estimates of a model's parameters (Jöreskog and Sörbom, 1976; Long, 1983). This is also true for latent-class models (Clogg, 1981; Goodman, 1974b). In general the number of nonredundant cells in the original cross-tabulation (i.e., # cells – 1) must be at least as large as the number of nonredundant model parameters to be estimated. Model H_1 in panel B of Table 3, for example, defines 26 nonredundant parameters to be estimated (two for $\pi_{ts}^{\bar{X}G}$, nine for $\pi_{its}^{\bar{F}XG}$, three for $\pi_{jts}^{\bar{R}XS}$, and twelve for π_{kts}^{LXG}), and has 36 (= $2 \times 2 \times 3 \times 3$) total observed cells with one of them being redundant given that the sample size is known. The degrees of freedom for H_1, then, should be 35 – 26 = 9.

There is an additional redundancy in the parameters, however, which is not initially apparent. Analogous to the problem of multicollinearity in regression analysis, two parameters essentially provide equivalent information. A model is estimated with p (apparently) nonredundant parameters on a table with n cells. A matrix with p rows and (n – 1) columns is created where each element is the first derivative, with respect to a given parameter, of the observed cell count (π_{ijk}) as obtained from the model (i.e., from equations 1 and 3 in the single group case or by summing out the latent variable in equation 13 for multiple group models). Where the rank of this matrix equals p, the model is properly identified; when the rank is less than p, (p – [rank]) redundancies are indicated. See Clogg (1981) and Goodman (1974b). Improperly identified models typically require one or more of the model parameters to be restricted in order to achieve proper identification.

As a case in point, Model H_1 was thought to be identified with 9 degrees of freedom, but upon examination of the matrix of derivatives, it was found to have a rank of 25 rather than 26 as was expected. This suggests that the number of estimated parameters must be reduced by one to remove the redundancy. The restriction should in theory be chosen on a priori grounds, and should at a minimum be a reasonable substantive constraint. The restriction imposed here is $\pi_{111}^{\bar{F}XG} = \pi_{121}^{\bar{F}XG}$, that within the first group the probability of being interviewed face-to-face is the same for those actually NILF as for those actually unemployed.

DESCRIBING THE LATENT STRUCTURE OF
RESPONSE BIAS AND LF STATUS

The parameter estimates computed under model H_1 can be used to specify the exact pattern of response error and how it differs in the first group from the sixth and seventh. Perhaps most important from the adjustment perspective, we can obtain estimates of the "true" distribution of labor force statuses in the population, including the latent unemployment rate. These data are displayed in Table 5. The corresponding EASDs are reported in Table 6. Note that due to the large sample size all of the coefficients are quite significant with respect to the extreme values of 0.0 or 1.0.

Consider Panel A of Table 5. The restrictions on the conditional probabilities regarding interview and respondent types are evident. Briefly, the predominance of face-to-face interviewing in the first group (nearly universal) is clearly contrasted with the use of telephones in each of the remaining groups (between 70% and 85% of all interviews). Also, note that proxy respondents are utilized most for the unemployed (64%), least for those NILF (40%), and that this is the same regardless of which rotation group is considered (recall the imposed homogeneity constraint). The pattern of response error (as seen from the relationship between observed and latent labor force statuses—L and X—in Panel A of Table 5) shows that unemployment is by far the least accurately recorded status, with less than 75% of the unemployed being correctly reported in the interview (π_{22s}^{LXG} = .7446). Across groups, however, the most important result is the greater degree of error in classifying persons as NILF in the first rotation—14% (= .0306 + .1097) in the first group compared with 8% (= .0086 + .0677) in the sixth and seventh groups. Although the bulk of these errors in classification were expected to result from an exchange between NILF and unemployment, much of the misclassification appears to occur among those who are observed in an employed status in Table 5.

It may be more appropriate to turn this analysis around and ask what percentage of the population is estimated to be in each latent labor force status given a particular observed status (i.e., $\pi_{kts}^{L\overline{X}G}$—note the change in location of the "bar"). Using the basic rules of conditional probability:

TABLE 5
Parameters Estimated Under Model H1′[a]

	Rotation Group I			Rotation Group VI			Rotation Group VII		
	NILF	UNEMP	EMP	NILF	UNEMP	EMP	NILF	UNEMP	EMP
A. Conditional probabilities:									
Interview type									
1. telephone	.0166[b]	.0166[b]	.0277	.7918	.7036	.8127	.8313	.7399	.8516
2. face-to-face	.9834	.9834	.9723	.2082	.2964	.1873	.1687	.2601	.1484
Respondent type[c]									
1. proxy	.4010	.6371	.5855	.4010	.6371	.5855	.4010	.6371	.5855
2. self	.5990	.3629	.4145	.5990	.3629	.4145	.5990	.3629	.4145
Observed LF status[d]									
1. NILF	.8597	.1182	.0502	.9237	.1418	.0411	.9237	.1418	.0411
2. unemployed	.0306	.7446	.0101	.0086	.7143	.0094	.0086	.7143	.0094
3. employed	.1097	.1372	.9396	.0677	.1439	.9495	.0677	.1439	.9495
B. Probability of unobserved LF status given observed LF status:									
1. NILF	.9106	.1850	.0643	.9115	.0628	.0440	.9115	.0628	.0440
2. unemployed	.0019	.7126	.0127	.0200	.8221	.0134	.0200	.8221	.0134
3. employed	.0875	.1024	.9230	.0685	.1151	.9466	.0685	.1151	.9446
C. Distribution of latent labor force statuses:	.3529	.0557	.5913	.3529	.0557	.5913	.3529	.0557	.5913

a. All parameter estimates are significant beyond the .05 level.
b. Parameters constrained to equality.
c. Parameters constrained to equality across all groups.
d. Parameters constrained to equality across groups VI and VII.

312

TABLE 6
Standard Errors for Parameter Estimates in Table 5

	Rotation Group I			Rotation Group VI			Rotation Group VII		
	NILF	UNEMP	EMP	NILF	UNEMP	EMP	NILF	UNEMP	EMP
A. Conditional probabilities:									
Interview type									
1. telephone	.00164	.00405	.00163	.00522	.01478	.00387	.00482	.01423	.00353
2. face-to-face	.00164	.00405	.00163	.00522	.01478	.00387	.00482	.01423	.00353
Respondent type									
1. proxy	.00630	.01555	.00489	.00630	.01555	.00489	.00630	.01555	.00489
2. self	.00630	.01555	.00489	.00630	.01555	.00489	.00630	.01555	.00489
Observed LF status									
1. NILF	.00446	.01043	.00217	.00341	.01129	.00197	.00341	.01129	.00197
2. unemployed	.00221	.01410	.00099	.00119	.01462	.00096	.00119	.01469	.00096
3. employed	.00401	.01112	.00236	.00323	.01136	.00217	.00323	.01136	.00317
B. Unobserved labor force status:	.00142	.00060	.00175	.00142	.00060	.00175	.00142	.00060	.00175

NOTE: See text for discussion of model constraints and standard error computations.

$$\pi_{kts}^{L\bar{X}G} = \pi_{kts}^{\bar{L}XG}(\pi_{ts}^{\bar{X}G}/\pi_{ks}^{\bar{L}G})$$

Once the conditional probabilities are reversed in this manner, the nature of the error in classifying the unemployed becomes clearer (see Panel B). Again most of the error falls among those reported as unemployed, but now mostly those who are actually NILF. More important in terms of the hypotheses concerning rotation-group bias, the error in classifying those who say they are unemployed is greatly diminished in the sixth and seventh groups and due entirely to the reduction in NILF respondents being reported as unemployed (18.5% in group I reduced to 6.3% in groups VI and VII).

To this point the model has provided information concerning the response-error mechanism active in the three CPS rotations under study. The purpose of applying latent-class models here, however, is to obtain an estimated partitioning of the population without the effects of such bias present. This information is found in Panel C of Table 5. Recall that the unobserved distribution of labor force status is assumed under the model to be equal in each rotation. From Table 5 we find that 5.57% ($\hat{\pi}_{2s}^{\bar{X}G} = .0557$) of each group (and thus of the population as a whole given the model) is unemployed; taking the proportion of each group in the labor force to be those employed and unemployed combined (.0557 + .5913), the adjusted rate of unemployment under the model is (100% × [.0557]/[.0557 + .5913]) = 8.61%. This subset of the CPS data has an observed unemployment rate of 8.00% (taken from the data), thus the model in effect raises the unemployment rate by 0.61 percentage points.

CONCLUSIONS

The presentation of latent-class models in this chapter is an introduction to the models and concepts used in the analysis of latent categorical variables. Many types of latent-class models have not been discussed, including latent distance models (Lazars-feld and Henry, 1968), models for the analysis of Guttman scales (Goodman, 1978; Proctor, 1970), and various quasi-latent struc-ture models (Goodman, 1978; Clogg, 1981). One particularly important group of models omitted are those that posit multiple latent variables. The multiple latent variables may be assumed either independent or associated, once again drawing the analogy with factor analysis (Clogg, 1985; Clogg and Becker, 1984; see also Goodman, 1978; Haberman, 1979). Clogg (1985) has shown that this latent association can be modeled using a class of models combining the latent structure approach with ANOAS (Analysis of Association) models (see Goodman, 1984). A final set of extensions to the latent class model deals with the latent variables that are categorical representations of underlying continuous variables. One popular model of this type—the Rasch model (Andersen, 1980; Duncan, 1984; Rasch, 1960; Rost, 1985)—is closely related to the latent-class model.

These extensions, as well as portions of the earlier discussion, help to point out the close linkage between latent-class analysis and log-linear analysis, latent-trait analysis, and (on a conceptual level) factor analysis. As a general set of tools for describing the latent structure manifested in an observed multivariate association, they can examine a tremendous range of hypotheses, assumptions, and data formats. Unfortunately, models are often applied routinely without much thought for the nature of the variables under consideration. The present chapter has attempted to provide an introduction to latent-class models as an alternative to factor analysis when the data, both observed and unobserved, are measured on an ordinal or a nominal scale. New developments are being made to extend the applicability of the latent class approach further, and in contrast to the difficulties encountered in estimating these models as recently as 10 years ago, computer programs are increasingly available to the researcher.

NOTES

1. No distributional assumptions are required for latent trait models that are concerned only with the relationships between observed and latent factors; the added assumptions are only necessary when the latent classification itself is of interest.

2. The program MLLSA can be obtained for a small fee to cover costs from Clifford C. Clogg, Department of Sociology, Pennsylvania State University, University Park, PA 16802.

3. Those familiar with log-linear analysis may be tempted to compare M_1, M_2, and M_3 by computing the difference between L^2 values and treating the difference as a statistic itself distributed as a chi-square variate. It has been shown, however, that this cannot be done when comparing models with different numbers of latent classes.

4. Model H_1, also defined in Panel B of Table 2, will be defined below.

References

AGRESTI, A. (1984) Analysis of Ordinal Categorical Data. New York: John Wiley.

AITCHISON, J. and D. C. SILVEY (1958) "Maximum likelihood estimation of parameters subject to restraints." Annals of Mathematical Statistics 29: 813-828.

AITKIN, M. and D. R. RUBIN (1985) "Estimation and hypothesis testing in finite mixture models." Journal of the Royal Statistical Society 47: 67-75.

ALBA, R. D. (1986) "Cohorts and the dynamics of ethnic change." Presented at the 1986 Meetings of the American Sociological Association in New York; forthcoming in M. W. Riley et al. (eds.) Social Structures and Human Lives, Vol. 1. Newbury Park, CA: Sage (ASA Presidential Series).

ALBA, R. D. and R. GOLDEN (1986) "Patterns of ethnic marriage in the United States." Social Forces 65 (September).

ALDRICH, J. H. and F. D. NELSON (1984) Linear Probability, Logit, and Probit Models. Quantitative Applications in the Social Sciences No. 45. Newbury Park, CA: Sage.

ALLISON, P. D. (1977) "Testing for interaction in multiple regression." American Journal of Sociology 83: 144-153.

ALLISON, P. D. (1984) Event History Analysis: Regression for Longitudinal Event Data. Newbury Park, CA: Sage.

ALTHAUSER, R. P. (1971) "Multicollinearity and non-additive regression models," pp. 453-472 in H. Blalock (ed.) Causal Models in the Social Sciences. Chicago: Aldine.

ALWIN, D. F. (1973) "The use of factor analysis in the construction of linear composites in social research." Sociological Methods and Research 2: 191-214.

ALWIN, D. F. (1976) "Attitude scales as congeneric tests: a re-examination of an attitude-behavior model." Sociometry 39: 377-383.

ALWIN, D. F. (forthcoming) Design, Measurement and Analysis: A Structural Equations Approach.

ALWIN, D. F. and R. M. HAUSER (1975) "The decomposition of effects in path analysis." American Sociological Review 40: 37-47.

ALWIN, D. F. and D. J. JACKSON (1979) "Measurement models for response errors in surveys: issues and applications," pp. 68-119 in K. F. Schuessler (ed.) Sociological Methodology 1980. San Francisco: Jossey-Bass.

ALWIN, D. F. and D. J. JACKSON (1981) "Applications of simultaneous factor analysis to issues of factorial invariance," in D. J. Jackson and E. F. Borgatta (eds.) Factor Analysis and Measurement in Sociological Research. Newbury Park, CA: Sage.

ALWIN, D. F. and A. THORNTON (1984) "Family origins and the schooling process: early vs. late influence of parental characteristics." American Sociological Review 49: 784-802.

AMEMIYA, T. (1981) "Qualitative response models: a survey." Journal of Economic Literature 19: 1483-1536.

AMEMIYA, T. (1985) On the Goodness-of-Fit Tests for Linear Statistical Relationships. Technical Report No. 10, Econometric Workshop. Stanford, CA: Stanford University.

AMEMIYA, T. (1986) Advanced Econometrics. Cambridge, MA: Harvard University Press.

ANDERSEN, E. B. (1980) Discrete Statistical Models with Social Science Applications. Amsterdam: North-Holland.

ANDERSON, J. C. and D. W. GERBING (1984) "The effect of sampling error on convergence, improper solutions, and goodness-of-fit indices for maximum likelihood confirmatory factor analyses." Psychometrika 49: 155-173.

ARMINGER, G. (1986) "Linear stochastic differential equation models for panel data with unobserved variables." Sociological Methodology, 187-212.

ARMINGER, G. and U. KUSTERS (1986) "Latent trait and correlation models with indicators of mixed measurement level." (manuscript)

AVERY, R. B. and V. J. HOTZ (1983) HOTZTRAN User's Manual. Chicago, Economics Research Center/NORC. (unpublished manuscript)

BAILAR, B. A. (1975) "The effects of rotation group bias on estimates from panel surveys." Journal of the American Statistical Association (March): 25-30.

BARTLETT, M. S. (1935) "Contingency table interactions." Journal of the Royal Statistical Society (Supp.) 2: 248-252.

BAUMRIND, D. (1983) "Specious causal attributions in the social sciences: the reformulated stepping-stone theory of heroin use as exemplar." Journal of Personality and Social Psychology 45: 1289-1298.

BEARDEN, W. O., S. SHARMA, and J. E. TEEL (1982) "Sample size effects on chi-square and other statistics used in evaluating causal models." Journal of Marketing Research 19: 425-430.

BECKER, M. P. and C. C. CLOGG (1987) "A note on approximating correlations from odds ratios." Sociological Methods and Research.

BELSEY, D. A., E. KUH, and R. E. WELSCH (1980) Regression Diagnostics: Identifying Influential Data and Sources of Collinearity. New York: John Wiley.

BENTLER, P. M. (1980) "Multivariate analysis with latent variables: causal modeling." Annual Review of Psychology 31: 419-456.

BENTLER, P. M. (1982) "Linear systems with multiple levels and types of latent variables," pp. 101-130 in K. G. Jöreskog and H. Wold (eds.) Systems Under Indirect Observation: Causality, Structure and Prediction. Amsterdam: North-Holland.

BENTLER, P. M. (1983) "Some contributions to efficient statistics in structural models: specification and estimation of moment structures." Psychometrika 48: 493-517.

BENTLER, P. M. (1985) Theory and Implementation of EQS, a Structural Equations Program. Los Angeles: BMDP Statistical Software.

BENTLER, P. M. (1986a) "Structural modeling and Psychometrika: an historical perspective on growth and achievements." Psychometrika 51: 35-51.

BENTLER, P. M. (1986b) Lagrange Multiplier and Wals tests for EQS and EQS/PC. Los Angeles: BMDP Statistical Software.

BENTLER, P. M. (1987a) "Drug use and personality in adolescence and young adulthood: structural models with nonnormal variables." Child Development 58: 65-79.

BENTLER, P. M. (1987c) "Structural modeling and the scientific method: comments on Freedman's critique." Journal of Educational Statistics 12: 151-157.

BENTLER, P. M. and M. BERKANE (1985) "Developments in the elliptical theory generalization of normal multivariate analysis." Proceedings of the Social Statistics Section, American Statistical Association, 291-295.

BENTLER, P. M. and D. G. BONETT (1980) Significance tests and goodness of fit in the analysis of covariance structures." Psychological Bulletin 88: 588-606.

BENTLER, P. M. and C. P. CHOU (1986) "Statistics for parameter expansion and contraction in structural models." Presented at the meeting of the American Educational Research Association, San Francisco.

BENTLER, P. M., C. P. CHOU, and S. Y. LEE (1986) "Distributional consequences of linear latent variable structures." (manuscript)

BENTLER, P. M. and T. DIJKSTRA (1985) "Efficient estimation via linearization in structural models," in P. R. Krishnaiah (ed.) Multivariate Analysis VI. Amsterdam: North-Holland.

BENTLER, P. M. and E. H. FREEMAN (1983) "Tests for stability in linear structural equation systems." Psychometrika 48: 143-145.

BENTLER, P. M. and S. Y. LEE (1983) "Covariance structures under polynomial constraints: applications to correlation and alpha-type structural models." Journal of Educational Statistics 8: 207-222, 315-317.

BENTLER, P. M., S. Y. LEE, and J. WENG (1987) "Multiple population covariance structure analysis under arbitrary distribution theory. Communications in Statistics Theory 16: 1951-1964.

BENTLER, P. M. and W. PEELER (1979) "Models of female orgasm." Archives of Sexual Behavior 8: 405-423.

BENTLER, P. M. and J. S. TANAKA (1983) "Problems with EM algorithms for ML factor analysis." Psychometrika 48: 247-251.

BENTLER, P. M. and D. G. WEEKS (1980) "Linear structural equations with latent variables." Psychometrika 45: 289-308.

BERK, R. A. (1983) "An introduction to sample selection bias in sociological data." American Sociological Review 48: 386-398.

BERKANE, M. and P. M. BENTLER (1987a) "Distribution of kurtoses, with estimators and tests of homogeneity of kurtoses." Statistics & Probability Letters 5: 201-207.

BERKANE, M. and P. M. BENTLER (1987b) "Characterizing parameters of multivariate elliptical distributions." Communications in Statistics 16: 193-198.

BERRY, W. D. (1984) Nonrecursive Causal Models. Newbury Park, CA: Sage.

BIELBY, W. T. (1986) "Arbitrary metrics in multiple indicator models of latent variables." Sociological Methods and Research 5, 1-2: 3-23.

BIELBY, W. and R. M. HAUSER (1977a) "Structural equation models." Annual Review of Sociology 3: 137-161.

BIELBY, W. and R. M. HAUSER (1977b) "Response error in earnings functions for nonblack males." Sociological Methods and Research 6: 241-280.

BIELBY, W. T., R. M. HAUSER, and D. L. FEATHERMAN (1977a) "Response errors of nonblack males in models of the stratification process." Journal of the American Statistical Association 72: 723-735.

BIELBY, W. T., R. M. HAUSER, and D. L. FEATHERMAN (1977b) "Response errors of black and nonblack males in models of status inheritance and mobility." American Journal of Sociology, 1282: 1242-1282.

BIRCH, M. W. (1963) "Maximum likelihood in three-way contingency tables." Journal of the Royal Statistical Society, Ser. B., 25: 220-233.

BISHOP, Y.M.M., S. E. FIENBERG, and P. F. HOLLAND (1975) Discrete Multivariate Analysis: Theory and Practice. Cambridge: MIT Press.

BLALOCK, H. M., Jr. (1961) "Evaluating the relative importance of variables." American Sociological Review 26: 866-874.

BLALOCK, H. M., Jr. (1964) Causal Inferences in Nonexperimental Research. Chapel Hill: University of North Carolina Press.

BLALOCK, H. M., Jr. (1965) "Some implications of random measurement error for causal inferences." American Journal of Sociology 71: 37-47.

BLALOCK, H. M., Jr. (1967a) "Path coefficients versus regression coefficients." American Journal of Sociology 72: 675-676.

BLALOCK, H. M., Jr. (1967b) "Causal inferences, closed populations, and measures of association." American Political Science Review 61: 130-136.

BLALOCK, H. M., Jr. (1972) Social Statistics. New York: McGraw-Hill.

BLAU, J. R. and P. M. BLAU (1982) "The cost of inequality: metropolitan structure and violent crime." American Sociological Review 31: 114-129.

BLAU, P. M., O. D. DUNCAN, and A. TYREE (1967) The American Occupational Structure. New York: John Wiley.

BOCK, R. D. and M. AITKIN (1981) "Marginal maximum likelihood estimation of item parameters: Application of an EM algorithm." Psychometrika 46: 443-459.

BOHRNSTEDT, G. W. and T. M. CARTER (1971) "Robustness in regression analysis," in H. L. Costner (ed.) Sociological Methodology 1971. San Francisco: Jossey-Bass.

BOLLEN, K. A. (1986) "Sample size and Bentler and Bonett's nonnormed fit index." Psychometrika 51: 375-377.

BOLLEN, K. A. (1987) Outliers and improper solutions: a confirmatory factor analysis example. Sociological Methods & Research 15: 375-384.

BOLLEN, K. A. and K. G. JÖRESKOG (1985) "Uniqueness does not imply identification: a note on confirmatory factor analysis." Sociological Methods & Research 14: 155-163.

BONETT, D. G., J. A. WOODWARD, and P. M. BENTLER (1985) "Some extensions of a linear model for categorical variables." Biometrika 41: 745-750.

BOOMSMA, A. (1983) On the Robustness of LISREL (Maximum Likelihood Estimation) Against Small Sample Size and Nonnormality. Amsterdam: Sociometric Research Foundation.

BOOMSMA, A. (1985) "Nonconvergence, improper solutions, and starting values in LISREL maximum likelihood estimation." Psychometrika 50: 229-242.

BOWDEN, R. J. (1986) "Self-selection biases in correlation studies based on questionnaires." Psychometrika 51: 313-325.

BRADBURN, N. M. (1984) "Response effects," pp. 289-328 in P. H. Rossi et al. (eds.) Handbook of Survey Research. New York: Academic Press.

BREEN, R. (1984) "Fitting nonhierarchical and association log-linear models using GLIM." Sociological Methods & Research 13 (August): 77-108.

BROWN, G. W. and T. HARRIS (1978) Social Origins of Depression: A Study of Psychiatric Disorder in Women. New York: Free Press.

BROWNE, M. W. (1982) "Covariance structures," pp. 72-141 in D. M. Hawkins (ed.) Topics in Applied Multivariate Analysis. London: Cambridge University Press.

BROWNE, M. W. (1984) "Asymptotically distribution free methods for the analysis of covariance structures." British Journal of Mathematical and Statistical Psychology 37: 62-83.

BROWNE, M. W. (1985) "Robustness of the likelihood ratio rest of fit of a factor analysis model against nonnormality distributed common factors." Presented at Fourth European meeting of the Psychometric Society and Classification Societies, Cambridge, July.

BURT, R. S. (1976) "Interpretational confounding of unobserved variables in structural equation models." Sociological Methods and Research 5: 3-49.

BUSE, A. (1982) "The likelihood ratio, Wald, and Lagrange Multiplier tests: an expository note." American Statistician 36: 153-157.

BYE, B. V., S. J. GALLICCHIO, and J. M. DYKACZ (1985) Multiple-indicator, multiple-cause models for a single latent variable with ordinal indicators." Sociological Methods & Research 13: 487-509.

CAIN, G. G. and H. W. WATTS (1970) "Problems in making policy inferences from the Coleman Report." American Sociological Review 35: 228-242.

CARMINES, E. G. and J. P. McIVER (1981) "Analyzing models with unobserved variables: analysis of covariance structures," in G. W. Bohrnstedt and E. F. Borgatta (eds.) Social Measurement: Current Issues. Newbury Park, CA: Sage.

CHAMBERLAIN, G. (1982) "Multivariate regression models for panel data." Journal of Econometrics 18: 5-46.

CHATTERJEE, S. and A. S. HADI (1986) "Influential observations, high leverage points, and outliers in linear regression." Statistical Science 1: 379-416.

CHUA, T. A. and W. A. FULLER (1987) "A model for multinomial response error applied to labor flows." Journal of the American Statistical Association 82, 397: 46-51.

CLEARY, P. D. and R. C. KESSLER (1982) "The estimation and interpretation of modifier effects." Journal of Health and Social Behavior 23: 159-169.

CLIFF, N. (1983) "Some cautions concerning the application of causal modeling methods." Multivariate Behavioral Research 18: 115-126.

CLOGG, C. C. (1977) "Unrestricted and restricted maximum likelihood latent structure analysis: a manual for users." Working Paper No. 1977-09. University Park: Pennsylvania State University, Population Issues Research Center.

CLOGG, C. C. (1978) "Adjustment of rates using multiplicative models." Demography 15: 523-539.

CLOGG, C. C. (1979a) Measuring Underemployment: Demographic Indicators for the United States. New York: Academic Press.

CLOGG, C. C. (1979b) "Some latent structure models for the analysis of Likert-type data." Social Science Research 8: 287-301.

CLOGG, C. C. (1981) "New developments in latent structure analysis," pp. 215-248 in D. J. Jackson and E. F. Borgatta (eds.) Factor Analysis and Measurement in Sociological Research. Newbury Park, CA: Sage.

CLOGG, C. C. (1982) "Some models for the analysis of association in multi-way cross-classifications having ordered categories." Journal of the American Statistical Association 77: 114-134.

CLOGG, C. C. (1985) "Latent class models for measuring," in R. Langeheine and J. Rost (eds.) Latent Trait and Latent Class Models. Kiel, Federal Republic of Germany: Institute for Science Education.

CLOGG, C. C. (1986) "Quasi-independence," in Encyclopedia of Statistics, Vol. 7. New York: John Wiley.

CLOGG, C. C. and M. P. BECKER (1984) "An approximate relationship between the odds ratio and the tetrachoric correlation." Presented at the annual meetings of the American Statistical Association, Social Statistics Section, Philadelphia.

CLOGG, C. C. and M. P. BECKER (1986) "Log-linear modeling with SPSS^x," in D. M. Allen (ed.) Computer Science and Statistics: 17th Symposium on the Interface. Amsterdam: North-Holland.

CLOGG, C. C. and L. A. GOODMAN (1984) "Latent structure analysis of a set of multidimensional contingency tables." Journal of the American Statistical Association 79: 762-771.

CLOGG, C. C. and L. A. GOODMAN (1985) "Simultaneous latent structure analysis in several groups," pp. 81-110 in N. Tuma (ed.) Sociological Methodology 1985. San Francisco: Jossey-Bass.

CLOGG, C. C. and L. A. GOODMAN (1986) "On scaling models applied to data from several groups." Psychometrika 51, 1: 123-135.

CLOGG, C. C., D. B. RUBIN, N. SCHENKER, B. SCHULTZ, and L. WEIDMAN (1986) "Simple Bayesian methods for logistic regression." Presented at the annual meetings of the American Statistical Association.

CLOGG, C. C. and J. W. SHOCKEY (1986) "Multivariate analysis of discrete data," in J. R. Nesselroade and R. B. Cattell (eds.) Handbook of Multivariate Experimental Psychology. New York: Plenum.

CLOGG, C. C., J. W. SHOCKEY, and S. R. ELIASON (1986) "A general statistical framework for adjustment of rates." (manuscript)

COHEN, A. (1983) "Comparing regression coefficients across subsamples." Sociological Methods and Research 12: 77-95.

COHEN, J. (1968) "Multiple regression as a general data-analytic system." Psychological Bulletin 70: 426-443.

COHEN, J. (1978) "Partialed products are interactions; partialed powers are curved components." Psychological Bulletin 85: 856-866.

COHEN, J. and P. COHEN (1975) Applied Multiple Regression/Correlation Analysis for the Behavioral Sciences. Hillsdale, NJ: Lawrence Erlbaum.

COLEMAN, J. S. et al. (1966) Equality of Educational Opportunity. Washington, DC: Government Printing Office.

COLLINS, L. M., N. CLIFF, D. J. McCORMICK, and J. L. ZATKIN (1986) "Factor recovery in binary data sets: a simulation." Multivariate Behavioral Research 21: 377-391.

COMREY, A. (1985) "A method for removing outliers to improve factor analytic results." Multivariate Behavioral Research 20: 273-282.

COX, D. R. (1970) The Analysis of Binary Data. London: Methuen.

COX, D. R. and D. HINKLEY (1974) Theoretical Statistics. London: Chapman and Hall.

CRESSIE, N. and T.R.C. READ (1984) "Multinomial goodness-of-fit tests." Journal of the Royal Statistical Society, Ser. B., 46: 440-464.

CUDECK, R. and M. W. BROWNE (1983) "Cross-validation of covariance structures." Multivariate Behavioral Research 18: 147-167.

DARLINGTON, R. B. (1968) "Multiple regression in psychological research and practice." Psychological Bulletin 69: 161-182.

DEMPSTER, A. P., N. M. LAIRD, and D. B. RUBIN (1977) "Maximum likelihood from incomplete data via the EM algorithm (with discussion)." Journal of the Royal Statistical Society, Ser. B., 39: 1-38.

DIGBY, P.G.N. (1983) "Approximating the tetrachoric correlation coefficient." Biometrics 39: 753-757.

DUNCAN, O. D. (1966) "Path analysis: sociological examples." American Journal of Sociology 72: 1-16.

DUNCAN, O. D. (1969) "Some linear models for two-wave, two-variable panel analysis." Psychological Bulletin 72: 177-182.

DUNCAN, O. D. (1970). "Partials, partitions and paths," in E. F. Borgatta and G. W. Bohrnstedt (eds.) Sociological Methodology 1970. San Francisco: Jossey-Bass.

DUNCAN, O. D. (1971). "Path analysis: sociological examples (addenda)," pp. 136-138 in H. M. Blalock, Jr. (ed.) Causal Models in the Social Sciences. New York: Aldine-Atherton.

DUNCAN, O. D. (1972) "Unmeasured variables in linear models for panel analysis," in H. L. Costner (ed.) Sociological Methodology 1972. San Francisco: Jossey-Bass.

DUNCAN, O. D. (1975a) Introduction to Structural Equation Models. New York: Academic Press.

DUNCAN, O. D. (1975b) "Does money buy satisfaction?" Social Indicators Research, 2: 267-274.

DUNCAN, O. D. (1984a) Notes on Social Measurement: Historical and Critical. New York: Russell Sage.

DUNCAN, O. D. (1984b) "Rasch measurement in survey research: further examples and discussion," in C. F. Turner and E. Martin (eds.) Surveying Subjective Phenomenon, Vol. 2. New York: Basic Books.

DUNCAN, O. D., D. L. FEATHERMAN, and B. DUNCAN (1972) Socioeconomic Background and Achievement. New York: Seminar Press.

DUNCAN, O. D., A. O. HALLER, and A. PORTES (1968) "Peer influence on aspiration." American Journal of Sociology 74: 119-137.

DWYER, J. H. (1983) Statistical Models for the Social and Behavioral Sciences. New York: Oxford University Press.

EFRON, R. (1982) The Jackknife, the Bootstrap, and other Resampling Plans. Philadelphia: Society for Industrial and Applied Mathematics.

ETEZADI-AMOLI, J. and R. P. McDONALD (1983) A second generation non-linear factor analysis. Psychometrika 48: 315-342.

FAY, R. E. and L. A. GOODMAN (1975) ECTA Program. Chicago: University of Chicago, Department of Statistics.

FEATHERMAN, D. L. (1971) "A social structural model for the socioeconomic career." American Journal of Sociology 77: 293-304.

FEATHERMAN, D. L. and R. M. HAUSER (1978) Opportunity and Change. New York: Academic Press.

FEATHERMAN, D. L. and R. M. LERNER (1985) "Ontogenesis and sociogenesis: problematics for theory and research about development and socialization across the lifespan." American Sociological Review 50: 659-676.

FELLER, W. (1968) An Introduction to Probability Theory and Its Application. New York: John Wiley.

FIENBERG, S. E. (1980) The Analysis of Cross-Classified Categorical Data. Cambridge: MIT Press.

FINNEY, J. W., R. E. MITCHELL, R. C. CRONKITE, and R. H. MOOS (1984) "Methodological issues in estimating main and interactive effects: examples from coping/social support and stress field." Journal of Health and Social Behavior 25: 85-98.

FLEISS, J. L. (1981) Statistical Methods for Rates and Proportions. New York: John Wiley.

FORMANN, A. K. (1982) "Linear logistic latent class analysis." Biometric Journal 24: 171-190.

FOX, J. (1980) "Effect analysis in structural equation models: extensions and simplified methods of computation." Sociological Methods and Research 9: 3-28.

FOX, J. (1984) Linear Statistical Models and Related Methods: With Applications to Social Research. New York: John Wiley.

FOX, J. (1985) "Effects analysis in structural-equation models II: calculation of specific indirect effects." Socioilogical Methods and Research 14: 81-95.

FREEDMAN, D. A. (1985) "Statistics and the scientific method," pp. 345-366 in W. Mason and S. Fienberg (eds.) Cohort Analysis in Social Research. New York: Springer.

FREEDMAN, D. A. (1987) "As others see us: a case study in path analysis." Journal of Educational Statistics 12, 2: 101-128.

FREEMAN, E. H., Jr. (1982) "The implementation of effect decomposition methods for two general structural covariance modeling systems." Ph.D. dissertation, University of California, Los Angeles.

GAMORAN, A. (1987) "The stratification of high school learning opportunities." Sociology of Education 60: 135-155.

GAMORAN, A. and R. D. MARE (1987) "Secondary school tracking and stratification: compensation, reinforcement, or neutrality?" Presented at the annual meetings of the American Educational Research Association, Washington, DC.

GAREN, J. (1984) "The returns to schooling: a selectivity bias approach with a continuous choice variable." Econometrica 52: 1199-1218.

GERBING, D. W. and J. C. ANDERSON (1985) "The effects of sampling error and model characteristics on parameter estimation for maximum likelihood confirmatory factor analysis." Multivariate Behavioral Research 20: 255-271.

GERBING, D. W. and J. C. ANDERSON (1987) "Improper solutions in the analysis of covariance structures: their interpretability and a comparison of alternative respecifications." Psychometrika 52, 1: 99-111.

GEWEKE, J. F. and K. J. SINGLETON (1980) "Interpreting the likelihood ratio statistic in factor models when the sample size is small." Journal of the American Statistical Association 75: 133-137.

GOLDBERGER, A. S. (1971) "Econometrics and psychometrics: a survey of communalities." Psychometrika 36: 83-107.

GOLDBERGER, A. S. (1972) "Structural equation models in the social sciences." Econometrica 40l: 979-999.

GOLDBERGER, A. S. (1973) "Structural equation models: an overview," pp. 1-18 in A. S. Goldberger and O. D. Duncan (eds.) Structural Equation Models in the Social Sciences. New York: Seminar Press.

GOLDFELD, S. M. and R. E. QUANDT (1973) "The estimation of structural shifts by switching regressions." Annals of Economic and Social Measurement 2: 475-486.

GOLDSCHMID, M. and P. M. BENTLER (1968) Concept Assessment Kit—Conservation. San Diego, CA: Educational and Industrial Testing Service.

GOLLOB, H. F. and C. S. REICHARDT (1987) "Taking account of time lags in causal models." Child Development 58, 1: 80-92.

GOODMAN, L. A. (1964a) "Interactions in multidimensional contingency tables." Annals of Mathematical Statistics 35: 632-646.

GOODMAN, L. A. (1964b) "Simultaneous confidence limits for cross-product ratios in contingency tables." Journal of the Royal Statistical Society, Ser. B., 26: 86-102.

GOODMAN, L. A. (1968) "The analysis of cross-classified data: independence, quasi-independence, and interactions in contingency tables with or without massing entries." Journal of the American Statistical Association 63: 1091-1131.

GOODMAN, L. A. (1972) "A modified multiple regression approach to the analysis of dichotomous variables." American Sociological Review 37: 28-46.

GOODMAN, L. A. (1974a) "Exploratory latent structure analysis using both identifiable and unidentifiable models." Biometrica 61: 215-231.

GOODMAN, L. A. (1974b) "The analysis of systems of qualitative variables when some of the variables are unobservable. Part I—A modified latent structure approach." American Journal of Sociology 79: 1179-1259.

GOODMAN, L. A. (1978) Analyzing Qualitative/Categorical Data. Cambridge, MA: Abt Books.

GOODMAN, L. A. (1984) The Analysis of Cross-Classifications Having Ordered Categories. Cambridge, MA: Harvard University Press.

GOODMAN, L. A. and W. H. KRUSKAL (1954) "Measures of association for cross classifications, Part I." Journal of the American Statistical Association 49: 732-764.

GORDON, M. (1964) Assimilation in American Life. New York: Oxford University Press.

GORDON, R. A. (1968) "Issues in multiple regressions." American Journal of Sociology 73: 592-619.

GRAFF, J. and P. SCHMIDT (1982) "A general model for decomposition of effects," pp. 131-148 in K. G. Jöreskog and H. Wold (eds.) Systems Under Indirect Observation, Part 1. Amsterdam: North-Holland.

HABERMAN, S. J. (1974) "Log-linear models for frequency tables derived by indirect observations: maximum-likelihood equations." Annals of Statistics 2: 911-924.

HABERMAN, S. J. (1977) "Product models for frequency tables involving indirect observation." Annals of Statistics 5: 1124-1147.

HABERMAN, S. J. (1978) Analysis of Qualitative Data: Introductory Topics, Vol. 1. New York: Academic Press.

HABERMAN, S. J. (1979) Analysis of Qualitative Data, Vol. 2. New York: Academic Press.

HANUSHEK, E. A. and J. E. JACKSON (1977) Statistical Methods for Social Scientists. New York: Academic Press.

HARGENS, L. L. (1976) "A note on standardized coefficients as structural parameters." Sociological Methods and Research 5: 247-256.

HARLOW, L. L. (1985) "Behavior of some elliptical theory estimators with nonnormal data in a covariance structures framework: A Monte Carlo study." Ph.D. dissertation, University of California, Los Angeles.

HARRE, R. (1972) The Philosophies of Science. London: Oxford University Press.

HAUSER, R. M. (1972) "Disaggregating a social-psychological model of educational attainment." Social Science Research 1: 159-188.

HAUSER, R. M. and D. L. FEATHERMAN (1977) The Process of Stratification: Trends and Analyses. New York: Academic Press.

HAUSER, R. M. and A. S. GOLDBERGER (1971) "The treatment of unobservable variables in path analysis," in H. L. Costner (ed.) Sociological Methodology 1971. San Francisco: Jossey-Bass.

HAUSER, R. M., S.-L. TSAI, and W. H. SEWELL (1983) "A model of stratification with response error in social and psychological variables." Sociology of Education 56: 20-46.

HAYS, W. L. (1981) Statistics. New York: Holt, Rinehart & Winston.

HECKMAN, J. J. (1978) "Dummy endogenous variables in a simultaneous equation system." Econometrica 46: 931-960.

HECKMAN, J. J. and R. ROBB, Jr. (1985) "Alternative methods for evaluating the impact of interventions," pp. 156-245 in J. J. Heckman and B. Singer (eds.) Longitudinal Analysis of Labor Market Data. Cambridge: Cambridge University Press.

HECKMAN, J. J. and R. ROBB, Jr. (1986) "Alternative methods for solving the problems of selection bias in evaluating the impact of treatments on outcomes." Economics Research Center Discussion Paper, 86-9. Chicago: NORC.

HEISE, D. R. (1968) "Problems in path analysis and causal inference," in E. F. Borgatta (ed.) Sociological Methodology 1969. San Francisco: Jossey-Bass.

HEISE, D. R. (1972) "Employing nominal variables, induced variables, and block variables in path analyses." Sociological Methods and Research 1: 147-174.

HEISE, D. R. (1975) Causal Analysis. New York: John Wiley.

HEISE, D. R. (1986) "Estimating nonlinear models: correcting for measurement error." Sociological Methods & Research 14: 447-472.

HENRY, N. W. (1981) "Jackknifing measures of association." Sociological Methods and Research 10: 233-240.

HOELTER, J. W. (1983) "The analysis of covariance structures: goodness of fit indices." Sociological Methods and Research 11: 325-344.

HOLT, D. (1979) "Log-linear models for contingency table analysis: on the interpretation of the parameters." Sociological Methods & Research 7 (February): 330-336.

HOTCHKISS, L. (1976) "A technique for comparing path models between subgroups: standardized path-regression coefficients." Sociological Methods and Research 5: 53-76.

HOUT, M. (1977) "A cautionary note on the use of two-stage least squares." Sociological Methods and Research 5: 335-345.

JACKMAN, M. R. (1973) "Education and prejudice or education and response set?" American Sociological Review 38: 327-339.

JACKSON, D. J. and D. F. ALWIN (1980) "The factor analysis of ipsative measures." Sociological Methods and Research 9: 218-238.

JENCKS, C. et al. (1972) Inequality: A Reassessment of the Effect of Family and Schooling in America. New York: Basic Books.

JENSEN, A. R. (1969) "How much can we boost IQ and scholastic achievement?" Harvard Educational Review 39: 1-123.

JOHNSON, D. R. and R. L. MEILE (1981) "Does dimensionality bias in Langner's 22-item index affect the validity of social status comparisons? An empirical investigation." Journal of Health and Social Behavior 22: 415-432.

JOHNSTON, J. (1972) Econometric Methods (2nd edition). New York: McGraw-Hill.

JOHNSTON, J. (1984) Econometric Methods (3rd edition). New York: McGraw-Hill.

JONES, C., M. CLARK, G. MOONEY, H. McWILLIAMS, I. CRAWFORD, B. STEPHENSON, and R. TOURANGEAOU (1983) High School and Beyond 1980: Sophomore Cohort First Follow-Up (1982) Data File User's Manual. Washington, DC: National Center for Education Statistics.

JÖRESKOG, K. G. (1971) "Simultaneous factor analysis in several populations." Psychometrika 36: 409-425.

JÖRESKOG, K. G. (1973) "A general method for estimating a linear structural equation system," pp. 85-112 in A. S. Goldberger and O. D. Duncan (eds.) Structural Equation Models in the Social Sciences. New York: Seminar Press.

JÖRESKOG, K. G. (1977) "Structural equation models in the social sciences: specification, estimation and testing," pp. 265-287 in P. R. Krishnaiah (ed.) Applications of Statistics. Amsterdam: North-Holland.

JÖRESKOG, K., and A. S. GOLDBERGER (1975) "Estimation of a model with multiple causes of a single latent variable." Journal of the American Statistical Association 70: 631-639.

JÖRESKOG, K. G. and D. SÖRBOM (1979) Advances in Factor Analysis and Structural Equation Models. Cambridge, MA: Abt Books.

JÖRESKOG, K. G. and D. SÖRBOM (1981) LISREL V User's Guide. Chicago: National Educational Resources.

JÖRESKOG, K. G. and D. SÖRBOM (1984) LISREL VI User's Guide. Mooresville, IN: Scientific Software, Inc.

JÖRESKOG, K. G. and D. SÖRBOM (1986) LISREL—Analysis of Linear Structural Relationships by the Method of Maximum Likelihood. User's Guide, Version VI. Chicago: National Educational Resources.

JÖRESKOG, K. G. and M. VAN THILLO (1972) LISREL. Research Bulletin. Princeton, NJ: Educational Testing Service.

KAPLAN, A. (1964) The Conduct of Inquiry. San Francisco: Chandler.

KAUFMAN, R. L. and P. G. SCHERVISH (1986) "Using adjusted crosstabulations to interpret log-linear relationships." American Sociological Review 51: 717-733.

KELLEY, J. (1973) "Causal chain models for the socio-economic career." American Sociological Review 38: 481-493.

KENNY, D. A. (1979) Correlation and Causality. New York: John Wiley.

KENNY, D. A. and C. M. JUDD (1984) "Estimating the nonlinear and interactive effects of latent variables." Psychological Bulletin 96: 201-210.

KERLINGER, F. N. and E. J. PEDHAZUR (1973) Multiple Regression in Behavioral Research. New York: Holt, Rinehart & Winston.

KESSLER, R. C. and D. F. GREENBERG (1981) Linear Panel Analysis. New York: Academic Press.

KIM, J. and C. W. MUELLER, Jr. (1976) "Standardized and unstandardized coefficients in causal analysis: an expository note." Sociological Methods and Research 4: 423-438.

KMENTA, J. (1971) Elements of Econometrics. New York: Macmillan.

KMENTA, J. and R. F. GILBERT (1968) "Small sample properties for alternative estimators of seemingly unrelated regressions." Journal of the American Statistical Association 63: 1180-2000.

KNOKE, D. and P. BURKE (1980). Log-Linear Models. Newbury Park, CA: Sage.

KOEHLER, K. (1986) "Goodness-of-fit tests for log-linear models in sparse contingency tables." Journal of the American Statistical Association 81.

KOHN, M. L. and C. SCHOOLER (1973) "Occupational experience and psychological functioning: an assessment of reciprocal effects. American Sociological Review 38: 97-118.

KOHN, M. L. and C. SCHOOLER (1982) "Job conditions and personality: a longitudinal assessment of their reciprocal effects." American Journal of Sociology 87: 1257-1286.

KOHN, M. L., C. SCHOOLER, J. MILLER, K. A. MILLER, C. SCHOENBACH, and R. SCHOENBERG (1983) Work and Personality: An Inquiry into the Impact of Social Stratification. Norwood, NJ: Ablex.

LAIRD, N. and D. OLIVIER (1981) "Covariance analysis of censored survival data using log-linear analysis techniques." Journal of the American Statistical Association 76: 231-240.

LAND, K. C. (1968) "Principles of path analysis," in E. F. Borgatta (ed.) Sociological Methodology 1969. San Francisco: Jossey-Bass.

LAND, K. C. (1973) "Identification, parameter estimation, and hypothesis testing in recursive sociological models," pp. 19-49 in A. S. Goldberger and O. D. Duncan (eds.) Structural Models in the Social Sciences. New York: Seminar Press.

LAZARSFELD, P. F. and N. W. HENRY (1968) Latent Structure Analysis. Boston: Houghton Mifflin.

LEAMER, E. E. (1978) Specification Searches: Ad Hoc Inference with Nonexperimental Data. New York: John Wiley.

LEE, S. Y. (1985a) "Analysis of covariance and correlation structures." Computational Statistics & Data Analysis 2: 279-295.

LEE, S. Y. (1985b) "On testing functional constraints in structural equation models." Biometrika 72: 125-131.

LEE, S. Y. (1985c) "Maximum likelihood estimation of polychoric correlation in $r \times s \times t$ contingency tables." Journal of Statistical Computation and Simulation 23, 1-2. 53-67.

LEE, S. Y. (1986) "Estimation for structural equation models with missing data." Psychometrika 51: 93-99.

LEE, S. Y. and P. M. BENTLER (1980) "Some asymptotic properties of constrained generalized least squares estimation in covariance structure models." South African Statistical Journal 14: 121-136.

LEE, S. Y. and W. Y. POON (1986) "Maximum likelihood estimation of polyserial correlations." Psychometrika 51: 113-121.

LEE, S. Y., W. Y. POON, and P. M. BENTLER (1987) "Analysis of structural equation models with polytomous variables," (under review).

LEE, S. Y. and K. L. TSUI (1982) "Covariance structure analysis in several populations." Psychometrika 47: 297-308.

LIEBERSON, S. (1985) Making It Count: The Improvement of Social Research and Theory. Berkeley: University of California Press.

LIEBERSON, S. and M. WATERS (1985) "Ethnic mixtures in the United States." Sociology and Social Research 70 (October).

LINCOLN, J. R., J. OLSEN, and M. HANADA (1978) "Cultural effects on organizational structure: the case of Japanese firms in the United States." American Sociological Review 43: 829-847.

LINN, R. L. and C. E. WERTS (1969) "Assumptions in making causal inferences from part correlations, and partial regression coefficients." Psychological Bulletin 72: 307-310.

LITTLE, R.J.A. (1985) "A note about models for selectivity bias." Econometrica 53: 1469-1474.

LITTLE, R.J.A. (1986) "Robust estimation of the mean and covariance matrix from data with missing values." (manuscript)

LONG, J. S. (1976) "Estimation and hypothesis testing in linear models containing measurement error." Sociological Methods & Research 5, 2: 157-206.

LONG, J. S. (1983a) Confirmatory Factor Analysis: A Preface to LISREL. Newbury Park, CA: Sage.

LONG, J. S. (1983b) Covariance Structure Models: An Introduction to LISREL. Newbury Park, CA: Sage.

LONG, J. S. (1984) "Estimable functions in log-linear models." Sociological Methods & Research 12 (May): 399-432.

LORD, F. M. and M. R. NOVICK (1968) Statistical Theories of Mental Test Scores. Reading, MA: Addison-Wesley.

MacCALLUM, R. (1986) "Specification searches in covariance structure analyses." Psychological Bulletin 100: 107-120.

MADDALA, G. S. (1977) Econometrics. New York: McGraw-Hill.

MADDALA, G. S. (1983) Limited-Dependent and Qualitative Variables in Econometrics. Cambridge: Cambridge University Press.

MARDIA, K. V. (1970) "Measures of multivariate skewness and kurtosis with applications." Biometrika 57: 519-530.

MARSDEN, P. V. (1981) "Conditional effects in regression models," pp. 97-116 in P. Marsden (ed.) Linear Models in Social Research. Newbury Park, CA: Sage.

MASON, W. M., G. Y. WONG, and B. ENTWISLE (1983) "Contextual analysis through the multilevel linear model," pp. 72-103 in S. Leinhardt (ed.) Sociological Methodology 1983-1984. San Francisco: Jossey-Bass.

McCLEARY, R. and R. A. HAY (1980) Applied Time Series Analysis. Newbury Park, CA: Sage.

McCULLAGH, P. (1985) "The conditional distribution of goodness-of-fit statistics for discrete data." Journal of the American Statistical Association 81: 104-107.

McDONALD, R. P. and W. R. KRANE (1979) "A Monte Carlo study of local identifiability and degrees of freedom in the asymptotic likelihood ratio test." British Journal of Mathematical and Statistical Psychology 32: 121-132.

MERTON, R. K. (1957) Social Theory and Social Structure. New York: Free Press.

MIETHE, T. D. and C. A. MOORE (1986) "Racial differences in criminal processing: the consequences of model selection on conclusions about differential treatment." Sociological Quarterly 27: 217-237.

MILLER, R. G. (1984) "The jackknife—a review." Biometrika 61: 1-17.

MOOIJAART, A. (1982) "Latent structure analysis for categorical variables," pp. 1-18 in K. G. Jöreskog and H. Wold (eds.) Systems Under Indirect Observation: Causality, Structure, Prediction. Amsterdam: North-Holland.

MOOIJAART, A. (1985) "Factor analysis for nonnormal variables." Psychometrika 50: 323-342.

MOOIJAART, A. and P. M. BENTLER (1985) "Random polynomial factor analysis." Proceedings of Fourth International Symposium: Data Analysis and Informatics (Versailles).

MOOIJAART, A. and P. M. BENTLER (1986a) "Random polynomial factor analysis," in E. Diday et al. (eds.) Data Analysis and Informatics. Amsterdam: North-Holland.

MOOIJAART, A. and P. M. BENTLER (1986b) "Robustness of M.L. estimates in exploratory factor analysis." (manuscript)

MUTHÉN, B. (1984) "A general structural equation model with dichotomous, ordered categorical, and continuous latent variable indicators." Psychometrika 49: 115-132.

MUTHÉN, B. and D. KAPLAN (1985) "A comparison of some methodologies for the factor analysis of non-normal Likert vaiables." British Journal of Mathematical and Statistical Psychology 38: 171-189.

NEWCOMB, M. D. and P. M. BENTLER (1983) "Dimensions of subjective female orgasmic responsiveness." Journal of Personality and Social Psychology 44: 862-873.

OLSSON, U. (1979) "On the robustness of factor analysis against crude classification of the observation." Multivariate Behavioral Research 14: 485-500.

PAGE, W. F. (1977) "Interpretation of Goodman's log-linear model effects: an odds ratio approach." Sociological Methods & Research 5 (May): 419-435.

PEARLIN, L. I., Z. G. MENAGHAN, M. A. LIEBERMAN, and J. T. MULLAN (1981) "The stress process." Journal of Health and Social Behavior 22: 337-356.

PESCOSOLIDO, B. A. and R. MENDELSOHN (1986) "Social causation or social construction of suicide? An investigation into the social organization of official rates." American Sociological Review 51: 80-100.

PLACKETT, R. L. (1981) The Analysis of Categorical Data. New York: Macmillan.

PREGIBON, D. (1981) "Logistic regression diagnostics." Annals of Statistics 9: 705-724.

PROCTOR, C. A. (1970) "A probabilistic formulation and statistical analysis of Guttman scaling." Psychometrika 35: 73-78.

RAO, C. R. (1973) Linear Statistical Inference and Its Applications. New York: John Wiley.

RASCH, G. (1960) Probabilistic Models for Some Intelligence and Attainment Scores. Copenhagen: Danish Institute for Educational Research.

REICHARDT, C. S. and H. F. GOLLOB (1986) Satisfying the constraints of causal modeling," pp. 91-107 in W.M.K. Trochim (ed.) Advances in Quasi-Experimental Design and Analysis. San Francisco: Jossey-Bass.

RESKIN, B. F. and L. L. HARGENS (1979) "Scientific advancement of male and female chemists," pp 100-122 in R. Alvarez et al. (eds.) Discrimination in Organizations. San Francisco: Jossey-Bass.

RINDSKOPF, D. (1983) "Parameterizing inequality constraints on unique variances in linear structural models." Psychometrika 48: 73-83.

RINDSKOPF, D. (1984) "Structural equation models: empirical identification, Heywood cases, and related problems." Sociological Methods & Research 13: 109-119.

ROSENBERG, M. (1968) The Logic of Survey Analysis. New York: Basic Books.

ROST, J. (1985) "Test theory with qualitative and quantitative latent variables," in R. Langeheine and J. Rost (eds.) Latent Trait and Latent Class Models. Kiel, Federal Republic of Germany: Institute for Science Education.

RUBIN, D. B. and N. SCHENKER (1987) "Logit-based interval estimation for binomial data using the Jeffrey's prior," in C. C. Clogg (ed.) Sociological Methodology, 131-145.

RUBIN, D. B. and D. T. THAYER (1982) "EM algorithms for ML factor analysis." Psychometrika 47: 69-76.

SAMPSON, R. J. (1986) "Urban black violence: the impact of male joblessness and family disruption." University of Illinois, Department of Sociology. (unpublished)

SATORRA, A. (in press) "Alternative test criteria in covariance structure analysis: a unified approach." Psychometrika.

SATORRA, A. and P. M. BENTLER (1986) "Some robustness properties of goodness of fit statistics in covariance structure analysis." Presented at the annual meeting of the American Statistical Association, Chicago, August.

SCHOENBERG, R. (1972). "Strategies for meaningful comparisons," in H. L. Costner (ed.) Sociological Methodology 1972. San Francisco: Jossey-Bass.

SCHOENBERG, R. (1981) Documentation for MILS (Multiple Indicator Linear Structural Models). Bethesda, MD: National Institute of Mental Health.

SCHOENBERG, R. (1987) LINCS: A User's Guide. Kent, WA: Aptech Systems, Inc.

SCHUMAN, H. and S. PRESSER (1981) Questions and Answers in Attitude Surveys. New York: Academic Press.

SEWELL, W. H. and R. M. HAUSER (1975) Education, Occupation and Earnings: Achievement in the Early Career. New York: Academic Press.

SHAPIRO, A. (1985) "Asymptotic distribution of test statistics in the analysis of moment structures under inequality constraints." Biometrika, 72: 133-144.

SHAPIRO, A. (1986) "Asymptotic theory of overparameterized structural models." Journal of American Statistical Association 81: 142-149.

SHOCKEY, J. W. (1985) "Job satisfaction and underemployment," ch. 4 in Utilization of Labor: Composition and Consequences of Underemployment in the United States. Ph.D. dissertation, Pennsylvania State University, University Park, PA, Department of Sociology.

SHOCKEY, J. W. (1986) "Adjusting for response error in panel surveys: a latent class approach." (unpublished)

SILVEY, S. D. (1959) "The Lagrangian multipler test." Annals of Mathematical Statistics 30: 389-407.

SMELSER, N. J. (1962) Theory of Collective Behavior. New York: Free Press.

SMITH, K. W. and M. S. SASAKI (1979) "Decreasing multicollinearity: a method for models with multiplicative functions." Sociological Methods and Research 8: 35-56.

SOBEL, M. E. (1982) "Asymptotic confidence intervals for indirect effects in structural equation models," pp. 290-313 in S. Leinhardt (ed.) Sociological Methodology 1982. San Francisco: Jossey-Bass.

SOBEL, M. E. (1986) "Some new results on indirect effects and their standard errors in covariance structure analysis, pp. 159-186 in N. B. Tuma (ed.) Sociological Methodology 1986. San Francisco: Jossey-Bass.

SOBEL, M. E. and G. W. BOHRNSTEDT (1984) "Use of null models in evaluating the fit of covariance structure models," pp. 152-178 in S. Leinhardt (ed.) Sociological Methodology 1985. San Francisco: Jossey-Bass.

SOBEL, M. E., M. HOUT, and O. D. DUNCAN (1986) "Saving the bath water: an invited comment on Krauze and Slomczynski's 'Matrix representation of structural and circulation mobility.'" Sociological Methods and Research 14: 271-284.

SOCKLOFF, A. L. (1976) "The analysis of nonlinearity via linear regression with polynomial and product variables: an examination." Review of Educational Research 46: 267-291.

SÖRBOM, D. (1974) "A general method for studying differences in factor means and factor structures between groups." British Journal of Mathematical and Statistical Psychology 27: 229-239.

SÖRBOM, D. (1978) "An alternative to the methodology for analysis of covariance." Psychometrika 43: 381-396.

SÖRBOM, D. (1982) "Structural equation models with structured means," pp. 183-195 in K. G. Jöreskog and H. Wold (eds.) System Under Indirect Observation—Causality, Structure, Prediction. Amsterdam: North-Holland.

SOUTHWOOD, K. E. (1978). "Substantive theory and statistical interaction: five models." American Journal of Sociology 83: 1154-1203.

SPEARMAN, C. (1904) "'General intelligence' objectively determined and measured." American Journal of Psychology 15: 201-292.

SPECHT, D. A. and R. D. WARREN (1976) "Comparing causal models," pp. 46-82 in D. R. Heise (ed.) Sociological Methodology 1976. San Francisco: Jossey-Bass.

STEIGER, J. H., A. SHAPIRO, and M. W. BROWNE (1985) "On the multivariate asymptotic distribution of sequential chi-square statistics." Psychometrika 50: 253-264.

STELZL, I. (1986) "Changing a causal hypothesis without changing the fit: some rules for generating equivalent path models." Multivariate Behavioral Research 21: 309-331.

STEVENS, G. (1985) "Nativity, intermarriage, and mother-tongue shift." American Sociological Review 50 (February): 74-83.

STOLZENBERG, R. M. (1974) "Estimating an equation with multiplicative and additive terms, with an application to analysis of wage differentials between men and women in 1960." Sociological Methods and Research 2: 313-331.

STOLZENBERG, R. M. (1980) "The measurement and decomposition of causal effects in nonlinear and nonadditive models," pp. 459-488 in K. F. Schuessler (ed.) Sociological Methodology 1980. San Francisco: Jossey-Bass.

STONE, C. A. (1985) "CINDESE: computing indirect effects and their standard errors." Educational and Psychological Measurement 45: 601-606.

STOTO, M. A. and J. D. EMERSON (1983) "Power transformations for data analysis," pp. 126-168 in S. Leinhardt (ed.) Sociological Methodology 1983-1984. San Francisco: Jossey-Bass.

STROTZ, R. H. and H.O.A. WOLD (1960) "Recursive vs. nonrecursive systems: an attempt at synthesis." Econometrica 33: 1-41.

SWAFFORD, M. (1980) "Three parametric techniques for contingency table analysis: a nontechnical commentary." American Sociological Review 45 (August): 664-690.

TANAKA, J. S. (1984) "Some results on the estimation of covariance structure models." Ph.D. dissertation, University of California, Los Angeles.

TANAKA, J. S. and P. M. BENTLER (1985) "Quasi-likelihood estimation in asymptotically efficient covariance structure models." 1984 Proceedings of the American Statistical Association, Social Statistics Section, 658-662.

TANAKA, J. S. and G. J. HUBA (1985) "A fit index for covariance structure models under arbitrary GLS estimation." British Journal of Mathematical and Statistical Psychology 38: 197-201.

THEIL, H. (1971) Principles of Econometrics. New York: John Wiley.

THEIL, H. and K. LAITINEN (1980) "Singular moment matrices in applied econometrics," pp. 629-649 in P. R. Krishnaiah (ed.) Multivariate Analysis-V. Amsterdam: North-Holland.

THORNDIKE, R. L. (1985) "The central role of general ability in prediction." Multivariate Behavioral Research 20: 241-254.

TOBIN, J. (1958) "Estimation of relationships for limited dependent variables." Econometrica 26: 24-36.

TUKEY, J. W. (1969) "Causation, regression and path analysis," in O. Kempthorne et al. (eds.) Statistics and Mathematics in Biology. Ames: Iowa State College Press.

TUMA, N. B. (1976) "Rewards, resources, and the rate of mobility: a nonstationary multivariate stochastic model." American Sociological Review 41: 338-360.

TUMA, N. B. and D. CROCKFORD (1976) Invoking Rate. Program Documentation. Stanford, CA: Stanford University, Department of Sociology.

TYLER, D. E. (1983) "Robustness and efficiency properties of scatter matrices." Biometrika 70: 411-420.

VAN PRAAG, B.M.S., T. K. DIJKSTRA, and J. VAN VELZEN (1985) "Least squares theory based on general distributional assumptions with an application to the incomplete observations problem." Psychometrika 50: 25-36.

VELICER, W. F. and J. L. FAVA (1987) "An evaluation of the effects of variable sampling on component, image, and factor analysis." Multivariate Behavioral Research 22: 193-209.

WALD, A. (1943) "Tests of statistical hypothesis concerning several parameters where the number of observations is large." Transactions of the American Mathematical Society 54: 426-482.

WERTS, C. E., K. G. JÖRESKOG, and R. L. LINN (1973) "Identification and estimation in path analysis with unmeasured variables." American Journal of Sociology 78: 1469-1484.

WERTS, C. E. and R. L. LINN (1970) "Path analysis: psychological examples." Psychological Bulletin 74: 194-212.

WERTS, C. E., R. L. LINN, and K. G. JÖRESKOG (1974) "Quantifying unmeasured variables," in H. M. Blalock (ed.) Measurement in the Social Sciences. Chicago: Aldine.

WERTS, C. E., R. L. LINN, and K. G. JÖRESKOG (1977) "A simplex model for analyzing academic growth." Educational and Psychological Measurement 37: 745-756.

WHEATON, B. (1985a) "Models for the stress-buffering functions of coping resources." Journal of Health and Social Behavior 26: 352-364.

WHEATON, B. (1985b) "Personal resources and mental health: can there be too much of a good things," pp. 139-184 in J. M. Greenley (ed.) Research in Community and Mental Health, Vol. 5. Greenwich, CT: JAI Press.

WHEATON, B., B. MUTHEN, D. F. ALWIN, and G. F. SUMMERS (1977) "Assessing reliability and stability in panel models," pp. 84-136 in D. R. Heise (ed.) Sociological Methodology 1977. San Francisco: Jossey-Bass.

WIGGINS, J. S. (1972) Personality and Prediction: Principles of Personality Assessment. Reading, MA: Addison-Wesley.

WILLIS, R. J. and S. ROSEN (1979) "Education and self-selection." Journal of Political Economy 87, Part 2: S7-S36.

WILSON, K. L. (1981) "On population comparison using factor indexes or latent variables." Social Science Research 10: 301-313.

WINSHIP, C. and R. D. MARE (1983) "Structural equations and path analysis for discrete data." American Journal of Sociology 89: 54-110.

WINSHIP, C. and R. D. MARE (1984) "Regression models with ordinal variables." American Sociological Review 49: 512-525.

WOLFLE, L. M. and C. A. ETHINGTON (1985a) "SEINE: standard errors of indirect effects." Educational and Psychological Measurement 45: 161-166.

WOLFLE, L. M. and C. A. ETHINGTON (1985b) "GEMINI: program for analysis of structural equations with standard errors of indirect effects." Behavior Research Methods, Instruments, and Computers 17: 581-584.

WONNACOTT, R. J. and T. H. WONNACOTT (1979) Econometrics. New York: John Wiley.

WRIGHT, S. (1934) "The method of path coefficient." Annals of Mathematical Statistics 5: 161-215.

WRIGHT, S. (1954) "The interpretation of multivariate systems," pp. 11-33 in O. Kempthorne et al. (eds.) Statistics and Mathematics in Biology. Ames: Iowa State College Press.

WRIGHT, S. (1960) "Path coefficients and path regressions: alternative or complementary concepts?" Biometrics 16: 189-202.

YULE, G. U. (1900) "On the association of attributes in statistics." Philosophical Transaction of the Royal Society of London 194A: 257-319.

ZELLNER, A. (1962) "An efficient method of estimating seemingly unrelated regressions and tests for aggregation bias." Journal of the American Statistical Association 57: 348-368.

ZELTERMAN, D. (1987). "Goodness-of-fit tests for a large sparse multinomial distributions." Journal of the American Statistical Association 57: 348-368.

About the Contributors

Richard D. Alba is Professor of Sociology and Director of the Center for Social and Demographic Analysis, State University of New York at Albany. His recent research has been exploring the twilight of ethnicity among American whites.

Duane F. Alwin is Professor and Research Scientist in the Institute for Social Research at the University of Michigan, Ann Arbor, where he directs the Survey Research Center's Summer Institute in Survey Research Techniques. His research and teaching interests focus primarily on issues of socialization and inequality throughout the life cycle.

P. M. Bentler is Professor of Psychology at the University of California, Los Angeles. His research deals with theoretical and statistical problems in psychometrics, especially structural equation models, as well as with personality and applied social psychology, especially drug use and abuse.

Chih-Ping Chou is Research Associate in the Department of Psychology, University of California, Los Angeles. His research interests are statistical and computational problems in covariance structure modeling, multivariate statistical analysis, and measurement.

Clifford C. Clogg is Professor of Sociology and Statistics and Senior Research Associate of the Population Issues Research Center at Pennsylvania State University. He is currently editor of *Sociological Methodology*. His research interests include the social demography of the labor force and statistical models for categorical data.

Scott R. Eliason is a graduate student in the Department of Sociology at Pennsylvania State University. His research interests include the sociology of labor markets and quantitative methodology.

Gene A. Fisher is Assistant Professor at the University of Massachusetts, Amherst. His substantive research interests include the effects of mental illness on the family, and the sociology of emotions. In the area of statistics and methodology, he is currently working on single-equation methods of adjusting for measurement error and two-stage procedures for specifying structural equation models with latent variables.

Lowell L. Hargens is Professor of Sociology at the University of Illinois at Urbana-Champaign. His research interests are in the sociology of science. He is coeditor, along with Andrew Pickering and Robert Alun Jones, of the JAI Press Annual series *Knowledge and Society*.

J. Scott Long is Associate Professor of Sociology and Statistics and Director of the Social Data Processing Center at Washington State University. His recent substantive research is on gender stratification in science.

Terance D. Miethe is Assistant Professor of Sociology at Virginia Polytechnic Institute and State University. His current research interests are in criminal victimization, criminal court sentencing practices, and evaluation research.

Robert D. Mare is Professor of Sociology at the University of Wisconsin at Madison. His recent research focuses on changes in schooling, work, and marriage for young persons since 1940 (with C. Winship); trends in educational stratification; the effects of career patterns on the timing of mortality; and models of tracking within schools.

James W. Shockey is Assistant Professor of Sociology at the University of Arizona. His research interests are in demography, labor market sociology, and the use of latent structure models. His most recent work deals with the demographics of discouraged workers, the measurement and consequences of overeducation, and statistical models to adjust for response error in panel survey data.

Michael E. Sobel is Associate Professor of Sociology and of Applied Mathematics at the University of Arizona. In addition to his work in the area of latent variable models, he is working on models for the study of agreement and disagreement and on averaging models for decision-making processes.

Blair Wheaton is Associate Professor in the Department of Sociology at McGill University in Montreal. His primary research is in the area of social structure, stress, and mental health. He is currently involved in a study designed to evaluate a magnitude-scaling procedure for the social comparison component of chronic stress, and is beginning a study on the personal well-being of children in dual-career families.

Christopher Winship is Professor of Sociology, Statistics, and Economics at Northwestern University. His recent research focuses on changes in the transition from youth to adult with particular attention to black-white differences in employment and marriage (with R. Mare); and statistical models for the analysis of choice among roles and activities over the life cycle.

NOTES

DATE DUE